Invisible Visual Effects

This book offers a systematic introduction to essential visual effects (VFX) production, addressing both the internal operations of VFX studios and the external collaborations between facilities. It is designed to equip readers with a solid understanding of production pipelines, workflows, and industry standards, enabling them to apply this knowledge to personal projects, professional development, and job applications. With its alignment to university-level teaching standards, the book also serves as a practical textbook for VFX courses at various academic levels.

Structured across six chapters, the book covers a wide range of topics from professional terminology and project collaboration to operating platforms, software tools, and the structure of production workflows. It also includes the author's perspective on recent technological advancements in the creative industries, such as AI integration and virtual production, addressing common concerns about how these changes may impact learning and career development.

To support applied learning, the book includes hands-on exercises tied to real-world projects and features eight detailed case studies. Each case study is accompanied by pre-recorded demonstration videos, designed to bridge theoretical knowledge with practical execution through a clear, step-by-step progression. The final chapter offers professional advice on building VFX demo reels for entry-level roles, helping readers craft compelling portfolios and strengthen their career prospects.

Dr Jin Zhi is a tenured faculty member and a practitioner of film visual effects based in the United States. He is a Certified Nuke Trainer accredited by Foundry and a Teaching Fellow recognized by Advance HE in the UK. Over the past 15 years, he has worked as both a full-time academic and a VFX artist at leading universities and world-renowned visual effects studios in the United Kingdom and the United States.

Invisible Visual Effects

The Hidden Magic of Film VFX

Dr. Jin Zhi

Routledge
Taylor & Francis Group
NEW YORK AND LONDON

Designed cover image: Jin Zhi

First published 2027
by Routledge
605 Third Avenue, New York, NY 10158

and by Routledge
4 Park Square, Milton Park, Abingdon, Oxon, OX14 4RN

Routledge is an imprint of the Taylor & Francis Group, an informa business

ISBN: 978-1-032-12455-1 (hbk)
ISBN: 978-1-032-12453-7 (pbk)
ISBN: 978-1-003-22461-7 (ebk)

DOI: 10.4324/9781003224617

Typeset in Univers
by Apex CoVantage, LLC

Access the Support Material: www.routledge.com/9781032124537

Contents

Online tutorials for case studies are available at www.youtube.com/@InvisibleFilmVFX

Acknowledgments

As I dedicate this book to esteemed readers, I would like to take this opportunity to express my sincere gratitude to the following friends and organizations. They are outstanding professionals in their respective fields and dedicated contributors tirelessly working to nurture the next generation of filmmakers and artists. Writing this book has been a challenging journey, and without their support, it would not have been completed in a timely manner.

Hey-Kyoung Kim | Yun Fei Fu (CG Supervisor, Digital Domain) | Katherine Kadian Lowe (Editor) | Daniel Kershaw (Editor, Taylor & Francis) | Alyss Barraza (Editorial Assistant, Taylor & Francis) | Stacey Carter (Deputy Production Editorial Manager, Taylor & Francis) | Danielle Zarfati (Squad Manager of Editorial, Taylor & Francis) | Kate Fornadel (Senior Project Manager | Apex CoVantage)

Amy Smith (Framestore, UK) | Kathleen Ruffalo (Framestore, USA) | Rory Campbell (Filmmaker and Motion Graphic Artist, UK) | Adam Cant (Senior Motion Graphic Designer, UK) | Michael Ruvo (Independent filmmaker, NYC) | Corentin Kopp (Director and DOP) | Massimo Moretti (StudioCanal) | Weidi Chen (VFX Supervisor) | Malcolm Finnie (Photographer, Scotland, UK) | FXphd.com | Photobash.co | Hugh Harford (Producer) & North London Film Fund, UK | mango.blender.org | Walt Disney Animation Studios

Prof. Nigel Johnson (University of Dundee, UK) | Dr. Christopher Brown (University of Sussex, UK) | Prof. Gregory Sporton (University of Westminster, UK) | Prof. Ashif Tejani (University of Westminster, UK) | Prof. John DiMarco (St. John's University, NY) | Prof. Richard R. Thomas (St. John's University, NY) | Dr. Luca Iandoli (St. John's University, NY) | Prof. Myung-Jin Baek (Seoul National University)

Preface

Visual effects (VFX), as an important form of visual artistic expression in contemporary cinema, have rapidly taken root and flourished, particularly over the past two decades. With advanced technology and substantial developments, the high-quality output of visual effects continuously extends the boundaries of creative potential. Creating visual effects for film production involves a significant amount of skill, expertise, and creativity, all rooted in an understanding of traditional visual effects processes. A team of highly skilled professionals, including knowledgeable visual effects artists, supervisors, production crews, and management teams, is required to plan, execute, and deliver high-quality visual results. Additionally, factors such as the director's vision, the film's storyline, and the budget play crucial roles in the outcome of the visual effects.

Visual effects play a crucial role in storytelling by enhancing the visual impact and adding subtlety to films and other forms of media. With the rise of AI-driven tools and advanced technologies like virtual production in recent years, diverse viewpoints have emerged. However, for learners seeking to grasp the principles of film production, visual effects, 3D animation, and other creative disciplines while staying informed about emerging technologies, this transformative era presents both challenges and opportunities. This evolving landscape empowers filmmakers and content creators to harness revolutionary tools effectively, enriching storytelling and fostering innovation.

While the visual effects industry has experienced significant growth over the past few decades, higher education institutions have responded by offering various VFX-related majors and courses. These programs play a crucial role in nurturing the next generation of visual effects artists and filmmakers. However, some teaching approaches in higher education focus solely on software training, overlooking the broader scope of production pipelines. As a result, students often prioritize learning specific software, mistakenly believing that mastering these tools is the goal in this field. But is this what the industry expects from new entry-level professionals? Despite the large number of film majors graduating each year, a significant knowledge gap remains in understanding visual effects production pipelines, which are deeply embedded in modern filmmaking. This raises concerns about whether the new generation of filmmakers has the necessary knowledge to collaborate effectively with VFX production teams. As a result, VFX companies often invest additional time and resources in recruiting and training promising newcomers. However, not all graduates secure these opportunities. Success in recruitment and training applications depends on an applicant's comprehensive understanding of the profession, demonstrated through the quality of their work and their proficiency in both hard and soft skills.

This book aims to provide readers with a systematic understanding of essential visual effects production, covering both the internal operations of VFX studios and the external collaborations between visual effects facilities. It also seeks to familiarize readers with production pipelines, workflows, and industry standards, enabling individuals to apply the knowledge gained from the book to personal projects, enhance their professional expertise, and improve their chances of success in job applications or project collaborations. Furthermore, with a deep understanding of university-level teaching standards, this book is well-suited as a textbook for guiding and teaching relevant courses at various levels.

The book is divided into six chapters, covering a range of topics – from professional definitions of the field to internal project collaboration, operating platforms, software usage, industry standards, and production pipelines and workflows. Additionally, it presents the author's perspective on recent technological advancements in the film and creative industries, including the application of AI technology and virtual production, aiming to address some of the confusion and anxiety learners may have regarding the industry's future development and the impact of these advancements on their studies. Furthermore, to enhance the learning experience, the book includes hands-on exercises within specific projects. Additionally, it presents eight case studies accompanied by pre-recorded demonstration videos that bridge the book's written content with the Intuitive Media learning experience, following a simple-to-advanced progression. Lastly, to help build a strong demo reel and improve job prospects, the final chapter offers professional guidance and advice on creating VFX-related demo reels for entry-level positions in visual effects studios.

Chapter One

A professional understanding of film visual effects and related subjects

Learning objectives

> Understand the origins and historical development of visual effects (VFX) in film.

> Distinguish visual effects from other related professional disciplines.

DOI: 10.4324/9781003224617-1

• The origin and historical background of film visual effects

The evolution of cinematic visual effects can be traced back to the early days of filmmaking. In this section, the author will highlight several iconic films that have played a significant role in the history of visual effects.

The first special effects film recognized by the film industry to date is *The Execution of Mary, Queen of Scots (also known as The Execution of Mary Stuart)*, a short film directed by Alfred Clark and produced by Thomas Edison Studios in the United States in 1895 (Figure 1.1). The film was one of the earliest historical reenactments captured on film. It is a 35-mm silent film, shot at 30 frames per second and 15 seconds long. The moment that the executioner beheads Queen Mary is made using an in-camera substitution cut.

Although the shot film was brief and had technical limitations, *The Execution of Mary, Queen of Scots* was groundbreaking and established a precedent for historical reenactments and dramatic recreations in cinema, contributing to the medium's recognition as a powerful tool for storytelling.

Figure 1.1 is a still from the film, taken from an open-source motion picture shared by the Library of Congress Motion Picture, Broadcasting, and Recorded Sound Division in Washington, D.C. 20540, USA. The image can be viewed on the following website: www.loc.gov/item/00694120

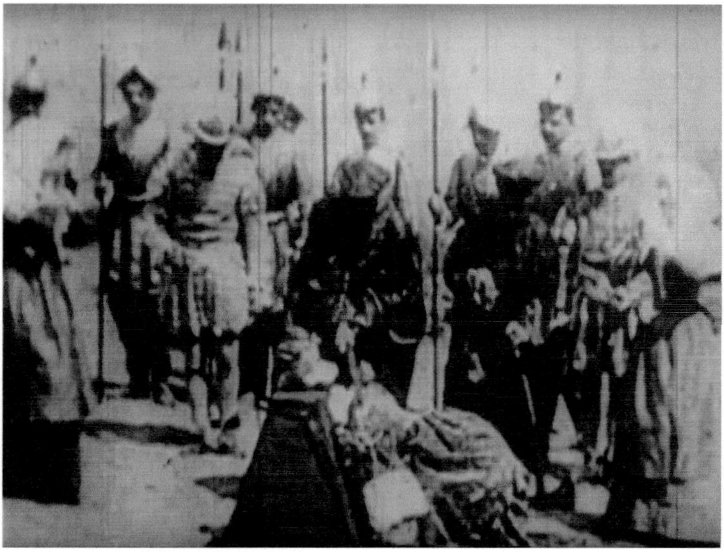

FIGURE 1.1 The Execution of Mary Queen of Scots (1895)

King Kong is considered a revolutionary film of its time, released in 1933 and co-produced by Merian C. Cooper and Ernest B. Schoedsack. It was a pioneering work of art that utilized the innovative stop-motion animation technique, which enabled the realistic portrayal of a colossal ape that dominated the silver screen. Despite the film's archaic technology compared to modern-day movies, it was a significant milestone in early special effects films. These films aimed to create realistic invisible visual effects, enhancing the authenticity and appeal of the storytelling. *King Kong* successfully achieved this goal by seamlessly integrating visual effects with the film's narrative, ultimately enhancing the story. Its impact is evident in today's films, where advanced technologies create visually stunning effects that have become essential to modern storytelling. *2001: A Space Odyssey* (1968), directed by Stanley Kubrick, employed practical and optical effects to depict space travel and futuristic technology realistically. *Star Wars*, released in 1977, revolutionized visual effects using miniatures and practical effects to create a vast and immersive sci-fi world. Finally, *Tron* (1982) was the first film to use CGI elements extensively and is considered a landmark in the history of visual effects. Each of these films played an integral role in advancing the art of visual effects, and their influence can still be seen in modern cinema. In 1989, the release of *Indiana Jones and the Last Crusade* signaled a significant shift in the film industry. The movie delivered a thrilling adventure and marked a major milestone in visual effects technology, featuring the first use of full-screen digital compositing of live-action footage in a movie. Industrial Light & Magic (ILM)'s groundbreaking work on the film inspired filmmakers and visual effects artists alike to push the boundaries of what was possible, ultimately transforming how movies were made and experienced by audiences around the world. Film visual effects and digital compositing technologies evolved rapidly in the 1990s. During this period, filmmakers gained access to a variety of visual effects tools and techniques that allowed them to bring their imaginative ideas to life with unprecedented realism and precision. Today, ongoing technological advancements have further enhanced the creation of invisible visual effects and significantly expanded the possibilities of visual storytelling.

• Definition of VFX and related professional disciplines

Visual effects is a process crucial to film production, especially in modern filmmaking. It allows filmmakers to create scenes that do not exist in reality, simulate hazardous conditions, and produce effects that are impossible to achieve with practical methods. However, to fully understand VFX, we must delve deeper into its definition and creative processes.

To explain VFX literally, it is the process of creating and manipulating images during various stages of filmmaking. However, in contemporary film production, the creative processes of visual effects are deeply involved in pre-production, on-set data collection during shooting, and comprehensive post-production workflows. These processes ensure the seamless integration of various types of assets with live-action footage. This implies that the final output must be created as realistically as possible in all aspects to meet both the artistic and scientific requirements of each shot. High-quality visual effects should be convincing enough for the audience to believe that all elements in the scene were present during filming rather than added in post-production. In other words, the ultimate goal is to create the illusion that everything existed on set during the shoot. A basic understanding of the history of film visual effects is crucial for distinguishing visual effects from similar topics that might confuse beginners.

• Professional definition of film special effects

Special effects, also known as practical effects, involve the use of physical materials such as props, special makeup, and various tangible elements to create effects during on-set filming. These effects have been a cornerstone of cinematic storytelling for over a century, playing a pivotal role in bringing fantastical and otherworldly scenes to life. For instance, prosthetic makeup was used in the Harry Potter film series to transform actors into completely different characters. Other examples of special effects include stunts, explosions, puppetry, and various other elements.

The use of special effects in films can be traced back to the late 1800s and early 1900s, with Georges Méliès' *A Trip to the Moon* being the first science fiction film to utilize them. This pioneering work incorporated stop-motion animation, hand-painted color, and multiple special exposure techniques, setting a new benchmark in cinema history.

In contemporary times, the term "special effects blockbusters" often refers to movies featuring high-intensity visual components. Modern films frequently combine practical effects with digital visual effects, such as computer-generated imagery (CGI), to create immersive and realistic worlds on screen. However, it is important to distinguish between special effects and visual effects in production. While special effects are achieved using physical materials and practical methods, visual effects are created using computer-generated techniques.

To summarize, special effects have been a vital aspect of cinema production for over a century and continue to evolve alongside technological advancements. Understanding the difference between special effects and visual effects allows us to better appreciate the artistry and skills involved in creating stunning film visuals. Both practical and digital effects share the goal of crafting an engaging and immersive cinematic experience for the audience.

• Professional definition of motion graphic design

Motion graphic design is an extension of traditional graphic design, incorporating motion elements and rhythm. Motion graphics designers apply traditional graphic design principles and animation techniques to create the illusion of motion using various forms of visual elements, such as text, graphics, video clips, and background music. These elements must be harmoniously and dynamically integrated to support the overall design. Motion graphics are commonly used in TV advertisements, explainer videos, title sequences, and across media platforms.

While motion graphic design and film visual effects share similarities, they differ significantly. Both incorporate various visual elements, but motion graphic design does not necessarily aim for photorealism. In contrast, film visual effects must adhere to strict industry standards and be seamlessly integrated, especially with live-action footage. This requires careful consideration of multiple aspects, such as color science, image bit depths, light principles, camera movements, lens information, physical laws in animation, and other components related to film technology.

Overall, motion graphic design is a dynamic and versatile field that combines creativity and technical expertise to produce visually appealing content that effectively communicates complex ideas and concepts. The discipline covers a range of styles and techniques, from 2D and 3D animation to typography design.

An example of motion graphic design is shown in the upper image of Figure 1.2. It features multiple scenes within a 30-second duration, seamlessly integrating a series of 2D and 3D elements into background images, accompanied by music to create a captivating visual experience. Like many stylized motion graphics, this piece blurs the line between motion graphic design and visual effects. Motion graphic design offers an exciting career path for those passionate about creativity and visual storytelling.

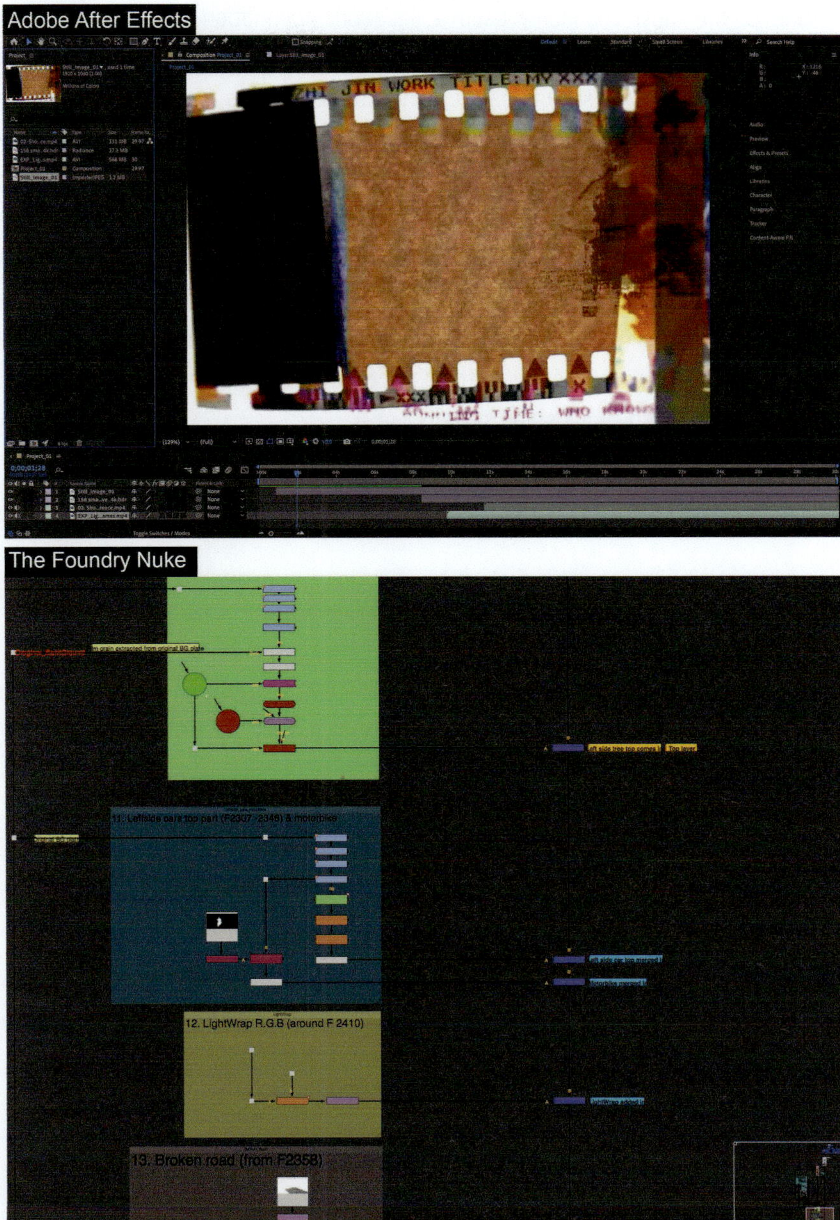

FIGURE 1.2 Comparison of user interfaces and workflows in After Effects and Foundry NukeX

One of the most commonly used applications for motion graphics design is Adobe After Effects (AE). This popular, layer-based professional software offers users a comprehensive set of features and add-on plugins for creating stunning motion graphics. However, for high-end visual effects integration, particularly in films and TV commercials, The Foundry's NukeX is the preferred choice among visual effects studios. Unlike layer-based applications, Nuke is node-based software specifically designed for high-end compositing. It has established itself as the industry-standard tool, offering efficient and reliable solutions for managing complex visual effects shots within production pipelines. Figure 1.2 highlights the structural differences between Adobe After Effects, a layer-based tool, and Foundry's NukeX, a node-based compositing system.

• Understanding effects assets

In filmmaking, visually stunning effects (FX) are essential for establishing a movie's atmosphere. FX assets play a pivotal role in this process and can be categorized into two main types: live-action FX assets and computer-generated (CG) FX assets.

As the name suggests, live-action FX assets refer to elements captured on camera during filming. These include natural phenomena like fire, smoke, rain, and other practical effects incorporated into a scene during shooting. In contrast, CG FX assets are created through computer simulations and can be manipulated to produce unique effects that are difficult or impossible to achieve with live-action techniques. CG FX assets can also interact with the main characters or environment within a scene. For example, a spaceship might appear to disturb the surrounding clouds as it flies through the sky, generating airflow that alters their shapes and movements. These kinds of interactions help bring a shot to life, making it more immersive and engaging for the audience.

Visual effects studios often create and maintain internal digital libraries containing a wide range of FX assets tailored to specific projects during film production. These assets can include both live-action and CG FX elements, which are used to integrate with hero live-action footage in compositing and help create the breathtaking visuals we see on screen.

Despite the clear distinctions between various fields within the industry, confusion can still arise, especially in educational settings. Some schools offer courses that conflate different areas, such as special effects (SFX), visual effects, FX, motion graphics, and post-production. This overlap can lead to misleading learning outcomes and unclear goals. Therefore, having a clear understanding of the different categories is essential for anyone looking to master the art of visual effects in filmmaking.

• Understanding traditional post-production

Post-production is critical in creating a media product, such as a film or television show. It involves several main stages, including editing, color grading, audio mixing, digital intermediate, and other tasks. Traditionally, post-production was seen as a single process. However, the rise of visual effects in film and television has led to its subdivision into various specialized departments. One such department is the VFX editorial department. This team is responsible for editing raw client footage, which consists of untouched files with metadata from cameras. These raw files are divided into individual shots based on the structure of each project and eventually exported as sequential images – called "plates" – in the required formats for use across departments. This process requires a scientific understanding of moving images, including color spaces, digital image formats, and production pipelines.

It is worth noting that editorial duties in the VFX industry may differ from those in traditional editorial processes within the broader film and television industry. For instance, editing in post-production houses often emphasizes storytelling, while VFX editorial work primarily focuses on technical aspects. Nevertheless, both types of editing play a crucial role in shaping the final version of a media product. Therefore, understanding the differences between these two processes is important in both fields.

The importance of VFX editing and the level of precision it demands in production cannot be overstated. Figure 1.3 shows a typical VFX editorial datasheet that includes essential production details and technical specifications, such as image format, bit depth, aspect ratio, color space, and more. It also provides important information about the sequence length, which is key to ensuring seamless editing in the final product. One of the most critical elements in VFX production is the plate. The datasheet features an example of a background plate delivered as a 10-bit DPX (Digital Picture Exchange) file. The start frame of this plate is 1001, and the end frame is 1069.

Due Date: (In Cut?)	IN	Notes	Plate Name	Slate Name	Camera Aperture Resolution	Extraction Resolution	Bit Depth	Color Space	File Type
			BB0030_bg_v001	V26N - 1*	6560 x 3100	5513 x 2310	10 bit	Log C	DPX
		Comp Frames:	**1001**	1009				1061	**1069**
Plate1 10Bit DPX	**BB0030 _bg_v0 01**	Plate Frames: Description:	1025 First Frame Of Work Handle	1033 First Frame In Cut →				1085 Last Frame In Cut	1093 Last Frame Of Work Handle

FIGURE 1.3 Example of a datasheet for a VFX plate, showing assigned sequence frames and specific shot information

In this chapter, we have explored several professional concepts that are essential for understanding the world of visual effects, special effects, motion graphic design, and FX assets. Our primary objective is to clarify these concepts for our readers and help them gain a deeper understanding of these creative and technical fields. Additionally, we have explained the role of editorial in visual effects studios and how it differs from that in traditional post-production houses. By providing a detailed explanation of these topics, we aim to equip our readers with the foundational knowledge needed to excel in the field of visual effects.

Over more than a decade of studying, working, and teaching the same subject in the UK, I spent a significant amount of time in London engaging with department heads at some of the world's most renowned visual effects facilities. A recurring theme in these conversations was the quality of visual effects courses offered by higher education institutions. One particularly striking question that often arose was whether these programs truly focused on visual effects production or merely on "visuals and effects".

In modern film and television production, visual effects are integrated into every stage: pre-production, production, and the complex, time-consuming processes that follow filming. This work spans the entire production pipeline, especially in films and high-end television commercials that rely heavily on visual effects.

The concerns raised by industry experts have led me to believe that students must receive an education that is both current and aligned with industry demands. Staying informed about trends and developments is crucial to equipping them with the skills and knowledge needed for success. To cultivate next-generation and industry-ready professionals, higher education institutions should realistically integrate production pipelines into their curricula and continuously adapt their courses to reflect the actual needs of the industry.

Chapter Two

VFX project concepts and emerging trends

> **Learning objectives**
>
> - Understand the concept and importance of collaboration in visual effects production.
> - Analyze and interpret shot scripts for visual effects planning.
> - Understand the role of live-action footage in visual effects production.
> - Thoughts on the application of AI in visual effects and creative production industries.
> - The impact of virtual production (VP) on visual effects (VFX) production.

The realm of modern film visual effects has rapidly expanded beyond the conventional scope of "post-production". Today, visual effects facilities assume multifaceted roles that extend far beyond merely creating stunning pictures. Visual effects production processes now include script analysis to identify VFX requirements and determine necessary shots, collaboration with internal and external production teams, on-site supervision, and data measurement and collection. These diverse responsibilities require a wide array of expertise, ranging from creative and technical skills to management and communication abilities. Visual effects companies now play a crucial role in filmmaking by working closely with the creative team to identify opportunities for seamlessly incorporating VFX elements into the story. In addition, they help determine the cost of VFX shots and prepare accurate budgets to ensure the project stays on track. During filming, the VFX team supervises on-site shooting to ensure that everything is correctly captured for VFX creation and collects valuable data to facilitate the visual effects production process.

The VFX industry is a fast-paced, ever-evolving sector that demands a wide range of skills and knowledge. Successful VFX professionals possess a mix of technical expertise, artistic talent, project management skills, and effective communication abilities. With the demand for high-quality VFX in the film industry rising, visual effects companies must adapt quickly to the changing landscape and continually enhance their capabilities to remain competitive.

DOI: 10.4324/9781003224617-2

• The concept and importance of collaboration in VFX production

Visual effects production is a highly collaborative endeavor involving many artists and technicians working together to create stunning visual imagery, especially for high-end feature films. While collaboration between different departments within a visual effects company is crucial, collaboration extends well beyond organizational boundaries. Working effectively with other studios and production companies is often the key to success in the highly competitive world of visual effects.

When bidding on a project, visual effects studios typically compete against one another to secure the contract. Once a studio is chosen, they may lead the project and work with other studios to complete the required tasks based on their expertise. For example, in the Harry Potter series and The Jungle Book films, the Moving Picture Company (MPC) led the visual effects work. At the same time, other studios – such as DNEG, Framestore, and Cinesite – also made significant contributions to many of the same VFX shows.

One of the challenges for project collaborations across visual effects studios is sharing specific project files. Fortunately, many studios have similar workflow and production pipelines, which make shared VFX shots easier to fit into all collaborating studios. Therefore, sharing portions of scripts and assets with other peer studios working on the same shot is not uncommon. The ability to work collaboratively across organizational and geographic boundaries is an essential skill for all studios and professionals working in visual effects production.

Creating VFX-intensive films is a highly intricate and time-consuming process that demands the collaboration of individuals and companies to bring a shared vision to life. The final product represents the collective efforts of numerous talented artists, technicians, and production management teams, each contributing their skills and expertise across various stages of the production pipeline – including concept art, storyboarding, pre-production planning, filming, visual effects, post-production, and final delivery. Each stage requires meticulous coordination and communication among departments and collaborating studios. As a result, the extensive credits at the end of VFX-heavy films serve an important purpose: they acknowledge the contributions of the many individuals and companies involved in the production. These credits showcase the hard work and dedication of the talented artists and production crews who played pivotal roles in crafting visually striking and complex projects.

• Interpreting shot scripts for VFX planning

At visual effects studios, there are typically two types of supervisor roles: on-site supervisors and in-studio supervisors. Both are responsible for overseeing and coordinating various aspects of the production process, including analyzing film scripts to determine the visual effects required. On-set VFX supervisors work closely with the film production team and other key crew members to develop shooting plans, ensuring accurate capture of on-set data during filming for the creation of necessary VFX assets. To support this process, VFX supervisors often prepare detailed notes and plans for each scene that requires visual effects. These notes might include information such as HDR images, textures, green screens, clean plates, tracking, survey camera settings, on-set survey data scans, and more. The following script describes an interior scene for a short film. Based on the visual effects elements required for this shot, a set of notes can be prepared in advance to guide on-set data capture. These may include HDR images, environmental survey data and scans, green screens, backlit shadows, camera tracking details, and multiple reference camera setups. These components are essential for accurately and effectively creating the desired VFX scene. Such notes help guide the production team, including directors, cinematographers, and crew members, during filming, ensuring they remain aligned with the intended vision.

Analyzing film scripts for VFX shots aims to identify potential issues in the scenes and develop solutions ahead of the shoot. The ultimate goal is to capture a successful plate with accurate on-set data, enabling the creation of seamless and realistic visual effects. Through careful planning, preparation, and execution, VFX supervisors and artists can bring even the most complex and seemingly impossible scenes to life on the big screen.

The following screenplay excerpt is copyrighted by Dr. Christopher Brown, University of Sussex, United Kingdom.

INT. HALLWAY, APARTMENT – EVENT

The large hallway is furnished in traditional mahogany. It is dark and quiet, except for the sound of a thunderstorm outside. In a small window at the end of the hall, the leaves of a tree can be seen fluttering madly in the breeze.

Lighting flashes, illuminating a strange sight. Splattered over the middle of the wooden floorboards lies a pile of red jelly. The plastic mould lies upturned nearby.

The handle of the front door moves softly up and down. There is the subtle sound of metal being forced, followed by a clicking noise. The door opens quietly.

SAMI (20s) enters and closes the door. He is wearing joggers and a hoodie, over which an old sports jacket is zipped up tightly. He places a small crowbar back into his pocket, then pulls away his hood, wiping his hand across his wet face.

Spotting the jelly, Sami pulls out a flashlight and runs the beam across the floor to check that he is seeing things correctly. Perplexed, he shrugs and creeps past the jelly.

• Understanding the role of live-action footage in VFX production

The success of modern film visual effects relies heavily on preproduction, on-site visual effects supervision, and accurate data measurement. Seamlessly integrating visual effects with live-action scenes to achieve invisible effects requires precise, physically based calculations involving 3D modeling, animation, lighting, dynamics simulations, rendering, color management, and compositing. In later chapters, we will explore the technical details of this process, which involves a substantial amount of professional knowledge.

One fundamental aspect of visual effects production is the use of live-action footage. The VFX industry primarily employs two types of live-action footage files provided by clients. For instance, if traditional film cameras were used for shooting, 10-bit scanned DPX (Digital Picture Exchange) format sequence files would be utilized during VFX production. In modern productions, however, various digital cinema cameras are more commonly used. In such cases, clients typically provide native raw files, such as those from ARRI cameras (in ARRI format), RED cameras (in R3D format), or other digital formats. Additionally, clients usually supply color data information, such as the American Society of Cinematographers Color Decision List (ASC CDL), lookup tables (LUTs), and any other relevant color metadata embedded during filming.

In the early stages of VFX production, requesting and sharing files between VFX studios and film production studios is essential. Figure 2.1 illustrates a simplified version of this workflow. The primary goal of the process is to preserve the highest possible image quality of the live-action footage throughout visual effects production while also referencing the original metadata embedded in the raw footage during production.

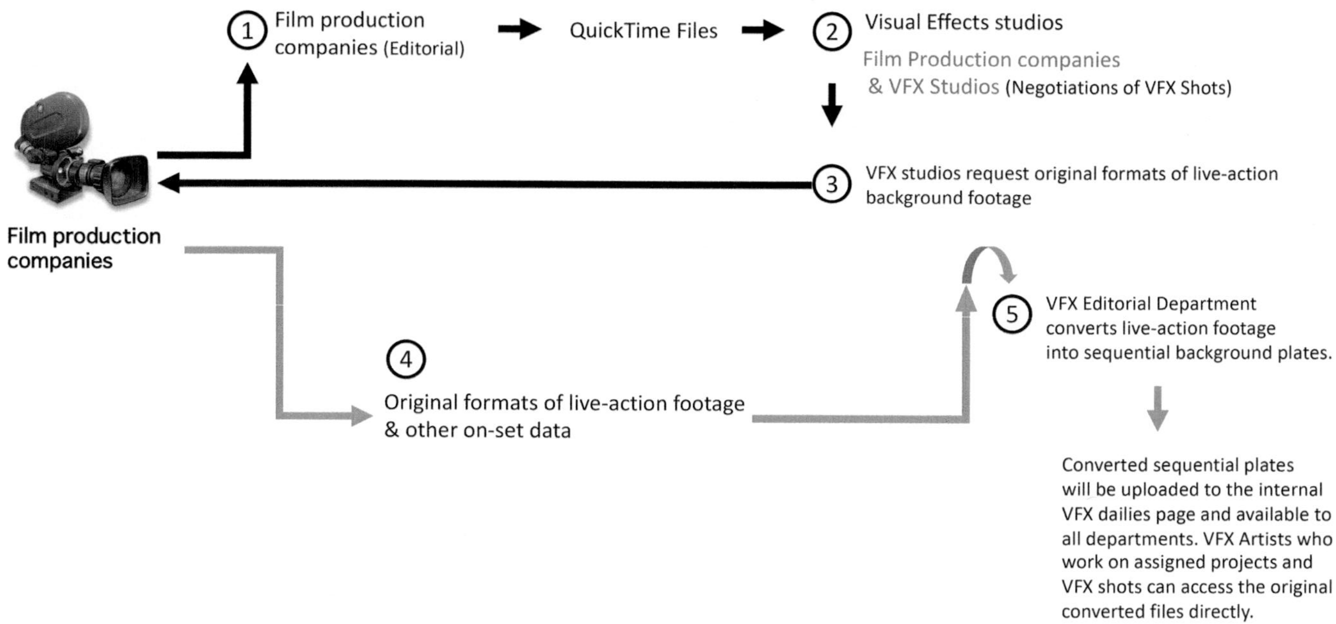

FIGURE 2.1 Concept for sharing live-action footage between the film production team and VFX studios

Notes:

The QuickTime file format has been a preferred option for digital creators to store media files for several decades. Its introduction in 1991 revolutionized the storage of multimedia content, such as video and audio, in a single file. QuickTime was developed with the capability to support a vast range of codecs for file compression, making it a versatile choice for media professionals. QuickTime still holds its place in the film and video production industry, attesting to its efficiency and reliability in delivering high-quality media content. Furthermore, the ease of editing and exporting QuickTime files using a wide range of professional editing software has made it the preferred choice for many media studios. However, it is worth noting that the QuickTime format is primarily intended for previewing media content and production dailies. It is not suitable for use as a VFX production format or for final-quality delivery for the following reasons:

1. One of the primary concerns regarding QuickTime is its compression capabilities. Although QuickTime supports various codecs for file compression, not all are suitable for handling high-resolution videos with complex visual effects. As a result, this may lead to a loss of quality and detail, which can be especially problematic for visual effects shots that require precision and accuracy.
2. Another challenge in visual effects production when using QuickTime is its limited color management capabilities. Visual effects workflows typically follow a scene-referred approach, often involving linear color spaces and the Academy Color Encoding System (ACES). ACES is widely adopted in the industry to ensure consistent and accurate color representation across different devices and platforms. However, QuickTime lacks built-in support for advanced color management systems like ACES. This absence can lead to color shifts and inconsistencies in the final output, posing a significant issue for visual effects shots that require precise color grading and matching.

In summary, visual effects productions require raw files to work with VFX shots rather than QuickTime format files.

• AI in VFX and the creative industries: perspectives

The term "AI" has already permeated the entire industry in recent years. Like all emerging phenomena, opinions on the proliferation of AI vary. On one hand, there is awe and excitement about its powerful capabilities; on the other, concern about its impact across various industries. From a human development perspective, AI undoubtedly holds immense potential for significant progress. Conversely, from a business operations standpoint, its rapid rise has also fueled numerous commercially hyped expectations.

As someone working in the field of visual effects in film and higher education, I believe there's no need to be overly excited or alarmed about the arrival of the AI era. Similar to the invention and subsequent application of the steam engine in the 1820s, humanity transitioned from the era of horse-drawn carriages to gradually evolve into the machine industry age. In our closely related industry of film and creative arts, AI, as an advanced tool of the future, can significantly assist our creative processes and maximize time savings, allowing artists to focus more on their creations. I wonder if you feel the same when dealing with tasks such as rotoscoping, creating high-quality Z-depth and clean plates for live-action shots, UV unwrapping after modeling, working with on-set photographed textures, or rigging before 3D animation, and how valuable it would be if AI could fully assist with these seemingly tedious technical processes. Given the current state of AI development, particularly in terms of precision and flexibility, these technologies still require further development and testing. Ultimately, they should support rather than replace the artistic and technical decision-making of VFX artists. At the same time, overestimating the substitutability of AI is not entirely beneficial for students currently in education or for existing educational systems. Excessive reliance on elements and operations produced by so-called artificial intelligence may lead students to undervalue fundamental training, thereby weakening their ability to think and act critically and ultimately hindering their future professional growth. Fortunately, amid the excitement surrounding the rise of AI, an increasing number of people are beginning to recognize the importance of maintaining this balance and are approaching this technological progress with greater calm and rationality, learning how to use these tools more wisely to enhance both current and future creative endeavors.

• The impact of virtual production on VFX production

Virtual production has rapidly become a popular trend in film and TV commercial production in recent years, thanks to advancements in technology. However, its origins can be traced back to the 1930s, when back projection was first used in films. As the term suggests, a background image was projected onto a large translucent screen from behind, creating the illusion that the foreground elements were filmed together with the background on set.

Nowadays, the development of high-end technology and corresponding hardware has greatly expanded the possibilities for creating specific scenes in film production. Virtual production involves the use of dynamic LED screens, whose main feature is the ability to provide not only real-time background updates but also HDR ambient lighting to a certain extent. This advancement significantly enhances the experience and efficiency of filming on location, marking a major improvement in the filmmaking process. Additionally, for smaller-scale film projects – especially those by independent filmmakers and students – this technology enables the creation of scenes that were previously unachievable due to technical, financial, and other constraints typically associated with large-scale productions. Reflecting on my experience in large-scale film visual effects production, I realize that some simple green/blue screen keying shots could have been handled through virtual production. If the current VP technology had been available, visual effects artists could have focused more on complex VFX scenes, thereby working more efficiently. While the rapid development of virtual production has expanded possibilities for film and television, it also presents a unique set of advantages and challenges. For example, when large-scale VFX scenes require numerous visual elements, such as set extensions or complex interactions with the protagonist, the limitations of virtual production become apparent. Additionally, current LED virtual production technology still faces technical constraints, and the costs remain prohibitively high.

With the continued development and broader adoption of virtual production, visual effects in film and television can be broadly categorized into two types: those planned and executed on set using in-camera visual effects (ICVFX) through virtual production and those requiring intensive interaction with main characters, which necessitate traditional visual effects techniques. This shift does not fundamentally alter the role of visual effects facilities; rather, it places greater emphasis on pre-production planning and on-set execution for shots that were previously reliant on post-production. These stages still require substantial input and guidance from visual effects companies.

Overall, the widespread adoption of virtual production has the potential to create a qualitative leap in the production of visual effects for film and television – significantly enhancing both efficiency and quality for all parties involved while ultimately serving the essence of storytelling.

Chapter Three

Understanding department operations at leading VFX studios

Learning objectives

> Understand internal departments and functions.
> Understand the operating systems and software used in VFX studios.
> Understand the framework and process of project operations.

DOI: 10.4324/9781003224617-3

• An overview of leading film visual effects studios

When audiences marvel at the stunning visual effects of Hollywood blockbusters, they often assume these remarkable creations are produced solely in the United States. However, many renowned visual effects companies from around the world contribute to these impressive and visually striking sequences. Undoubtedly, numerous outstanding visual effects companies are located around the world. Following is an overview of some of the largest and most well-known VFX studios, listed in alphabetical order.

DNEG (Double Negative) | www.dneg.com

DNEG, founded in 1998, is a multiple Academy and BAFTA Award-winning VFX studio based in London, UK. It operates studios in major global cities, including Vancouver, Los Angeles, Montréal, Toronto, Sydney, and various locations across India. These studios have contributed to some of the most visually stunning scenes in film and television.

Framestore | www.framestore.com

Framestore was founded in London in 1986 and has since opened additional studios in New York, Los Angeles, Chicago, Montréal, Melbourne, and Mumbai. Framestore's work can be seen in numerous outstanding feature films and TV commercial productions, winning major industry awards, including the BAFTAs, Academy Awards, Emmys, Cannes Lions, D&AD, Clio, and VES.

Industrial Light & Magic (ILM) | www.ilm.com

ILM, one of the most well-known VFX companies, was founded by George Lucas and is headquartered in San Francisco, California. It has since expanded to include studios in Vancouver, London, Sydney, Singapore, and Mumbai.

The Moving Picture Company (MPC) | www.mpcvfx.com

MPC is part of Technicolor Creative Studios and is one of the world's VFX studios to have won multiple Academy and BAFTA Awards.

(The shocking news of Technicolor's financial difficulties shook the entire VFX industry in 2025. As affiliated visual effects studios, MPC and The Mill were also affected. Wishing the very best to the talented VFX artists and colleagues who grew alongside these studios and helped shape the industry.)

Sony Pictures Imageworks | www.imageworks.com

Sony Pictures Imageworks is headquartered in Vancouver, B.C., and has studios in Montreal, QC, and Los Angeles, CA.

Wētā FX | www.wetafx.co.nz

Weta FX created the visual effects for *The Lord of the Rings and The Hobbit trilogies*, as well as many other renowned films, including the *Avatar* series. The company is based in Wellington, New Zealand.

It is worth noting that London is one of the world's leading centers for visual effects (VFX). In the heart of the city, several top facilities thrive, including DNEG, Framestore, Industrial Light & Magic (London), MPC, and many other VFX and post-production studios. Additionally, the Foundry, which develops the industry-standard compositing software Nuke, is headquartered nearby. London's reputation as a hub for visual effects and the broader creative industry is expected to continue growing. While Hollywood may be the heart of the film industry, it is important to recognize that visual effects creation is a global effort.

Exploring the official websites of leading visual effects companies reveals astonishing examples of their remarkable work. Naturally, this sparks curiosity about the inner workings of these companies and raises questions such as: What processes are involved in producing such extraordinary visual effects? How do they operate on a daily basis? What are their industry standards and guiding principles? Which professional software and tools do they use to achieve these impressive results? Since each studio has its own unique culture, workflow, and organizational structure, addressing these questions is essential for gaining a comprehensive understanding of the industry.

• Operating platforms for film VFX production

Visual effects companies in the film industry rely on specific operating platforms and software to produce high-quality work. Typically, studios use 64-bit Linux distributions such as CentOS, Rocky Linux, Fedora, and other Linux-based operating systems. These open-source platforms offer extensive customization and development flexibility, making them particularly well suited to VFX production pipelines.

While Linux is the predominant operating system in the VFX industry, Windows or macOS may also be used, depending on specific software requirements. However, a strong understanding of Linux remains highly advantageous for those aspiring to work in VFX studios. In some cases, large-scale VFX studios may be invited to test visual effects applications on Linux systems before their official release.

• Departmental division: internal functions at leading VFX studios

Although the specific tasks performed by each department may vary across different studios, VFX facilities generally categorize their departmental operations as follows (listed in alphabetical order):

o Art department and virtual art department

The art department is a crucial part of visual effects studios. They are responsible for creating the visual representation of a project, playing a vital role in the filmmaking process, and translating the director's ideas into a visual format through sketches or digital renderings. This step is crucial in establishing the look and feel of each VFX scene and guides the production design process. Concept art and storyboards serve as a roadmap for creating physical elements such as sets, props, and costumes. The role of the art department extends beyond traditional skills like drawing and painting. Artists also use digital tools essential to the production pipeline to enhance the final representation of VFX scenes. In addition to technical skills, art department artists must have a thorough understanding of the production's visual style. They are required to work within budget and timeline constraints while creating immersive worlds and captivating characters that leave a lasting impression on audiences. Their work is indispensable in producing memorable films and TV shows, regardless of the production's scale. The art department also collaborates with other departments across studios to ensure the project's visuals are cohesive and aligned with the director's vision.

The Virtual Art Department (VAD) works closely with various teams within visual effects studios, including previsualization, 3D assets, lighting, and compositing. It captures physical sets and integrates computer-generated (CG) elements created by other departments into virtual environments for use by on-set production teams. These final visual environments are mapped to on-set cameras using real-time software such as Unreal Engine. As a relatively new addition to visual effects studios, the VAD offers promising job opportunities for entry-level artists who have a strong general understanding of film production, along with solid skills in both 3D and 2D.

◦ Animation department

Visual effects studios are known for their distinct focus on photorealism, especially in feature films. This contrasts with traditional animation studios, which often prioritize more stylized or exaggerated visuals. The difference stems from the goal of visual effects studios to create a seamless and realistic experience for the audience – something that's particularly important in films with heavy visual effects. If viewers notice any deviations from photorealism, their immersion in the story can be disrupted, resulting in a less satisfying viewing experience.

One prominent example of achieving photorealism is the creation of 3D digital doubles. These digital versions of real-life actors must be indistinguishable from their real counterparts to achieve the desired level of realism. Achieving this level of detail and accuracy requires meticulous attention to every aspect of the digital double, including precise modeling of the actor's features, accurate representation of their skin and clothing materials, realistic lighting to mimic the on-set conditions, lifelike animation to capture their movement, and seamless compositing to integrate the CG characters with live-action footage. In fact, it is not only the creation of digital doubles that requires this level of detail and precision. All visual elements must be crafted to achieve photorealism, from the smallest details to the grandest set pieces. Even something that seems simple, like a digital fire or explosion, must be carefully designed to ensure it looks and behaves realistically.

Before beginning animation, it is essential to have a clear and comprehensive brief outlining the shot requirements, provided either by the client or an internal VFX supervisor. This brief should cover key aspects such as the number of characters, their intended actions and emotions, any required CG or green screen elements, and the preferred creative and technical approach to the shot. It is important to clearly define the responsibilities of the animation team versus those handled by other departments, including the use of motion references, holdouts for integrating CG elements behind live-action, and whether the shot requires card animation or simple re-racking of existing elements. The brief should also clarify which team – layout, animation, or compositing – is responsible for each aspect of the work. To ensure smooth workflow and downstream production, naming conventions and upstream requirements (such as prop variations) must be finalized, and all relevant cuts and audio should be available to provide necessary context. As animation is a critical component of VFX production, its quality and success are heavily reliant on upstream departments such as matchmove and rotoAnim, puppet rigging, roto/prep, environments/set geometry, and editorial.

○ Compositing department

Compositing is an essential process that integrates various elements into a cohesive and realistic visual composition, enhancing visual storytelling. Visual effects studios rely heavily on their compositing departments to deliver high-quality results, making it essential to have a team of skilled and experienced compositors who thoroughly understand digital image manipulation and visual effects production pipelines. Compositors should possess a strong grasp of film language, an in-depth knowledge of the science behind moving digital images, and a keen eye for natural detail. They must be able to work under the pressure of tight production schedules and meet deadlines without compromising quality. The number of compositors required for a project depends on its complexity, and for large-scale visual effects productions, hundreds may be employed during peak periods to ensure timely and high-quality completion. To excel as a compositor, one must have both technical and artistic skills, a solid understanding of the necessary tools and techniques, and strong communication abilities, as collaboration with other departments – such as roto/prep artists, compositing supervisors, coordinators, and fellow team members – is a key part of the role.

○ Crowd department

The Crowd Department is responsible for creating computer-generated characters, typically consisting of large numbers of crowds or creatures that would be impractical or impossible to produce using practical effects or live actors. These 3D digital crowds or creatures are strategically placed in the background or middle ground of visual effects scenes. The department typically seeks skilled 3D artists who often use specialized in-house tools to create digital characters that meet the required standards of precision and realism. When executed effectively, these digital characters can enhance the presence of the main characters in the foreground and contribute meaningfully to the storytelling.

○ 3D digital matte painting/environment department

The techniques used in matte painting have evolved over the past century, but many of its fundamental principles remain integral to today's visual effects pipelines. Technically, the architecture, landscapes, and other elements in the distant background do not require complex three-dimensional models due to the absence of a noticeable parallax effect. Instead, a carefully painted digital background image can effectively satisfy the human eye's perception when captured by virtual cameras. Digital matte painting (DMP) is a sophisticated technique that has transformed the creation of movie backgrounds and environments. It involves using digital manipulation software to create highly realistic landscapes, cities, and other imaginary background settings that play a crucial role in establishing the overall atmosphere of visual effects scenes and transporting audiences to different worlds.

The DMP department works closely with the compositing department. It creates digital matte painting renders using software such as Adobe Photoshop and then projects them in Foundry's NukeX to produce environment background images that are used in compositing. Therefore, the final package delivered by the DMP department should include various outputs and test files, such as DMP renders, environment renders, the camera used for projecting the environment images, a test projection Nuke script, and other related assets.

◦ Data capture department

In modern film production, both invisible and visible visual effects have become integral to the filmmaking process. They are no longer mere add-ons or afterthoughts but are intricately woven into every aspect of production. This integration is particularly evident in the data capture departments of visual effects companies, which play a crucial role in ensuring that the effects are of the highest quality and seamlessly integrated into the final output of each shot.

The data capture department is responsible for capturing and measuring all on-set data required for the successful production of visual effects. During on-site shooting, the team collects critical information, including on-set survey data, camera data, reference images, high-dynamic-range (HDR) images, photogrammetry, turntable object captures and scans, lens grids, and more. On-set survey data is essential, as it provides a detailed representation of the set's dimensions, including the positions of cameras, lights, and actors. Camera data contains information about the camera's position, movement, and lens settings, enabling artists in the matchmove department to align the virtual camera accurately with the live-action footage. Reference images are another vital component, offering all departments a clear understanding of the set and allowing artists to work precisely on the required assets throughout the project.

◦ Editorial department

The editorial department at VFX studios is the first to handle client footage in the visual effects production process. Unlike traditional post-production roles, VFX editorial focuses primarily on the technical aspects of digital moving images. This includes expertise in color spaces, LUTs, image formats, compression codecs, and other elements essential for image input and output in VFX production. The department's main responsibility is to edit and organize the raw live-action footage into meaningful VFX plates, categorized into the following areas:

- Color grade reference: The input color grade reference is extracted from supplied reference QuickTime files.
- VFX plate: Sequence images of live-action footage will be delivered to all departments, including the actual working resolutions (image aspect ratio) and the original resolutions.
- LUTs: The department creates LUT files, shot-specific LUTs, and American Society of Cinematographers Color Decision List (ASC CDL) color correction values based on the LUTs provided by clients. Ultimately, a package containing the ASC color-corrected neutral grade and shot LUTs will be delivered to all departments.

VFX editors work with image sequences output as DPX and OpenEXR files, typically starting from frame 1001 for each shot. Once the VFX plates are prepared, they are uploaded in two formats to separate locations. QuickTime files are sent to the internal VFX dailies page for preview purposes, shot details, and review by all departments and VFX artists involved in the project. However, the actual working image formats remain EXR and DPX.

◦ FX department

In previous chapters, we discussed FX assets, including 2D live-action elements and 3D dynamics simulations, which play a vital role in enhancing the overall visual experience and making other visual components appear more realistic and interactive within the scene. While 2D FX assets are typically filmed and later modified during the compositing process, 3D FX assets are created using specialized software such as Houdini, along with custom in-house tools to fine-tune simulations until they achieve the desired look and feel. An FX render delivery package usually includes FX renders, associated scripts, and cameras – all essential components for the compositing department.

∘ Groom department

The responsibility of this department is to ensure that the fur or hair of digital creatures looks as authentic as possible. To achieve this, visual effects studios often develop their in-house specialized tools and software, allowing groom artists to meticulously design and manipulate fur and hair. These tools enable groom artists to enhance the detail and realism of CG characters and creatures, bringing them to life on screen.

∘ Imaging department

VFX studios work on multiple feature films every year, with each project presenting its unique challenges and requirements. From fantasy worlds to realistic scenes, the demands of the industry never cease. To ensure that every project strictly meets industry standards during production and satisfies the expectations of various client requirements, the imaging department establishes specific image and color pipelines tailored to each project. These pipelines encompass color configurations, ingest image pipelines (including image resolutions and reference QuickTime files), color grading pipelines, and client submissions. This intricate process involves comprehensive color management, including the use of specific color spaces and LUTs for each project, implemented via OpenColorIO (OCIO) in conjunction with the Academy Color Encoding System (ACES). Furthermore, managing colors across all monitors, projectors, and screening rooms within departments and studios is critical. It ensures that artists view consistent color results across all displays while working on the same project and that the output remains uniform between departments and studios. The imaging department collaborates closely with all teams to maintain the high level of color accuracy demanded by each production.

∘ Layout and previsualization department

Layout and previsualization departments can be separated in some VFX studios. In VFX-intensive feature films, the on-set production team from visual effects studios typically scans every scene involving visual effects during filming. Once the on-set survey data and scanned environments are delivered to the visual effects studios, layout artists reconstruct clean 3D models of these environments and any necessary set extensions. These models are then aligned with the corresponding live-action background plates and virtual cameras, as provided by upstream departments such as editorial and matchmove. The layout department works closely with the matchmove, 3D animation, and lighting departments.

The previsualization department is responsible for visualizing VFX scenes, exploring creative ideas, determining camera positioning, conducting technical simulations when needed, and meeting client requirements as VFX shots progress.

○ Lighting department

The lighting department is responsible for producing realistic lighting for CG elements to match the lighting with live-action plates in visual effects scenes. Lighting artists must understand how light behaves and interacts with colors, especially in VFX productions that operate in a linear color space. Additionally, lighting artists are responsible for creating HDRIs (High Dynamic Range Images) and using them to light CG elements within VFX scenes. Foundry's Katana is a commonly used professional application in the lighting department.

The lighting department collaborates with various upstream departments at different stages of the lighting process, including matchmove, 3D animation, techAnim, groom, FX, and others. Additionally, lighting artists use powerful rendering engines, such as Pixar's RenderMan, to generate lighting and volume passes for the compositing department to use in the final stage of compositing.

○ Modeling department

The modeling department creates photo-realistic 3D models for visual effects shots, including CG human characters, animals, creatures, mechanical objects, and more. In high-profile feature films, key creatures are sometimes first sculpted as miniatures, which are then digitized using 3D scanning technology. As one of the earliest stages in the visual effects pipeline, 3D modeling involves the use of specialized software such as Maya and ZBrush for modeling and digital sculpting, alongside tools like Foundry's Mari and Adobe Substance Painter to create procedural textures. Concept designs provided by the art department guide the modeling process as part of an upstream workflow, while downstream departments, such as rigging, animation, texturing, and lighting, build upon the models to bring them to life on screen.

◦ Motion capture department

To enhance the realism of traditional 3D character animation, the motion capture department captures the movements of stunt actors wearing capture suits equipped with ball-shaped markers during scene performances. Once the data is recorded, it is transferred to the animation department, where animators apply the captured motion data to 3D characters. The use of motion capture has significantly enhanced the authenticity and realism of 3D character animation.

◦ Matchmove department

The term "matchmove" refers to the process of tracking a camera's movement in order to integrate computer-generated elements into live-action footage during film visual effects production. The ultimate goal of this process is to realistically integrate CG elements into live-action plates in every aspect, including seamless camera movement. 3D camera tracking is critical to achieving this goal because it captures the camera motion from the original live-action plate. By accurately capturing the camera motion in the scene, a virtual camera can be created whose movement is consistent with the live-action plate. Artists across departments can then use the virtual camera to refilm and reproject elements within the scene. This approach is particularly important for integrating VFX assets into live-action plates. Additionally, the matchmove department provides accurate 3D camera tracking and matchmoving data to the rotoAnim team to precisely match the movements of live-action plates with 3D models, known as "digital doubles", which can replace actors in scenarios that would be impossible to shoot in the real world.

The upstream department of matchmove is editorial, which provides the original resolutions of live-action plates, camera formats, film back (sensor size) settings, actual work plate resolutions, and other essential data. Matchmove artists use this information to track the original plate in specialized applications such as 3DEqualizer, a widely adopted tracking tool across VFX studios. Once 3D camera tracking is completed, the resulting camera and lens distortion data becomes crucial for subsequent visual effects work.

◦ Photography department

This department is focused on on-set and in-studio filming, as indicated by its name. However, its responsibilities primarily involve capturing additional shots to assist with on-site data collection. These tasks include capturing reference images, filming lens grids, recording on-set references, documenting internal and external events, and other related activities.

○ Production department

The department coordinates and manages resources to ensure the timely delivery of visual effects shots that meet or exceed client expectations. Additionally, it liaises between various internal departments, including art, editorial, and technical departments, and external partners, such as film studios, producers, and vendors. The production department plays a vital role in coordinating communication across teams.

The production department usually has three key roles: VFX producers, production managers, and production coordinators. VFX producers focus on creating bids to persuade film (or TV series) producers to hire their VFX studio for projects. They assemble teams of VFX artists and other technical staff, establish work schedules, and manage budgets. VFX production managers work closely with VFX producers to ensure effective decisions are implemented. They develop detailed schedules for projects, allocate resources, and oversee manage budgets. Production coordinators work alongside with the production manager or producer to oversee the daily operations of the VFX team, facilitate the movement of assets through VFX pipelines, and communicate updates on project status and any alterations that may impact their work, all in the interest of ensuring seamless execution of VFX projects.

○ Rigging department

The rigging department in VFX studios creates digital skeletons or structures for 3D characters and objects. The department works closely with the animation and modeling departments to ensure that the characters and objects are rigged correctly and are ready for animation. The department typically consists of artists specializing in different aspects of rigging, such as character rigging, prop rigging, and environment rigging. These artists work together to create complex and realistic rigs that enable animators to achieve the desired movements and expressions for the characters and objects in each VFX project. Rigging in film VFX shots often focuses on creating realistic movement and behavior for characters and creatures. Therefore, rigging artists in VFX need a deeper understanding of human and animal anatomy to create believable and realistic rigs. In contrast, rigging in stylized animation may focus more on creating exaggerated movements and expressions to align with the animation style.

The workflow for rigging in VFX is highly collaborative and closely integrated with other departments, such as modeling, texturing, and animation.

○ Roto/prep department

Rotoscoping involves manually creating mattes (masks) for elements in live-action plates, which are then used for compositing purposes. When unwanted elements are removed or fixed, the resulting plates are called clean plates. In the visual effects industry, a traditional professional development route often starts with rotoscoping and preparation artists before progressing to junior compositor positions. Therefore, an excellent digital compositor should possess strong knowledge and skills in rotoscoping and preparation tasks, enabling them to handle simple tasks independently and avoid burdening the roto/prep department. These skills are especially important when working with a small visual effects team, as compositors may occasionally need to participate in roto and prep production.

There are several factors to consider when promoting roto and prep artists at each level, including work quality, time management, technical knowledge, communication efficiency, work ethic, and attitude. Roto and prep artists use specialized tools such as Silhouette (Boris FX) and Foundry's NukeX to complete and review their daily assignments. Senior-level roto and prep artists are expected to demonstrate strong shot assessment skills and advanced proficiency in Nuke. This includes creative problem-solving, blue/green screen keying, and a solid understanding of color spaces and camera projections, among other skills.

The editorial department functions as the upstream stage for roto and prep, while the compositing department acts as the downstream department for roto/prep.

○ Shading and rendering department

As the title suggests, the department is responsible for writing shaders and managing rendering pipelines for 3D elements. The leading members of this department are primarily professional engineers with strong backgrounds in computer graphics and computer science. However, there is also room for talented 3D artists with highly technical programming skills to transition into this department.

Creating stunning visual effects for films and TV commercials involves complex creative processes that require varying levels of coding knowledge at different stages within professional software packages. Therefore, visual effects artists with coding skills are highly sought after. Coding is integral to every stage of the visual effects pipeline, from asset creation and animation to lighting, rendering, and compositing. As a result, excellent artists with coding expertise are always in high demand.

Traditionally, visual effects companies have relied on Pixar's RenderMan rendering engine for rendering 3D assets, particularly CG elements in feature films. However, over the past decade, the emergence of several new rendering engines has prompted VFX studios to diversify their pipelines. For example, high-end TV commercial projects now incorporate other physically based rendering (PBR) engines such as Autodesk Arnold and Chaos V-Ray, into their workflows. Although these tools are widely used, the choice of rendering engine ultimately depends on the specific needs of the production pipeline.

o Software research and development

Leading VFX facilities also invest considerable time and resources in developing in-house software tools to streamline production workflows and enhance creative capabilities. These tools include plugging, improved rendering engines, real-time simulation software, and advanced animation systems, among others. Such innovations enable studios to produce more complex and realistic visual effects, ultimately raising the overall quality of their work. Additionally, in-house software development allows studios to meet the specific needs of their clients. By creating custom tools and solutions, they can deliver unique visual effects that distinguish them from competitors. Software research and development is essential to the visual effects industry, requiring ongoing investment for studios to stay competitive and offer cutting-edge solutions.

o Stereoscopic department

The stereoscopic department is responsible for 3D stereoscopic production and 2D to 3D stereoscopic conversion. There are two common technical approaches used to achieve 3D stereoscopic effects.

The first approach involves the use of two cameras mounted side by side to capture scenes directly. Positioned horizontally, these cameras simultaneously record the left and right views, effectively replicating the visual experience of human binocular vision. As with natural eyesight, the slight difference in perspective between the two views is interpreted by the brain to produce a three-dimensional perception of the observed scene.

The second approach to creating 3D stereoscopic film involves traditional shooting, followed by converting mono-camera footage to stereo in post-production. This method was widely used in feature films during the early 2000s due to its lower cost and the technical challenges of shooting stereoscopic footage directly at the time. However, the 2D-to-3D conversion process is complex and demands significant time and resources. It involves using precise roto shapes to isolate all elements within each scene, which are then reprojected by a pair of rigged virtual cameras onto roughly constructed 3D models in a virtual space to produce stereoscopic images. Thanks to advances in technology, such production processes are no longer necessary today.

○ Texturing department

Textures define the visual appearance of 3D objects, making them essential for achieving realism. There are two primary approaches to creating textures for 3D elements: procedurally generating them using professional applications or capturing real-world references to create specific textures. As a result, the department must adhere to strict standards for texture creation.

During texture shoots, a key focus of the texturing department is managing the resolution and lighting of cross-polarized images, which capture surface textures while minimizing glare and reflections. The captured textures must be of sufficiently high resolution to preserve even the smallest surface details, with consistent lighting that avoids self-cast shadows.

Texture creation is a complex process that demands a deep understanding of digital color pipelines in production. Texturing artists must be well versed in linear color space and the ACES color pipeline to ensure accurate color representation across various applications. This expertise is essential for producing textures that not only look visually appealing on their own but also integrate seamlessly into the broader production workflow. Collaboration is key, as the texturing department works closely with other teams, such as 3D modeling and lighting, to maintain consistency and align with the overall creative vision. VFX studios commonly rely on industry-standard texture painting tools like Foundry Mari and Adobe Substance for 3D texturing.

In general, texture artists rely on existing photo libraries to create textures for personal or small-scale projects. However, for large-scale productions, particularly in film visual effects, many specific textures must be captured directly in the studio or on location. For example, when creating a digital double, the textures must match the appearance and level of detail of the original character as closely as possible to maintain visual consistency.

• Professional software and file formats used in film VFX production

Those interested in learning film visual effects may be curious about the software used by top visual effects studios around the world. This section explores the applications commonly employed in the film VFX industry, along with the relevant standards and concepts.

o Rotoscoping and prep software

Silhouette, software developed by Boris FX, has established itself as an indispensable tool for rotoscoping in the visual effects industry. It allows for the creation of precise masks and mattes, which are essential for seamlessly integrating live-action footage with digital elements. While Silhouette is a powerful standalone application, mastering it alone is not sufficient for rotoscoping and prep artists aiming to succeed in the industry. Rotoscoping artists also need to possess a certain level of proficiency in Nuke for testing roto and prep assets before final delivery to other departments.

As pipelines evolve in visual effects studios, performing rotoscoping directly in NukeX is becoming increasingly effective. This shift is primarily driven by the need to streamline workflows and simplify processes. While Silhouette remains a popular choice, rotoscoping in NukeX has gained significant traction. Furthermore, ongoing advancements in machine learning tools such as Copycat in NukeX have introduced powerful new features that further enhance the efficiency of the rotoscoping process.

o 3D camera tracking software

Advanced software applications, such as 3D Equalizer developed by Science-D-Visions, have become indispensable for visual effects studios worldwide. With precise camera tracking capabilities, these applications can accurately replicate real-world camera movements extracted from live-action footage.

3D Equalizer is not the only software application that has gained widespread adoption in the VFX industry. Other popular matchmoving and 3D camera tracking tools, such as SynthEyes by Boris FX and PFTrack by The Pixel Farm, are also widely used by professionals. These applications offer features that allow users to efficiently solve complex camera movements, making them valuable assets in visual effects production.

◦ Compositing software

The Foundry's NukeX is highly regarded compositing software used extensively in the film and TV commercial industries. With its node-based architecture, NukeX offers artists an intuitive workflow that enables flexible handling of complex visual effects shots. For over a decade, Nuke has been the preferred choice of compositing departments at leading visual effects studios. Its strong reputation stems from its ability to deliver outstanding results with exceptional flexibility. Equipped with a rich set of features and tools, Nuke empowers artists to create sophisticated compositions by seamlessly integrating 2D and 3D elements. Additionally, it supports a wide range of plugin gizmos, allowing for a highly customizable user experience.

◦ 3D software

- Autodesk Maya and SideFX Houdini are essential 3D software packages used to create assets in the visual effects industry. Since its initial release in 1998, Maya has undergone over two decades of development and is now deeply embedded in visual effects and 3D animation production pipelines. Depending on specific project requirements, VFX studios may also use other 3D software to support artists in completing particular tasks. For example, Houdini, procedural-based 3D software, is increasingly becoming the primary tool for creating FX assets. Blender is another frequently used 3D tool for asset creation; however, it is not yet fully integrated into film VFX production pipelines.
- Maxon ZBrush is widely used for digital sculpting in character workflows.
- The Foundry's Mari is essential for texture creation and is commonly used in major VFX studios. Additionally, familiarity with Adobe Substance Painter is almost mandatory for texture artists.
- The Foundry's Katana is the industry-leading software for digital lighting and look development.

Additionally, larger-scale VFX facilities extensively develop and use in-house tools to produce high-quality VFX shots for specific tasks within the VFX pipeline, such as realistic simulations of human hair or animal fur, rigid body dynamics for 3D animation, digital crowd simulations, and internal systems for simulating the destruction of buildings and 3D models.

○ Common file formats used for storing CG assets

OpenEXR is a file format developed by Industrial Light & Magic (ILM) specifically for storing high-dynamic-range images. It was designed to meet the demanding requirements of VFX production, including high image quality and native support for linearized color space. One of OpenEXR's key advantages is its ability to support multiple layers. This feature enables artists to store various image passes within a single OpenEXR file, simplifying the management of large volumes of image data. Additionally, OpenEXR can store extensive color information in a linear color space, which is essential in VFX pipelines. As a result, it has become an industry-standard file format for visual effects production.

Another crucial aspect of the visual effects workflow is the use of arbitrary output variables (AOVs). AOVs allow artists to separate images into individual passes, such as reflections, shadows, specular highlights, and many others. This separation enables precise control and manipulation of specific elements during compositing. The preferred format for rendering AOVs is the EXR file format, as certain utility AOV passes require 32-bit image depth.

○ Live-action footage formats used in visual effects

Visual effects studios often work with a variety of footage formats and image aspect ratios during production. These may include 10-bit DPX scans, ARRI camera native formats, RED camera R3D files, and many other image formats captured by different cameras. However, the editorial department typically converts the original digital formats of live-action footage into 16-bit EXR sequences to integrate them into the linear color production pipeline. Despite the predominance of digital formats today, 10-bit DPX scans may still appear in compositing when footage is sourced from scanned negative films.

• Examples of the operational framework between departments

While internal departmental structures and collaborative processes may vary across VFX studios, the following section aims to illustrate the interconnected production operations across various departments during VFX production.

Editorial is the first department to receive the original live-action footage from the client. At this stage, the department creates the following assets and outputs data.

∘ Key operations in the editorial department

– *Color grade reference*

This data is extracted from each shot provided by the client and is used to ensure color accuracy in the output plates, matching them to the client's reference QuickTime files. At this stage, the editorial department will deliver the following files, which will be shared across departments:

Plate resolutions

Plate at working resolution (2K)

Plate at original resolution

These plates will be delivered to the matchmove and compositing departments. Notably, the editorial department should also provide the Nuke scripts used to generate these plates. This aspect of the workflow differs from traditional editorial processes in most post-production houses.

– *LUTs and metadata*

(ASC CDL) Color correction

Client-provided color correction value data from EDL, metadata, etc.

File LUT

Client-provided LUTs.

Shot LUT

A LUT file is produced for various displays across departments.

– *Final delivery package*

Pack the assets and data produced previously into an "InputPlate Package" that includes the following items:

Original plate

Work plate

Plate metadata

Nuke scripts

Element color grade

This package will be delivered to other departments, such as roto/prep, matchmove, stereoscopic, and compositing, for further operations. As an example, let's look at how the roto/prep department handles the data obtained from the "InputPlate Package".

◦ Key operations in the roto/prep department

– *Roto team*

Roto artists use Boris FX Silhouette to create pixel-accurate roto shapes according to shot requirements and deliver mattes that are crucial for compositing.

– *Silhouette tasks*

Roto artists create roto shapes based on specific instructions and export mattes. They also provide roto splines in compatible formats for the compositing department, allowing compositors to make additional adjustments directly in NukeX. This minimizes the need to frequently request minor changes from the roto team.

– *Nuke tasks*

After completing the rotoscoping process in Silhouette, roto artists need to create a series of combined mattes by assigning red, green, and blue channels (R, G, and B) to different roto shapes in NukeX. These mattes are categorized into two types: those with motion blur and those without. This classification allows compositors to flexibly use the roto shapes for various compositing needs.

– *Roto package*

The output at this stage will include a combined render of mattes (both with and without motion blur), Nuke-compatible roto splines, and Silhouette-generated Nuke scripts.

– *Prep team*

The prep team uses Nuke and Silhouette to create clean plates tailored to the specific requirements of each shot in the project.

– *Prep package*

The final delivery of this package should include clean plates that have been processed to remove any unwanted elements from the original work plates, along with metadata containing details such as resolution and frame rate. Additionally, the package should include Nuke scripts used to create the clean plates, ensuring the work can be easily reproduced or modified.

o Key operations in the compositing department

Usually, compositing leads or supervisors create Nuke templates for generating input Maya data, neutral plates, and flattened (lens undistorted) plates. Additionally, the department also builds templates for further operations, such as denoising, dispelling, and keying the input plates, as well as generating a neutral grade for each shot. The neutral-grade node is applied at the end of each compositing script as a reference for future color grading. Consequently, at the end of the Nuke script, two separate outputs can be seen: one is the neutral-grade output, and the other is the result with the original client LUT applied.

– *Comp asset package*

After completing the preparation of assets, the compositing team will pack the rendered assets and scripts into an asset package, which includes denoise, despill, key, lens distortion data, and stereo camera convergence files. Additionally, the package contains plates with neutral-grade flattened plates and files compatible with Autodesk Maya. The finalized package will then be handed over to the lighting department.

o Key operations in the lighting department

The lighting department uses Foundry's Katana to create two types of output files: scene-referred linear OpenEXR image sequences and lighting renders. A package of lighting renders should include the following elements: lighting renders, noise-free lighting renders, Katana scripts, cameras, Nuke relight files, and holdout renders.

Stereoscopic films have become increasingly common, especially in VFX-intensive productions that often require both 3D stereo and 2D versions.

○ Key operations in the stereoscopic department

The stereoscopic team manages two types of assets related to the working plate provided by the editorial department: vertical alignment and color alignment.

– *Vertical alignment*

When capturing stereoscopic shots using two horizontally aligned cameras, slight vertical position shifts between the cameras may occur, causing the footage from the left and right cameras to misalign. The stereoscopic team must rectify these misalignment issues for each shot before proceeding with additional tasks.

– *Color alignment*

Color shift is a common issue in stereoscopic footage, so correcting color alignment is important. The Foundry's Ocula plug-in for Nuke is a powerful tool for this task.

– *Stereo alignment package*

The final delivery package from the stereoscopic team includes vertical alignment maps, aligned working plates, and Nuke scripts. The package should also contain aligned disparity and occlusion maps, along with assets prepared by the roto/prep, editorial, and compositing departments. These assets are gathered in the package and are ready for the department to proceed with further stereo operations.

Meanwhile, other departments continued working on their respective responsibilities. The matchmove department uses the original plate supplied by the editorial department to track camera movements and create virtual cameras and lens distortion data, which can be imported directly into Nuke for further use.

At this stage, an "Input Package" is created, containing elements provided by the editorial, roto/prep, matchmove, stereoscopic, and compositing departments.

○ Key operations in the digital matte painting department

When the "Input Package" contains prepackaged elements delivered by the editorial, roto/prep, stereoscopic, matchmove, and compositing departments,

DMP artists use a variety of professional tools to create matte painting renders. They then deliver an environment render package that includes DMP renders, environment renders, camera packages, Nuke scripts, and other necessary components.

After this extensive journey through various departments and collaborative efforts, the next step is to create a comprehensive "Compositing Package". This package integrates prepackaged elements from the DMP environment, lighting, FX, and other input packages. This integrated package plays a vital role in the final compositing process and is essential for securing client approval in the next phase.

Chapter Four

Analysis of the core components in invisible film visual effects

Learning objectives

> Understand the difference between linear color space and human vision.

> Understand ACES color management in visual effects production.

> Understand image color depth and its applications in visual effects production.

> Understand the importance of on-set data in high-end visual effects production.

DOI: 10.4324/9781003224617-4

• Understanding the color spaces of digital images and VFX color pipelines

◦ Additive color vs. subtractive color

There are two color principles involved in dealing with digital color primitives: the additive color principle and the subtractive color principle.

It is important to note that the additive color principle, which uses the R, G, and B color primitives, primarily applies to digital images displayed on monitors, such as computer displays, TV panels, smartphones, and similar devices. In contrast, the subtractive color principle is used when the final product is physically printed, as in books and magazines. This system uses the C (cyan), M (magenta), Y (yellow), and K (key/black) colors.

With this distinction clarified, the color theories and practices discussed throughout this book specifically relate to the additive color principle. The images in Figure 4.1 compare the visual differences between the additive and subtractive color principles.

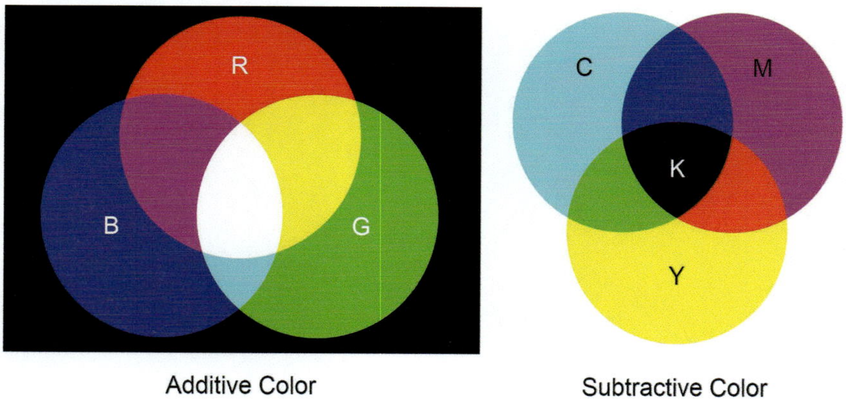

FIGURE 4.1 Comparison of additive and subtractive color principles

◦ Scene-referred and display-referred workflows

A thorough comprehension of image colors is crucial in high-end visual effects production, such as in feature films and TV commercial projects. The field of computer science delves deeply into color spaces, which can be confusing for artists. In visual effects production, especially when live-action footage is involved, color pipelines require an understanding of two significant categories: scene-referred and display-referred workflows.

A scene-referred workflow is a critical color management solution in visual effects production. It ensures consistent color accuracy throughout the production pipeline, from image capture to final delivery. In this workflow, images are processed in a linear color space that preserves their original characteristics without early conversion. This approach differs from a display-referred workflow, where images are immediately transformed into a color space optimized for a specific display device, such as Rec. 709.

Throughout the VFX production pipeline, images are processed to preserve their scene-referred nature rather than being adjusted for display on a particular device. After VFX production, the final output is transformed into a display-referred color space optimized for viewing on a specific device. This transformation uses a color management system to ensure accurate color representation, given the limitations of the display device.

VFX studios utilize scene-referred workflows to preserve the originality of image data and the dynamic range of live-action footage. Therefore, CG renders and assets should also be processed in a scene-referred workflow. Image A in Figure 4.2 illustrates an initial conceptual comparison between scene-referred and display-referred workflows.

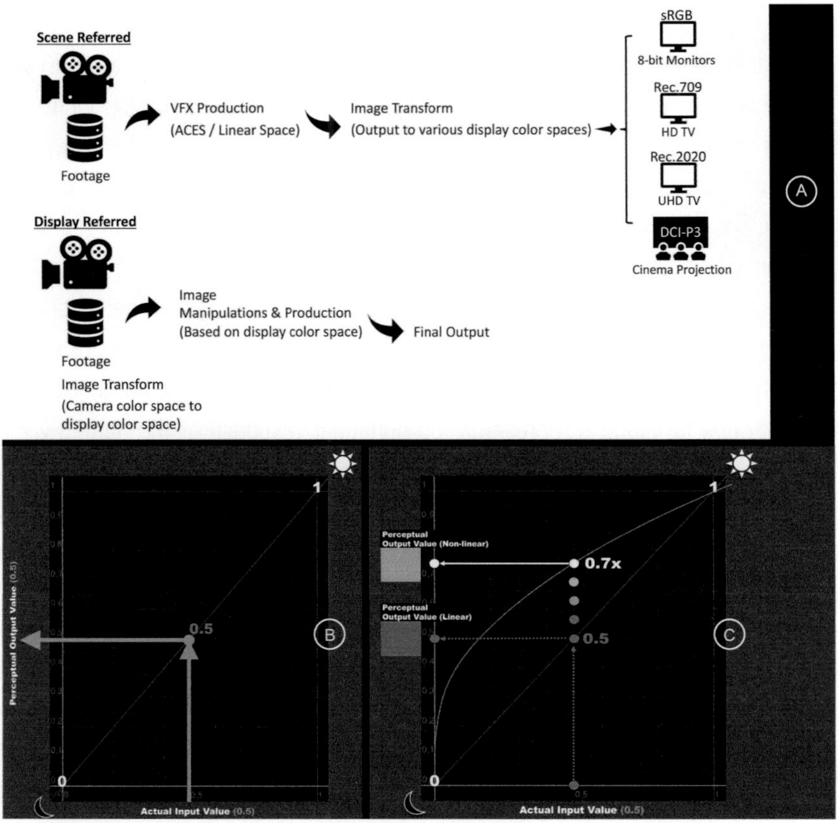

FIGURE 4.2 Scene referred vs. display referred (A); linear color space (B) vs. human vision (C)

The following section explores the distinctions between linear space and human vision and their relevance to color perception, as demonstrated in Images B and C in Figure 4.2. Understanding this principle is especially important in visual effects production when integrating live-action footage and CG elements.

◦ Linear space vs. human vision and color perception

Light is essential for us to perceive colors within the visible spectrum. It is widely known that the physical world exists in a linear color space. Digital cameras also record images in a linear color space, where intensity values directly correspond to the actual amount of light in the scene. However, human vision does not perceive light in a strictly linear manner. Our eyes have a non-linear response to light, meaning the perceived brightness of a light source is not directly proportional to its actual intensity. To address this, scientists use gamma compensation to analyze digital images in linear space while accounting for the non-linear response of the human visual system.

Gamma compensation is a technique used to adjust the intensity values in digital images to make them more visually pleasing to human perception while preserving the physical properties of the natural world. It involves applying a power function to these values to account for the nonlinear response of the human visual system. The degree of this adjustment is determined by the exponent of the power function, known as gamma.

Image B in Figure 4.2 shows a diagonal line representing the linear light law in the real world. An input value of 0.5 from a linear light source corresponds proportionally to a perceptual output value of 0.5. In contrast, the curve above the diagonal line in Image C represents the nonlinear response of the human visual system. As a result, an actual input value of 0.5 maps to approximately 0.7x on the curved line, increasing the perceptual output from 0.5 to 0.7x. Consequently, the human eye perceives the 50% gray output as approximately 70% gray in Image C.

In summary, light plays a crucial role in how we perceive the world, and the nonlinear response of the human visual system poses a challenge for artists working in visual effects production. Gamma compensation is an essential technique used by scientists to address this issue.

◦ Understanding gamma compensation in digital images

Gamma compensation is key to accurately encoding and decoding luminance in digital images. This process involves applying a non-linear operation, typically represented by γ, to the image's luminance before it is saved or transmitted. When the image is displayed on a screen, a decoding gamma is applied to ensure the original luminance is rendered correctly.

Figure 4.3 shows three images (A, B, and C). Images A and B illustrate non-linear curves corresponding to the encoding and decoding processes. Image C demonstrates how gamma compensation operates in the context of digital images and display devices.

The upper curve in Image A represents the non-linear nature of human visual perception, encoded with a gamma value of 0.45 ($\gamma = 1/2.2 \approx 0.45$). This curve reflects how our eyes perceive brightness levels. In contrast, the lower curve in Image B represents a decoding gamma of 2.2, which closely aligns with the standard sRGB gamma value commonly used in digital devices such as cameras, computer monitors, smartphones, and more.

The gamma compensation process occurs in two stages to accurately encode and decode an image's luminance, as shown in Figure 4.3, Image C. This process is also visible in Images A and B, which use gamma values of 0.45 and a compensation value of 2.2 to represent the encoding and decoding process.

The first stage involves encoding a lookup table (LUT) into the image when it is saved or transmitted. The encoding LUT value (0.45) ensures that the image's luminance is accurately represented and can be precisely decoded later.

The second stage involves decoding the image using a LUT embedded in display devices. In this example, the LUT value (2.2) ensures that the image's original luminance is faithfully rendered on the computer screen, which uses an sRGB LUT with a value of 2.2.

LUTs embedded in images and display devices can vary. For instance, ARRI and RED cameras have specific LUTs embedded in their footage, which require corresponding LUTs on monitors for proper decoding and display.

Understanding gamma compensation and LUTs is essential for professionals working with digital images. By applying the correct LUTs during the encoding and decoding stages, images can be accurately represented and appear as intended on any device.

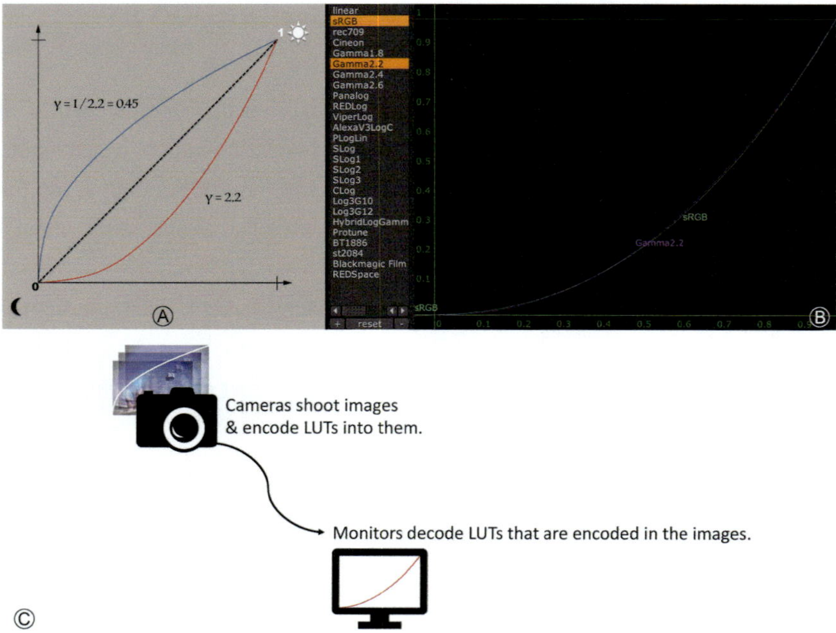

FIGURE 4.3 Process of compensating for gamma encoding and decoding in images and display devices

◦ Linear color workflow in VFX production

In Nuke's default color management, there is an sRGB dropdown menu called "viewerProcess" located at the top left of the Viewer1 panel. As the industry-standard compositing tool, NukeX is designed to operate primarily in linear color space, which is essential for visual effects production. When an image is loaded into the Viewer1 panel, the default color management system automatically applies an sRGB LUT, ensuring the image is displayed correctly on computer monitors that use an embedded sRGB LUT.

As a practical example, Figure 4.4 illustrates how different LUTs can alter the appearance of the same image. The upper image shows the result with the default sRGB LUT applied in the Viewer1 panel. In contrast, the lower image displays the same content with "None" selected from the dropdown list of LUTs, indicating that the image is viewed in linear space without any specific LUT applied. This comparison highlights how the choice of LUT influences the visual output, emphasizing the importance of color management and a solid understanding of color spaces when selecting LUTs.

Notes:

1. The default sRGB LUT in the Viewer1 panel can be changed and customized to meet production requirements. It is important to note that footage captured by different cameras and formats may have varying color profiles. Therefore, using the appropriate LUT in the Viewer1 panel is essential for accurate image color representation.
2. The default LUTs or customized LUTs applied to the Viewer1 panel only affect how images are displayed on different monitors without altering the inherent properties of the original images.

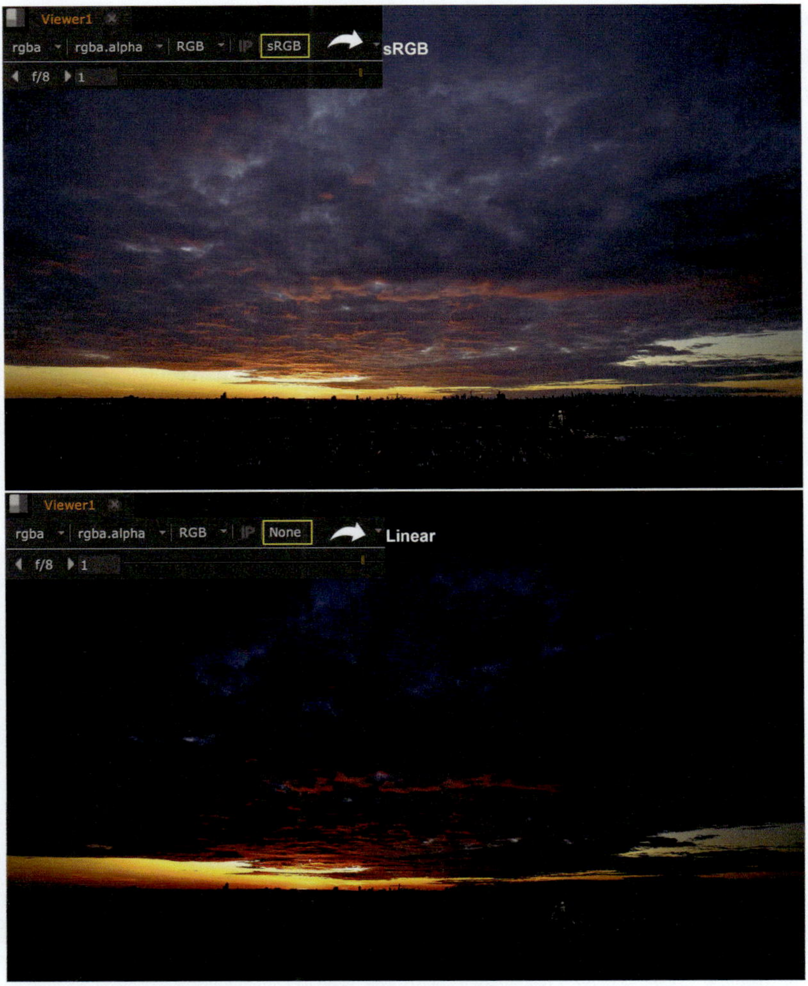

FIGURE 4.4 Comparison of sRGB and linear color spaces when viewing the same image in Nuke's Viewer panel

With an understanding of how Nuke displays images in different color spaces, let's explore how LUTs can be configured for visual effects projects at this stage. In visual effects production, clients often provide predefined LUTs for use in VFX shots. These specially designed LUT files must be consistently applied to all computer displays across departments when working on VFX projects. To achieve this, the image department (or a relevant department) configures LUTs to ensure that computer monitors automatically switch to a custom LUT when artists access a specific project or scene.

Visual effects studios often use dual computer displays. One display is typically calibrated to match the standard color LUT of the device on which the project will be displayed, such as the DCI-P3 LUT used for digital cinema projections. In contrast, the other display is usually calibrated natively and adjusted with project-specific LUTs. This dual-display setup allows visual effects artists to continuously observe and compare image colors, enabling real-time adjustments as necessary.

A visual comparison of the dual display setup in visual effects productions is shown in Figure 4.5, where a blank white document is displayed across two side-by-side computer monitors. Considering the lighting environment of the standard theater where the final film will be shown, the left monitor has been color-calibrated to match the DCI-P3 color temperature commonly used for cinema projectors. In contrast, the right monitor is calibrated to the native computer color temperature with the client project LUT applied. As a result, the difference in color temperature between the two monitors is clearly observable.

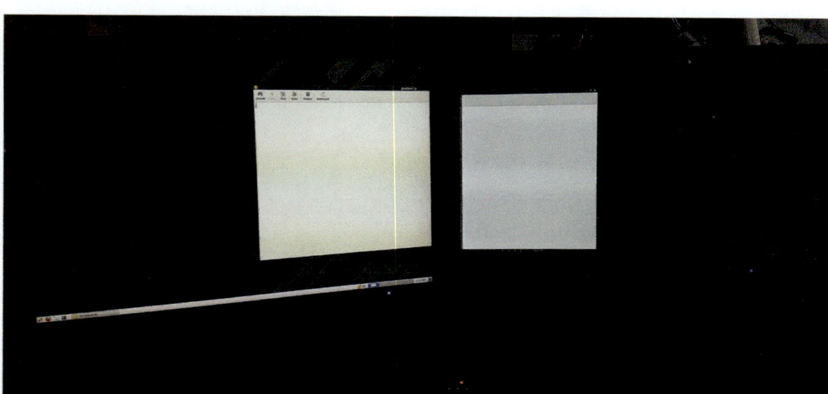

FIGURE 4.5 Example of color temperature comparison on dual computer displays used in VFX studios

It is worth noting that the dimly lit working environment shown in Figure 4.5 is typical of compositing departments, especially for color-critical projects in high-end film and TV commercials that require precise color accuracy. This is because working in low-light conditions helps minimize issues such as color bleeding and reflections from external light sources, allowing artists to focus on the color details of the image without distractions.

◦ Scene-referred workflow for integrating 3D assets into live-action footage

A "scene-referred" workflow means that all VFX assets are created within the linear color space. Let's briefly look at the concept of the scene-referred workflow, as shown in Figure 4.6.

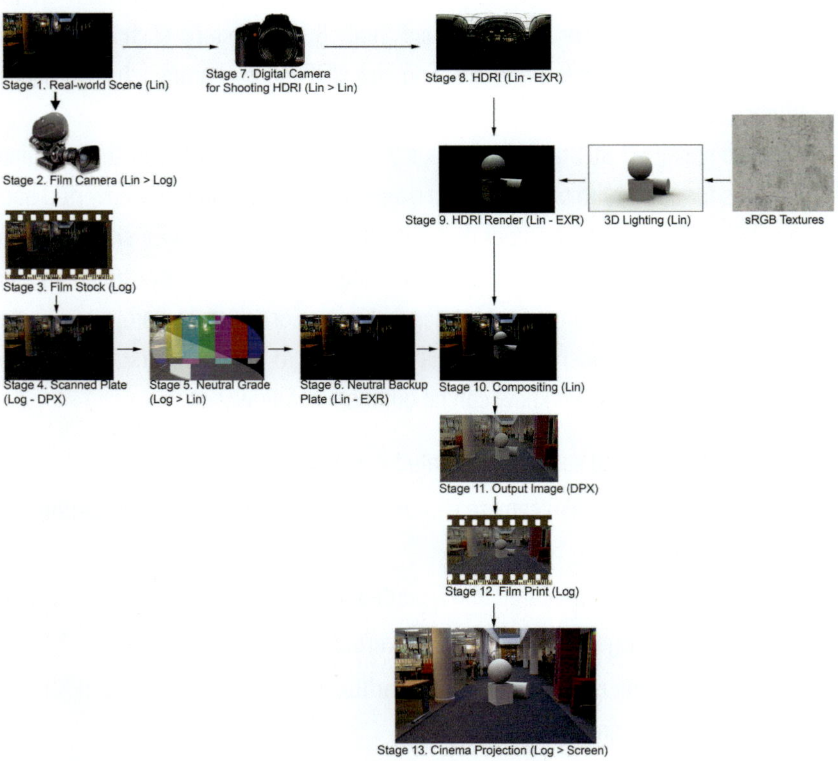

FIGURE 4.6 Scene-referred workflow for integrating 3D assets into live-action footage

Stage 1 (located in the upper left corner of Figure 4.6) visually represents a real-world linear space scene. Stage 2 (positioned below the Stage 1 image) shows the same scene being filmed using traditional film cameras, capturing it in a logarithmic format. This process naturally converts linear space into logarithmic space (Lin > Log), a transformation that occurs within the camera during filming.

In Stages 3, 4, 5, and 6, the scene is captured, scanned, and converted into 10-bit DPX (Digital Picture Exchange) format, which is the industry standard for digitizing traditional negative film. The resulting footage is then color-neutralized and saved in EXR (OpenEXR) format. Meanwhile, in Stages 7 and 8, a series of high dynamic range images (HDRIs) of the on-set environment are captured using still digital cameras. These HDR images are stitched together and converted into a 360-degree environment map in 32-bit EXR format. To seamlessly integrate 3D assets with live-action footage, it is important to light the 3D assets using an HDRI map that accurately reflects the lighting conditions of the live-action scene. This integration process involves several stages, which are explored in detail in the following case studies. For example, Case Study 8 covers steps such as capturing images with multiple exposures, creating the HDRI map, lighting the 3D scene, multi-pass rendering, and final compositing.

After compositing at Stage 10, output VFX shots are exported in their original file formats for delivery to clients. In this example, the final output is converted back to the DPX format and then integrated with the remaining non-VFX shots for subsequent processes such as color grading, editing, and more. Finally, the completed show is printed onto negative film in a logarithmic color space and projected in cinemas (Log > Screen space) using cinema projectors. To better understand this process, the scene-referred workflow can be outlined as follows:

Stage 1. A real-world scene is presented in linear space.

Stage 2. A traditional film camera captures the real-world scene in logarithmic (Log) format.

Stage 3. The scene is captured and recorded on film stock.

Stage 4. The footage is scanned and converted to 10-bit DPX format.

Stage 5. The scene is converted from logarithmic (Log) format to linear (EXR) and neutrally graded.

Stage 6. The neutralized plate of the scene is saved in OpenEXR format.

Stages 7–9 involve capturing HDR images of the real-world location where the live-action footage was filmed. These HDR images are taken using a digital camera and recorded in RAW format. Stages 10–13 illustrate the key steps involved in integrating the live-action plate with 3D assets and producing the final output.

Stage 7: A series of HDR images is captured, and a 360-degree HDRI map is created from them.

Stage 8: The 360-degree HDRI map is converted to OpenEXR format.

Stage 9: 3D assets are lit and rendered using the HDRI map in linear color space.

Stage 10: All elements are integrated through compositing in linear color space.

Stage 11: The final VFX shot is exported to DPX format. Then, integrated with other non-VFX shots for further post-production processes such as editing and color grading.

Stage 12: The completed film is printed onto negative film (Log).

Stage 13: The film is projected using cinema projectors (Log > Screen).

After developing a basic understanding of the concept of linear workflow, we will explore a more advanced color management system known as ACES, which is a standard in VFX production pipelines, in the upcoming sections.

• Analyses of digital image bit depths and applications in visual effects production

○ Understanding image bit depths

Image bit depth refers to the amount of color information stored in a digital image. The higher the bit depth, the more color information the image can contain. For example, a 1-bit image can only represent two color shades: black and white, as shown in Figure 4.7.

The mathematical formula for calculating the number of color shades in a bit depth is:

1 bit (2^1) = 2 shades.

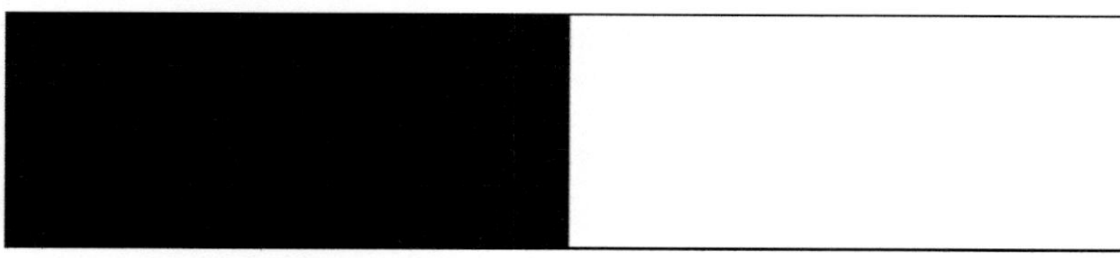

FIGURE 4.7 A 1-bit image contains only two colors: black and white

Most digital images encountered online are typically 8-bit depth images, such as JPEG and PNG files. These images include an embedded sRGB lookup table and are relatively small in size, making them suitable for online use. The mathematical representation of an 8-bit image is:

8-bit (2^8) = 256 color shades per channel.

When dealing with 8-bit digital images, we understand that each image consists of three channels: R, G, and B. With this in mind, the total number of possible color shades can be expressed as R × G × B, or 256 × 256 × 256, which equals 16,777,216. This large amount of color information stored in an 8-bit image is generally sufficient for basic image manipulation. However, in visual effects production, live-action plates typically require higher bit depths, such as 10-bit DPX, 12-bit, 16-bit, or high-end RAW digital formats.

Using the same equation, the color information in a 10-bit image can be calculated as follows: 10-bit (2^{10}) = 1024 values per channel. Consequently, the R × G × B (1024 × 1024 × 1024) gamut generates an impressive 1,073,741,824 possible colors. This significant increase in color data greatly impacts how digital images are processed.

As a result, 10-bit depth is widely considered the minimum requirement for effectively handling live-action footage in visual effects studios.

The images in Figure 4.8 explore how image bit depth affects digital images, particularly the rich detail in the highlights. The top images in Figure 4.8 compare a 16-bit image with an 8-bit image. To the human eye, the two images appear visually identical. However, when the f-stop (exposure value) is decreased in both images, the 16-bit image reveals more color detail in the highlights, whereas the 8-bit image loses these details. For example, the texture of the glass lampshade is lost in the highlights of the 8-bit image. This difference is also evident in the R, G, and B values measured at the same position in both images.

Why do the same highlights produce different sets of R, G, and B values, and why are the texture details of the glass lampshade lost in the 8-bit image?

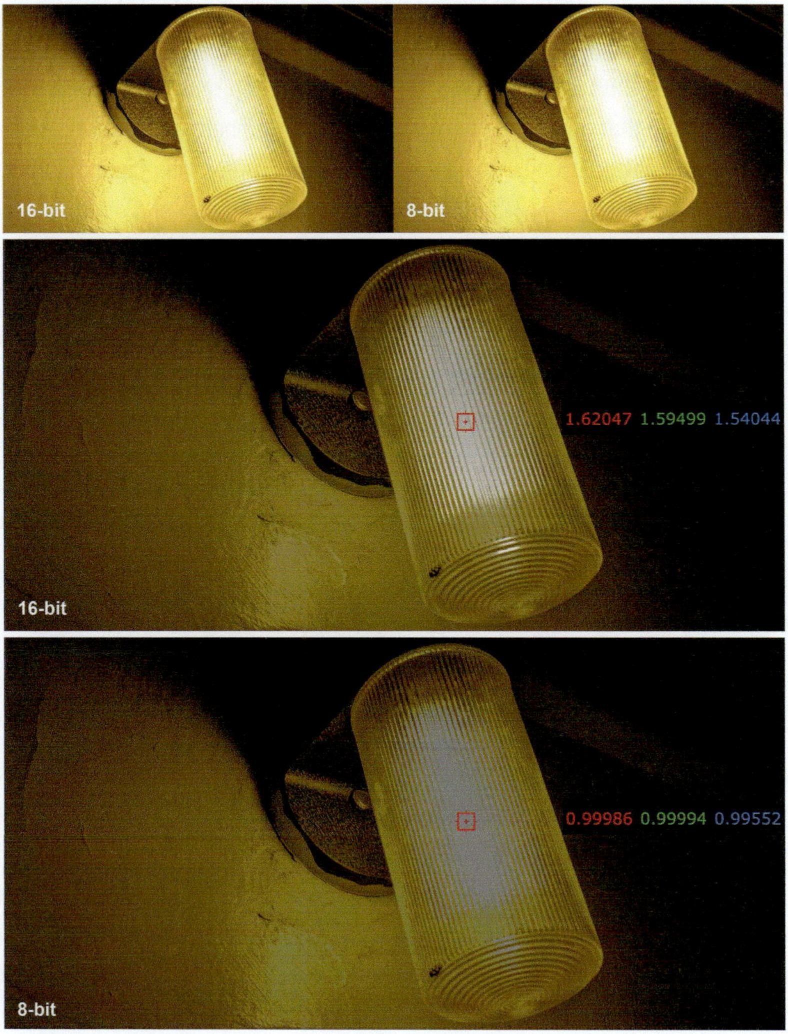

FIGURE 4.8 Comparison of the same image rendered at two different bit depths, highlighting variations in highlight color values

To address the questions raised here, it is important to recognize the limitations of 8-bit images. Due to their limited color range, 8-bit images clamp color values above 1. In this example, the R, G, and B values in the highlights are clamped to 0.99986, 0.99994, and 0.99552, respectively. However, images with a bit depth of 10 or higher can store values that exceed 1. For instance, in the 16-bit image shown in Figure 4.8, the R, G, and B values analyzed in the same area are 1.62047, 1.59499, and 1.54044, respectively. This allows highlight color values greater than 1 to be retained. As a result, these details are properly displayed when the exposure is decreased.

Figure 4.9 compares how 10-bit and 8-bit images handle color values above 1. In this context, 0 and 1 represent the minimum and maximum displayable color values. As shown in the 8-bit image, the diagonal line in the top right flattens after reaching 1, indicating that any values greater than 1 are clamped. In contrast, the 10-bit image allows values beyond 1 to continue increasing, preserving highlight information more accurately.

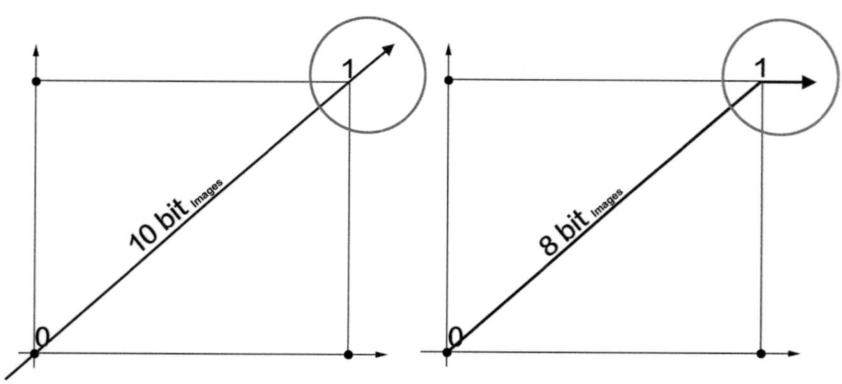

FIGURE 4.9 How color values in highlights are preserved between 10-bit and 8-bit images

This raises another question: why must exposure be decreased to reveal image details in the highlights when viewing 10-bit or higher bit-depth images on many computer displays?

To answer this, it is important to understand the relationship between bit depth and display capabilities. Displays in common devices such as computers, TV sets, and mobile phones have traditionally used 8-bit color depth. Even if a 10-bit or higher bit-depth image is shown on an 8-bit monitor, details with values above 1 may not be displayed properly, particularly in the highlights. These details still exist in the image data, but they cannot be accurately rendered due to the limitations of 8-bit display technology.

In visual effects production, artists often need to accurately perceive image details with values greater than 1 while working on 8-bit screens. To properly visualize color information in highlights that exceed this range, specific LUTs can be applied using professional software.

◦ Applications of image bit depths in VFX production

This section provides a practical example of applying image bit depth in live-action footage for visual effects projects. The primary focus is on understanding how the finer details captured in 10-bit or higher bit-depth images can be effectively visualized on standard 8-bit computer displays, with particular emphasis on color detail in the highlights.

As an industry-standard compositing tool, NukeX is widely used in major visual effects studios and will be used for hands-on practice throughout this book. A non-commercial version of NukeX is available from Foundry's official website at foundry.com. If you're unfamiliar with how Nuke operates, please watch the pre-recorded introductory video at the following link:

www.youtube.com/@InvisibleFilmVFX
Video title: The initial concept of node-based compositing in NukeX

Additionally, for an in-depth study of the software, it is recommended to watch the official Nuke training videos released by Foundry, available at:

https://learn.foundry.com/nuke

• Hands-on example (I): creating a custom LUT in Nuke's color management

The hands-on sections include step-by-step instructions provided in the following section, along with video demonstrations. Additionally, Nuke project scripts and assets are available to support the practical exercises.

Watch the hands-on example (I) pre-recorded video at the following link:

www.youtube.com/@InvisibleFilmVFX

Video title: Hands-On Example (I) | Creating a Custom LUT in Nuke's Color Management

The footage used in this section is an open-source asset provided by the Blender Foundation under a Creative Commons (CC) license, available at https://mango.blender.org/download/. Alternatively, the green screen plate demonstrated in this example can also be downloaded from the project folder associated with this book on the Routledge online system.

The hands-on example (I) serves the following purposes:

1. To reveal hidden details in the highlights of a 16-bit green screen plate, ensuring that all color information is visible on 8-bit computer displays for further tasks.
2. To apply a client-predefined LUT to Nuke's Viewer1 panel.

The background plate used in this example can be downloaded directly from the following link:

https://media.xiph.org/tearsofsteel/linear-exr/04_5f/

Background plate information:

File format: 16-bit OpenEXR

Color space: Linear RGB

Aspect ratio: 4K_DCP (4096 × 2160)

Step 1 | Launch NukeX and set up a new project.

– To set up a new project, go to the menu Edit > Project Settings . . .

  Alternatively, place your mouse cursor in the Node Graph area and press the S key to open the Project Settings. The Project Settings parameters will then appear in the Properties panel.

Note:

Nuke's hotkey operations work interactively with the mouse cursor. This means the position of the cursor determines which specific operations are accessible via hotkeys. As a result, the same hotkey can trigger entirely different actions depending on where the cursor is located within Nuke's user interface.

- In the Project Settings dialog box, set the following knobs (option slots):

  frame range: 1 to 100

  (The default frame range is set from 1 to 100. However, it may be adjusted as needed to match the start and end frames of the image sequence contained in the background plate.)

  fps: 24

  full size format: 4K_DCP 4096x2160

To import external images, position the mouse cursor within the Node Graph area and press the R key. This will open a dialog window titled Read File(s). Navigate to the folder where the plate is stored, select the file, and click the Open button at the bottom of the dialog window to import it into NukeX. Once imported, the plate will appear in the Node Graph area.

Step 2 | Loading the background plate into the Viewer1 panel.

- After importing the background plate, a Read1 node appears in the Node Graph area, highlighted in orange.
- With the plate (Read1 node) still selected, press the 1 key (numeric) on your keyboard to load the plate into Nuke's Viewer1 panel. This action creates a connection between the Viewer1 node and the plate (Read1 node), indicated by a dotted line. At the same time, Nuke's default color management, sRGB (LUT), is automatically applied to the Viewer1 panel.

  To gain a more intuitive understanding of this section, please watch the hands-on example video (I) available on YouTube at @InvisibleFilmVFX.

Step 3 | Analyze the details in the highlights of the background plate.

Hover the mouse cursor over the highlights on the green screen plate to analyze the RGB color values of the selected areas. As you move the cursor across the image highlights, the corresponding RGB values appear at the bottom of the Viewer1 panel.

Figure 4.10 shows two analyzed areas on the green screen plate, marked with red squares. The corresponding R, G, and B values within the marked area of Image A are 3.64792, 2.33867, and 1.55111. In Image B, the RGB values are 5.49466, 4.43077, and 3.69639, respectively.

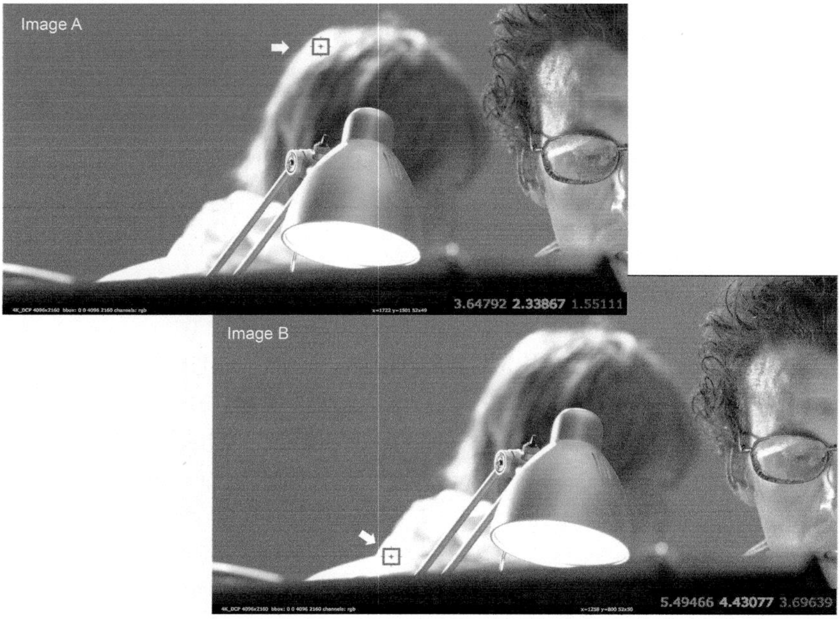

FIGURE 4.10 Analyzing the R, G, and B values in the highlights of the image. Original footage © Mango.blender.org

As shown in Figure 4.10, the color information in the highlight areas of the image cannot be accurately displayed on standard 8-bit computer monitors, as the color values exceed 1. To display these details, a monitor with a higher bit depth, such as a 10-bit display, is required. However, true 10-bit professional monitors remain relatively expensive, even for VFX studios, especially when used in large numbers. Therefore, a workaround is needed to visualize the out-of-range color information on standard 8-bit displays.

Step 4 | View color details in highlights on an 8-bit computer display.

Move the gain slider (located at the top left of the Viewer1 panel) to the left to reveal more color detail in the highlights of the green screen plate. This adjustment doesn't alter the image's attributes; it simply helps us inspect the color information in the highlights. See Figure 4.11.

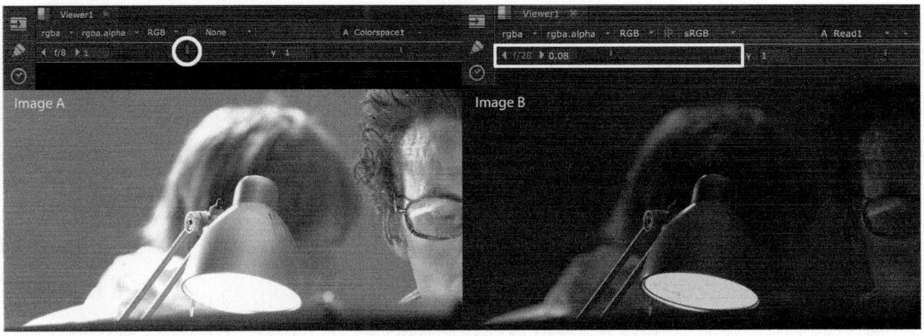

FIGURE 4.11 Comparison of the same image at different gain (f-stop) values in the Viewer panel

Figure 4.11 compares the 16-bit green screen plate displayed in the Viewer1 panel. Image A (left) shows the plate with the default gain setting of 1, while Image B (right) displays it with a lower gain setting. By comparing the images at both gain settings, we can see that Image B reveals more color detail in the highlights, whereas Image A exhibits blown-out highlights.

To properly display color details in the highlights of this 16-bit plate on an 8-bit computer display during production, we need to apply a customized LUT to the Viewer1 panel. This ensures that all color information in the plate is accurately visible before proceeding with further VFX tasks.

Step 5 | Create a custom LUT for the Viewer1 panel.

- In the Node Graph, select the green screen plate (Read1 node) by clicking on it.
- Press the Tab key on your keyboard to open the search bar.
- In the search bar, type Colorspace [Color] and select it from the drop-down menu. This will add a Colorspace node connected to the green screen plate.

Note:

Position the mouse cursor within the Node Graph area when performing these operations, as its location can affect the outcome. For example, toggling the Tab key while the cursor is over the Viewer1 panel will switch between the Viewer1 panel and Nuke's 3D space.

- Double-click the Colorspace node to load its parameters in the Properties panel. Then, set the input and output settings as follows:

  input: Linear

  output: Cineon

These settings in the Colorspace node convert the green screen plate from linear color space to Cineon color space, revealing rich detail in this 16-bit image, especially in the highlights. However, the green screen plate appears milky when viewed through the Viewer1 panel. This result is due to the inherent characteristics of the Cineon color space combined with the sRGB LUT (gamma 2.2) applied in Nuke's Viewer1 panel.

To accurately visualize the color of the green screen plate in the Cineon color space without being affected by the default sRGB LUT automatically applied in the Viewer1 panel, change the viewerProcess setting from "sRGB" to "None." This option is indicated by a white-rectangle wireframe at the top of the Viewer1 panel, as shown in Figure 4.12.

Note:

Switching from the default "sRGB" to "None" disables the sRGB LUT applied to the Viewer1 panel, allowing the image to be viewed in its native color space without the sRGB correction.

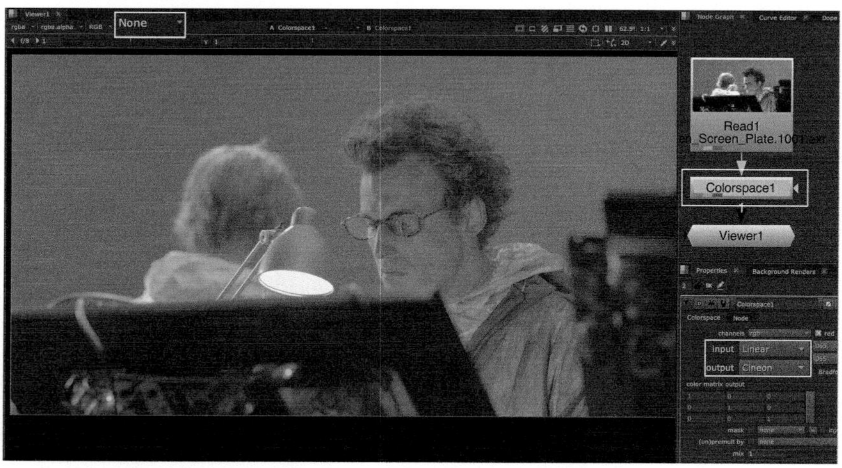

FIGURE 4.12 Image converted from linear to Cineon color space and displayed in the Viewer1 panel without the default sRGB LUT applied

As the details in the highlights of the image become visible in the Viewer1 panel, we can now create a custom color LUT for this shot.

Considering the storytelling aspects, we assume that this scene takes place inside a spaceship. Additionally, based on the shot's metadata, the white balance is set to 3200K, creating a warm and inviting atmosphere. We can therefore envision an environment surrounded by heads-up displays emitting warm light around the characters. With this concept in mind, a bluish-tinted custom LUT will be added to enhance the overall mood of the scene. In the following steps, we will use a Grade node to further enrich the visual impact of this custom LUT.

Step 6 | Connect a Grade node after the Colorspace node.
Press the G key to add a Grade node connected after the Colorspace node.
In the Properties tab of the Grade node, enter the following values into the respective knobs (option slots):

Gain: 1.15 (blue channel)

Multiply: 1.2

Gamma: 0.7

These adjustments in the Grade node result in a customized color with a blue tint.

So far, the issues with displaying highlight details have been resolved. We can now combine these nodes, including the Colorspace and Grade nodes, and use them as a custom LUT in the Viewer1 panel.

Step 7 | Select the Colorspace and Grade nodes, then group them (Ctrl/Cmd + G).

Step 8 | Select the newly created Group node (automatically labeled "Group1"), press the N key on your keyboard, and rename it to VIEWER_INPUT. Make sure the name is written in all capital letters and includes an underscore between the two words.

Step 9 | Once the custom LUT named VIEWER_INPUT is created, the IP (input_process) icon in the top-left corner of the Viewer1 panel should automatically activate and turn yellow-orange. If needed, refer to the hands-on example video (I) for a more intuitive understanding of the operations in this section.

Step 10 | After the IP (input_process) icon is activated, the green screen plate can be viewed in the Viewer1 panel using the custom LUT. Finally, disconnect the VIEWER_INPUT node from the green screen plate (Read1 node). See Figure 4.13.

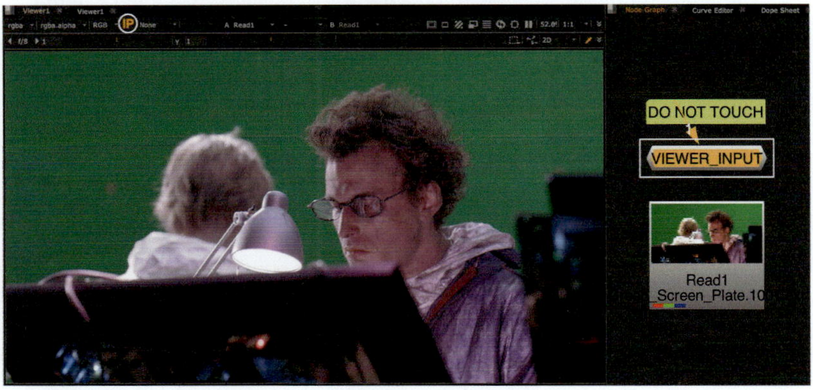

FIGURE 4.13 The IP (input_process) icon is activated by the customized VIEWER_INPUT LUT node

Note:
The customized VIEWER_INPUT node has been applied to the Viewer1 panel to accurately display highlight details in the green screen plate on 8-bit monitors. However, to prevent the custom LUT from altering the image attributes of the original plate, it is essential to disconnect the VIEWER_INPUT node from the plate (Read1 node); otherwise, the LUT will affect the appearance of the original image.

In real-world production, color decisions involve both creative and technical elements and are often predetermined by clients to match the specific requirements of each scene. As a result, altering client-provided content during production is strictly prohibited without prior approval.

Up to this point, we have created a custom LUT for the green screen plate using a straightforward method available in NukeX. It is important to note that this custom LUT node should not be modified during production, as any changes may lead to color inconsistencies and affect all departments.

In this example, we have created a simple custom LUT using Nuke's default linear color system. However, when working with live-action footage and assets in visual effects production, we inevitably encounter the following challenges:

1. Live-action footage and assets are often captured and created using various formats and color spaces. When VFX artists work on these assets using computer displays, the images may appear incorrect due to differing input color spaces, typically defined as input transform (or input device transform [IDT]).
2. Clients typically request the application of both creative and technical LUTs to the final visual effects shots. As a result, custom or predefined LUTs must be applied to monitors across all departments during VFX production.
3. The final output will be viewed on a variety of devices, including cinema projectors, UHD TV monitors, and computer displays used for online streaming platforms. Therefore, it is essential to convert each show to the appropriate color space, known as the output device transform (ODT), to ensure the images appear correctly on different devices.

Considering these scenarios, let's now explore how the Academy Color Encoding System (ACES) is used in visual effects production.

• ACES color management in VFX projects

The filmmaking industry often requires a color management system that ensures consistency and accuracy in color imaging across various devices and platforms. The Academy Color Encoding System is an innovative solution to this need. ACES is free, open, and device-independent, making it accessible and adaptable to a wide range of workflows and productions. By employing a standardized approach to color management, ACES has become the industry standard for managing color in filmmaking and visual effects. Its adoption helps streamline workflows and eliminates discrepancies that can arise from using different devices and software applications in production. As a result, many mainstream professional software packages have adopted ACES color management and integrated it into production pipelines.

OpenColorIO (OCIO) is a comprehensive color management solution widely used in visual effects and computer animation production pipelines. It is compatible with the Academy Color Encoding Specification. The latest versions of OpenColorIO can be found at https://opencolorio.org. At the time of writing this book, we are using OpenColorIO (OCIO) v2.x with ACES versions 1.2 and 2.0 in NukeX. As ACES continues to evolve, this color management system is expected to become even more comprehensive and robust in future versions of Nuke.

○ Essential understanding of ACES and its applications

ACES operates within a scene-referred linear color space and is the industry-standard color management system. It handles input device transforms and output device transforms, ensuring that images are displayed accurately across different devices and perceived correctly by the human visual system. When working with visually critical images, such as high-end VFX shots, artists typically aim to use the widest possible color gamut, encompassing the full visible spectrum. This involves identifying the range of colors that can be faithfully represented during the processing of high-end imagery.

While the ACES color space standard is more comprehensive than those listed subsequently, artists working in everyday motion picture and television production typically encounter a few common color gamuts. These usually include ACES 2065–1, ACEScg, sRGB/Rec. 709, and DCI-P3.

- *ACES 2605–1*

The ACES 2065–1 color space, with its AP0 set of primaries, encompasses the entire visible color spectrum, making it the broadest color gamut available. This color space is commonly used for exchanging high-end moving images among post-production and visual effects facilities. For instance, post-production studios may export live-action raw footage in the OpenEXR sequence format using the ACES 2065–1 color space and provide the plates to visual effects studios for VFX production. Once the visual effects work is completed, typically using the ACEScg color space, the final VFX shots are converted back to ACES 2065–1 for further post-production processes, ensuring the integrity of the color data throughout the pipeline.

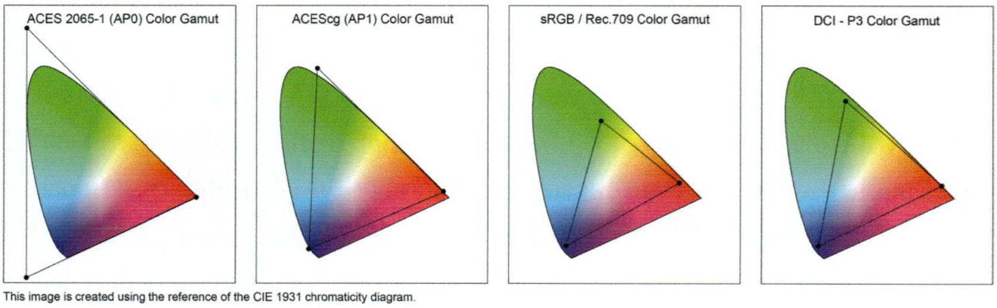

FIGURE 4.14 A comparison of color gamuts for four commonly used color spaces

- *ACEScg*

ACEScg is the standard color management system used in computer graphics and visual effects production. It is seamlessly integrated into many professional 3D animation, painting, lighting, and compositing applications. Unlike ACES 2065–1, which preserves the full range of the color spectrum captured by cameras, its color gamut is considered too wide for practical use. ACEScg, by contrast, uses the AP1 set of color primaries, maintaining the full spectrum of visible high dynamic range colors through RGB primaries, making it more suitable for production workflows.

Additionally, using the ACEScg color gamut can help reduce potential negative values and errors that occur across color spaces during data processing. Since negative values can cause significant issues in visual effects production, VFX artists should take care to avoid them in image colors throughout the production process.

- *sRGB/Rec709*

The sRGB/Rec.709 color primaries cover the smallest range of colors in the visible spectrum and are typically seen in 8-bit images, such as JPEG files. However, when working extensively with ACES color management in CG/VFX projects, it is important to process all potential assets in the ACEScg color space, including texture images for 3D models, HDR images for lighting, and 3D renders for compositing. The wide-ranging ACEScg color space encompasses the entire sRGB color range and ensures consistency in managing the color spaces of all assets. Additionally, it helps avoid confusion and rendering errors that may occur from mixing various color spaces in the production pipeline.

A comprehensive introduction to using the ACEScg color space across project assets will be presented in Chapter 5, Case Study 8.

- *DCI–P3*

DCI–P3 is an RGB color space that covers approximately 53.6% of the CIE 1931 chromaticity diagram. It is specifically designed for viewing images in a fully darkened environment, making it the preferred choice for distributing digital theatrical motion pictures (DCDM). As mentioned in previous paragraphs, we operate within the ACEScg color space during VFX production and subsequently render the necessary color spaces as required by output device transform sources. Therefore, it is always helpful to be aware of the color spaces associated with ODT sources, as they determine how our final work will be displayed.

• Hands-on example (II): creating a custom LUT using ACES color management

This section explores ACES color management in Foundry NukeX, including a pre-recorded video demonstration and accompanying Nuke scripts. Watch the pre-recorded video at the following link:

www.youtube.com/@InvisibleFilmVFX

Video title: Hands-On Example (II) | Creating a Custom LUT in ACES Color Management

Hands-on example (II) covers the following operations:

- Set up OCIO color management in NukeX.
- Import the original footage and apply the appropriate ACES color space using the correct Input Transform based on its native color space.
- Convert and export the footage as an OpenEXR image sequence in the ACES 2065–1 color space. Studio VFX production pipelines typically work with sequential image files, usually starting at frame 1001.

Download the MXF raw footage from the open-source database provided by mango.blender.org at the following link:

https://media.xiph.org/tearsofsteel/raw/

File name: A003C007_120507.mxf

Shot information:

Camera and color space: Sony F65 digital cinema camera with Sony Linear S-Gamut3.Cine color Gamut.

Frames per second (fps): 24

Footage resolution: 4K (4096 × 2160)

Image bit depth: 16-bit

Note:

The current version of Foundry NukeX includes ACES 1.2, 1.3, and 2.0 configuration files in its color management system. For a more intuitive understanding of setting up Nuke ACES 1.2 and 1.3 as you read the following sections, please watch the hands-on example video (II) available on YouTube at @InvisibleFilmVFX.

Setting up the OCIO ACES 1.2 config file in NukeX 15 and 16

- Step 1 | Launch NukeX version 15 or 16.

  Go to Edit > Preferences (or press Shift + S) to open the Preferences dialog window. Then, click Color Management from the list on the left-hand side.
- Step 2 | On the right-hand side of the Color Management, change the Default Color Management option from Nuke to OCIO using the drop-down menu. In the Default OCIO Config section, select ACES > aces_1.2 from the drop-down menu.

  Click OK to save the settings.

  Quit NukeX and relaunch the application to ensure that the newly defined config file is consistently applied in both the Preferences – Color Management panel and the Project Settings > Color tab.
- Step 3 | Import the MXF footage via a Read node.

  Ensure the mouse cursor is positioned within the Node Graph area. Press the R key to open the Read File(s) dialog window. Navigate to the folder where the MXF (Material Exchange Format) footage is saved, select the file, and click the Open button to import the footage. Once imported, Nuke will automatically label the footage as Read1.

  Double-click the imported footage (Read1 node) to load its parameters in the Properties panel. In the Read tab, click the Input Transform drop-down menu and select: Colorspaces > Input > Sony > Input – Sony – Linear – S-Gamut3.Cine.

  With the Read1 node still selected in the Node Graph, press the numeric key 1 on the keyboard to load the plate into the Viewer1 panel. By default, Viewer1 automatically applies an sRGB (ACES) LUT. When viewing the green screen plate in the Viewer1 panel, you'll notice that the image details in the highlights are properly displayed.

  Alternatively, click the sRGB (ACES) drop-down menu above the Viewer1 panel to preview how the image appears with different LUTs, if needed.

Setting up the OCIO ACES 2.0 config file in NukeX 17 or later

– Step 1 | Launch NukeX.

Go to Edit > Preferences (or press Shift + S) to open the Preferences dialog window. Then, click Color Management from the list on the left-hand side.

– Step 2 | On the right-hand side of the Color Management, change the Default Color Management option from Nuke to OCIO using the drop-down menu. In the Default OCIO Config section, choose ACES > fn-nuke_studio-config-v3.0.0_aces-v2.0_ocio-v2.4.

Click OK to save the settings.

Quit NukeX and relaunch the application to ensure that the newly defined config file is consistently applied in both the Preferences – Color Management panel and the Project Settings > Color (tab).

Note:

There are two ACES 2.0 config files listed:

fn-nuke_cg-config-v3.0.0_aces-v2.0_ocio-v2.4

fn-nuke_studio-config-v3.0.0_aces-v2.0_ocio-v2.4

The first is for the CG config, and the second is for the studio config. Since we're working with live-action footage in this example, you should choose the fn-nuke_studio-config-v3.0.0_aces-v2.0_ocio-v2.4 file.

– Step 3 | The steps for importing the MXF footage are identical to those in "Step 3" for setting up the OCIO ACES 1.2 config file.

After importing an MXF format file into NukeX, you may see an ERROR sign on the node thumbnail. This happens because Nuke automatically assigns a linear colorspace to the file. However, to display it correctly, you need to assign its native colorspace.

– Step 4 | Double-click the imported footage (Read1 node) to load its parameters in the Properties panel. In the Read tab, click the Input Transform drop-down menu and choose:

Colorspaces > Input > Sony > Linear S-Gamut3.Cine. This sets the correct color space for the MXF file.

– Step 5 | After setting the correct input transform color space for the imported footage (Read1 node), press the number key 1 to load the green screen plate into the Viewer1 panel. By default, a LUT titled ACES 2.0 - SDR 100 nits (rec.709) (sRGB - Display) is applied to Viewer1. This LUT is intended for standard computer monitors. At this stage, when viewing the green screen plate through Viewer1, the highlight details should display correctly.

- Step 6 | After the plate is properly displayed, convert it to an OpenEXR sequence using the ACES 2065–1 color space. To do this, select the Read1 node and press the Tab key to open the search bar. Type OCIO ColorSpace [OCIO] from the list and select it. This will create an OCIOColorSpace node connected to the Read1 node.
- Step 7 | Double-click the OCIOColorSpace node to load its parameters in the Properties panel. Then, set the input and output drop-down menus as follows:

  input: (Colorspaces - Input - Sony) Linear S-Gamut3.Cine

  output: (Color Spaces - ACES) ACES 2065-1

  These settings convert the MXF format footage from its original color space (Linear S-Gamut3.Cine) to ACES 2065–1.

  After converting the green screen footage to the ACES 2065–1 color space, we can observe some color changes. For instance, the overly saturated tone of the main character's face now appears more natural. At this stage, the footage should be exported in OpenEXR format as a VFX shot plate.
- Step 8 | While the OCIOColorSpace node is still selected, press W on the keyboard to connect a Write node. In its Properties panel, set the following options:

  file (slot)

  To save the renders, click the folder icon at the right end of the file slot at the top, then navigate to your desired location. Keep in mind that the original MXF file will be rendered as an OpenEXR sequence. Therefore, create a folder with an appropriate name to store the rendered sequence images. For demonstration purposes, the image sequence has been saved using the following name and format:

  GreenScreen_ACES2065–1.%04d.exr

  (The % indicates that this is a sequence file, with 04d specifying that the sequence uses four-digit frame numbers, such as 1001, 1002, and so on.)

  EXR Options

  ☒write ACES compliant EXR (make sure this checkbox is selected)

Output Transform

output transform (drop-down menu)

Click the drop-down menu, go to Colorspaces > ACES > ACES2065–1.

Next, click the Render button located below the drop-down menu to open the render dialog window, where you can adjust the frame range for the desired image sequence.

Click OK to start the render. See Figure 4.15 for details on these settings.

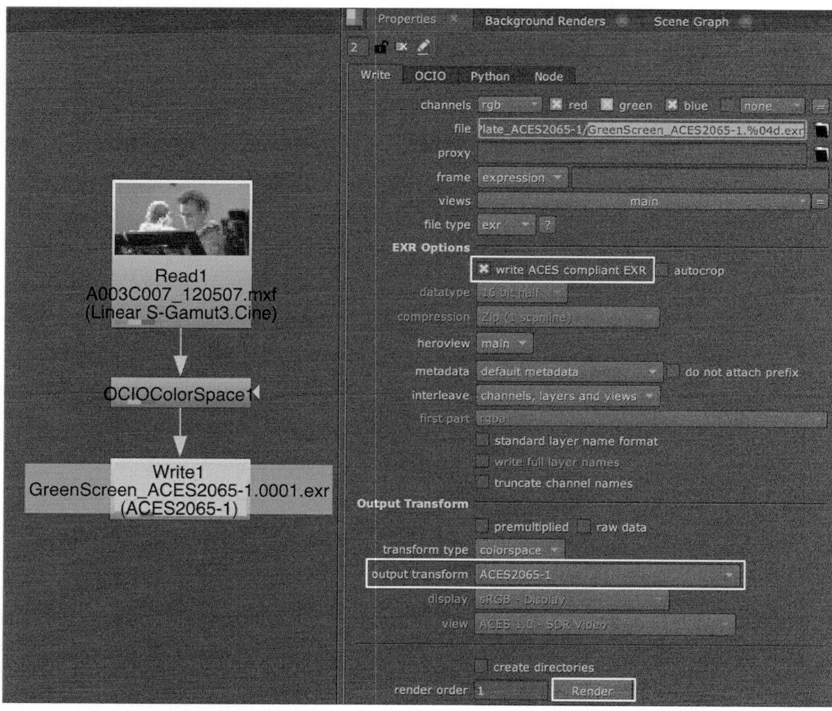

FIGURE 4.15 Settings of the Write node for exporting OpenEXR image sequences in the ACES2065–1 color space

– Step 9 | Once the rendering of the OpenEXR image sequence is complete, import the rendered sequence into NukeX using a Read node to double-check it. This time, Nuke will automatically assign the default color space (scene_linear) to the rendered plate, which corresponds to ACEScg. As a result, the newly rendered plate appears more neutral compared to the original MXF footage, with the difference especially noticeable in the main character's skin tones.

Note:

In this example, the MXF file format was converted and exported using NukeX. However, since post-production and visual effects pipelines can vary between studios, the conversion and export process can also be carried out using other software, such as DaVinci Resolve, which is capable of handling raw footage and delivering the required formats and color spaces to VFX studios.

• The importance of on-site data capture for VFX shots

On-site data capture is essential for creating seamless visual effects in film production. Accurate reference data that closely aligns with the on-set environment is crucial to achieving unmatched authenticity and attention to detail. Therefore, on-site measurements and data collection are vital to the success of visual effects shots. This process greatly assists visual effects artists in working between digital and real-world environments, ensuring precise alignment of virtual and physical elements. For this reason, on-set reference data must be carefully selected and recorded.

• Professional understanding of on-set data capture processes

A professional understanding of on-set data capture and measurement enhances the knowledge and expertise of artists across all departments in visual effects production. This section will explore a series of essential on-set data measurements, including:

- Total station survey
- Reference photos
- Witness camera
- Drift camera
- HDRI shoot
- Roundshot shoot
- Texture shoot for characters and props
- Environment and set shoot
- Photogrammetry shoot
- Capturing reference images for creating 3D models
- Capturing reference images for 3D texturing
- Understand lens distortion and shoot lens grids
- Lens vignetting

◦ Total station survey

With the rapid development of the motion picture industry, various techniques from multidisciplinary fields have become commonplace in visual effects production pipelines. Total station survey data is primarily used for match-moving, helping CG elements integrate realistically with live-action footage in terms of position, scale, motion, and other important aspects. Additionally, data from total station surveys can support other departments, including layout, modeling, lighting, and compositing. As such, total station surveys are an essential part of the data capture skill set.

Nowadays, many high-budget films use LiDAR (light detection and ranging) to scan on-set scenes, capturing real-scale layouts and spatial data. During location surveys, it is essential to prioritize areas such as the green screen and ground, especially if LiDAR scanning is not planned. The survey should be conducted meticulously, with particular attention to its role in camera solving, LiDAR alignment, and geometry construction. Arriving on set before filming begins is recommended to allow for a thorough and uninterrupted survey.

Select at least six key points and mark them using matchmove markers or reflective tape to support alignment during visual effects production. These points should be as small as possible while still easily recognizable and placed in elevated positions to avoid interference during filming. It is important to note that any key points caught on camera will be involved in VFX shots. In addition, the following factors should be carefully considered during site surveys:

Camera starting and ending positions
Witness camera positions
Tracking markers and LEDs
Actor positions
Light positions
Key props & vehicles
HDRI positions

○ Reference photos

Taking reference photos to document on-set information allows technical directors (TDs) to visually describe specific situations during filming. These images are especially useful during production when shots need to be revisited or recreated by different departments within VFX studios, such as matchmove and asset teams. They help provide a clearer understanding of the shot and support the digital reconstruction of the set. Without reference images, visual effects artists often struggle to envision the scene when relying solely on live-action footage.

Taking a good set of reference photos is important and depends on several factors, including time constraints, scene complexity, and the number of shots captured. A typical set of reference images includes five to ten photos per slate, so learning to work quickly and efficiently is essential.

To capture reference photos, data capture TDs should use a reliable digital camera with a standard zoom lens. They must also ensure that metadata, such as time and date, is correctly embedded in the images to prevent human error during the fast-paced on-set workflow.

Flash photography should only be used when necessary. If a data capture TD needs to use a flash, they must give an audible warning to alert others, as the flash can cause concern for the director of photography (DoP) or the lighting department, who may think one of their lights has failed. Flash photography can also disrupt a take and temporarily affect the vision of actors, directors, camera operators, and DoPs. Therefore, TDs should be cautious when using flash during a take and turn it off immediately afterward.

The following section outlines the key elements that should be carefully included in reference photos. Since there is often no time to annotate images on set, it is important to follow a logical shooting procedure to ensure that viewers can easily understand what was captured. Data capture TDs should photograph scenes in sequences that progress from wide-angle shots to detailed close-ups.

– *Slate reference photos*

Be sure to take a picture of the slate at the beginning or end of each setup.

Capturing the slate is always helpful, as it provides essential context for each shot. If possible, also photograph the monitor displaying relevant slate information and camera framing. Bookmarking these reference images can help clarify the context of each shot before the official editorial release.

– *Scene reference photos*

When LiDAR scanning or total station survey data is not planned, it is essential to take reference photos of the environment for the scene. Measuring key props and capturing real-world scale is particularly important when a scene involves CG creatures interacting with actors. In the absence of LiDAR scans or survey data, reference photos help visual effects artists accurately interpret scene scale, lighting, and camera positions. Figure 4.16 shows a reference photo of the on-set environment. This image is open source and provided by the Blender Foundation (CC) | mango.blender.org.

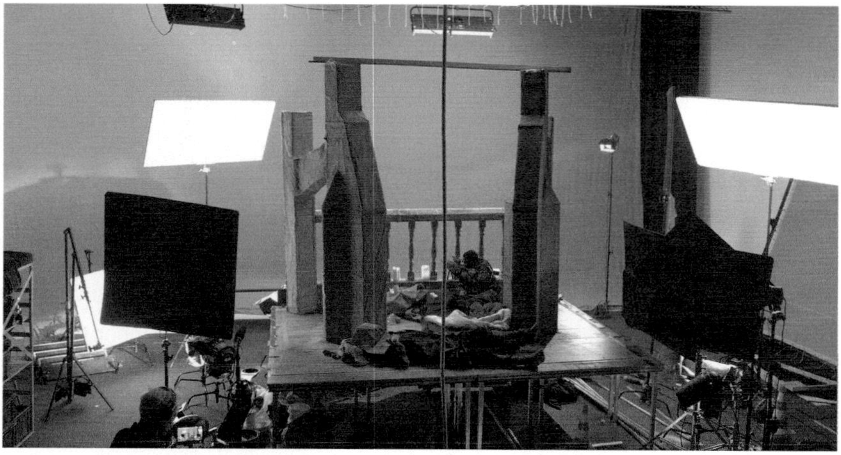

FIGURE 4.16 Reference photo of the on-set environment. © Mango.blender.org

– *Cameras reference photos*

When cameras are in position, take reference photos for each camera within a few minutes. Additionally, take reference photos if multiple cameras are involved in the same shot. Use a slate to label each take and explain the differences between them. If the camera has start and end positions, these should also be captured in the reference photos. For crane camera movements, also try to capture reference images of the camera's mid-position, as shown in the top image of Figure 4.17.

Wide shots

Capture reference photos from multiple camera angles that cover the entire scene, positioning the camera within the context of the LiDAR-scanned characters and the set environment. These reference images help viewers better understand the scene and its elements in context.

Tight shots

Take reference photos that show camera details, including the body, lens, and focal length, as illustrated in the bottom image of Figure 4.17. If possible, include the camera's position within the scene.

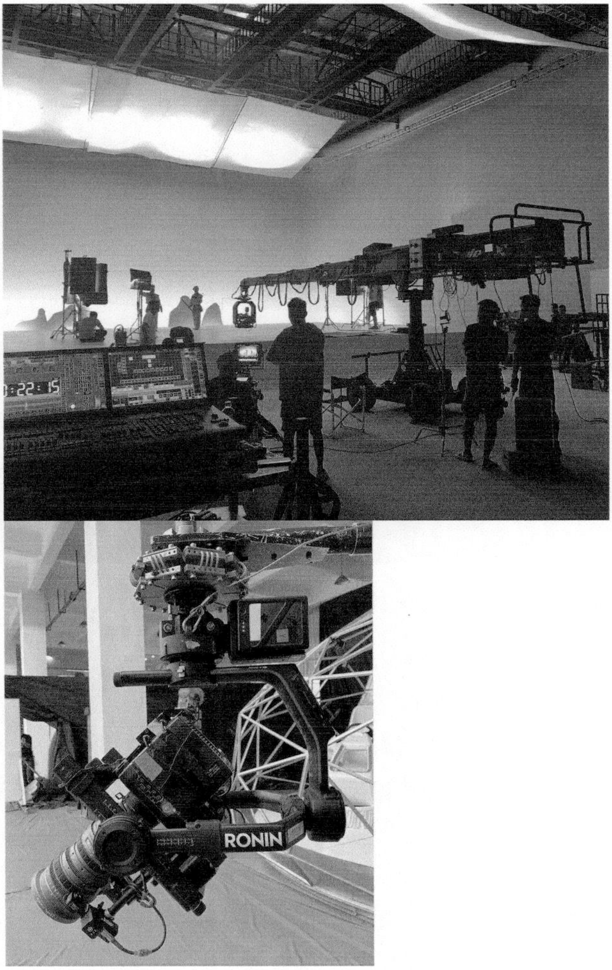

FIGURE 4.17 Reference photos showing camera details on set

– *Lighting reference photos*

To provide reference photos for lighting, take wide shots of the environment that include bounce cards and gobos. These photos can help the lighting department understand the on-set lighting setups. Figure 4.18 shows an on-set lighting reference image shared by Corentin Kopp, a director of photography based in Belgium.

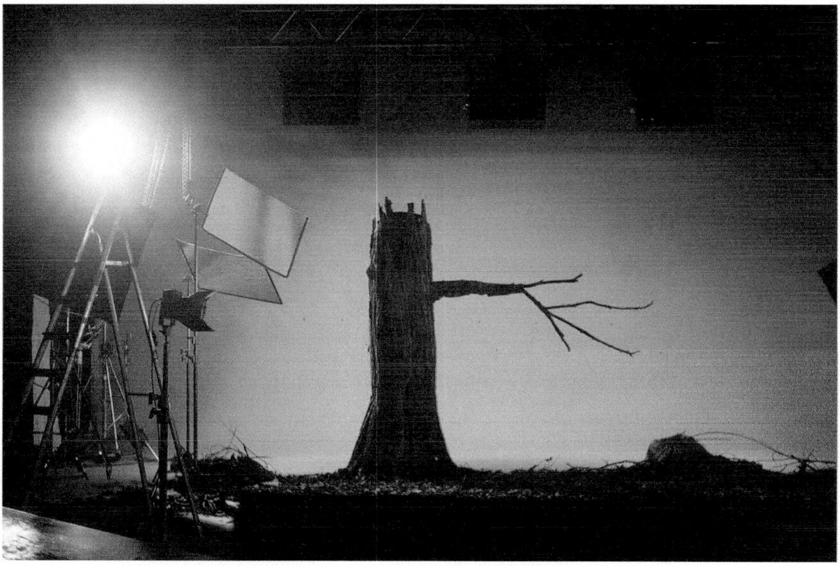

FIGURE 4.18 An example reference photo for on-set lighting. © Corentin Kopp

– *Witness cameras*

A few wide shots taken by witness cameras should capture the on-set components within the context of the environment. Witness cameras will be discussed in more detail in later sections.

– *Total station*

To document the position of the total station on the survey site and its relationship to the surrounding environment, take several medium and wide shots.

– *Tracking markers*

Ensure that the tracking markers are visible in the reference photos. If feasible, include a scale indicator, such as a tape measure placed next to or between the markers. Additionally, take wide shots to show the markers in context with the environment, followed by close-up shots to capture more detail.

– *Actors/Actresses*

If the lead actors interact with CG creatures in the scene, their starting and ending positions should be documented from multiple angles. Additionally, obtain permission to take reference photos of facial and body markers from various perspectives.

– *Stunt performers*

The same measurement techniques used for leading actors should also be applied when capturing reference photos of stunt performers, especially when scanning is not possible. In these cases, measurements such as full height, arm span, elbow to fingertip, and knee to foot should be recorded. These details are essential for rotoAnim (rotomation) in live-action footage. To achieve the physically impossible movements required by the scene, the main character must be paired with an identical digital 3D double. The 3D model must accurately follow each frame to replicate the actor's movements and performance.

o Witness camera

Setting up witness cameras is indispensable for modern VFX production, as it helps reconstruct each shot or scene in 3D space, particularly during the early stages of the pipeline, such as matchmove, rotoAnim, and layout. For an ideal setup, the witness camera should capture both the hero camera and any on-set action, including character movement and positioning during the take. Proper camera placement is essential, though it can sometimes be challenging. Therefore, it is important to aim for the best possible coverage, depending on the specific VFX requirements of the shot. Different angles should be tested from each camera, including slightly wider views, which can help VFX artists better understand everything happening in the scene. Figure 4.19 shows a pair of diagrams that illustrate the recommended camera angles for reference. Reference footage and images captured by witness cameras support all departments by providing a clearer understanding of each shot and the spatial placement of every element in 3D space, rather than requiring artists to rely solely on 2D VFX plates to interpret each scene.

For capturing on-set reference footage, witness cameras should follow the following guidelines:

1. Cover the position of the hero camera but prioritize capturing the actors and props for rotoAnim tasks. Be sure to include the positions and movements of the lead actors during each take.

2. Accurately record the FPS, timecode, resolution, frame rate, and codec for the hero cameras. FPS and timecode information are especially important for VFX editorial to synchronize footage from the hero cameras.
3. Note the details of the witness cameras used for the slate, including the date, slate number, take number, and camera name. Also, record whether any witness cameras were zoomed in or out.
4. Ensure that witness camera positions are locked off and remain unobstructed while capturing each take.

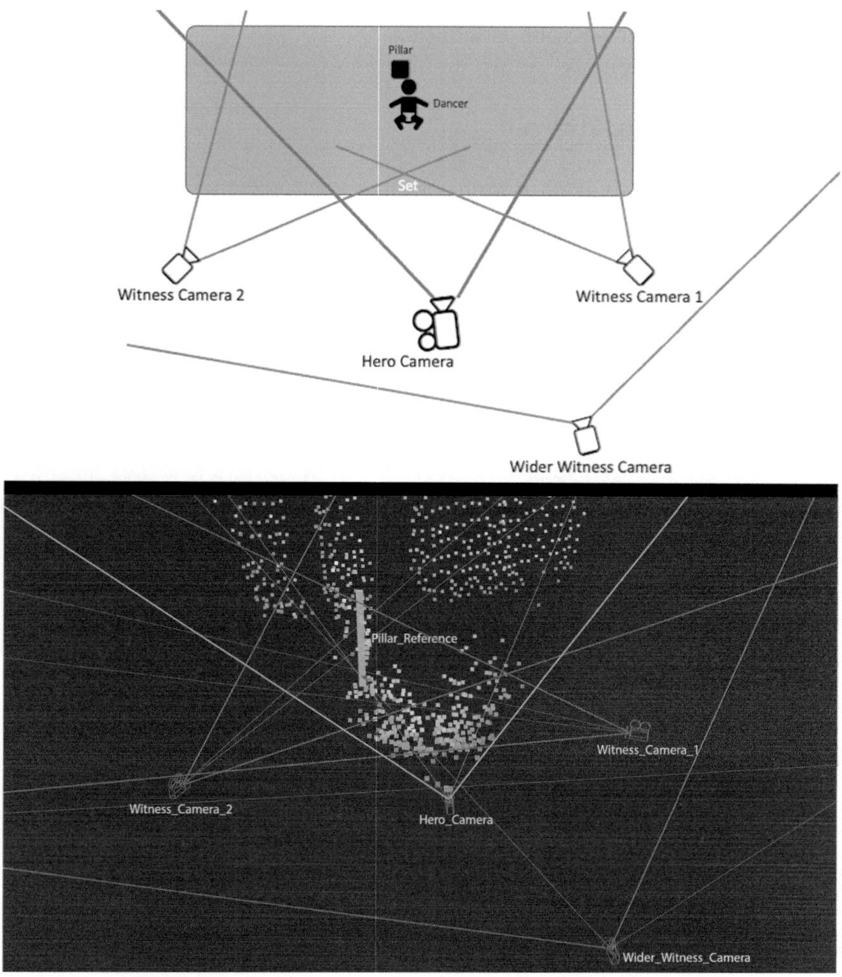

FIGURE 4.19 A comparison of witness camera position alignment between on-set and 3D space

∘ Drift camera

A drift camera is a small camera mounted on the main film camera body to capture tracking shots when the camera is handheld. It is used for tight framing or zooming. When using a drift camera, it is important to communicate effectively with the on-set camera crew during a lens grid shoot, as the device can add weight to the camera rig. The resolution of the drift camera is usually set to 720p at 60 fps to minimize the rolling shutter effect. Additionally, due to the large video files generated during the data processing stage, drift cameras should only record during takes.

∘ HDRI shoot

In the previous sections, we discussed the limitations of standard 8-bit monitors, which can only display a range of luminosity from 0 (black) to 255 (white). In visual effects production, this luminance range is often redefined to span from 0 to 1. However, these 0–255 (or 0–1) values do not accurately represent real-world luminosity. For example, sunlight has an intensity of approximately 107,527 lux (where one lux equals one lumen per square meter), which far exceeds the maximum value of 255 that 8-bit images can store. To address this limitation, a series of high dynamic range images is captured on set and merged to create a 32-bit, 360-degree environment map that contains extensive lighting and color information, particularly in the highlights. With approximately 4.3 billion possible values per channel, the 32-bit environment map has a dynamic range sufficient to represent real-world brightness levels. As a result, HDR images are widely used in visual effects production, especially for lighting 3D elements in VFX scenes.

To capture HDR images on set, the following equipment is recommended:

- A tripod with a nodal head that allows 3x horizontal and 2x vertical angles to cover the full 360° environment.
- Full-frame cameras and lenses
- 8-mm fisheye lens
- A ColorChecker chart

Shooting high dynamic range images on set is intended to recreate on-set lighting for integrating 3D elements into VFX shots. Therefore, when capturing HDRIs, the camera should be positioned (including its height) where potential CG elements will appear in the scene. Since time for capturing HDRIs on set is often limited, prepare the camera setup in advance and place a ColorChecker chart in view (on the ground) during the HDRI shoot. Be sure to capture a separate slate image. On-set light sources should never be obstructed by any element that is not part of the scene during HDRI capture.

Note:
The purpose of placing the ColorChecker chart in the environment during HDRI capture is to eliminate chromatic adaptation and neutralize the merged HDR environment map before using it to light a VFX scene. Therefore, the ColorChecker chart does not necessarily need to face the camera; instead, it should be positioned to receive neutral light from the environment on set.

– *Generic setting reference*

Stage & exterior (at night) | 7 brackets; 2/3 stops increment; f16/32; iso400; center bracket 1/45sec (8000–4).

Exterior day (with sun) | 7 brackets; 2/3 stops increment; f32; iso100; 1/60sec (8000–2).

Exterior sun capture | 7 brackets; 3 stops increment; f16; iso100; 1/15sec – using an ND 3.0 filter.

Figure 4.20 shows an example HDR image along with its exposure sequence from the shoot. In this instance, a mirror ball was used on set instead of a fisheye lens.

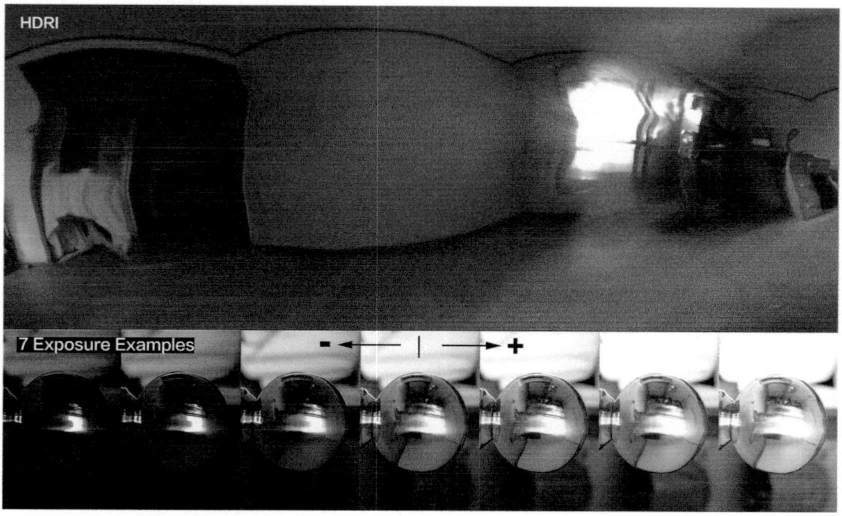

FIGURE 4.20 An example of an unwrapped HDR image and its exposure levels

○ Roundshot shoot

The Roundshot is a stitched panoramic image captured on set and used in compositing, HDR lighting, digital matte painting, and environment reconstruction. Some major VFX studios use the Roundshot VR Drive for automated stitching of cylindrical or spherical panoramas, time-lapses, video, object movies, and 32-bit HDR. Additionally, it generates a set of predefined VR Drive XML files for the panorama workflow in external stitching software, such as PTGui. These XML files are used in VFX studios to stitch panorama images in Foundry NukeX. Figure 4.21 shows an example of a Roundshot contact sheet, with each image block having a resolution of 8K.

To successfully capture 360-degree Roundshot images, it is recommended to use manual exposure and focus, as well as high-speed continuous shooting for bracketing. A complete 360-degree Roundshot typically consists of 74 images, which are frequently bracketed to produce a total of 222 images.

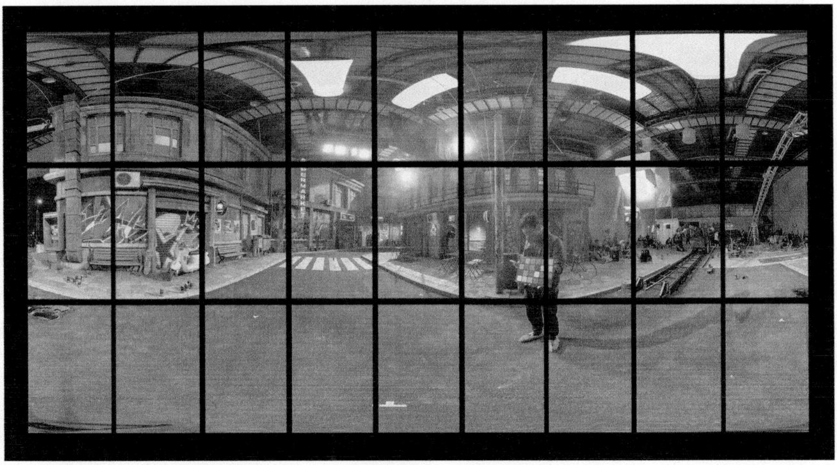

FIGURE 4.21 A Roundshot contact sheet

○ Texture shoot for characters and props

Different visual effects studios use various methods to capture textures. However, the process typically falls into two main categories: unpolarized and cross-polarized imaging for 3D assets. In the real world, materials reflect light and display colors due to the unpolarized nature of most light sources. For 3D elements, however, only the inherent color of the surface is needed. This can be achieved through cross-polarization, using polarized light sources and filters during the texture-capturing process.

Figure 4.22 compares an unpolarized image (left) and a cross-polarized image (right). While unpolarized images can be used as a reference for the look development of 3D assets, the cross-polarized image is used as a texture for 3D assets.

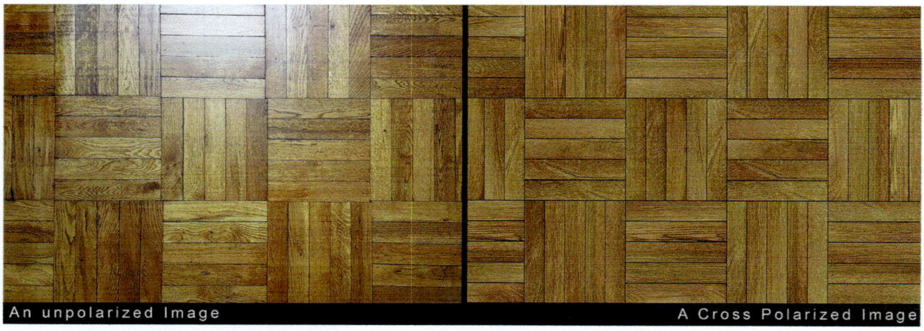

FIGURE 4.22 A comparison of an unpolarized image (left) and a cross-polarized image (right)

Texture shooting guidelines

- Environment

A minimum darkroom space of 5 by 8 meters is required. Doors and windows should be blocked to create a fully controlled environment with no ambient light sources. Ensure that the walls and floors are covered with non-reflective materials.

- Equipment

The equipment required includes a full-frame stills camera mounted on a tripod, and a lens no wider than 50 mm fitted with a polarizing filter. Lighting should consist of two 1500-W flashlights mounted on light stands. An 18% gray backdrop will be used as the background. A turntable, marked at its center with a clock face featuring eight evenly spaced markings at 45-degree intervals, is necessary for consistent positioning. An object of known dimensions should be included for scale reference or matchmove alignment. If available, a Leica FlexLine TS Series

Performance Total Station is recommended for precise spatial measurements. For optimal lighting, a beauty light setup should be arranged, consisting of two 2K spotlights, two 5K spotlights, and two 1K spotlights.

– *Before shooting textures for objects*

Place tracking markers on the backdrop, then survey the positions of the markers, turntable, light boxes, and camera. Capture reference photos of the entire setup for matchmoving, followed by still images of the turntable for photogrammetry. Next, photograph the gray ball, chrome ball, and color chart placed at the center of the turntable, aligned with the camera's height. Additionally, capture HDRI images for both beauty and standard lighting setups. If using a flash head for HDRI, consider applying an ND filter. Finally, include a known object in the frame to provide a scale reference.

Shooting textures involves several categories, such as full body, half body, head, detailed components, costumes, and props. Each category may require specific shooting setups. The following reference settings outline how to capture the main characters for digital doubles.

– *Example specifications of shooting main characters for digital doubles*

Flash heads
Shutter: 1/125
Aperture: f/16
ISO: 400
White balance: Flash
8x turns (polarized/non-polarized)
Beauty lights (for main digital doubles)
Shutter: 1/60
Aperture: f/5.6
ISO: 1600
White balance: Tungsten
8x turns (each light separately, then all lights)

Additionally, the turntable must be visible in the frame, and each shot should include a slate and a color chart. The character's name (as used in the show), height, and scene number should be included in the polarized images.

◦ Environment and set shoot

Images of environments and sets will be used primarily by the assets department for CG builds. These images serve two main purposes:

Modeling reference

Texture reference

Traditionally, capturing reference images involves using full-frame digital cameras along with scale measurements of the objects. For personal projects, this process can now be done using 3D scanning applications, including those available on smartphones. However, the final quality may be compromised due to bandwidth limitations for online data processing.

◦ Photogrammetry shoot

Photogrammetry involves creating 3D geometry and textures from a series of photographs. The Assets, Digital Matte Painting (DMP), and Environment departments use this technique to quickly construct props and sets, and to perform matchmoving when LiDAR scans are unavailable. Several widely used software packages in the industry include Agisoft Metashape, Autodesk ReCap Pro, Adobe Substance 3D Sampler, and RealityCapture. Additionally, newly developed tools based on machine learning, such as NeRF (Neural Radiance Field), and smartphone apps like Polycam can process photogrammetry data by reconstructing camera positions, focal lengths, and focal length distortions in 3D space based on common patterns found in the photos and their parallax.

There are some basic rules and guidelines to consider when shooting for photogrammetry:

– Begin by capturing wider images to gain a better overall perspective, as this will help reconstruct the spatial relationships between objects. Then move in closer to capture finer details. Ensure the camera lens frames the subject surface vertically to avoid parallax in the captured images. Additionally, pan the camera from one physical position to another after each shot, rather than rotating the camera head in a fixed position.

- Using a single focal length is preferred, although wide-angle shots can sometimes be useful. Prime lenses work best, but a 24–105-mm lens offers versatility.
- Avoid non-textured, flat objects or scenes, repeated patterns, shiny and transparent objects, moving elements in the foreground or background, and moving subjects.
- Significant overlap between photos and thoughtful shot planning is highly beneficial. Balanced exposure is recommended in diffused, overcast, or flat lighting conditions, where shadows are minimized. For photogrammetry to be successful, images must be sharp and in focus. Using appropriate equipment settings for each shoot is also important.
- Canon mirrorless or DSLR full-frame cameras and lenses are recommended, with an ISO setting no higher than 800, a minimum aperture of f/11, and a fast shutter speed.
- Shoot in RAW format, maintain consistent white balance and exposure, and use neutral camera settings.
- A ColorChecker chart and measuring tape are essential for accurate scaling. A tripod is recommended, although handheld shooting may be feasible under ideal conditions.

In Figure 4.23, three key stages in the creation of a set of 3D models are shown. The top image depicts a series of photographs taken on location. To reduce parallax, the camera was repositioned after each shot to keep the wall vertically framed and to minimize perspective distortion. The middle image shows a 3D model generated using the open-source reconstruction software AliceVision Meshroom. The bottom image features a retopologized and refined 3D model of the room, enhanced with additional elements created in Autodesk Maya.

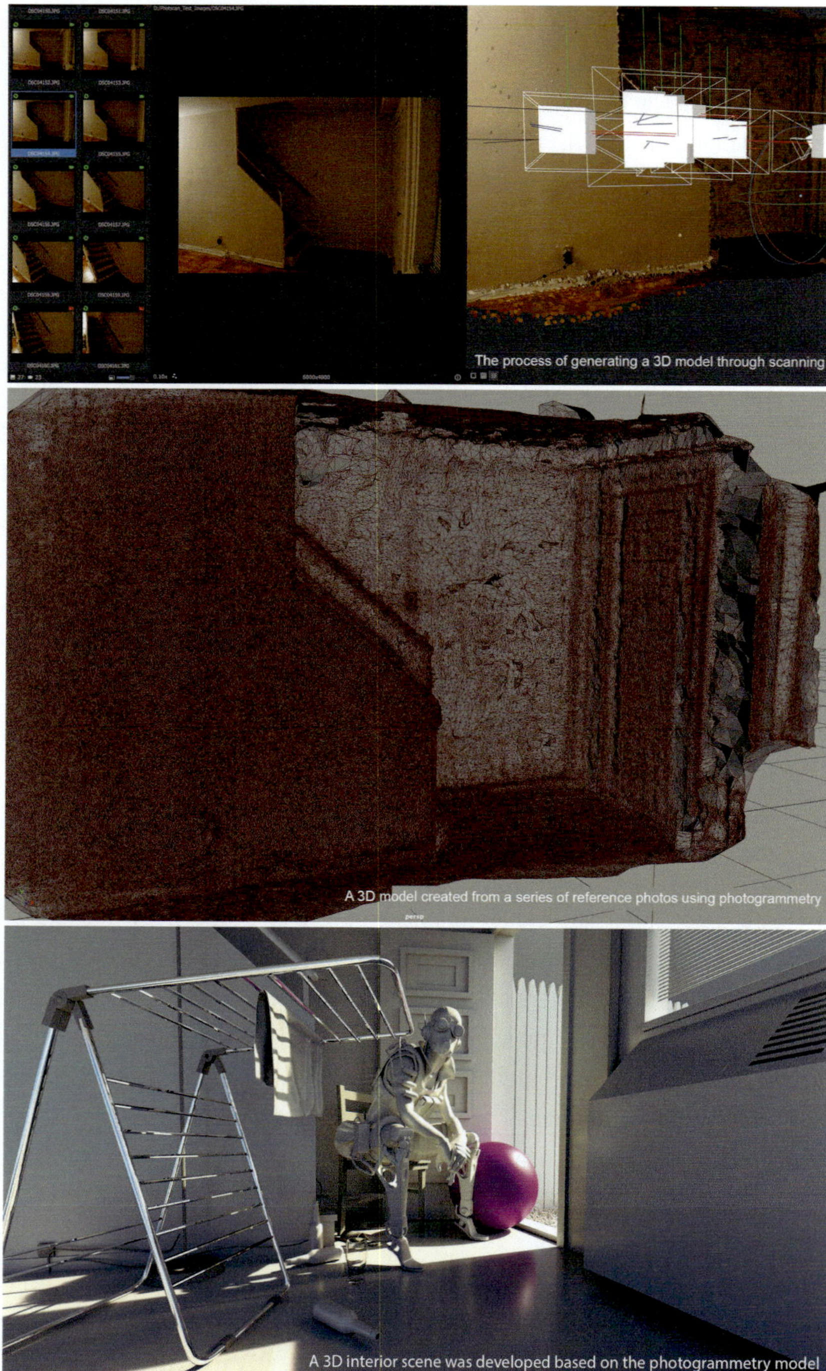

FIGURE 4.23 Three key stages of developing a 3D environment using photogrammetry

∘ Capturing reference images for 3D model creation

- Capture as many wide and medium close-up shots as possible of the geometries from multiple angles to provide valuable information for the assets department when creating accurate CG models, especially if survey data or scanned models are unavailable.
- Ensure that overlapping areas between positions are maintained in each shot. When done correctly, reference photos can be used for photogrammetry.

As an example, Figure 4.24 shows a contact sheet with multiple angles used for taking reference photos of a backpack. Each position includes three bracketed exposures spaced 2 stops apart. These images were taken with a full-frame camera and lens, with each image captured at 8K resolution.

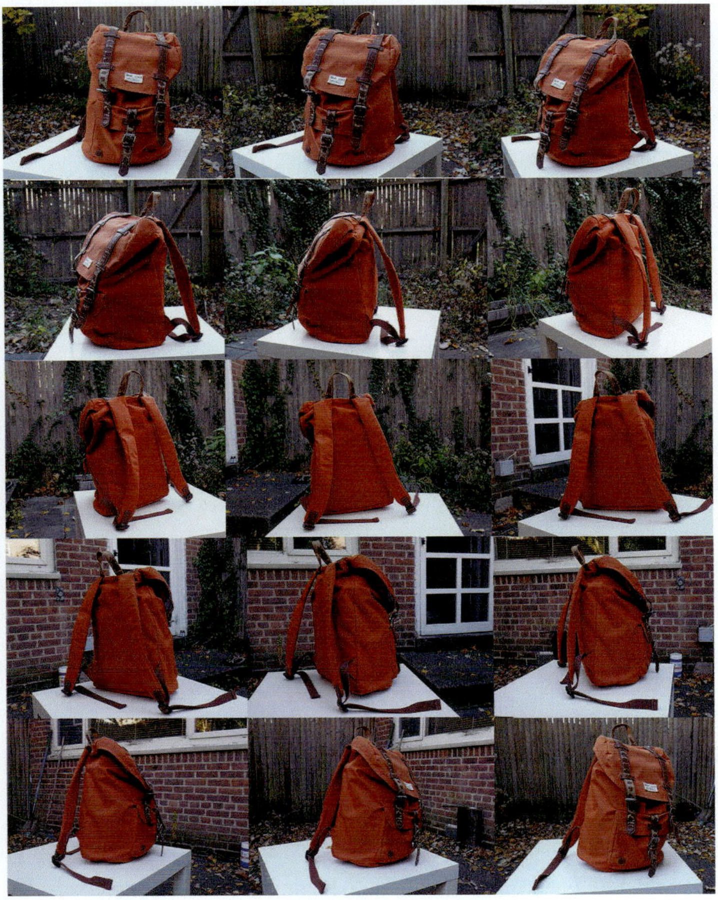

FIGURE 4.24 Multi-angle photos taken as a reference for 3D modeling

In recent years, smartphone applications have made it possible for individuals to scan 3D objects using just their phones. To do this, users simply walk around the object while recording, and the app generates 3D models in various formats and resolutions, along with associated 2D textures. This process is more straightforward than the traditional method of capturing reference images; however, the mesh details in the resulting scanned models are generally not as high as those produced using traditional offline methods. This reduction in quality is largely due to the limited bandwidth available for online data processing. A good example of this can be seen when comparing Adobe Substance 3D Sampler, a photogrammetry software, with Polycam, a 3D scanning smartphone app.

It is also worth noting that scanned 3D objects must undergo a retopology process to create clean polygonal meshes for various production purposes. Retopologizing is essential for digitally sculpted 3D models and scans, as they often contain high-density or distorted meshes. Clean meshes are particularly important when a 3D model undergoes deformation or physics simulations. Retopologizing may involve manually rebuilding the geometry based on the existing 3D model or using automated techniques available in professional 3D applications.

Figure 4.25 shows example snapshots of a scanned backpack captured using the Polycam application on a smartphone.

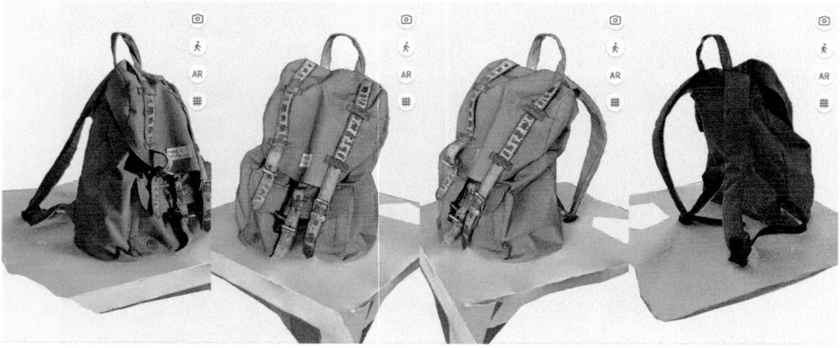

FIGURE 4.25 Examples of a backpack scanned using the Polycam application on a smartphone

∘ Capturing reference images for 3D texture creation

– Ensure important details such as windows, doors, and signs are captured in full frame to allow these elements to be duplicated if needed.

- Avoid tiling too closely. Include surrounding context to help artists better understand the environment.
- Shoot under flat lighting conditions (e.g., overcast skies or shade) for consistent results.
- Use appropriate exposure settings to ensure optimal image quality.
- Keep the aperture no wider than f/11. Wider apertures may be used for tile shots after verifying sufficient depth of field.
- Turn off image stabilization when using a tripod.
- If shooting handheld, set your shutter speed to at least double your focal length.
- Maintain a consistent ColorChecker chart, especially when shooting under changing lighting conditions.
- If on-set survey data is unavailable, record basic measurements for scale.

Figure 4.26 shows an approximately 9.5K raw texture image captured on an overcast day. The area within the dashed line will be used to create the texture. If a close-up VFX shot is required, texture artists can modify and seamlessly duplicate this portion of the image to generate much higher-resolution texture maps for 3D texturing, including base color, normal, displacement, roughness, and specular maps. In addition, the window is included in the full frame for reference, and the entire image provides sufficient context for understanding the environment.

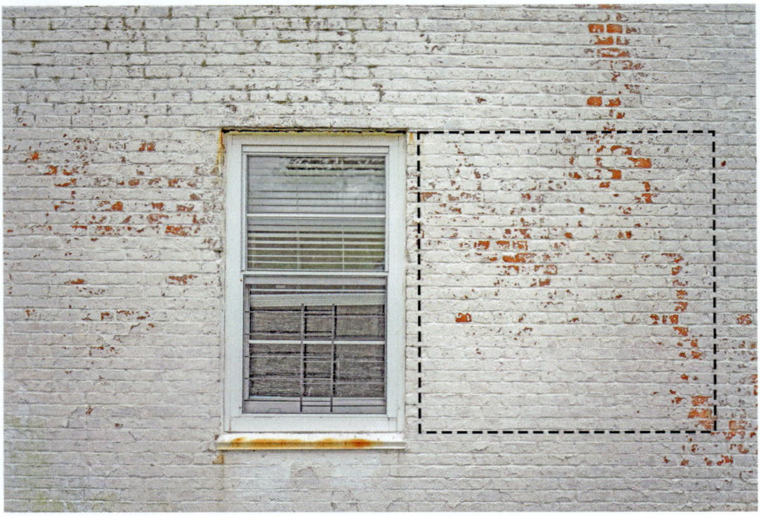

FIGURE 4.26 Wall texture captured at 9.5K under overcast lighting conditions

◦ Understanding lens distortion and shooting a lens grid

Lens distortion is a phenomenon caused by the inherent physical properties of camera lenses, which can lead to image distortion. This distortion is typically categorized into two types: barrel distortion and pincushion distortion. Barrel distortion is commonly observed in wide-angle lenses and results in a bulging effect at the edges, making subjects in those areas appear stretched or distorted. Conversely, pincushion distortion is more typical in telephoto lenses and creates an inward pinching effect toward the center, causing subjects in that region to appear similarly stretched or distorted.

As illustrated in Figure 4.27, three example images are presented side by side. Image A exhibits no lens distortion, resulting in an even distribution of the checker pattern across the entire image. Conversely, Image B shows barrel distortion, while Image C displays pincushion distortion. Lens distortion typically occurs in a subtle, spiral pattern originating from the center of the image. It becomes more pronounced toward the edges due to the spherical surface of the lens. Therefore, we can observe that the central areas of the checker patterns in Images B and C are less stretched than the border areas. Furthermore, different types of camera lenses can produce various forms of distortion.

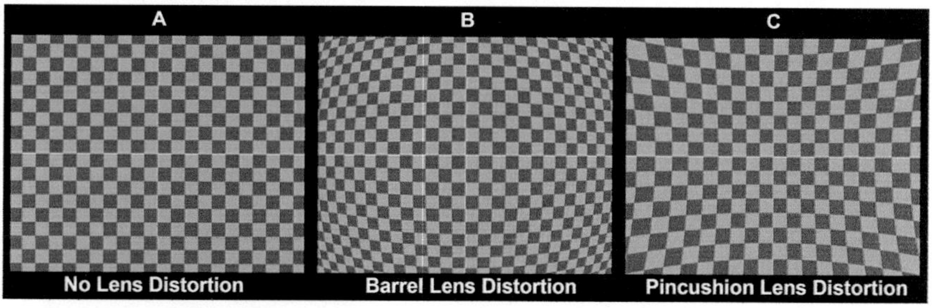

FIGURE 4.27 Comparison of different types of lens distortion in Images A, B, and C

To demonstrate the impact of lens distortion on real images, Figure 4.28 presents an example of barrel distortion in the upper image (A) and its corrected version in the lower image (B). The inward curvature of the edges of the concrete wall and door frames in the upper image illustrates the presence of distortion.

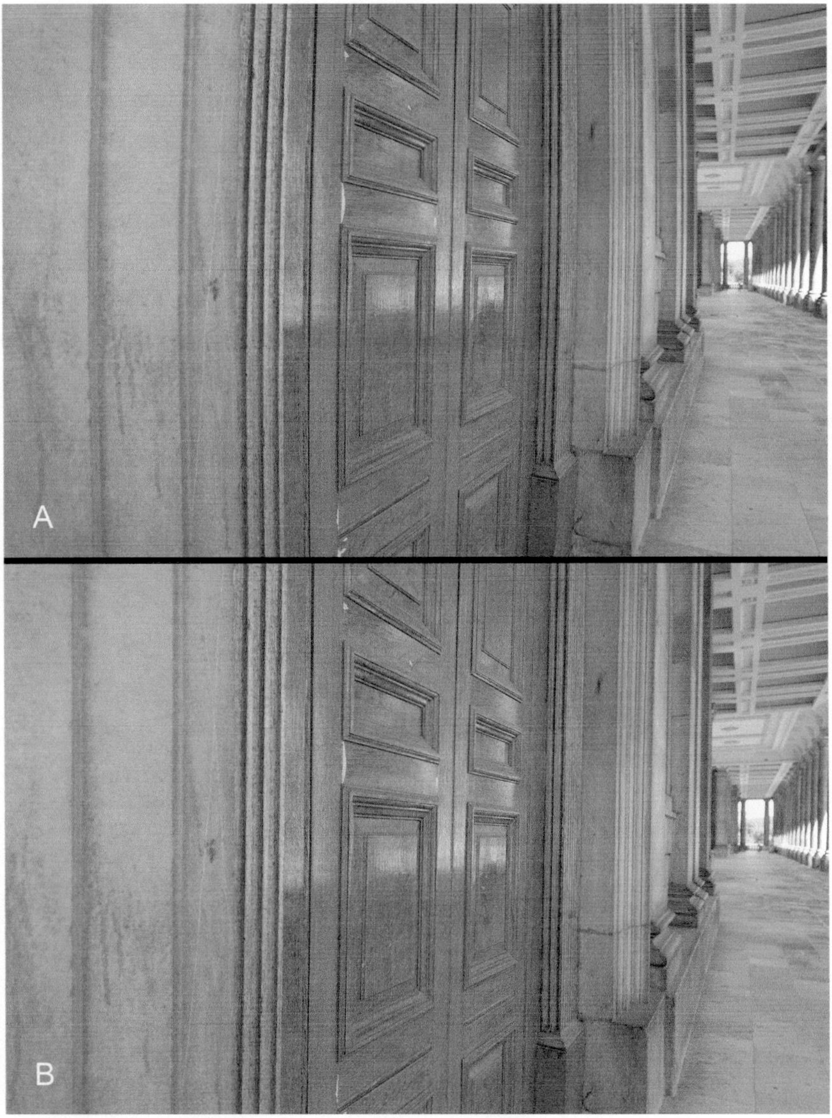

FIGURE 4.28 Comparison of lens distortion in the same Images A and B

Why is it important to consider lens distortion in visual effects projects?

Understanding and correctly applying lens distortion is crucial in visual effects production. Invisible visual effects, such as seamlessly integrating multiple assets into live-action footage, aim to create the illusion that all elements were captured by the same camera under identical conditions, without additional image processing.

Original live-action footage often contains lens distortion, which can be especially pronounced when using fisheye lenses. This distortion may result in footage that is unsuitable for certain visual effects operations, such as 3D modeling. For instance, if building pillars appear bent in a live-action scene due to lens distortion, the distortion must be corrected. To ensure consistency across all assets during production, it is essential to remove lens distortion from live-action footage before proceeding with subsequent tasks. In the final stage of VFX production, the original lens distortion must be reapplied to all CG assets before they are integrated with the live-action footage. Figure 4.29 illustrates the workflow for removing and reapplying lens distortion.

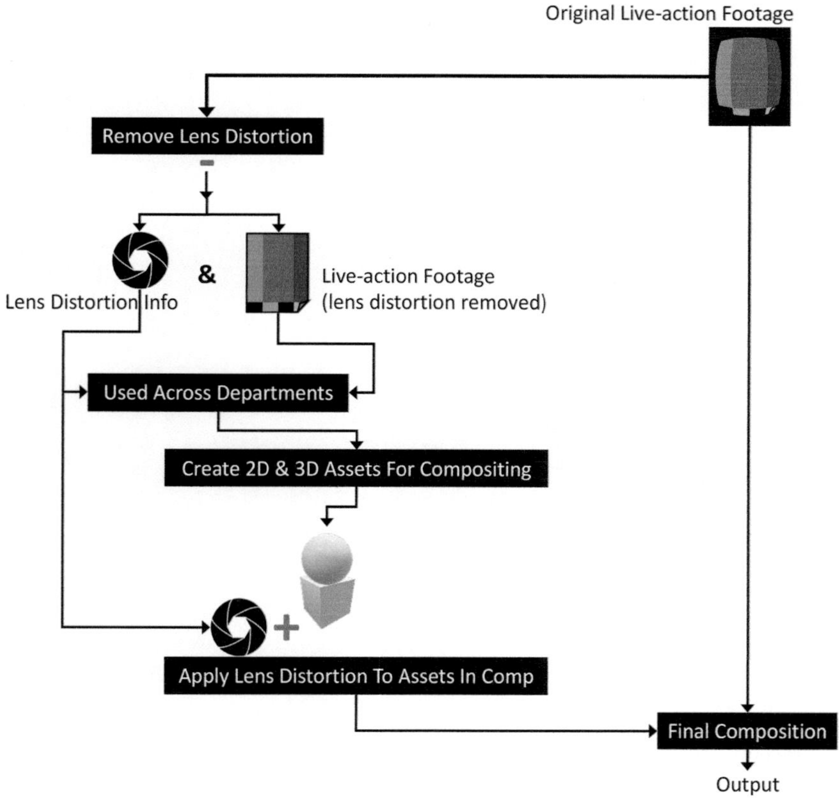

FIGURE 4.29 Workflow illustrating the processing of lens distortion data in VFX shots

– *Preparations for shooting a lens grid*

To accurately remove lens distortion from live-action footage, the recommended method is to film a lens grid and use the captured data to correct the distortion. Capturing camera lens distortion information is essential in VFX production. Major studios typically shoot various mainstream film lenses with different focal lengths and framing distances for this purpose. The collected data is then used to correct distortion in live-action footage. The process of shooting lens grids can vary depending on the camera type, lens type, and camera movement. These factors include whether the lens is prime or zoom, and whether the footage is shot with spherical or anamorphic lenses. Therefore, an appropriate shooting approach should be selected for each lens grid.

To illustrate the concept of shooting lens grids, we will demonstrate how to film lens distortion using a spherical prime lens. To experience how lens distortion is filmed, you can generate and download a lens grid template directly from BorisFX.com using the following link:

https://borisfx.com/grid-generator/

– *Essential setup of the lens grid and camera positioning*

1. Securely mount the lens grid image on a flat, stable surface, such as a wall or plywood board.
2. Ensure this surface is positioned vertically and perpendicular to the floor. In this example, a full-frame camera with a full-frame spherical prime lens is used. Whether mounted on a dolly track or tripod, the camera must be positioned perpendicular to the lens grid.
3. Aim the camera lens directly at the center of the lens grid. Avoid any rotation or tilting, as these can introduce perspective distortions that affect the accuracy of the capture.
4. Make sure the lens grid is evenly illuminated. If possible, use a light meter to confirm uniform lighting across the entire grid.
5. To accurately capture lens distortion, frame the board to maximally cover the inner area of the lens grid. Avoid including edges or any external objects. The goal is to capture a full-frame, edge-to-edge image of the evenly lit grid for precise distortion analysis.

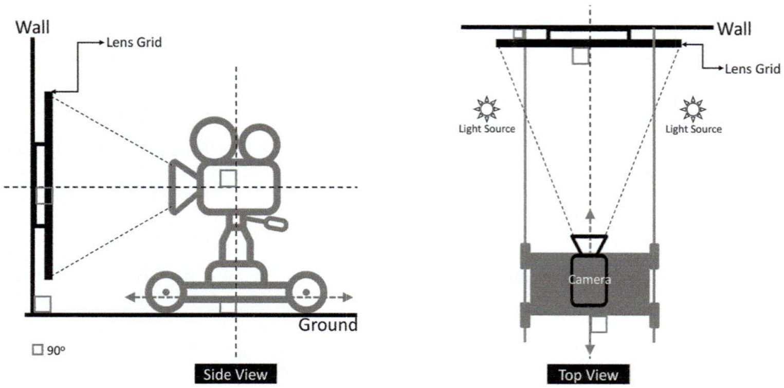

FIGURE 4.30 Multiple views of the lens grid, camera, and dolly track setups during shooting

– *Information needs on a slate*

Record a slate in front of the lens grid and include the following information on the slate:

Lens name (manufacturer included)

Lens focal length (in millimeters)

Lens serial number

Distance to film back (from lens grid to camera sensor)

Focus distance (in feet or inches)

Figure 4.31 shows the lens grid with two rectangular areas. For demonstration purposes, the green-coded area represents a large square grid, while the red-coded area indicates a medium square grid.

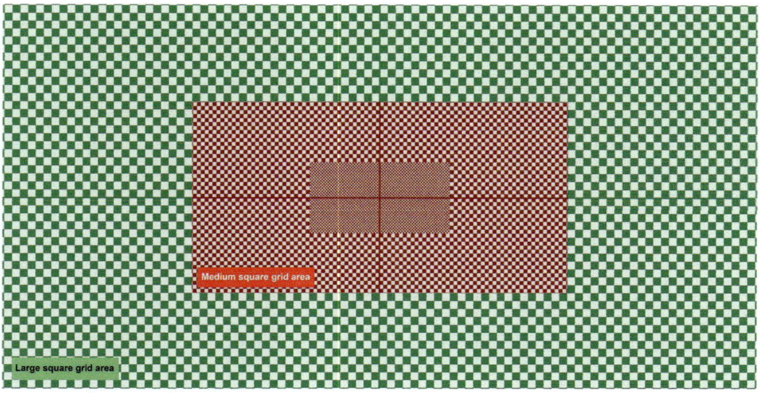

FIGURE 4.31 Large square grid shown in green; medium square grid shown in red

- *Correctly framing the lens grid*

Properly framing the lens grid is crucial for accurately capturing lens distortion, as the results depend on the framing area. Ensure that the entire lens grid is fully within the frame, excluding the edges and any areas outside the grid. Figure 4.32 shows an example of how to frame the lens grid using wide to medium focal length lenses. The dark gray area in Image A represents the recommended framing area. However, if the framing area is smaller than the semi-transparent dark green rectangle shown in Image B, shooting should be limited to the medium square grid area, indicated in red.

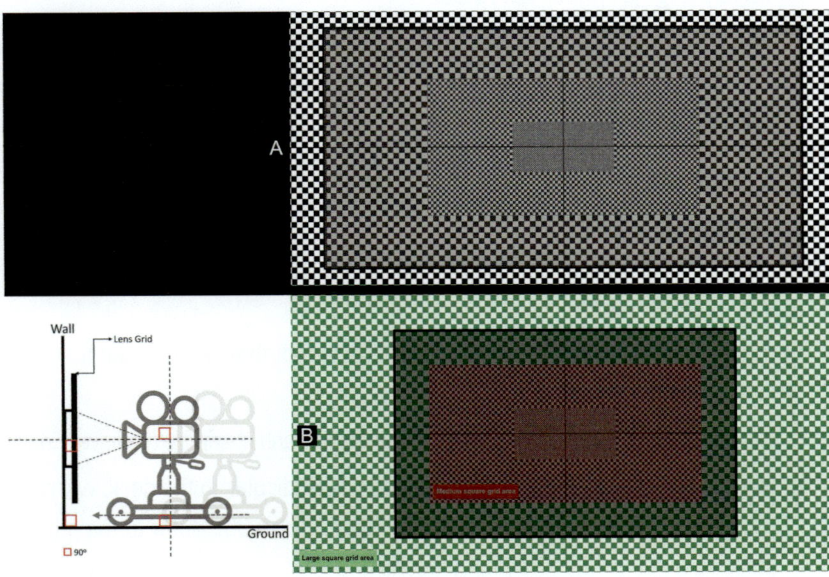

FIGURE 4.32 Recommended framing area for lenses with wide to medium focal lengths

Note:

Due to the varying focal lengths, if the framing area in Image B (the semi-transparent deep green area) is smaller than six large square checker patterns counted from the edges of the lens grid, it is recommended to move the camera closer to the lens grid and use the medium square grid area (in red) instead. In such cases, it is important to ensure that both framing and shooting are confined to the medium square grid area.

– *Shoot the lens grid*

When using a digital camera, record 5 to 10 seconds of the grid.

If you're using a film camera, stand approximately 3 feet away and cover the lens for 2 seconds before each shot to help distinguish between different focal lengths. Be sure to document all lens information and relevant details on a datasheet.

Download an example datasheet from the following link:

www.routledge.com/9781032124537

– *A simple alternative method for capturing a lens grid using prime lenses*

Professional approaches to shooting lens grids are always recommended. However, setting up a lens grid and camera rig for low-budget projects can be challenging. Given the complexities involved, it may be worthwhile to consider alternative methods, especially for personal visual effects work. The following method outlines a simplified approach to shooting lens grids using prime lenses. If executed correctly, it can be an efficient solution.

1. Use a full-frame digital camera.
2. Use the same camera body, lens, and focal length that will be used for filming the live-action scene.
3. Load the lens grid template on a computer display and maximize preview window.
4. Ensure the computer display is level and perpendicular to the desk, with no tilting forward, backward, or sideways (see Figure 4.33). Refer to the previous steps as a guide when framing the lens grid.
5. Record the lens grid for approximately 5–10 seconds.

Note:

To obtain accurate lens distortion information, use full-frame cameras when capturing the lens grid. APS-C cameras and crop lenses omit edge-to-edge distortion data due to their crop factors.

While the procedure for capturing lens distortion with zoom lenses is similar to that for prime lenses, the key difference lies in capturing images at each of the incremented focal lengths marked on the zoom lens barrel.

Ensure the camera is set to full-frame and full-gate formats.

Record the details of each lens on a data sheet and capture the slate.

At each marked focal length on the lens barrel, shoot while maximizing the number of visible grid squares in the frame by adjusting the camera dolly or tripod. If the framing includes fewer than six large grid squares surrounding the medium square grid, move the camera closer to the grid and reframe to center the medium square grid.

When using digital cameras, shoot for approximately 5 seconds. For film cameras, shoot approximately three feet of film, blocking the lens for 2 seconds between lenses to ensure separation between focal lengths.

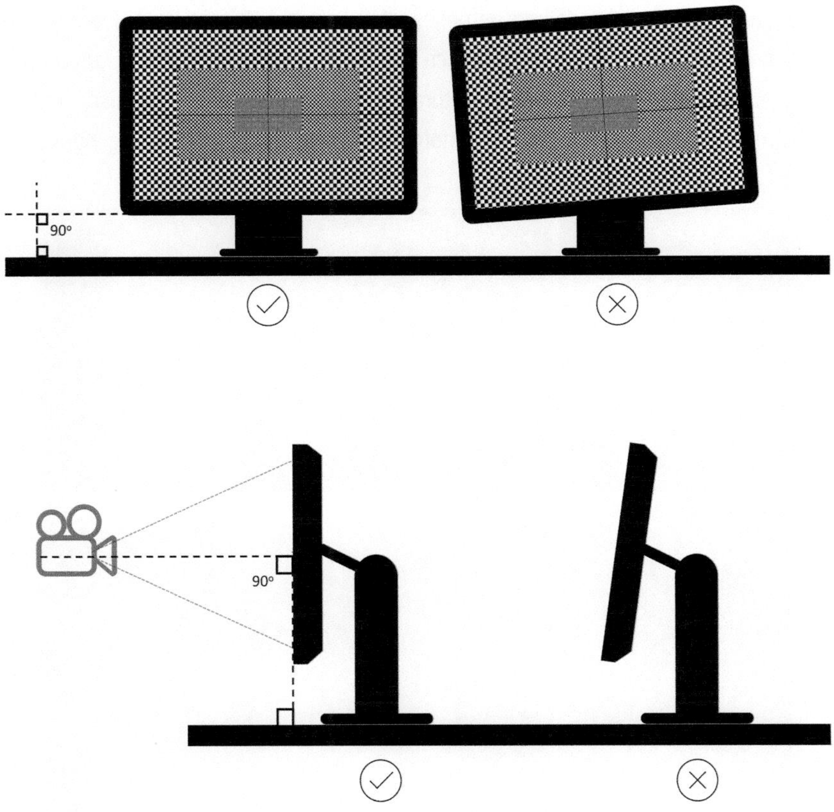

FIGURE 4.33 Visual guideline for filming a lens grid on a computer display

◦ Lens vignetting

Vignetting is a common optical phenomenon in lenses that can occur in natural, optical, and mechanical forms. Natural vignetting happens when light reaches the camera sensor at different angles and gradually fades from the center of the image to its edges. This occurs because the energy of the light diminishes as it travels farther from the center, causing the edges of the image to progressively dim (see Figure 4.34).

During VFX production, lens vignetting should be carefully addressed when present in the original footage. Typically, it is removed before VFX work begins and restored after all tasks are completed. VFX studios are typically meticulous when reproducing vignetting effects in VFX production, ensuring they match the original footage. The most effective way to create a lens vignette is to capture it in-camera. Doing so produces a more natural and authentic result.

In traditional filmmaking, "vignetting" often refers to the intentional darkening of an image's edges, commonly used to draw the viewer's attention toward the center of the frame for storytelling purposes. However, this effect is sometimes overused, particularly in student films, which can result in a forced and distracting look. By understanding the subtleties of natural vignetting, filmmakers can use the technique more deliberately to achieve a more authentic and natural-looking vignette.

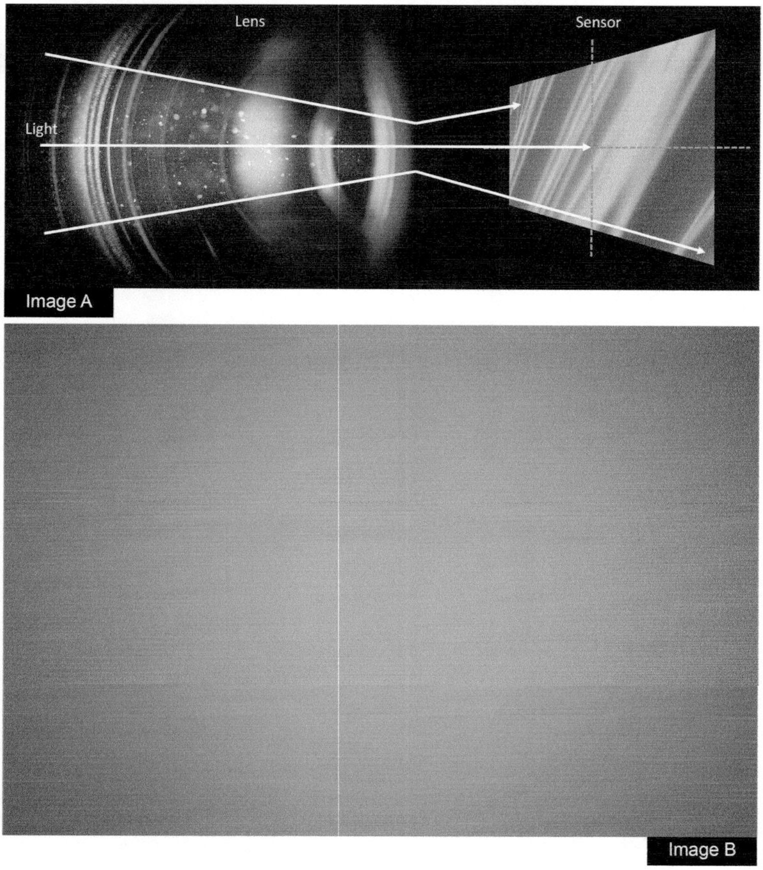

FIGURE 4.34 Image A illustrates the path of light through a camera lens to the sensor. Image B shows a lens vignette captured with a full-frame Sony G Lens

Chapter Five

Visual effects project case studies

Case studies:

> Case Study 1 – Rig removal in a stop-motion animation shot.
> Case Study 2 – Understanding the importance of 3D camera tracking.
> Case Study 3 – The library project.
> Case Study 4 – Sky replacement.
> Case Study 5 – Essential concepts of keying in compositing.
> Case Study 6 – Creating a VFX shot for the classic film *The Lavender Hill Mob.*
> Case Study 7 – The CG shoe project: seamless integration of CG elements with low-end footage.
> Case Study 8 – The space capsule project.
> Nuke Script examples for high-profile feature film shots.

Online tutorials for case studies are available at
www.youtube.com/@InvisibleFilmVFX

This chapter presents a series of case studies that demonstrate how the theories and workflows covered in previous chapters can be applied to personal VFX projects. To reduce the burden of learning multiple specialized software programs, we have minimized software dependencies as much as possible. The primary software

DOI: 10.4324/9781003224617-5

used in this chapter includes Foundry NukeX and Autodesk Maya. Additionally, we will reference the integration of Adobe Substance 3D Painter and Boris FX SynthEyes within the project workflows.

Don't worry, the focus of these projects is not on mastering the software itself, but rather on developing a deep understanding of visual effects workflows through the integration of various tools. While proficiency in software is important, having a clear grasp of the workflow is essential for long-term professional growth.

• Introduction to the primary applications used in the case studies

◦ The essential understanding of node-based compositing in NukeX

Understanding node-based compositing is essential for working effectively with NukeX. This process involves connecting individual nodes to create a comprehensive flowchart, which ultimately leads to the production of a composition. Therefore, it is important to think logically about node connections and layout. This section will explain the fundamental concepts involved in building compositing scripts in NukeX.

Foundry NukeX
Official website: www.foundry.com

As introduced in previous chapters, NukeX is an industry-standard compositing system widely used in visual effects studios. It is a standalone flagship application within Foundry's Nuke Studio, which includes both NukeX and Nuke. NukeX is available under both non-commercial and commercial licenses. To obtain a non-commercial license, simply sign up and download the Nuke Studio application package. Students may also be eligible for Foundry's free or discounted license programs. To learn more about downloading NukeX, watch the prerecorded video titled "Download NukeX" at www.youtube.com/@invisiblefilmvfx.

– *The concept of compositing layouts in NukeX*

Foundry NukeX is an essential tool in compositing workflows, featuring a specific script layout that facilitates seamless collaboration between studios.

The standard compositing structure in Nuke follows a top-to-bottom flow, starting with background elements at the top of the script, gradually incorporating middle-ground elements, and concluding with foreground elements at the bottom. This vertical layout mirrors our perception of elements in the real world, categorizing them clearly into background, middle ground, and foreground (see Figure 5.1).

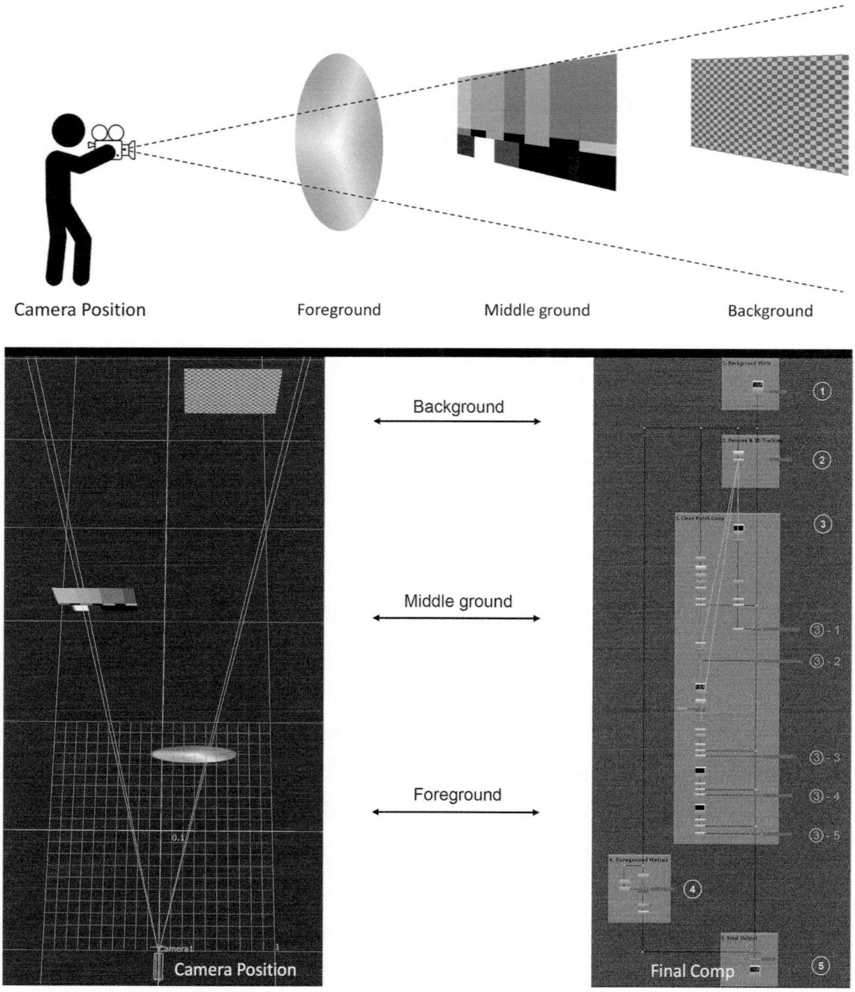

FIGURE 5.1 Comparison of the spatial arrangement of objects in the physical world versus the layout of elements in Nuke scripts

– *Mouse cursor interactions with Nuke operations*

After launching NukeX, the default user interface is divided into three main sections. It's important to note that the position of the mouse cursor determines which operations can be performed when using hotkeys. For example, placing the mouse cursor in the Node Graph panel and pressing the R key will open the Read File(s) dialog window, allowing users to import external footage into Nuke. However, if the cursor is positioned in the Viewer1 panel, pressing R will switch Viewer1 from its default RGB channel to the R (red) channel when viewing images. Therefore, always pay attention to the position of the mouse cursor during operations, especially if you are new to Nuke.

– *Project settings*

Like many other creative applications, setting up a project in NukeX is the first step before working on a composition. This setup involves specifying the image frame range, frame rate, and project format. These settings directly affect certain operations in the compositing scripts of each project. To open the Project Settings dialog box, place the mouse cursor in the Node Graph panel and press the S key. In the lower section of the Project Settings panel, confirm the following settings:

Confirm the frame range of the background plate.

The default frame range in Nuke is set from 1 to 100. However, each shot contains a different number of frames, so the frame range should match the required working frame range of the shot.

Double-check the fps.

The fps (frames per second) is set to 24 by default, aligning with the standard playback frame rate for films. In VFX projects, live-action footage may be captured at various frame rates, so setting the correct fps for each shot is also critical at this stage.

Confirm the full size format option.

The default project format in NukeX is 2K_Super_35 (full-ap) 2048 × 1556. Set the full size format option to match the required resolution of the live-action footage for the final compositing output. For example, if the live-action footage was originally filmed in 4K (4096 × 2160), but the actual working plate format in the pipeline is 2K (2048 × 1080), as indicated by the editorial department, then the final output should be 2K (2048 × 1080), so the full size format option should be set to 2K_DCP (2048 × 1080), not 4K (4096 × 2160). This is particularly important, as all node formats created in the compositing scripts will be aligned with the final output size.

Note

2K is still a common working resolution in visual effects production. Image resolution alone does not define image quality, which is also influenced by other important factors such as color gamut, high dynamic range, and various technical specifications. Therefore, larger image sizes do not necessarily equate to higher-quality images. Watch the pre-recorded Nuke introductory video for a more detailed demonstration at www.youtube.com/@ InvisibleFilmVFX

Video title: The Initial Concept of Node-Based Compositing in NukeX

○ The primary 3D applications used in the case studies

Although visual effects studios develop various in-house tools, major 3D applications like Autodesk Maya and SideFX Houdini have become fundamental building blocks, deeply integrated into their production pipelines. For the project case studies throughout this book, we will use Maya as the primary 3D tool to demonstrate the key workflows between NukeX and Maya.

– *Essential concepts of working in Autodesk Maya*

Autodesk Maya (www.autodesk.com) is industry-standard 3D animation software that has been deeply embedded in the production pipelines of visual effects and 3D animation studios for over two decades. It offers both indie and student versions for individual learners.

To download Autodesk Maya, search for "Students and Educators | Getting Started", which provides a guide video explaining how to access Autodesk educational licenses.

Maya's user interface consists of four working viewports (perspective, top, front, and side), each based on a different camera view. 3D artists can quickly access these viewports by pressing and releasing the spacebar. Each viewport responds to the position of the mouse cursor, similar to Foundry NukeX. Both Maya and Foundry NukeX require a three-button mouse, with the scroll wheel functioning as the middle mouse button, providing access to certain operational features.

In this section, you will be guided through setting up a new Maya project.

For more information about learning Maya, please visit Autodesk's official learning website and YouTube channel at www.youtube.com/@Autodesk_Maya/featured

– *Setting up new projects in Maya*

It is essential to set up new project directories in Maya before beginning any project. A project directory folder enables Maya to save projects and assets into appropriate subfolders. There are two options for creating a Maya project under the File menu > Project section:

Project Window

This option sets up a new project directory.

Set Project . . .

This option defines an existing Maya project and allows Maya to access the project directory to save project files and assets.

A pre-recorded introductory video on project settings in Maya is available at https://www.youtube.com/@InvisibleFilmVFX. The video is titled "Setting Projects in Maya".

• The essential understanding of matte in compositing

Each digital image has four channels: red (R), green (G), blue (B), and alpha (A). The alpha channel is often initially empty and visually appears as pure black, with a value of 0. Occasionally, certain operations may result in a solid white color with a value of 1 in the alpha channel. Pure black signifies complete transparency, while solid white indicates full opacity. Values between 0 and 1 represent varying degrees of transparency.

A matte is a grayscale image used to isolate a specific area in an image, typically stored in the alpha channel. In digital compositing, a matte can also be stored in individual red, green, blue, and alpha channels. For example, the matte of the bird in Figure 5.2 is stored in the red channel of the original footage.

There are three primary approaches to creating a matte, depending on the specific requirements of each shot.

○ Approach one: rotoscoping

Rotoscoping is a technique that traditionally involves tracing motion picture footage frame by frame. This method becomes essential in various scenarios, such as isolating specific objects when green or blue screens are not available in the shot, or when clean mattes cannot be extracted for certain parts of objects. The image on the left in Figure 5.2 illustrates the structure of roto shapes (depicted as red circular lines) based on the parrot's body structure and movement.

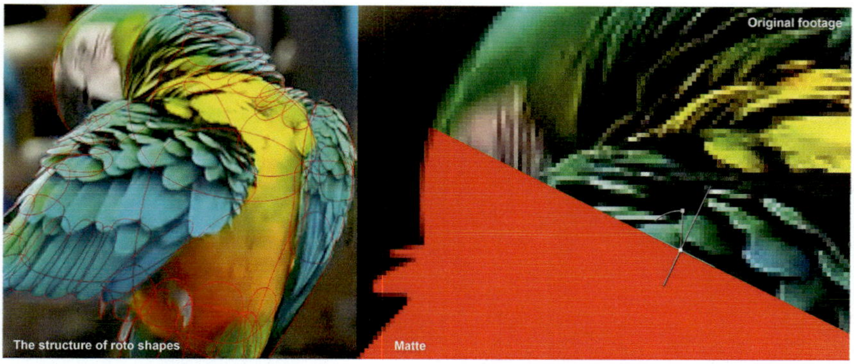

FIGURE 5.2 Rotoscoping structures of a parrot, with the resulting matte stored in the red channel

Notes

1. In visual effects production, mattes created through rotoscoping must precisely match the pixels of objects in the original footage.
2. Rotoscoping may still be necessary even when using green or blue screens, especially if the lighting is poor or if fine details such as hair in close-ups or objects with heavy motion blur need to be preserved. In these cases, green or blue screens may not produce a clean matte through keying. However, as the in-camera VFX (ICVFX) methodology is extensively used in virtual production, rotoscoping and keying may not be required for certain green/blue shots.

○ Approach two: CG assets rendered from 3D software

3D applications typically render alpha channels for computer-generated (CG) assets automatically. In Figure 5.3, a group of 3D shapes rendered using Autodesk Maya is shown. Additionally, a matte of the shapes is rendered and included in the alpha channel of the final output.

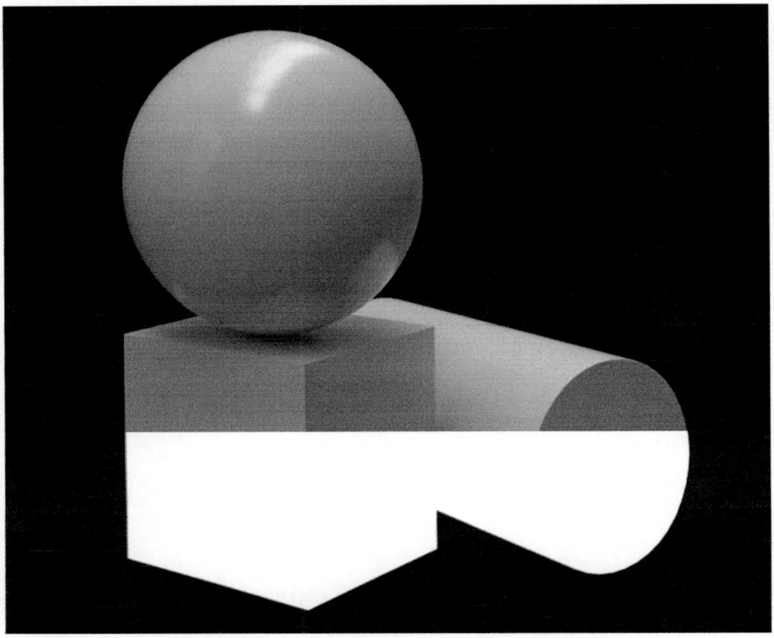

FIGURE 5.3 A set of rendered 3D geometries with a matte embedded in the alpha channel

○ Approach three: screen keying

The screen keying process creates mattes for objects filmed against a green or blue screen. With the growing popularity of virtual production (VP) technologies, many shots that once required green/blue screen filming can now be captured directly in an on-set LED "Volume." However, due to the complexity of VFX shots, green and blue screens are still widely used in modern film production. They are likely to remain essential in many on-set shooting scenarios, such as outdoor locations. Therefore, understanding the fundamentals of screen keying in VFX shots is highly beneficial for artists.

Case Study 5 will offer a detailed overview of green and blue screen keying techniques.

Case Study 1

Rig removal in a stop-motion animation shot

Key learning points:

> Fundamental techniques for creating clean plates and patches.
> Removing prop rigs from a stop-motion animation shot.
> Understanding professional compositing layouts and work approaches.

Notes

Each case study includes a pre-recorded video tutorial. Watching these videos alongside reading the case studies is strongly recommended to ensure a smooth and comprehensive learning experience for each hands-on project.

Video link: youtube.com/@InvisibleFilmVFX

Video title: Case Study 1 | Rig Removal in a Stop-Motion Animation Shot

Project file: Case_Study_1_Project_File

The project file is available for download on the book's official webpage. High-resolution color figures from this project are also available for download on the book's official webpage.

• Case Study 1: Shot analysis

○ Terminologies discussed in Case Study 1

- In visual effects production, live-action footage is commonly converted into an OpenEXR format image sequence by the editorial department prior to the start of production. The image sequence is referred to as a "plate".
- A "clean plate" is created from the original live-action footage (plate) with specific unwanted elements removed.
- A "clean patch" refers to a small area of the original plate from which certain elements have been removed.

Figure 5.4 illustrates the first and last frames of the short film *Fred's Meat* (2010), funded by the UK North London Film Fund. The film was shot using a RED camera. Special thanks to director Robert Darcy, producer Hugh Harford, and the production crew for their assistance in providing the footage used in this book.

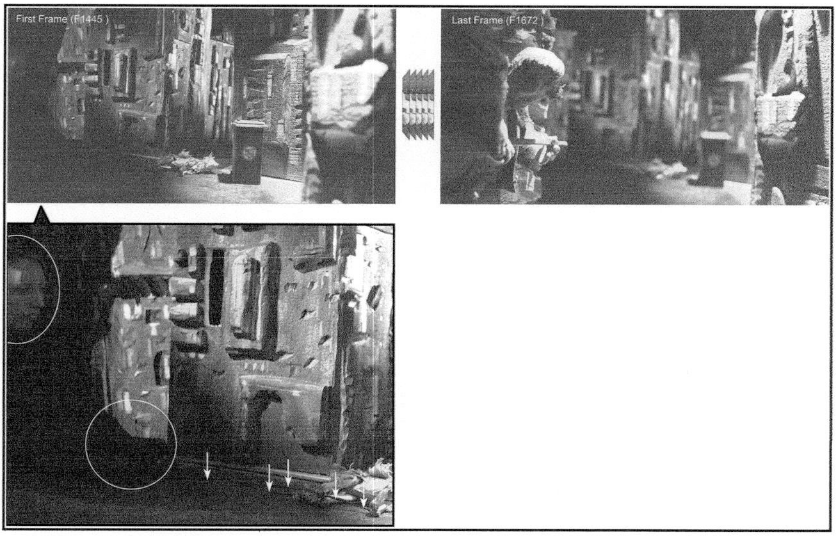

FIGURE 5.4 The elements highlighted by white circles and arrows should be removed from the scene. © Hugh Harford and the North London Film Fund

○ Client requirements

The shot begins with the puppeteer's face and hands visible in certain frames. Additionally, the puppet character's control ropes are visible beneath its legs and in the shadows. These elements should be removed from the final film.

○ Understanding camera movement in the shot

Camera movement: A dolly shot

In the original footage, a dolly shot is used. Starting from frame 1600, the camera performs a dolly-out, gradually defocusing the background character while simultaneously bringing the foreground object into sharp focus.

○ Production concept

To meet the client's requirements for the shot, the compositing process involves several steps. These include extracting still images, creating clean patches by removing unwanted elements from those images, applying 2D motion tracking to match the original camera movement, replicating the defocusing effect of the original shot, and finally integrating the clean patches into the original plate to cover problematic areas.

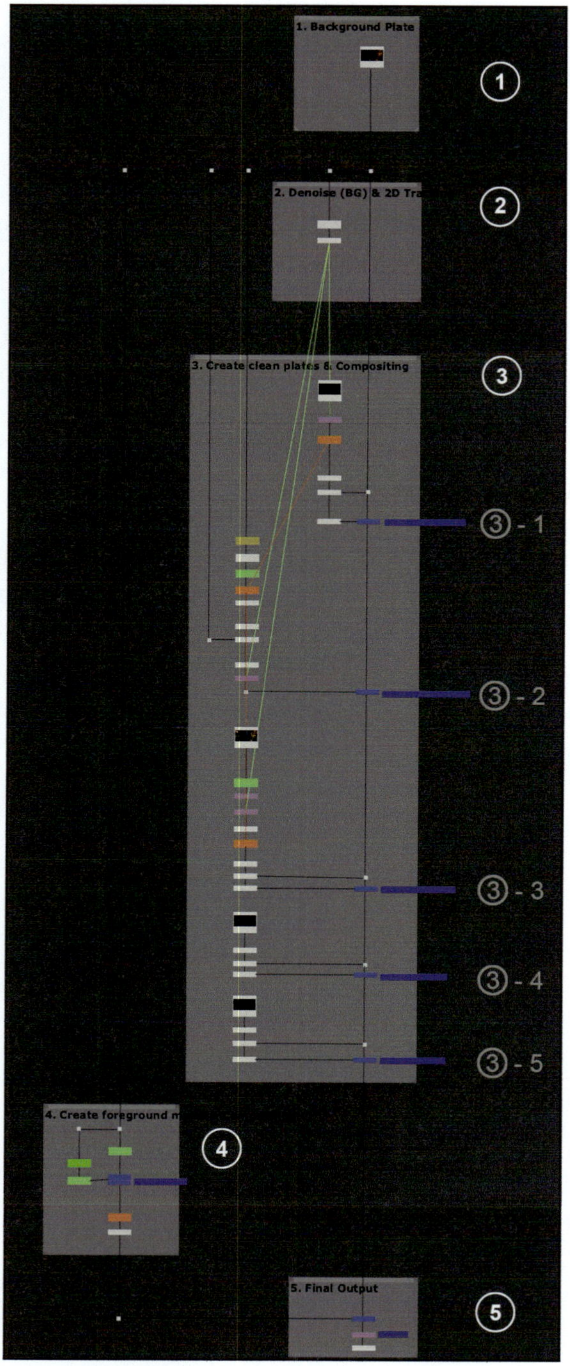

FIGURE 5.5 The overall Nuke script for Case Study 1

• Analyzing the Nuke compositing script for Case Study 1

The compositing script for Case Study 1 consists of five main sections:

Section ①: Original plate

Section ②: Denoise the background plate and perform 2D tracking

Section ③: Create clean patches and compositing

This section is subdivided into five subsections, numbered ③-1 through ③-5, to facilitate the generation of the necessary clean patches.

Section ④: Create the foreground matte and final composition

Section ⑤: Final output

∘ Section ①: Original plate

Position the mouse cursor in the Node Graph panel.

Press the R key.

Navigate to Case Study 1 project folder where the background plate is stored.

Import the background plate into NukeX.

Once the original background plate is loaded in Nuke using the Read node, the following information can be accessed in its Properties panel:

Double-check the following information in the Read tab of the Properties panel.

Format: 2K_LatLong 2048 × 1024

Frame Range: 1445–1672

Original Range: 1445–1672

Input Transform: default (linear)

The background plate is in OpenEXR format, which indicates that the color space is linear.

Double-check the information in the Metadata tab of the Properties panel.

input/bitsperchannel: 16-bit half float

◦ Section ②: Denoise the background plate and perform 2D tracking

This section includes two nodes:

Denoise node

This node is used to remove film grain from the original plate.

Tracker node

The Tracker node analyzes and calculates the camera movements in the original footage along the 2D X and Y axes. The resulting tracking data is then used to drive clean patches, allowing them to follow the camera movements in the shot.

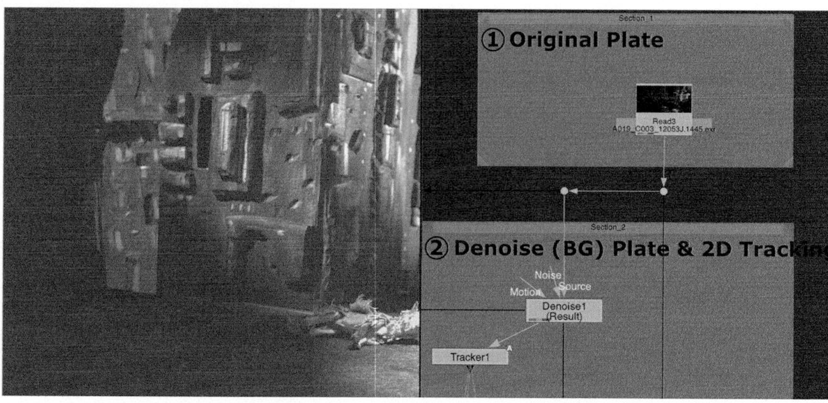

FIGURE 5.6 Nodes used in Sections 1 and 2

– *Analyzing the use of the Denoise node*

Before proceeding with 2D or 3D tracking, it is recommended to use a Denoise node to remove film grain from the original background plate (footage), especially if it appears grainy. This recommendation is based on the following reasons:

Reason one:

Traditional film grain is primarily caused by the photosensitive substances used in chemical film. With the advancement of digital camera technology, film grain can still appear in both still and moving images due to factors such as digital camera sensors, lenses, and lighting conditions. For instance, different ISO settings can produce varying levels of film grain in digital cameras, especially in low-light scenarios.

The appearance of film grain can vary from frame to frame, and this inconsistency can affect the accuracy of both 2D and 3D tracking, particularly in scenes with prominent film grain. To address this issue, it is important to remove the film grain from the background plate before starting the 2D tracking process.

Reason two:

The purpose of removing noise from extracted still frames is to eliminate the embedded static film grain from the original live-action footage and create clean patches.

To generate clean patches, we must first remove the film grain from the extracted images and then erase any unwanted elements. Afterward, the original film grain will be reintroduced to the generated clean patches to match the original plate during compositing.

When using the Denoise node, a square Analysis Region appears in the lower-left corner of the image, prompting the selection of an area for analysis. Drag this square over a flat region with uniform color and no distinct patterns to complete the analysis process.

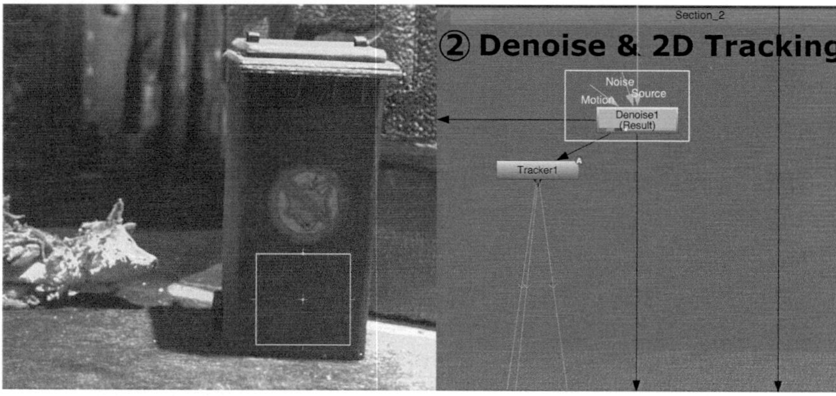

FIGURE 5.7 In this example, the Analysis Region (gray square) is sampled at the bottom of the trash can

- *Analyzing the use of the Tracker node*

NukeX provides two tracking nodes: the Tracker (Transform) node for 2D tracking and the CameraTracker (3D) node for 3D camera tracking tasks. In this project, we use the Tracker node to calculate 2D camera motion and apply the tracking data to drive the clean patches. This allows the clean patches to follow the camera's movement within the shot (see Figure 5.8).

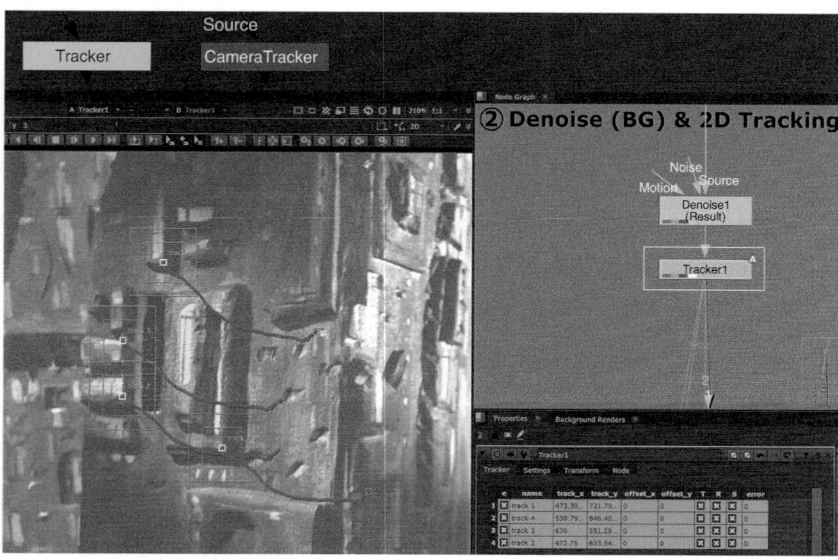

FIGURE 5.8 Four tracking features (left image) are selected on the same plane of the wall, near the puppeteer's face

Notes

1. Trackers should be placed around the elements that need to be erased. For example, in Figure 5.8, four tracking features were selected near the puppeteer's face on the same wall plane to ensure a consistent camera perspective. This approach helps reduce inaccuracies in the tracking results caused by varying camera angles. In contrast, selecting tracking features from walls with different camera perspectives may result in noticeable tracking errors.
2. It is worth noting that the order of counting (X, Y) positions in Nuke follows a counterclockwise direction. Nuke begins counting coordinates from the lower-left corner (0, 0), moves to the lower-right corner (1, 0), then to the upper-right corner (1, 1), and so on. This explains why certain operational icons default to appearing in the lower-left corner during operations.
3. It is important for tracking features to be unique and not have similar patterns nearby. For optimal results, high-contrast features should be used. For instance, in this case, we positioned four tracking markers on the high-contrast, hard corners of the bricks on the same wall plane (refer to Figure 5.9).

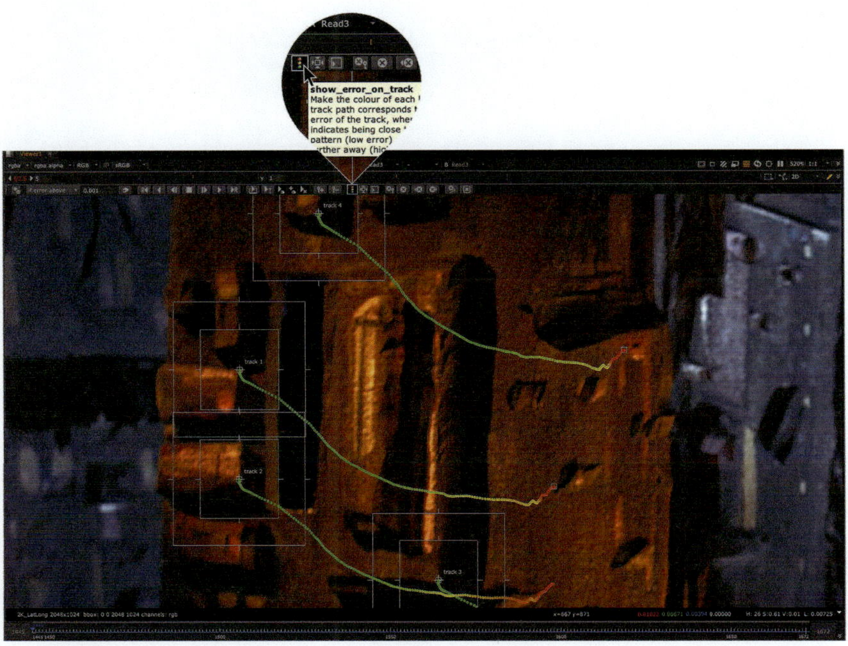

FIGURE 5.9 2D tracking results obtained from four high-contrast corners on the same wall plane

After completing the 2D tracking tasks, go to the Export section in the Properties panel of the Tracker1 node. From the dropdown menu, select Transform (match-move) and click the create button to generate a Transform_Matchmove node. This node will be used to drive the created clean patches, effectively replicating the camera motion from the original shot (see Figure 5.10).

Note

The Tracker1 node in Section ② should not be connected to the main compositing pipeline. This node is used solely to calculate the 2D movement of the camera from the shot.

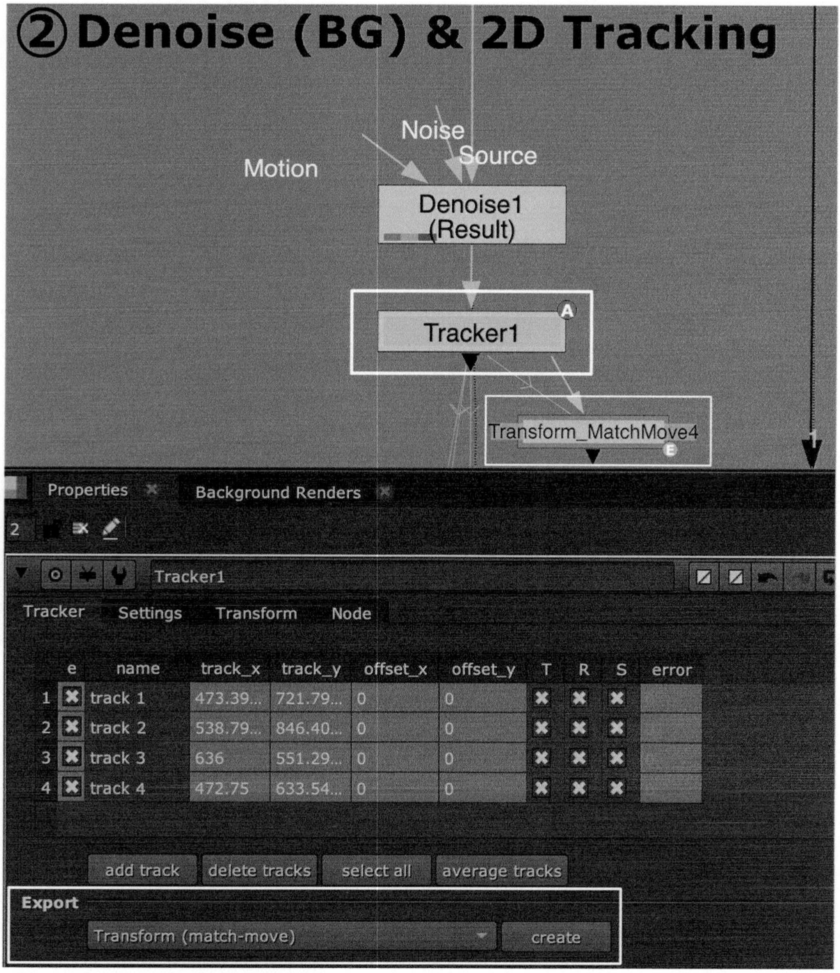

FIGURE 5.10 A separate Transform_Matchmove node is generated based on the 2D tracking results

○ Section ③ : Create clean patches and compositing

The process of creating clean patches involves extracting still frames that feature the puppeteer's face, hands, and prop ropes. Unwanted elements are then erased from these still frames to create clean patches. Lastly, the Transform_Matchmove node is used to apply 2D camera movements to the resulting clean patches.

– *Section ③–1: Create a clean patch for the puppeteer's face and hands*

Figure 5.11 shows the node connections used to create a clean patch for the puppeteer's face and hands.

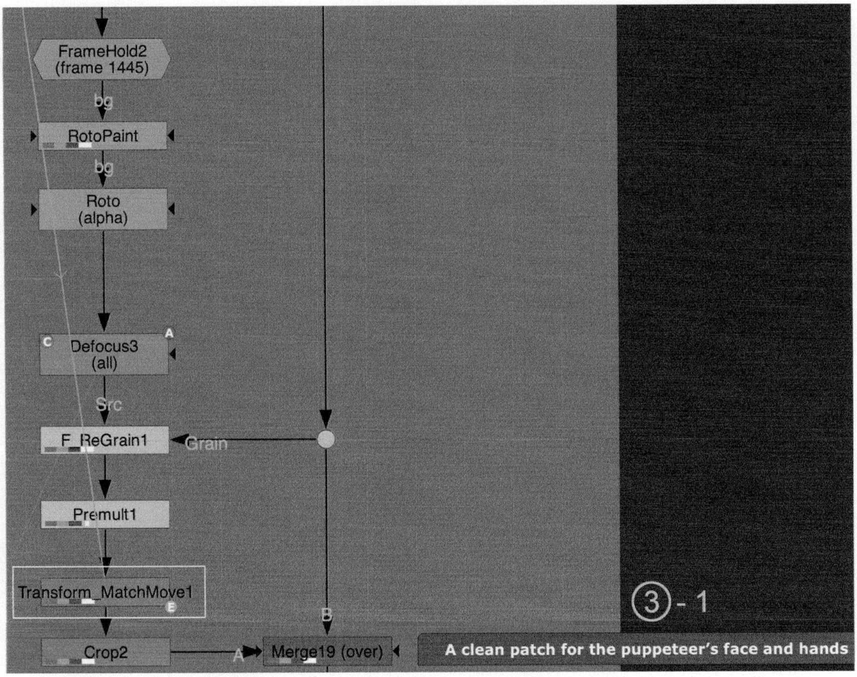

FIGURE 5.11 Node connections in Section 3–1

Step 1 | FrameHold node.

After the Denoise1 node, connect a FrameHold node to convert the denoised background plate sequence into a still image at frame 1445, which is the first frame of the plate. Refer to the first node in the script connections, as shown in Figure 5.11.

Step 2 | RotoPaint node.

Connect a RotoPaint node after the FrameHold node and use its Clone tool to erase the puppeteer's face and hands in the still image at frame 1445. Figure 5.12 shows the FrameHold and RotoPaint nodes connected after the Denoise1 node, along with a clean plate created using the Clone tool in the RotoPaint node (right).

Note

A Wacom Intuos Pro tablet is recommended for painting images. Pen tablets enable artists to take advantage of pressure sensitivity when painting subtle image details, whereas brush strokes made with a mouse can feel rigid. As a result, tablets are widely used across departments in VFX studios.

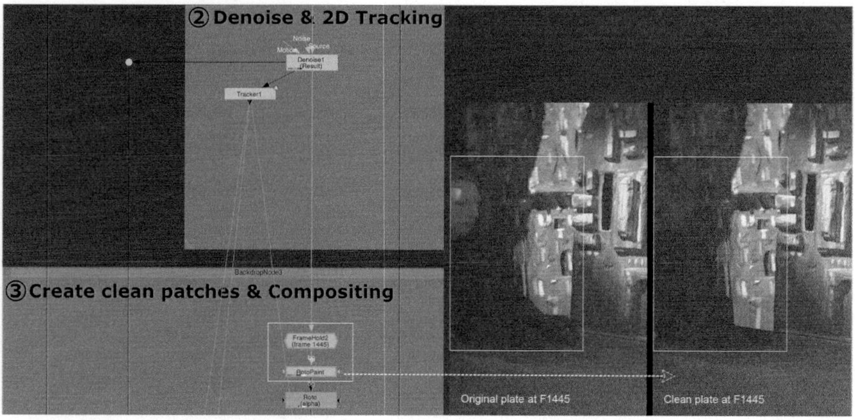

FIGURE 5.12 The FrameHold and RotoPaint nodes (left) are connected after the Denoise node. The clean plate created at frame 1445 is shown on the right

Step 3 | Roto node.

Connect a Roto node after the RotoPaint node. Use the Roto node to draw two shapes on the created clean plate: one covering the puppeteer's face and the other covering her hands.

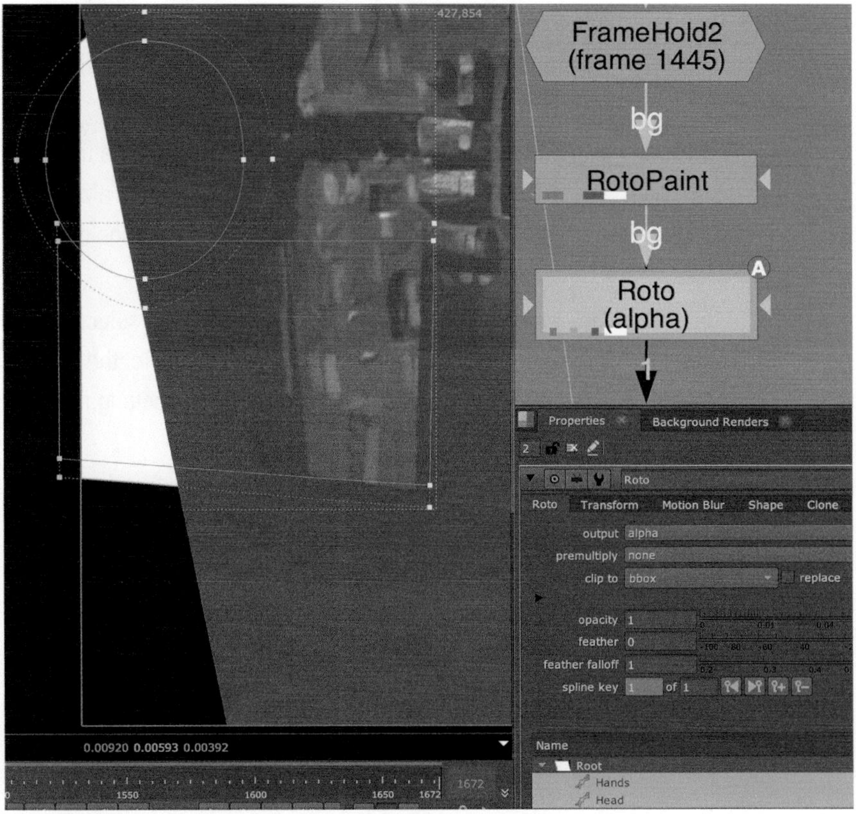

FIGURE 5.13 Connect a Roto node after the RotoPaint node and draw two separate roto shapes large enough to cover the puppeteer's face and hands

Step 4 | Defocus node.

We can see that the elements in the original background gradually go out of focus starting from frame 1600. However, the clean patch still image, created based on frame 1445, remains perfectly in focus. To match the original footage, especially the defocused look after frame 1600, the same defocus effect must be applied to the clean patch. To replicate the defocus observed in the original background plate from frame 1600 to the end of the shot, we need to determine how many pixels have shifted from a focused image to a completely defocused image. To calculate this, use a sharp, high-contrast corner of a brick on the wall in frame 1600 as a reference point. This detail helps us to measure the number of pixels transitioning from sharp focus at frame 1600 to the full defocus frame. Once the pixel range is identified, the same defocus effect can be accurately applied to the clean patch. Follow these steps to apply the defocus effect.

1. Add a Defocus node after the Roto node.
2. Zoom in on any sharp vertical edge or corner of the wall until it becomes pixelated.
3. Hold down Ctrl+Shift (or Cmd+Shift on macOS), then press and hold the left mouse button (LMB) and drag to sample a vertical region of pixels along a sharp edge. See the red highlighted region in the lower-left image of Figure 5.14.
4. Go to the last frame of the shot and count how many pixels the selected sharp edge has expanded after being defocused. In this example, the sharp edge has expanded by approximately 15 pixels. Refer to the rectangular shape in the bottom-right image of Figure 5.14.

   (You don't need to be too precise at this stage, as this only provides a basic idea of the expanded pixel count.)
5. Go to frame 1600 on the timeline. Double-click the Defocus node to open its Properties panel. We need to set two keyframes to animate the Defocus effect. First, right-click the Defocus slot and choose Set key to create a keyframe. Then, move to the last frame of the shot, type 15 into the Defocus field, right-click it again, and choose Set key. This will animate the Defocus value, starting at 0 on frame 1600 and increasing to 15 by the final frame.

   Figure 5.14 shows a Defocus node added after the Roto node, animated from frame 1600 to the end of the shot. The capital letter A in the top-right corner of the node indicates that it has animation.

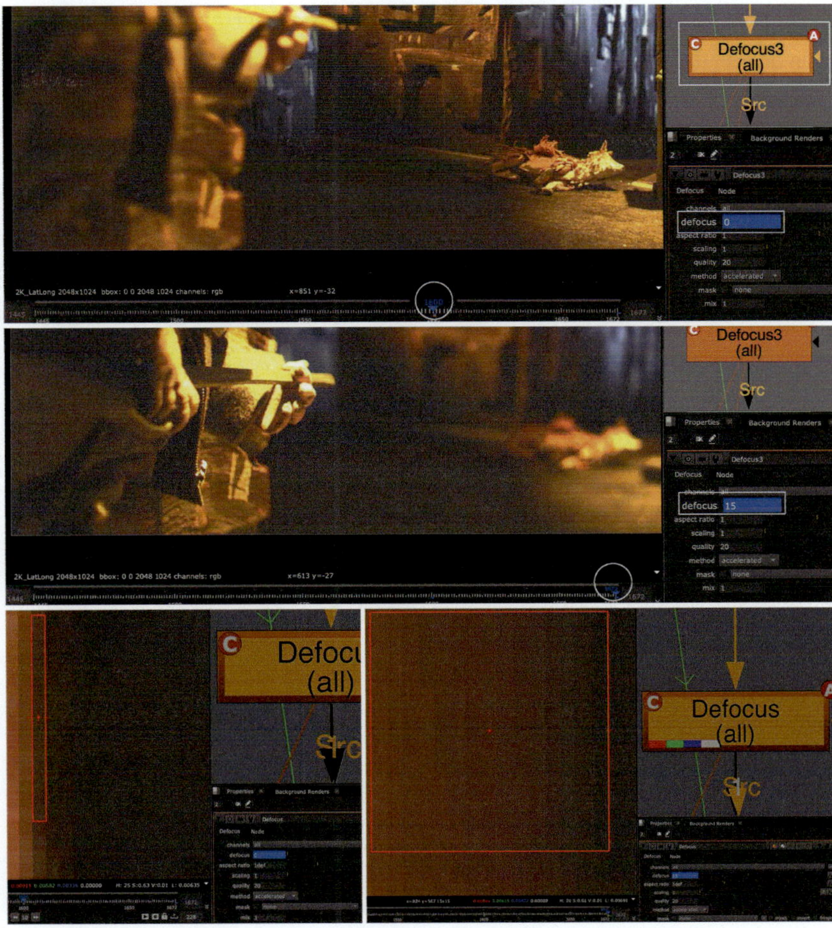

FIGURE 5.14 Add a Defocus node to mimic the defocusing effect of the original plate on the newly created clean plate

Step 5 | F_ReGrain node.

Up to this point, we have been working on creating a clean plate with a single frame from which the original film grain has been removed. Now, it is time to restore the original film grain.

1. Add an F_ReGrain node after the Defocus node.

   The F_ReGrain node has two inputs: connect the Grain input to the original plate and connect the Src input to the Defocus node.

2. By default, a gray analysis region will appear at the center of the original plate. Move this region to a flat, pattern-free area to analyze and extract the film grain from the original plate.

Figure 5.15 illustrates how the F_ReGrain node is connected in the script. The image on the left shows the location of the analysis region for the F_ReGrain node.

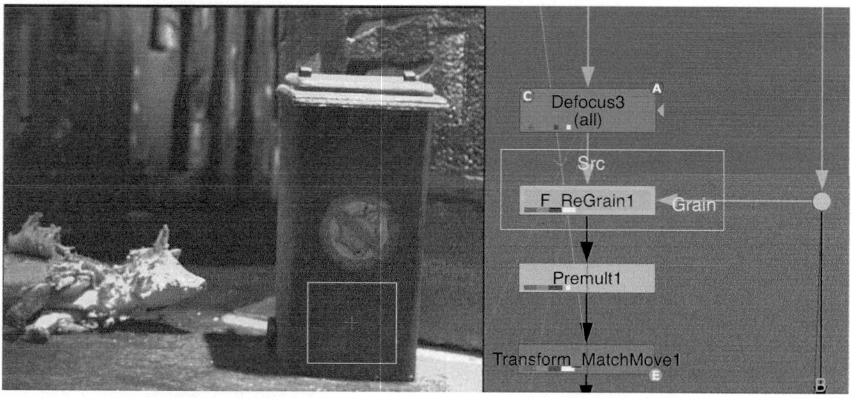

FIGURE 5.15 Film grain has been applied to the created clean plate

Step 6 | Premult node.

The Premult node uses the matte in the alpha channel of an image to multiply the image itself, creating a premultiplied image. In Figure 5.16, the top-right script illustrates the connection between the Premult node and the F_ReGrain node, along with the resulting output image on the left. The lower image demonstrates the multiplication equation used in the Premult node.

An in-depth demonstration of using premultiplied and unpremultiplied images in compositing will be provided in Case Study 7.

Note

As we delve deeper into the compositing process, managing scripts and nodes becomes increasingly important for computational efficiency. In VFX studios, a common approach to improving the processing speed of complex Nuke scripts is to render and export a completed portion, then import the render back into Nuke for downstream operations. This method is necessary because certain nodes require intensive computations, which can significantly slow down Nuke's performance, especially when working with complex scenes. By exporting and importing completed renders, Nuke can avoid recalculating the same nodes each time in upstream scripts, resulting in faster overall processing times.

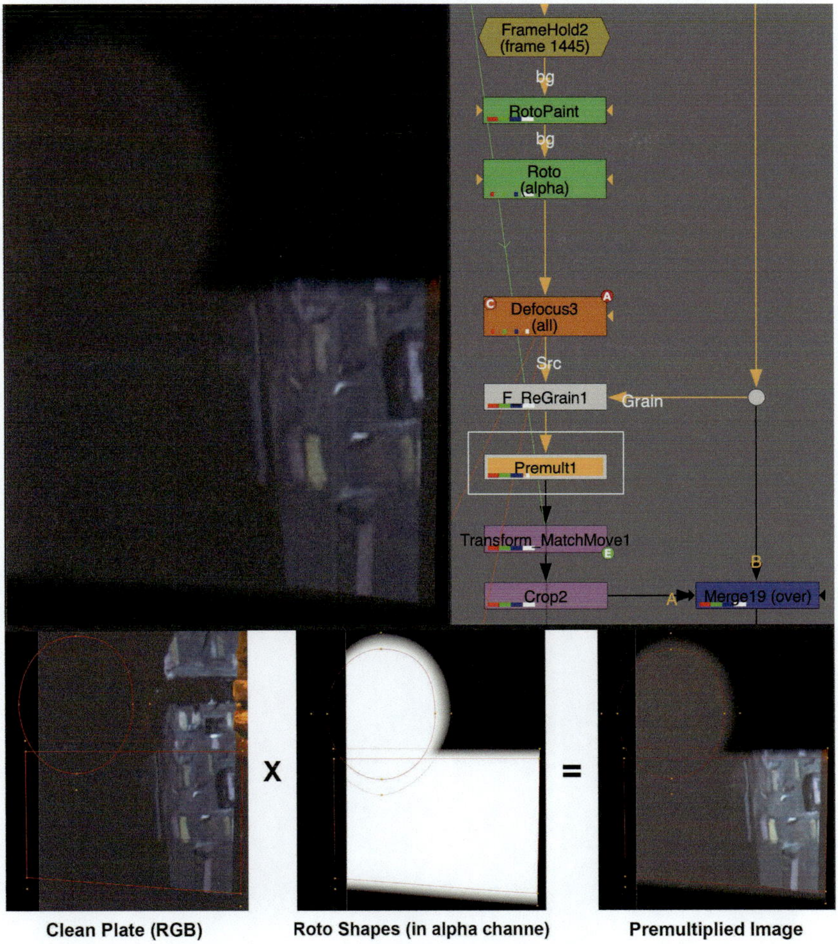

FIGURE 5.16 The Premult node in the script and its operational principles

To take advantage of this approach, add a Write node after the Roto node to render (export) the created clean patch as an OpenEXR image. Then, import the image back into Nuke for use in the downstream script. Figure 5.17 illustrates this process. As a result, Nuke will not repeatedly calculate the Denoise, FrameHold, RotoPaint, and Roto nodes, significantly speeding up the compositing process.

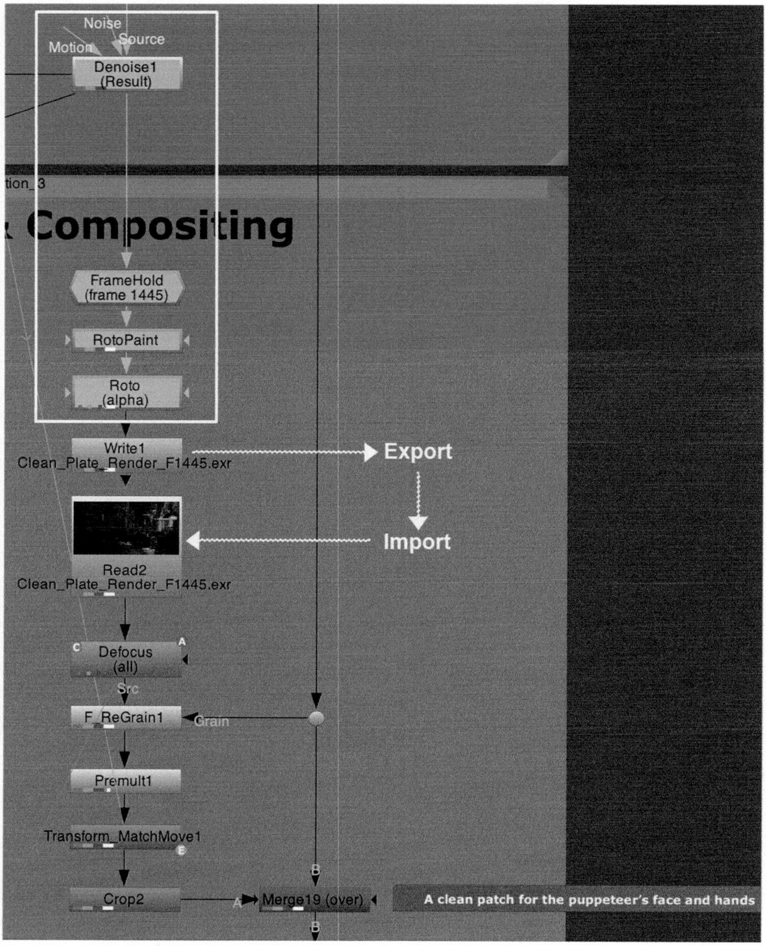

FIGURE 5.17 Exporting and importing part of the completed composition to speed up node calculation

Step 7 | Use the 2D tracking data generated by the Tracker1 node in Section 2 (Denoise & 2D Tracking) to drive the clean patch. This step involves replicating the original camera movement onto the clean patch image.

Figure 5.18 illustrates how the Tracker1 node uses Transform_MatchMove nodes to control the clean patches created in Section 3. As shown, three green lines extend from the Tracker1 node. One of these connects to the Transform_MatchMove1 node, which drives the movement of the clean patch created for the puppeteer's face and hands. This node applies the original 2D camera movement to the clean patch, and its result is then merged with the original footage using a Merge node. The same method is used to integrate additional clean patches into the downstream scripts.

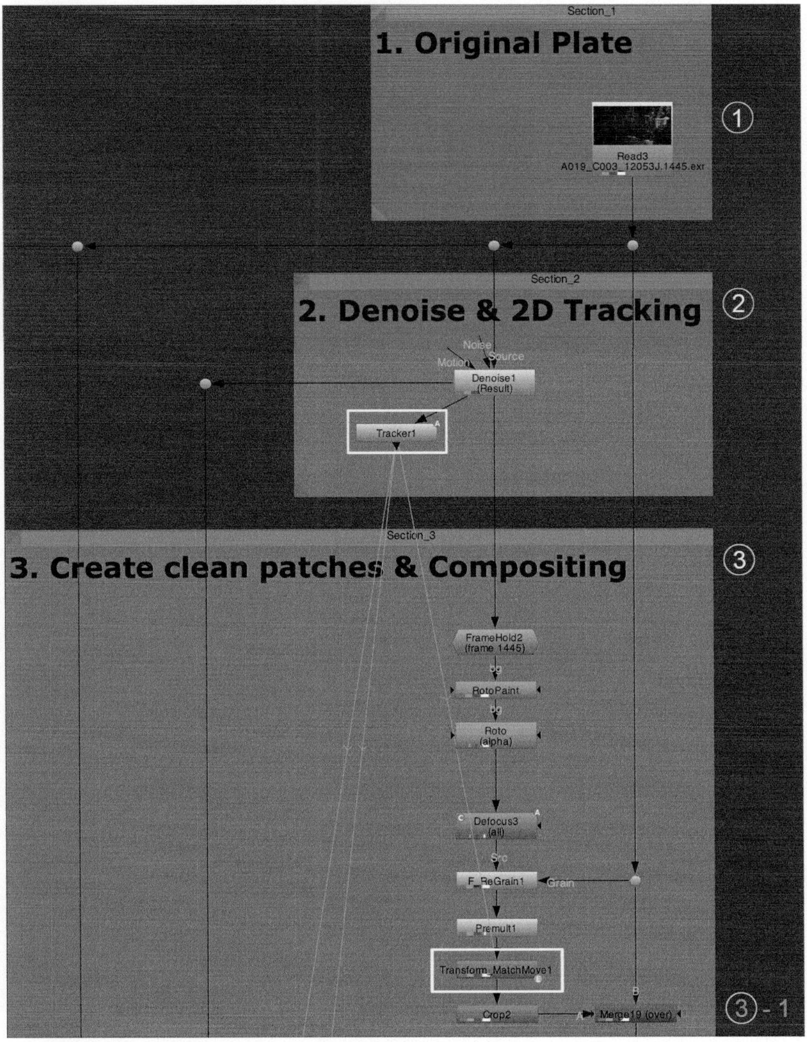

FIGURE 5.18 Node connections for using 2D tracker data to drive the created clean patch

- *Section ③–2: Remove shadows cast by the puppeteer's hands on the wall*

Although the puppeteer's hands were successfully removed from the original scene, their shadows remained on the background wall between frames 1500 and 15200. Figure 5.19 shows the hands and shadows in the original scene.

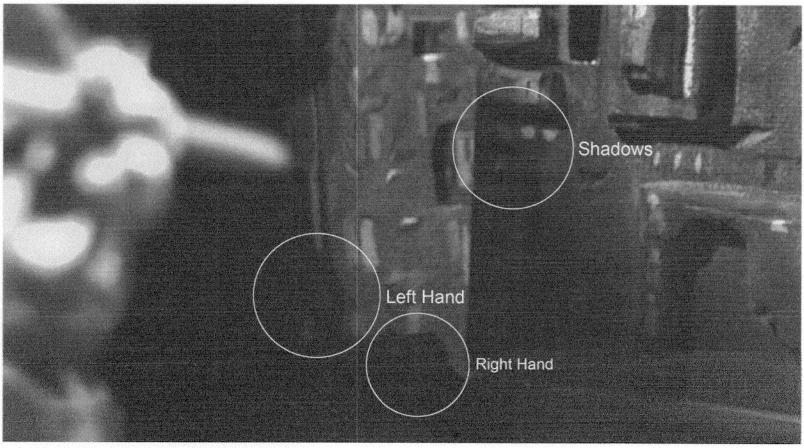

FIGURE 5.19 The movement of the hands casts shadows on the background between frames 1500 and 1520

Since the shape of the wall and the environmental lighting remain consistent throughout the entire shot, we can extract a nearby frame (a still image) from the original plate that does not have any shadows cast by the hands. For example, the same area in the first frame (1445) can be used as a clean patch to cover the parts of the original frames where the puppeteer's hands cast shadows. Figure 5.20 shows the node connections used to create a clean patch, based on frame 1445, to cover the original wall area where the hands cast shadows.

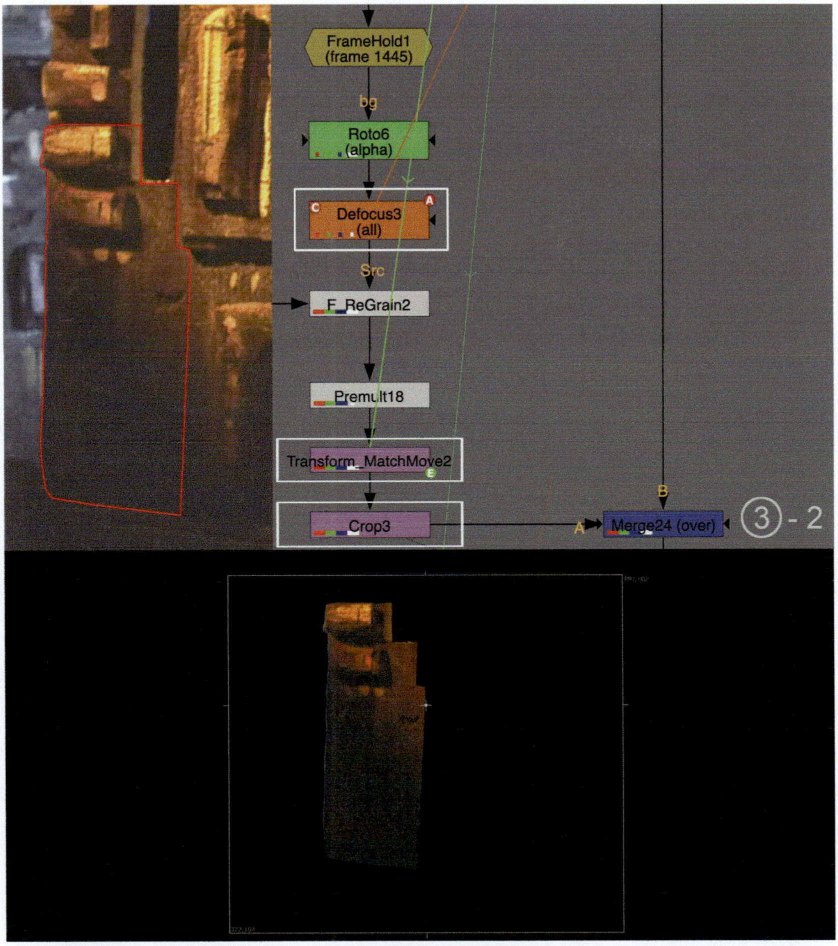

FIGURE 5.20 Node connections for creating a clean patch of the wall in Section 3–2

As shown in Figure 5.20, a FrameHold node is first used to hold the denoised plate at frame 1445, effectively turning the sequence into a still image. A Roto node is then connected to create a mask covering the shadows on the wall cast by the puppeteer's hands, which occur between frames 1500 and 1520. After the Roto node, a Defocus node is applied to recreate the out-of-focus effect that appears from frame 1600 to the end of the original shot. Then, an F_ReGrain node is used to restore the original film grain. Finally, a Premult node is employed to generate a premultiplied clean patch image.

Before merging the clean patch with the original plate, a Transform_MatchMove node, driven by the upstream Tracker1 node, is used to replicate the original shot's camera movement onto the clean patch.

Note

At the end of the node connections shown in Figure 5.20, a Crop node is used. This node reduces the size of the bounding box surrounding the generated clean patch. The size of the bounding box directly affects the time Nuke requires to process and render the image in the Viewer1 panel. If the bounding box is unnecessarily large, even when it contains no data in the black areas, Nuke will still scan the entire region by default, resulting in slower processing speeds in the Viewer1 panel. Therefore, it is always recommended to keep the bounding box around assets as small as possible during compositing.

– *Section ③–3: Create a clean patch for the ground*

In the original shot, two puppet ropes are used to control the stop-motion character lying on the ground. These ropes need to be removed from the scene. To achieve this, take a still frame from the denoised plate and carefully remove the ropes to create a clean patch. Then, use this clean patch to cover the ropes in the original shot. Figure 5.21 shows the nodes used to create the clean patch for the ground.

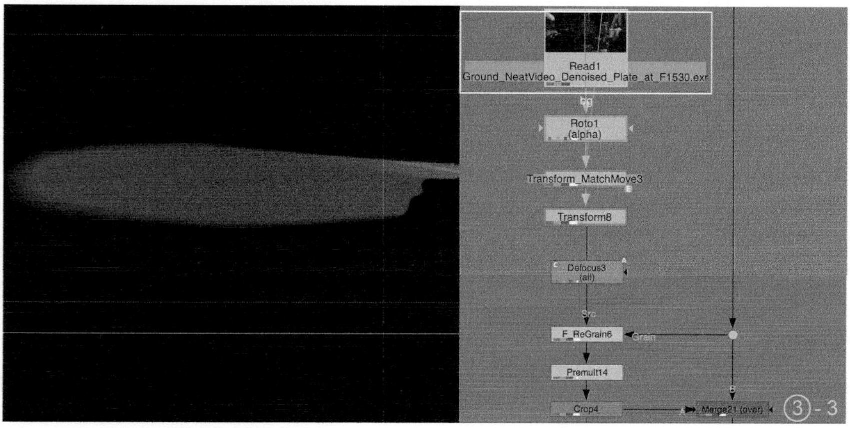

FIGURE 5.21 Node used to generate a clean patch on the ground in Section 3–3

Read1 (Ground_NeatVideo_Denoised_Plate_at_F1530.exr) in Figure 5.21 is a pre-rendered clean plate from which film grain and puppet ropes have been removed. The creation of this clean plate involves the following nodes:

FrameHold

Connect a FrameHold node directly to the original plate. In the Properties panel of the node, set the first frame (slot) to 1530. This operation freezes the original frame at frame 1530.

Denoise

After the FrameHold node, connect a Denoise node to remove film grain from the still frame.

RotoPaint

After removing the film grain from the still image at frame 1530, press the P key to connect a RotoPaint node. Carefully erase the puppet ropes from the still image using the Clone tool within the RotoPaint node.

Write

Once all operations are complete, connect a Write node to render the cleaned plate as an OpenEXR format image.

Note

In this example, a third-party plug-in (Neat Video Reduce Noise node) was used to remove film grain from the original plate. The Neat Video node is commonly employed for noise reduction in demanding VFX production shots. If the Neat Video plug-in is unavailable, please use the default Nuke Denoise node instead.

The process of creating a clean patch for the ground is shown in Figure 5.22.

Step 1 | Import the pre-rendered clean plate.

Place the mouse cursor in the Node Graph panel, press R to create a Read1 node, and import the file Ground_NeatVideo_Denoised_Plate_at_F1530.exr.

Step 2 | Connect a Roto node.

Connect a Roto node after the Read1 node and draw a shape to cover the ropes used to control the puppet on the ground.

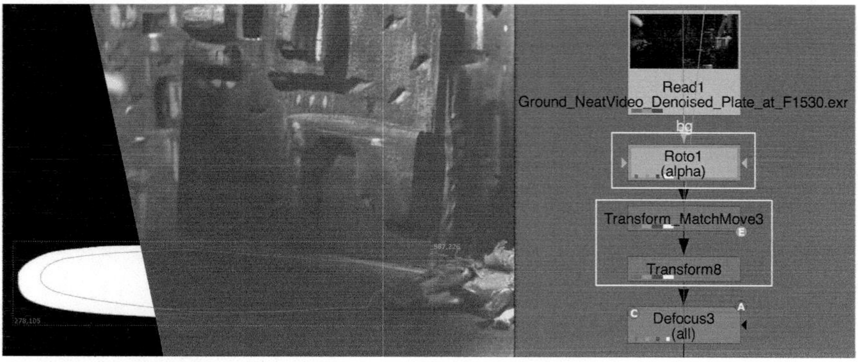

FIGURE 5.22 The main nodes used to create the clean patch, as described in Section 3–3

Step 3 | Transform nodes & node concatenation.

This step involves concatenating nodes in Nuke, as illustrated in Figure 5.22.

After the Roto1 node, connect a Transform_MatchMove node. This node is driven by the Tracker1 node generated in Section 2.

In earlier sections, we mentioned that to minimize camera parallax, 2D tracking features should be positioned as close as possible to the area requiring adjustment. In this example, we applied the 2D tracking data generated from the wall to the clean ground patch. However, due to camera parallax between the wall and the ground, the 2D tracking data showed a slight deviation when aligning the ground patch. To correct this, we added another Transform node for manual adjustment. These two Transform nodes are concatenated.

Understanding node concatenation in Nuke is essential for maintaining image quality during compositing. Improper use of concatenation nodes can excessively filter and smooth out image details. According to the Nuke documentation, when nodes are concatenated, they pass their adjacent operations to the last node, which then executes all operations at once. Figure 5.23 illustrates the concept of node concatenation and its results.

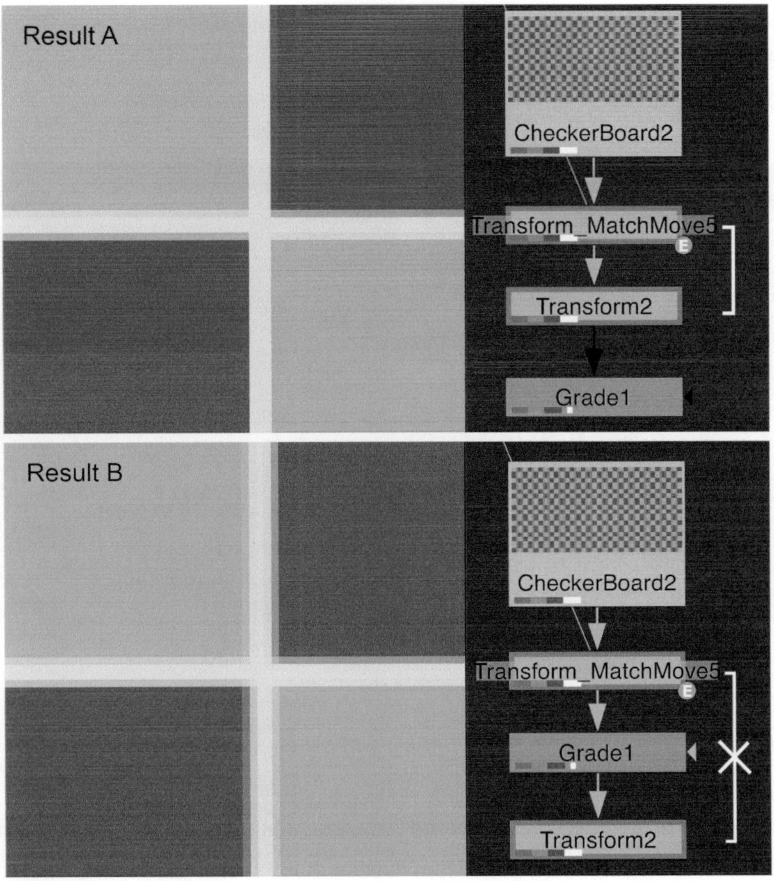

FIGURE 5.23 Comparison of node concatenation (Result A) and interrupted node concatenation (Result B)

In Figure 5.23, two Transform nodes are connected consecutively in Result A. Due to the principles of node concatenation, the filtering options from both nodes are applied only once, preserving the final quality of the image. In contrast, node concatenation is broken in Result B, causing the checkerboard to be filtered separately by each Transform node, resulting in a blurrier image.

Nuke has over 35 nodes related to node concatenation. For more information on concatenation nodes in Nuke, please refer to "How Nodes Concatenate" on the Foundry's official website.

– *Sections ③–4 & ③–5.*

The two additional clean patches created in Sections ③–4 and ③–5 employed the same methods outlined previously, including noise reduction, removal of control ropes, application of 2D transform data, defocus, premultiplication, and crop node operations. These clean patches were exported as OpenEXR format files and then reimported into NukeX for integration with other downstream assets.

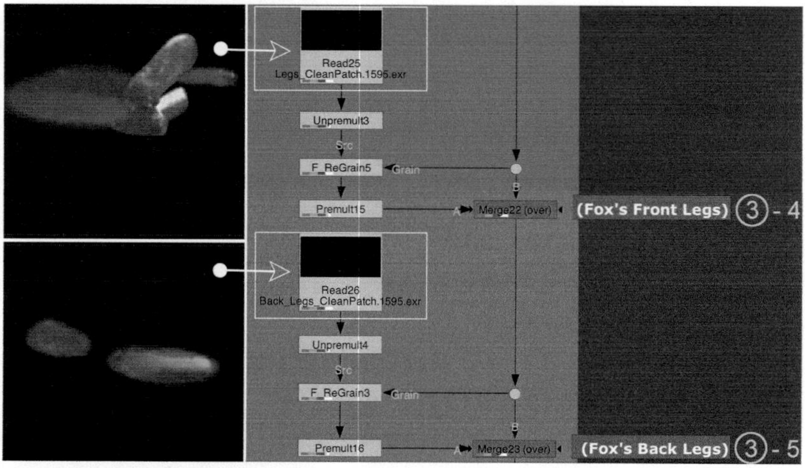

FIGURE 5.24 Node connections and results for creating clean patches in Sections 3–4 and 3–5

Note

Figure 5.24 also shows the connections for the Unpremult and Premult nodes. It is important to understand the difference between premultiplied and unpremultiplied images, which we will explain in detail in Case Study 7 when discussing CG assets.

○ Section ④: Create the foreground matte and final composition

Once clean patches have been created for the background wall and the elements on the ground, we can integrate them into the original plate. Figure 5.25 shows the integration of the rebuilt background wall and ground elements.

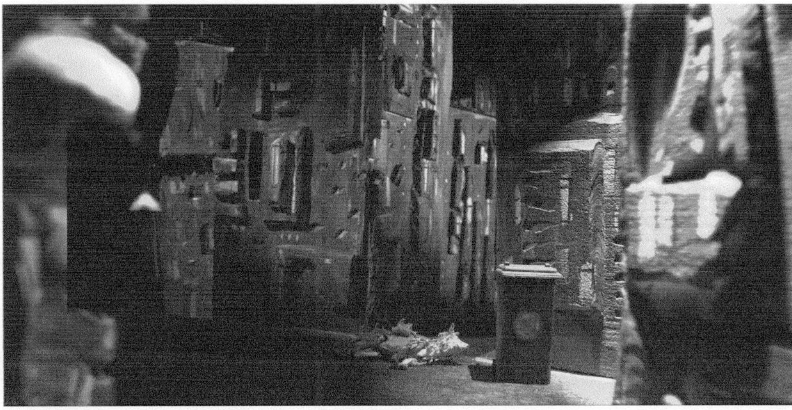

FIGURE 5.25 Background and middle-ground elements have been seamlessly integrated into the shot

Don't be alarmed by the large notch on the left foreground wall at this stage. It's normal to see results like this during compositing. We are currently disassembling the shot, starting with the background elements, and reconstructing the scene to fix issues and add new elements. The notch issue will be addressed as follows:

A combination of Roto and Keyer nodes will be used to create separate mattes for the foreground wall on the left, as well as for the hunter's hands and the gun barrel. These separated elements will then be merged back on top of the current result to complete the final VFX shot.

Figure 5.26 illustrates the node connections used to separate the foreground elements from the original plate. A detailed demonstration of this process is available in the prerecorded video.

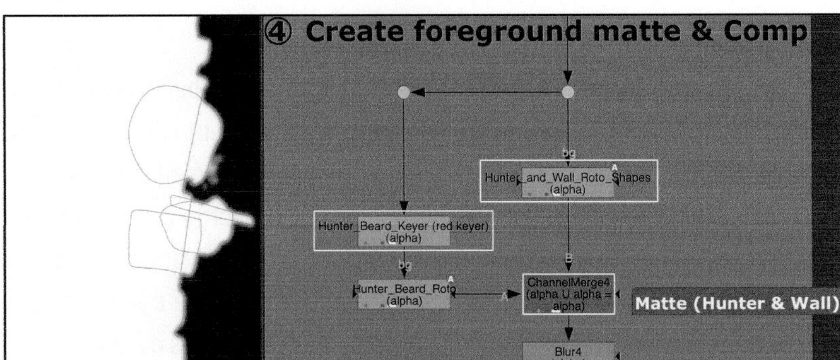

FIGURE 5.26 Node connections for rebuilding the foreground elements

In Figure 5.26, the Hunter_and_Wall_Roto_Shapes node is a Roto node containing animated roto shapes for the wall, the hunter's head, hands, and gun barrel. The hunter's mustache is keyed using a Keyer node. These two separate results are then combined using a ChannelMerge node to create a complete matte for the foreground elements on the left side of the shot.

Figure 5.27 shows the results generated from Sections ③ and ④, along with the Merge node used to combine both results.

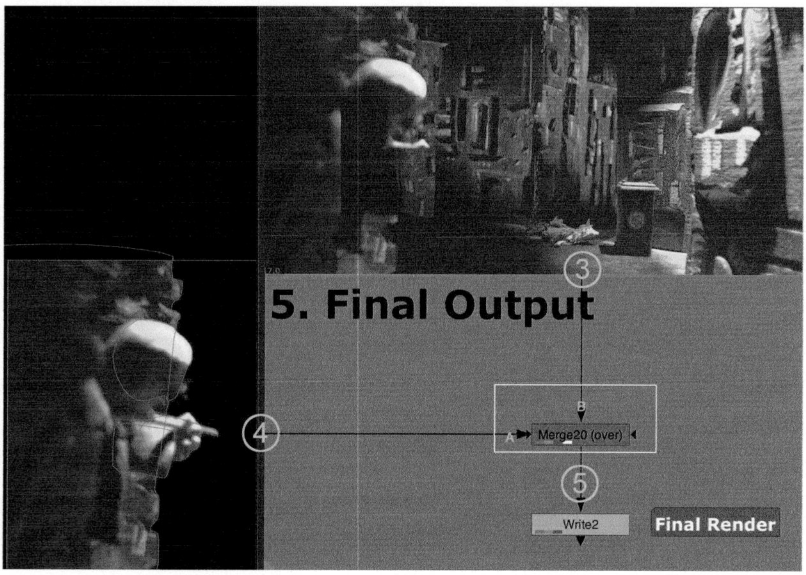

FIGURE 5.27 The premultiplied foreground element ④ is merged back into the composition ③ using a Merge node

Creating visual effects shots under tight deadlines can be both challenging and time-consuming for VFX artists, who often need to experiment with various methods to achieve the desired results. However, it is important to maintain a consistent compositing structure, starting with background elements, progressing through the middle ground, and concluding with foreground elements at the bottom of the script for each shot. Additionally, preserving the original quality of the client's content in the final composition is crucial for maintaining professionalism as a compositor.

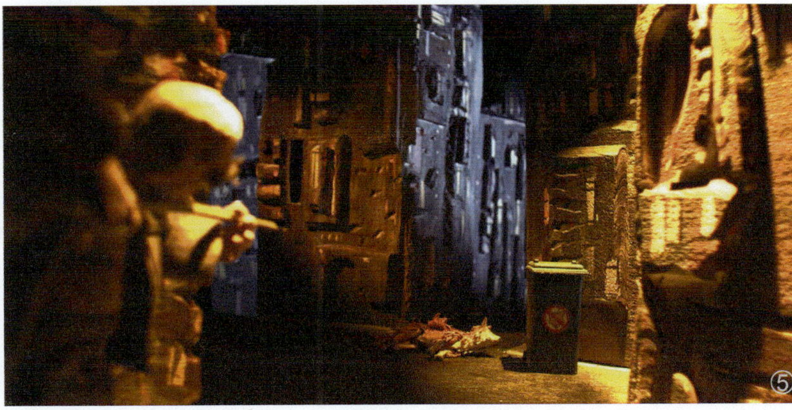

FIGURE 5.28 Final output of Case Study 1

Case Study 2

Understanding the importance of 3D camera tracking

Key learning points:

> Removing lens distortion from the background plate using a lens grid.
> Understanding the fundamental concepts of 3D camera tracking.
> Exploring basic workflows across applications for 3D camera tracking.

• Case Study 2 | Understanding the importance of 3D camera tracking

Notes

Each case study includes a pre-recorded video tutorial. Watching these videos alongside reading the case studies is strongly recommended to ensure a smooth and comprehensive learning experience for each hands-on project.

Video link: youtube.com/@InvisibleFilmVFX

Video title: Case Study 2 | Understanding the Importance of 3D Camera Tracking in Live-action Footage

Project file: Case_Study_2_Project_File

The project file is available for download on the book's official webpage.

High-resolution color figures from this project are also available for download on the book's official webpage.

• The concept of 3D camera tracking in visual effects shots

Understanding camera movement is crucial for creating visual effects shots. Whether the camera is moving or stationary, match-moving is essential for integrating 2D and 3D objects into live-action footage. Accurately tracking live-action footage allows for the extraction of a virtual camera from the scene, which can then be used to recreate the scene in 3D space and seamlessly add additional visual elements.

Notes

The LensDistortion and CameraTracker nodes used for 3D camera tracking are only available in NukeX.

Effective 3D camera tracking in visual effects production requires accurate on-set measurements and data collection, including details such as camera models, focal lengths, camera movement patterns, and properly captured lens grids. Collecting this information is essential for achieving precise 3D camera tracking.

• Shot analysis

◦ The purpose of this case study

This case study aims to demonstrate a 3D camera tracking workflow across multiple applications, testing the matchmoving of 3D elements with live-action footage. The software packages used in this project are Foundry NukeX and Autodesk Maya.

Figure 5.29 displays a series of test geometries within the scene to assess camera tracking accuracy. Each cone's apex is positioned at a specific pixel on the ground, allowing quick detection of any positional shifts during playback. For example, if a cone moves from its original position during playback, the amount of drift in pixels becomes easily noticeable by observing the apex's position. The ultimate goal of this test is to achieve a successful camera track that accurately represents the original camera movements in the live-action footage. Any potential drifting error of the test elements should be less than one pixel. With a precisely extracted virtual camera, 3D assets can then be added to the scene and refilmed by the virtual camera to create visual effects for the shot.

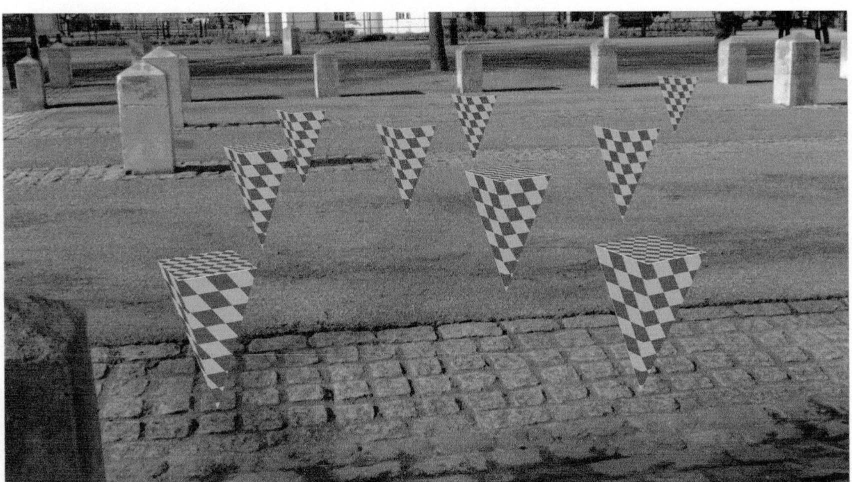

FIGURE 5.29 3D camera tracking test result

○ Understanding the scene

The background plate for this project was captured using a handheld camera, resulting in noticeable camera shake. Additionally, the lens grid was not captured precisely. However, these imperfections make this project a good example of how professional techniques can be effectively applied to track a challenging shot. The project assets shown in Figure 5.30 are provided by Adam Cant, a UK-based VFX artist.

○ Footage information

Lens grid

Frame range: 1001–1073 frames

The lens grid was filmed with a DSLR camera and later converted into a sequence of 8-bit images.

Background plate

Frame range: 1001–1192 frames

○ Camera information

Camera model: Canon EOS 550D (EOS Rebel T2i)

Sensor size: 22.3 × 12.54 mm

Focal length: 24 mm

Footage aspect ratio: 1920 × 1080

Frame rate: 24 fps

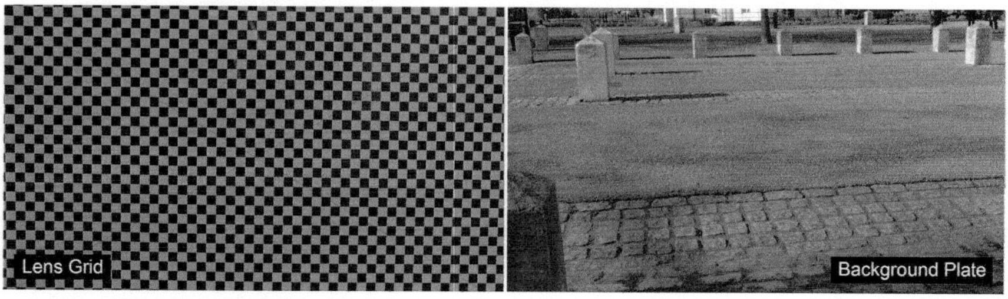

FIGURE 5.30 Lens grid and background plate used in Case Study 2. Photograph by Adam Cant

Notes

High-end consumer digital cameras, especially APS-C cameras, may have slightly different sensor dimensions for shooting still images and videos. For example, the camera used to capture the background footage in this project was the Canon EOS 550D (EOS Rebel T2i), which features two slightly different sensor sizes: one (22.3 × 14.9 mm) for still images and another (22.3 × 12.54 mm) for video recording. Therefore, the sensor size used for video recording should be employed for 3D camera tracking in these scenarios.

In large-scale VFX productions, standalone software solutions for 3D tracking tasks are commonly used, such as Science-D-Visions' 3D Equalizer. However, the fundamental principles of 3D camera tracking remain consistent, regardless of the software employed. For this project, we will use Foundry NukeX to perform 3D camera tracking tasks.

• Workflow analysis

Case Study 2 consists of seven sections that cover operations and workflows involving NukeX and Maya for camera tracking and 3D match-moving tasks.

- Section ①: Removing lens distortion
- Section ②: 3D camera tracking and testing
- Section ③: Exporting 3D camera tracking data from NukeX to Maya
- Section ④: 3D match-moving test in Maya
- Section ⑤: Testing geometries in NukeX
- Section ⑥: Restoring original lens distortion
- Section ⑦: Final output

Figure 5.31 shows the overall Nuke script for 3D camera tracking in Case Study 2.

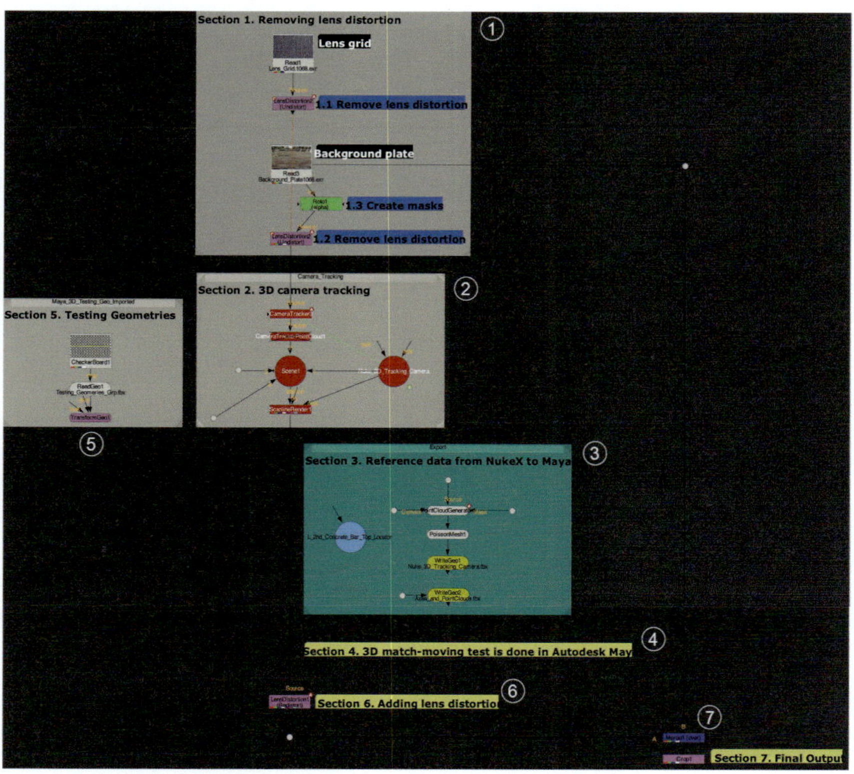

FIGURE 5.31 Overall script for 3D camera tracking in NukeX

Set up the project and load the plates:

Step 1 | Go to Edit > Project Settings . . .

Alternatively, you can use hotkeys: place the mouse cursor in the Node Graph panel and press the S key to bring up the Project Settings section.

Step 2 | Ensure the project has the following settings.

Set frame range slots to 1001–1192

fps: 24

full size format: HD_1080 1920 × 1080

Step 3 | Ensure the mouse cursor is inside the Node Graph panel, then press the R key to import the lens grid and background plates.

∘ Section ①: Removing lens distortion

The primary goal of this section is to remove the lens distortion information present in the original background plate.

– Remove lens distortion from the lens grid.

1. Position the mouse cursor in the Node Graph panel, then press the R key to open the Read File(s) dialog window. Navigate to the folder where the lens grid file is saved. Select the lens grid sequence file and click the Open button to import it into NukeX. After importing, the file will be assigned the default name Read1.
2. Connect a LensDistortion node to the lens grid, as shown in Figure 5.32.

   Select the Read1 node (Lens Grid) and press the Tab key on your keyboard to open the search field. Search for LensDistortion [Transform]. This will connect a LensDistortion node to the Read1 node.

   In the Properties panel of the LensDistortion node, navigate to the Analysis tab under the Grid Detect section, and click the Detect button. This will analyze and remove the lens distortion information from the original lens grid.

– Remove lens distortion from the background plate.

After extracting the lens distortion information from the lens grid using the LensDistortion (Undistort) node, clone the node (Alt/Option + K) and connect the cloned LensDistortion (Undistort) node to the original background plate. This applies the same correction data and removes the lens distortion from the original plate. Please refer to subsections 1.1 and 1.2 in Figure 5.32 for details. A demonstration of this operation is also available in the pre-recorded video.

- Create masks to ignore the moving elements in the shot.

There are two primary types of 3D camera tracking: object tracking and scene tracking.

Object tracking involves tracking moving objects in 2D or 3D spaces. The goal is to attach or replace additional elements onto these moving objects. Successful tracking enables these attached elements to follow the objects' movements within the scene seamlessly. However, for this project, our objective is to integrate several test 3D elements into the scene. Therefore, we specifically need to track only the static features and disregard any moving elements to ensure the accuracy of the 3D camera tracking.

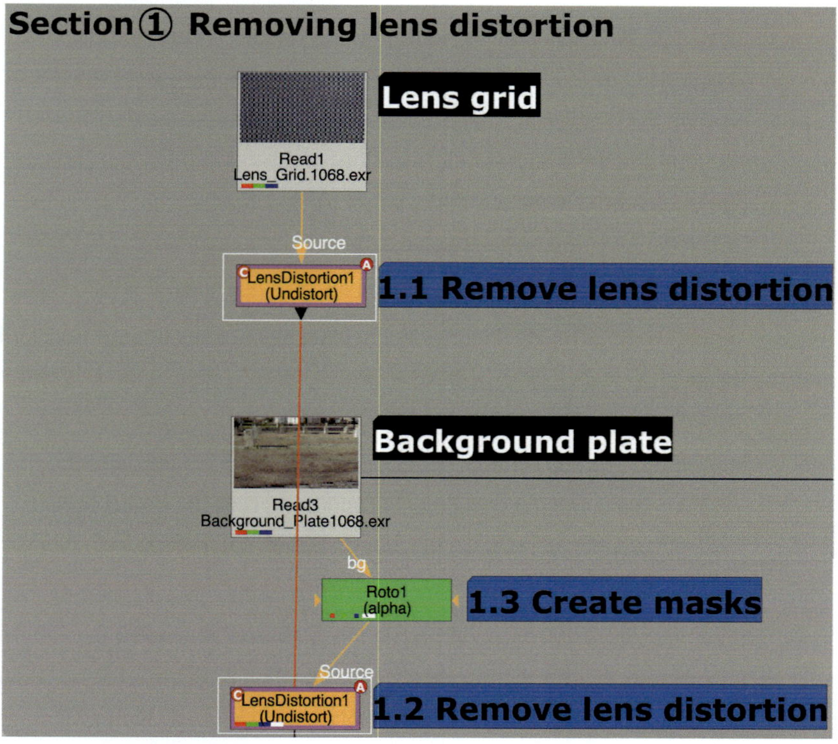

FIGURE 5.32 Removing lens distortion from the original background plate

Upon analyzing the plate, it is evident that several people are visible in the background, moving slightly. These moving elements must be excluded during the camera tracking process. To achieve this, insert a Roto node between the original background plate and the LensDistortion (Undistort) node, and create several roto shapes in the alpha channel to mask out the moving elements, as illustrated in section 1.3 of Figure 5.33.

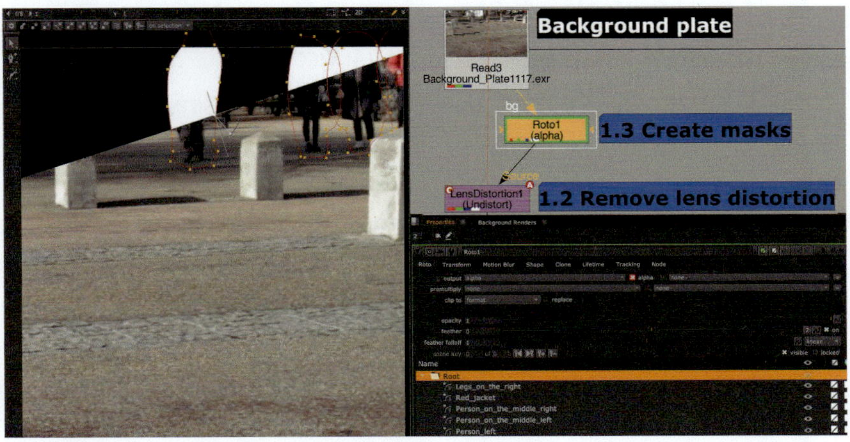

FIGURE 5.33 Using Roto nodes to create roto shapes in the alpha channel of the original background plate

Note

In node-based compositing applications, the order in which nodes are connected can significantly impact the results of image processing. For instance, if the Roto node (1.3) is connected before the cloned LensDistortion node (1.2 Remove lens distortion), any updates made to the LensDistortion node will not affect the upstream roto shapes. On the other hand, if the Roto node (1.3) is connected after the LensDistortion node (1.2), updates to the LensDistortion node will affect the roto shapes, requiring them to be redone. This outcome is undesirable, particularly in production.

◦ Section ②: 3D camera tracking in NukeX

– Setting up 3D camera tracking.

Press the Tab key, type CameraTracker [3D Classic] and select it from the dropdown list. This will insert a CameraTracker node after the cloned LensDistortion node (1.2), as shown in Figure 5.34.

Double-click the CameraTracker node to load its parameters into the Properties panel, and configure the settings under the CameraTracker tab as follows:

Source: Sequence

Mask: Source Alpha

Camera Motion: Free Camera

Lens Distortion: No Lens Distortion

Focal Length: Known | Length: 24

Film Back Preset: Rebel 550D 650D T2i T3i T4i Video

Film Back Size: × 22.3 | y 12.54 | Units: mm (camera sensor size)

Note

NukeX only includes mainstream camera models in its Film Back Preset list. To ensure accurate camera tracking, it is recommended to double-check the sensor size of your specific camera model on the manufacturer's official website and manually input the correct values into the Film Back Size fields.

Switch to the Settings tab and set the following parameters under the Features section.

Number of Features: 1000

Detection Threshold: 0.1

Feature Separation: 12

Tick the Preview Features option box. Enabling this option allows you to preview the number of tracking features in the Viewer panel before tracking.

Once all parameters are set, return to the CameraTracker tab and click the Track button under the Analysis section to start the 3D camera tracking process. The duration of this process may vary depending on your computer's hardware configuration.

In this project, the final solve error is 0.57.

For shots that are 1920×1080 (Full HD) or smaller, the 3D camera tracking solve error should be less than 1.

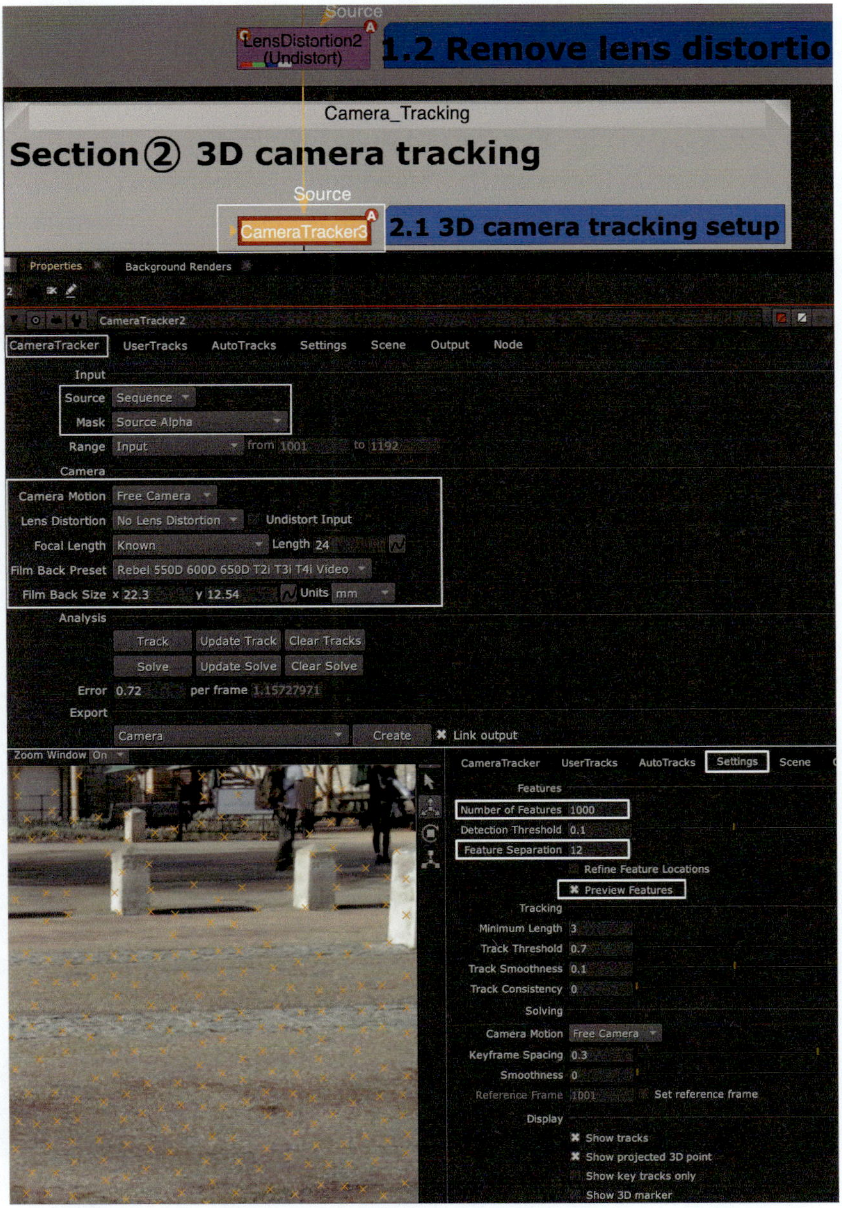

FIGURE 5.34 Settings of the CameraTracker node before performing 3D camera tracking

Upon completing the 3D camera tracking, select Scene from the dropdown list in the Export section, then click the Create button to generate a set of nodes, including CameraTrackerPointCloud, Scene, Camera, and ScanlineRender nodes. To view the tracking results in 3D space, position the mouse cursor in the Viewer1 panel and press the Tab key to switch to Nuke's 3D system.

To gain a comprehensive understanding of 3D camera tracking operations in this project, please watch the pre-recorded video included in Case Study 2.

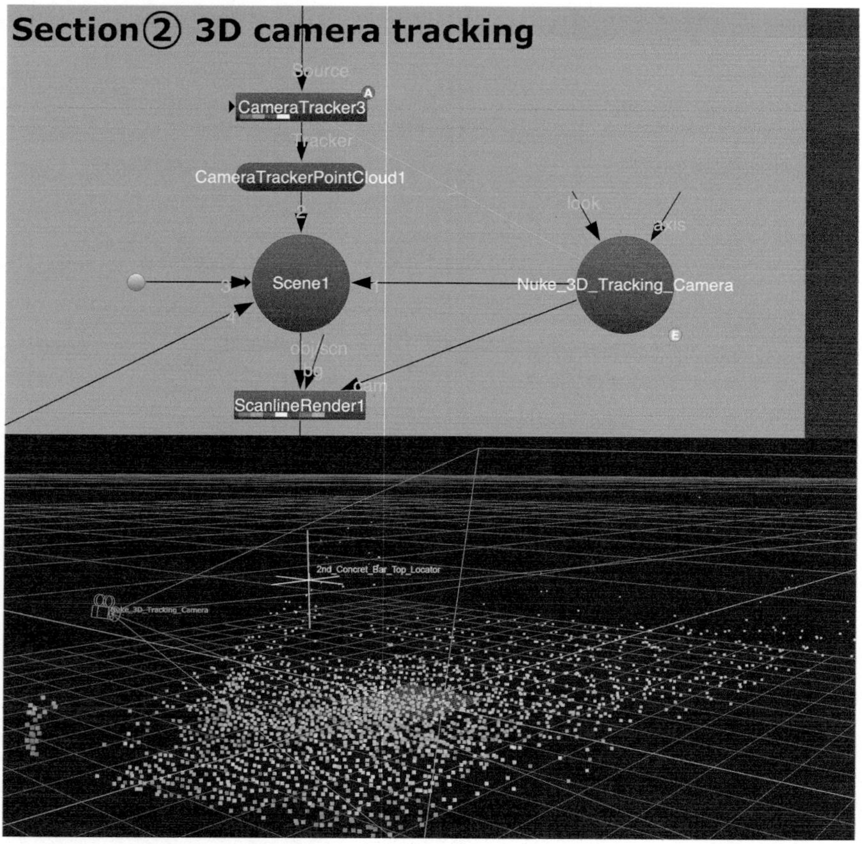

FIGURE 5.35 The initial nodes generated after the camera tracking process (top image) and the tracking output in Nuke's 3D space (bottom image)

○ Section ③: Exporting 3D camera tracking data from NukeX to Maya

After establishing a virtual 3D camera and the corresponding tracking reference data, the data will be exported for further 3D alignment tests in external applications such as Autodesk Maya. This process ensures that the camera movement accurately matches the live-action plate. In addition to the primary 3D camera tracking data, two additional nodes – PointCloudGenerator and PoissonMesh – are used to generate a 3D scene in NukeX. This 3D scene provides more detailed and precise visual references for match-moving work in Maya. Figure 5.36 shows the node connections and the resulting 3D scene.

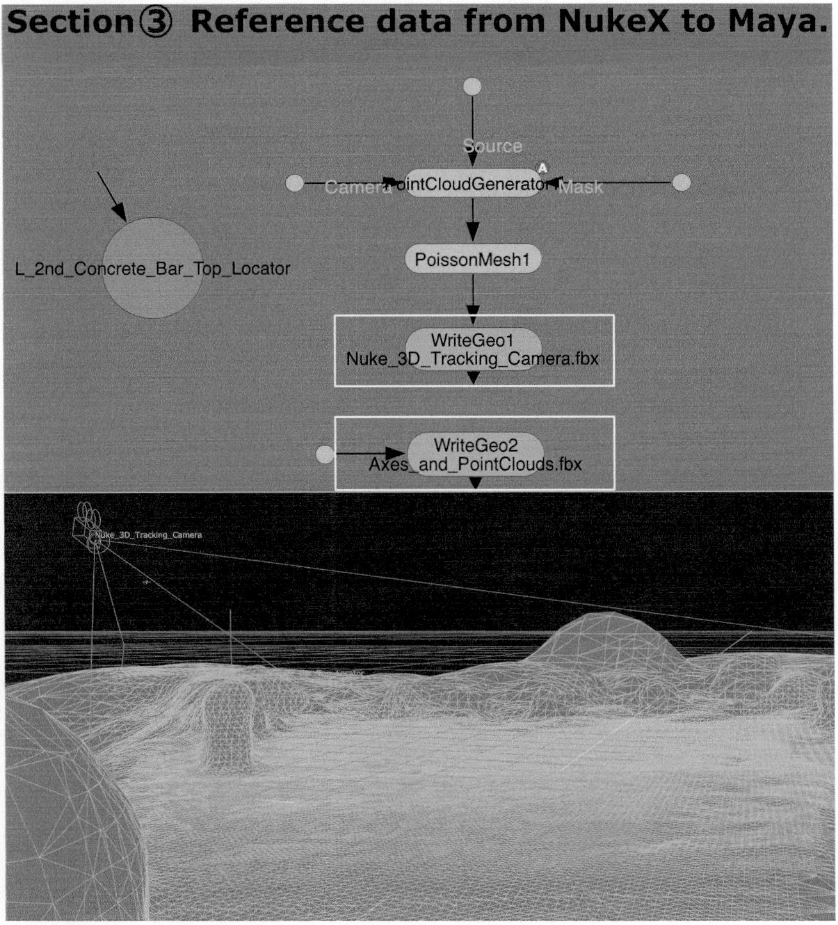

FIGURE 5.36 Node connections and the resulting 3D scene in NukeX

Once the 3D scene is generated in NukeX, two separate WriteGeo nodes are used to export all reference data, including the virtual camera, tracking point clouds, and the generated 3D model of the scene.

WriteGeo1 node

This node exports the virtual camera extracted from the live-action footage, as well as the generated 3D model of the scene.

WriteGeo2 node

This node is used to export tracking point clouds and a customized tracking axis.

Following are the FBX (Filmbox) format files exported for further matchmove tasks in Maya:

File 1: Nuke_3D_Tracking_Camera.fbx

File 2: Axes_and_PointClouds.fbx

◦ Section ④: 3D match-moving test in Autodesk Maya

1. Open Autodesk Maya.
2. Navigate to File > Import . . .

Import the Nuke_3D_Tracking_Camera.fbx file, which should include the following components:

- Nuke 3D tracking camera
- Ground (3D scene model)

After importing the FBX file into Maya, two separate components should be visible in the Outliner on the left side of the Maya user interface.

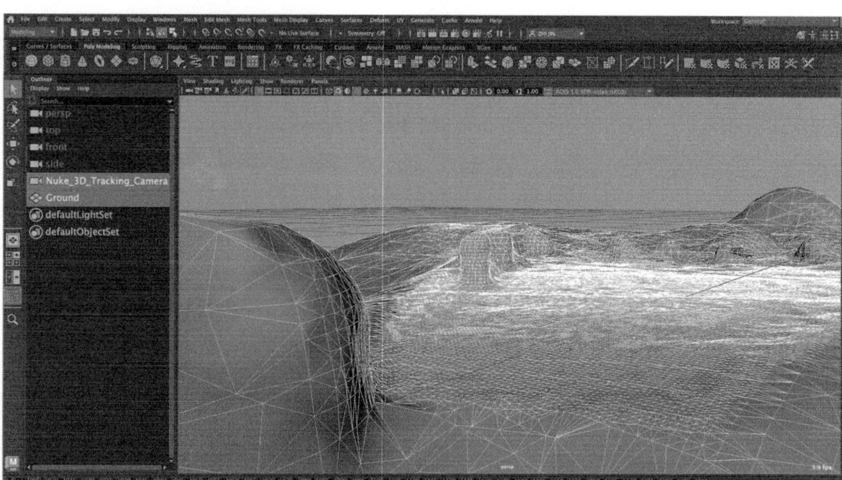

FIGURE 5.37 Screen capture of the Nuke_3D_Tracking_Camera.fbx file after it was imported into Maya

Notes

Please refer to the pre-recorded video on basic Maya navigation and project setup if you are new to the application. The good news is that Maya shares the same navigation features as those used in Nuke's 3D space, meaning that basic navigation is seamless across both applications.

Modern 3D applications utilize physically based rendering (PBR) systems, which measure objects at real-world scales and accurately render scenes in linear light space to achieve photorealistic results. Therefore, it is necessary to match the scene scale in 3D space to on-set data.

3. Import the Axes_and_PointClouds.fbx file into Maya. This file contains the following components:
   - L_2nd_Concrete_Bar_Top_Locator
   - Tracking_Features_Grp (this refers to a group of tracking locators that were defined during 3D camera tracking in NukeX)

In Image A of Figure 5.38, these two components are highlighted in Maya's Outliner. Below them, there is a long list of elements representing the tracking features defined during 3D camera tracking in NukeX. In Maya, these features are displayed as a group of cross-shaped locators.

Additionally, the imported 3D scene model can be viewed in the perspective (persp) viewport. From this viewpoint, we can observe that one of the bollards in the scene appears prominently in the foreground.

With the knowledge of on-set data measurements gained in earlier chapters, we understand that the actual scale of the concrete bollard can serve as a reference object for enlarging the entire 3D scene. For instance, the measured height of the concrete bollard on set is approximately 0.5 meters (50 centimeters). To match it to the real-world scale, use the Distance Tool (Create > Measurement Tools > Distance Tool) to measure the height from the ground to the top of the bollard in the 3D scene. Then, adjust the scale of the entire 3D scene accordingly. As the 3D scene scales up, the height of the concrete bollard measured by the Distance Tool will update in real time until it aligns with the actual scale. In this way, the scale of the entire 3D scene will match the scale of the real-world scene.

Image B in Figure 5.38 shows the enlarged scene, measured based on the actual height of the bollard.

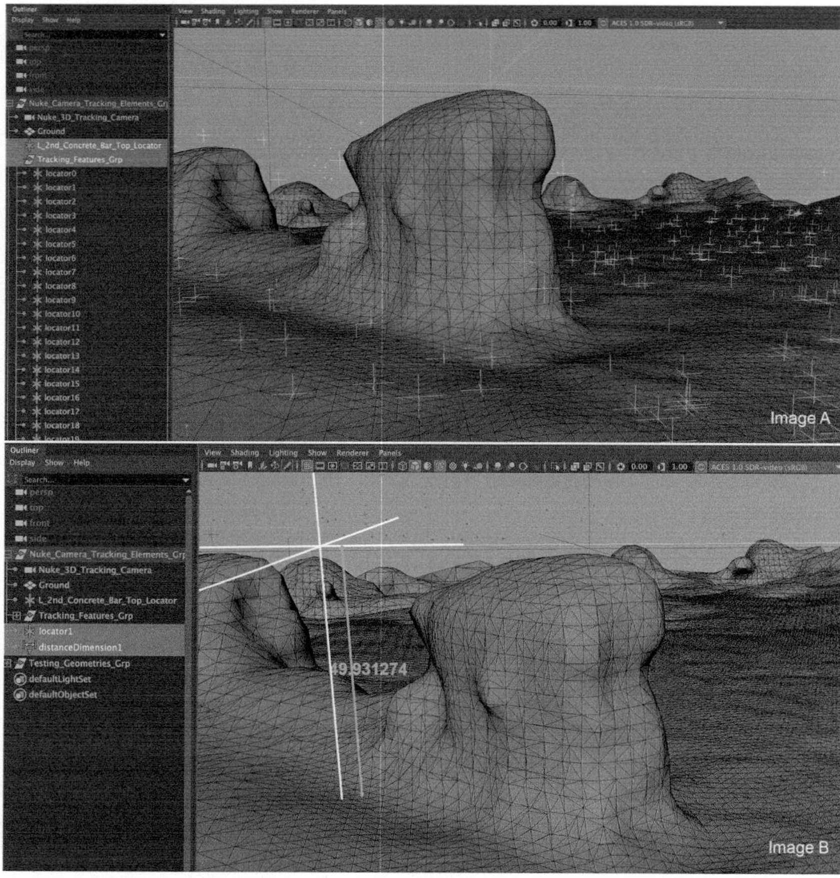

FIGURE 5.38 Camera tracking components imported into Maya (top image); 3D scene scaled to match real-world dimensions (bottom image)

4. Next, create a series of 3D cones and position the apex of each cone onto the surface of the 3D ground model, as shown in Figure 5.39.

Since the virtual camera accurately tracked in NukeX has been imported into Maya, we can view the 3D scene through the camera.

The upper right viewport in Figure 5.39 shows the 3D scene viewed through the camera. Play the scene to double-check if the 3D cones remain firmly attached to the ground without any drifting issues during playback.

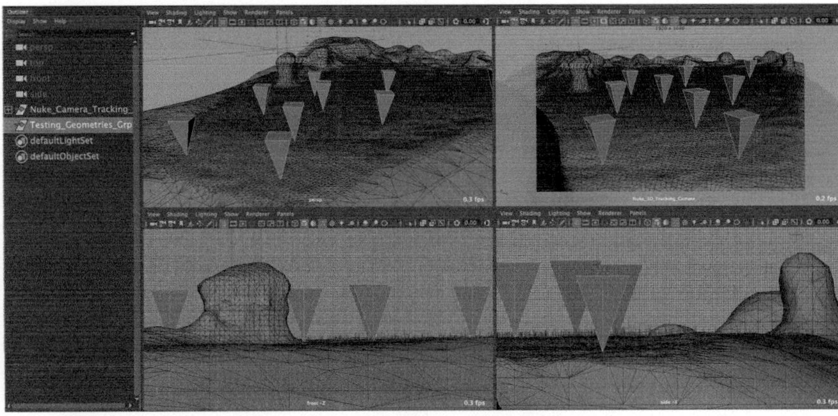

FIGURE 5.39 3D testing cones precisely attached to the surface of the 3D ground

Notes

The testing 3D cones in the scene are used for two purposes:

1. Drift checking: Turning the 3D cones upside down and snapping their apexes onto the surface of the 3D ground, generated based on feature tracking, allows for precise checking of drifting problems at the pixel level once the 3D cones are integrated with live-action footage. This approach accurately shows how many pixels each apex has drifted from its original position during playback, especially if the virtual camera is not precisely tracked.
2. Perspective validation: The distribution of the 3D cones throughout the scene provides a natural sense of perspective, determined by the distances between the objects and the camera. By using objects of the same size as references, it becomes evident that the cones in the foreground appear larger than those in the middle ground and background due to the perspective effect.

After completing the 3D matchmove process in Maya, the 3D test geometries will be exported to NukeX for further integration testing with the live-action plate. To do this, select all the 3D cones in the scene, go to File > Export Selection . . . , and export them as a single FBX file (Testing_Geomeries_Grp.fbx), which will be used in NukeX for additional testing.

◦ Section ⑤: Testing geometries in NukeX

1. Return to NukeX.
2. Put the mouse cursor in the Node Graph panel, and press the Tab key to search for the following nodes and bring them into the Node Graph:

   CheckerBoard [Image]

   ReadGeo [Geometry]

   The CheckerBoard node is used to apply a texture map to the 3D testing cones, while the ReadGeo node imports the FBX file into NukeX.
3. Connect the img input of the ReadGeo node to the CheckerBoard node to apply the texture to the 3D testing cones, as shown in Figure 5.40. Then, double-click the ReadGeo node to open its parameters in the Properties panel and load the FBX file (Testing_Geomeries_Grp.fbx) from the file slot.
4. Ensure all cones are properly loaded into the 3D space of NukeX.

   Next, press the Tab key and search for TransformGeo [Modify] to add a TransformGeo node after the ReadGeo node. The TransformGeo node allows us to rescale the imported 3D cones. This step is necessary because the entire scene was scaled up by 300 times when using the bollard as a reference to match real-world scale in Maya. However, the 3D cones must be uniformly scaled back down to their original size; otherwise, they will appear excessively large compared to the 3D camera tracking scene in NukeX. To uniformly scale down the 3D cones, navigate to the Properties panel of the TransformGeo node and enter 0.00333 in the Uniform Scale field. This scaling adjustment is crucial to prevent misalignment between the 3D cones and Nuke's original camera tracking scene. Refer to Figure 5.40 for the node connections and TransformGeo settings.

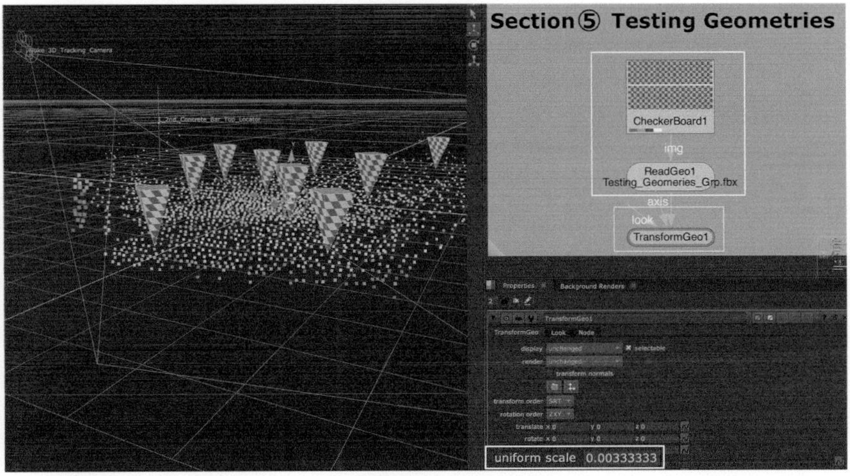

FIGURE 5.40 Node connections for importing the 3D testing cones and the Uniform Scale setting of the TransformGeo node

◦ Section ⑥: Restoring original lens distortion

Up to this point, we have been using an undistorted background plate for processing 3D camera tracking and matchmoving in NukeX and Maya. This cross-application process ensures that the 3D assets accurately match the camera movement in the scene. However, when integrating 3D elements into a live-action background, the 3D elements should incorporate the same lens distortion information as the live-action footage.

To apply lens distortion to the 3D cones, copy the LensDistortion node created in Section 1, which was originally used to remove lens distortion from the background plate before 3D camera tracking. Connect the duplicated LensDistortion node after the ScanlineRender node. Double-click the duplicated LensDistortion node, load its parameters in the Properties panel, and set the Mode to Redistort. This option re-applies the original lens distortion information to the 3D test cones. Figure 5.41 illustrates how the lens distortion is applied to the 3D cones.

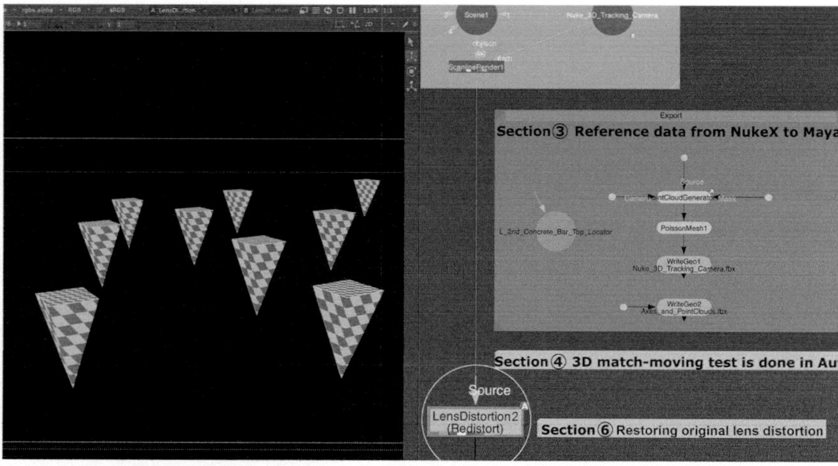

FIGURE 5.41 Adding the original lens distortion information to the 3D cones described in Section 6

Notes

1. The letter "C" in the upper left corner of a cloned node indicates that the node has been cloned. Please be cautious when using cloned nodes, as any attribute changes made to one cloned node will also affect all other cloned nodes.

   In Section 1, the LensDistortion (Undistort) node is used to remove lens distortion from the original background plate. However, in Section 6, we intend to add the original lens distortion to the 3D cones. Therefore, the cloned LensDistortion node from Section 1 will not work. Instead, create a new copy of that cloned node, remove its clone attribute (Edit > Declone), and switch the Mode to Redistort in its Properties panel.

2. Regardless of which 3D assets are ultimately used in the final shot, lens distortion information extracted from the original live-action footage must be applied to the 3D assets before integrating them with the live-action footage.

◦ Section ⑦: Final output

After successfully conducting camera tracking tests in Maya and Nuke, the 3D cones used for testing were replaced with a 3D bench. The lighting setup for the CG bench was then adjusted accordingly. Additionally, a series of multi-pass AOVs (Arbitrary Output Variables) were rendered in Maya and used during compositing to adjust the 3D bench and seamlessly integrate it into the original live-action footage.

In Figure 5.42, the upper image shows a Merge (over) node connected to the LensDistortion (Redistort) node, adding lens distortion information to the CG bench. Input B of the Merge (over) node is directly connected to the original background plate. The lower image shows the final render, with the 3D bench replacing the test 3D cones.

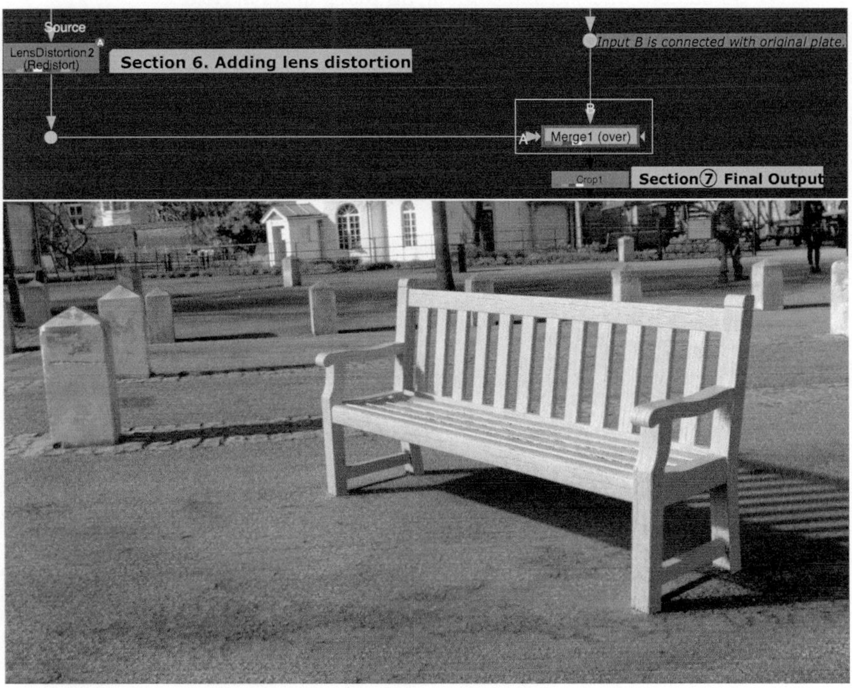

FIGURE 5.42 Final composition of Case Study 2

Case Study 3

The library project

Key learning points:

> Removing lens distortion without using a lens grid.

> 3D camera tracking and creating 3D test objects in NukeX.

> Match-moving and HDRI lighting in Maya.

> Integrating CG elements through compositing.

Notes

Each case study includes a pre-recorded video tutorial. Watching these videos alongside reading the case studies is strongly recommended to ensure a smooth and comprehensive learning experience for each hands-on project.

Video link: youtube.com/@InvisibleFilmVFX

Video title: Case Study 3 | The Library Project

Project file: Case_Study_3_Project_File

The project file is available for download on the book's official webpage.

High-resolution color figures from this project are also available for download on the book's official webpage.

• Creative concept and shot analysis

Recognizing the importance of 3D camera tracking, let's deepen our understanding by exploring a more comprehensive workflow, including 3D camera tracking, testing, lighting, and the integration of 3D assets into live-action footage. Figure 5.43 shows a comparison between a background plate and the final VFX shot based on the plate.

The 3D cloud used in this project is an open-source asset provided by Walt Disney Animation Studios.

◦ Creative concept

Case Study 3 showcases the workflow of visual effects production across two industry-standard applications, involving 3D camera tracking and match-moving in NukeX, lighting and rendering in Maya, and final compositing back in NukeX. Although the on-set information for this shot was not captured as professionally as in a typical production-level project, it serves as a practical example of how VFX can be achieved with limited resources, making it an ideal showcase for low-budget productions or student projects.

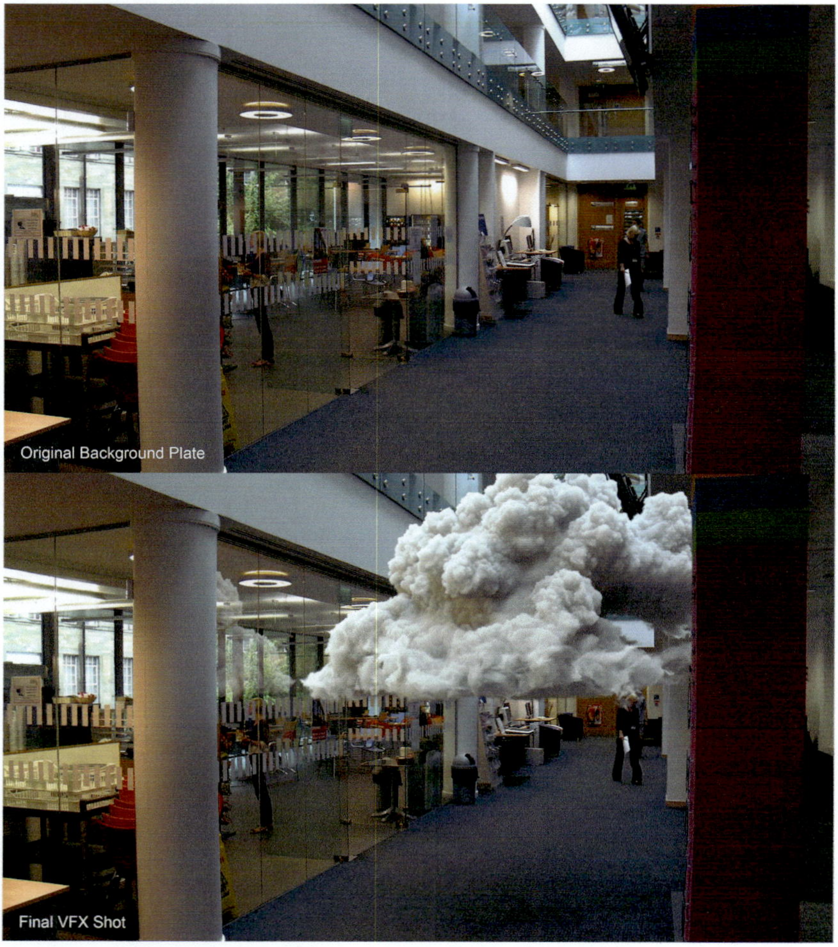

FIGURE 5.43 Comparison between the original plate and the final VFX output

- ## Shot analysis

– ### *Background plate*

Frame range: 1001–1190 frames

Footage aspect ratio: 1920 × 1080

Frame rate: 25 fps

Format: OpenEXR

Color space: Linear

– *Camera information*

Camera model and lens: Unknown

Lens grid: Not available.

Camera movement: Tilt shot

– *Additional elements*

A high dynamic range (HDR) image has been provided.

– *Moving elements in the scene*

Several moving elements are present in this shot, including three people walking in the center of the scene. Their reflections are occasionally visible on the glass door in certain frames. Additionally, two people intermittently appear behind the right pillar, while another two are seen standing behind the glass door on the left side of the shot.

- **Workflow analysis**
  - Part 1: Masking out moving elements, removing lens distortion, performing 3D camera tracking, and exporting tracking data in NukeX.
  - Part 2: 3D matchmoving, lighting and rendering in Autodesk Maya.
  - Part 3: Compositing 3D assets with the original background plate.

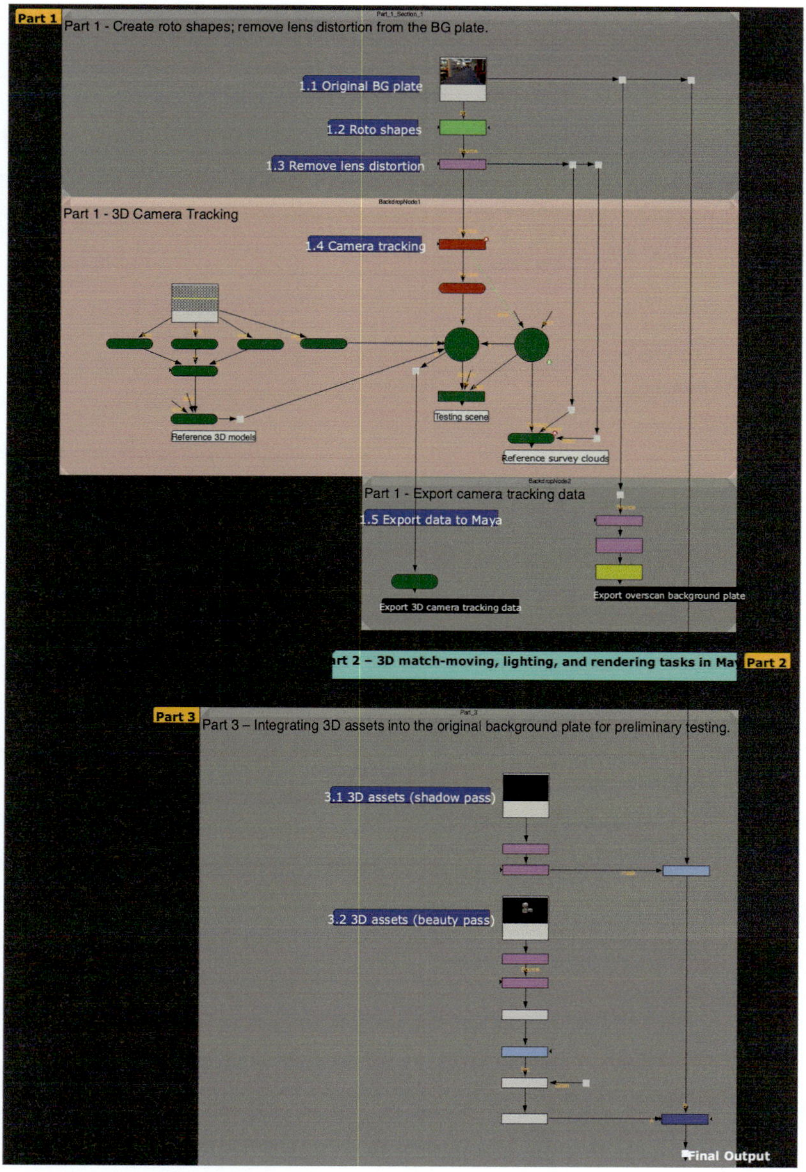

FIGURE 5.44 Compositing script for Case Study 3

○ Part 1: Masking out moving elements, removing lens distortion, performing 3D camera tracking, and exporting tracking data in NukeX

Nuke file: Case_Study_3_LibraryProject_3D_CameraTracking_v1.nk

– *Setting up the project*

Setting up a project with accurate shot information is crucial.

Project settings determine the correct working frame range, frames per second (FPS), and resolution of the original plate. It is also worth mentioning that the Project Settings window is usually grayed out (locked) in studios to prevent accidental alterations during production by artists.

Use the following information to set up the project in NukeX.

Press the S key to bring up the Project Settings window and configure the following settings:

frame range: 1001–1190

fps: 25

full size format: HD_1080 1920 × 1080

– *Import the original background plate*

To import the background plate into NukeX, follow these steps:

Position the mouse cursor in the Node Graph panel, press R to open the Read File(s) dialog window, and navigate to the folder where the background plate is saved. Select the sequence plate and click Open to import it. The plate will be loaded via a Read1 node in the Node Graph.

– *Creating roto shapes*

With the background plate (Read1 node) selected, press the O key to connect a Roto node to it. Use the Roto node to create a group of roto shapes for the moving elements in the scene, including the reflections on the glass door, as shown in the bottom image of Figure 5.45. The top image shows the Roto node connected to the Read1 node.

For a detailed explanation of the operations involved in creating roto shapes, please refer to the pre-recorded demonstration video in Case Study 3. For more

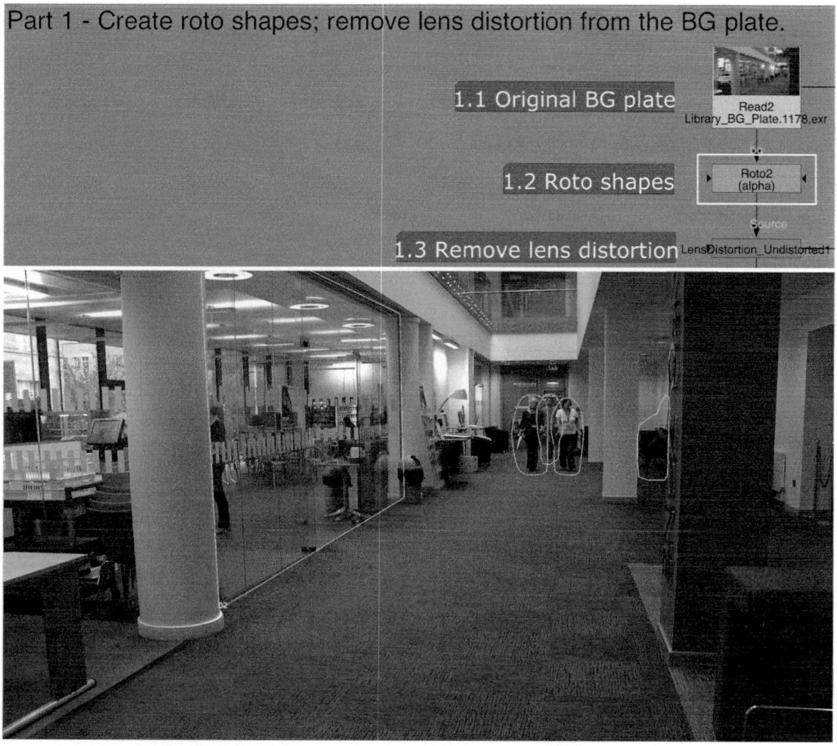

FIGURE 5.45 Roto shapes created to mask moving elements and reflections on the glass door in the scene

comprehensive guidance on node operations, watch the specific tutorials available on Foundry's official learning page.

– *Removing lens distortion*

Since no lens grid is available for this shot, we need to analyze the existing structures in the scene to calculate and remove lens distortion from the original footage. In this example, a legacy LensDistortion node was used in NukeX, as it is straightforward and beginner friendly.

By default, legacy nodes are not visible in NukeX. To enable them, click on Other in the left toolbar, then navigate to All Plugins > Update.

Next, position the mouse cursor in the Node Graph panel and press the Tab key. Search for LensDistortion [L] in the search bar. Figure 5.46 illustrates this process.

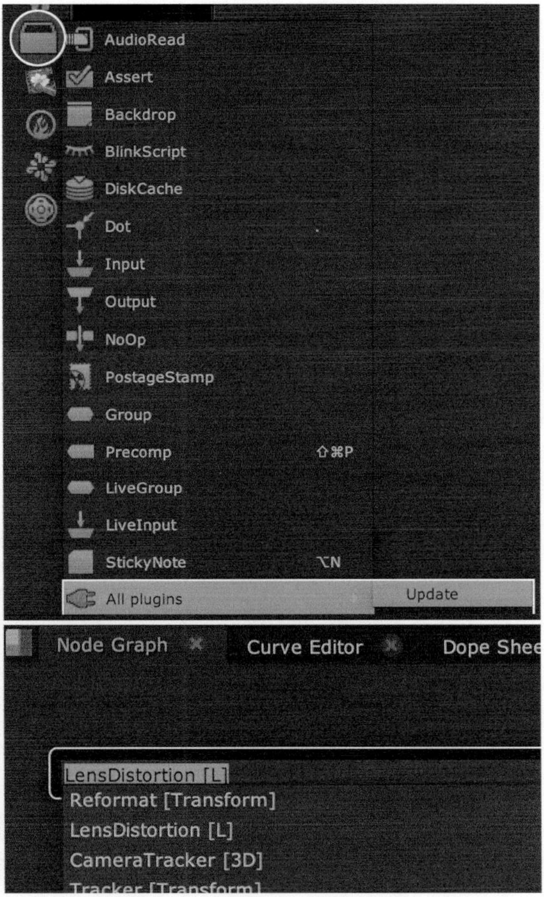

FIGURE 5.46 Activating the legacy node – LensDistortion [L]

After connecting the legacy LensDistortion node to the upstream Roto node, double-click the LensDistortion node to load its parameters in the Properties panel. Navigate to the Line Analysis tab and check the Drawing Mode On option, referring to the top image in Figure 5.47.

With the (legacy) LensDistortion node still selected, press any numeric key on the keyboard (e.g., 1) to load the background plate so that it becomes visible in the Viewer1 panel. By quickly scrubbing through the timeline back and forth, we can analyze the entire shot and observe a slight barrel-shaped lens distortion in the foreground pillars.

The most effective method to correct lens distortion in original live-action footage involves using lens grids, as introduced in Case Study 2. In this example, however, we will manually correct the lens distortion by drawing several vertical lines that follow the barrel-shaped curves of the pillars in the original plate.

As we learned in previous chapters, lens characteristics can make distortion more noticeable around the edges of an image compared to its center. Therefore, we focus our attention on shapes near the edges of the shot, such as the foreground pillars.

After carefully drawing four reference vertical lines along the shapes of the foreground pillars, as shown in the bottom image of Figure 5.47, click the Analyze Lines button in the Properties panel to analyze the lens distortion. NukeX will then calculate the lens distortion based on the reference lines and remove the corresponding distortion information from the original background plate.

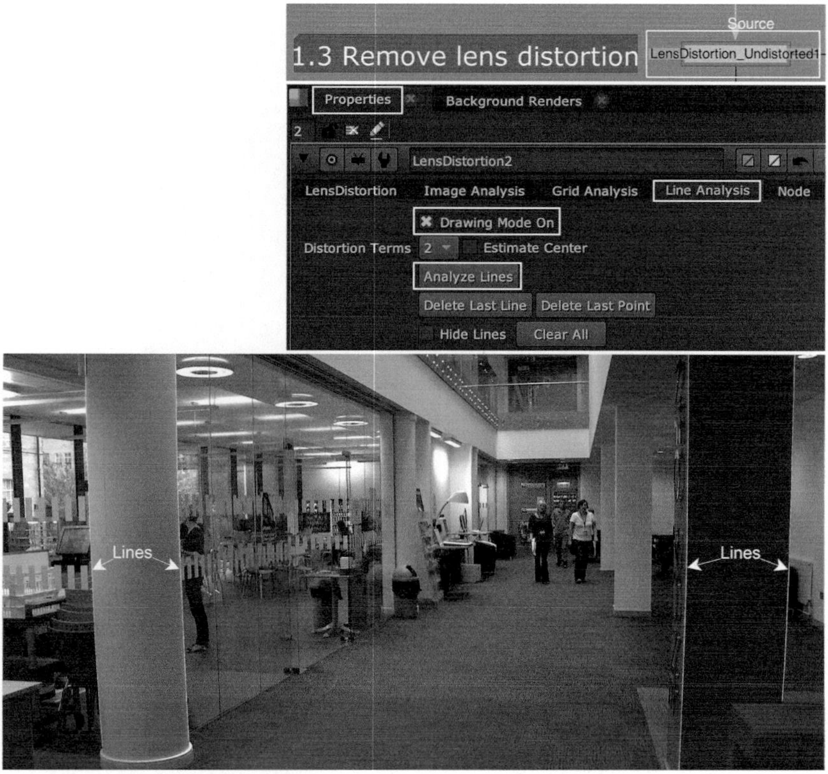

FIGURE 5.47 Four vertical lines along the pillars were drawn at frame 1130

Note

Carefully follow the original distorted shapes of the pillars when drawing the reference lines. These lines provide information to Nuke for calculating lens distortion. Therefore, the more precisely the shapes are drawn, the more accurate the resulting lens distortion calculation will be.

After removing lens distortion from the original background plate, a dotted wireframe appears beyond the original image size, as shown in the bottom image of Figure 5.48. This extended area represents the image overscan, which contains image information beyond the original boundaries.

Now that all preparations are complete, it is time to conduct 3D camera tracking.

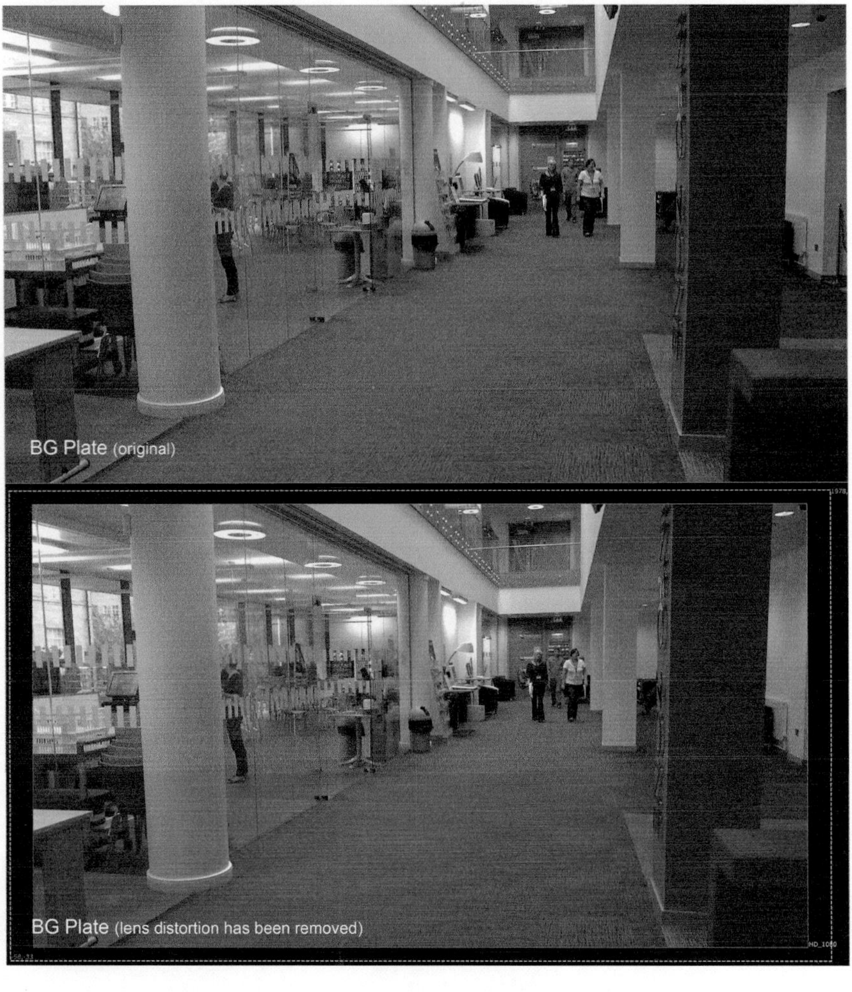

FIGURE 5.48 Comparison between the original background plate (top image) and the undistorted background plate (bottom image)

– *3D Camera tracking*

As explored in previous 3D camera tracking demonstrations, a virtual camera can be extracted from the background plate following successful 3D camera tracking. This allows the entire scene, integrated with VFX assets, to be re-filmed within the NukeX 3D system. The camera tracking process, shown in Figure 5.49 (top image), consists of three components: 3D models, a scene test, and reference survey clouds.

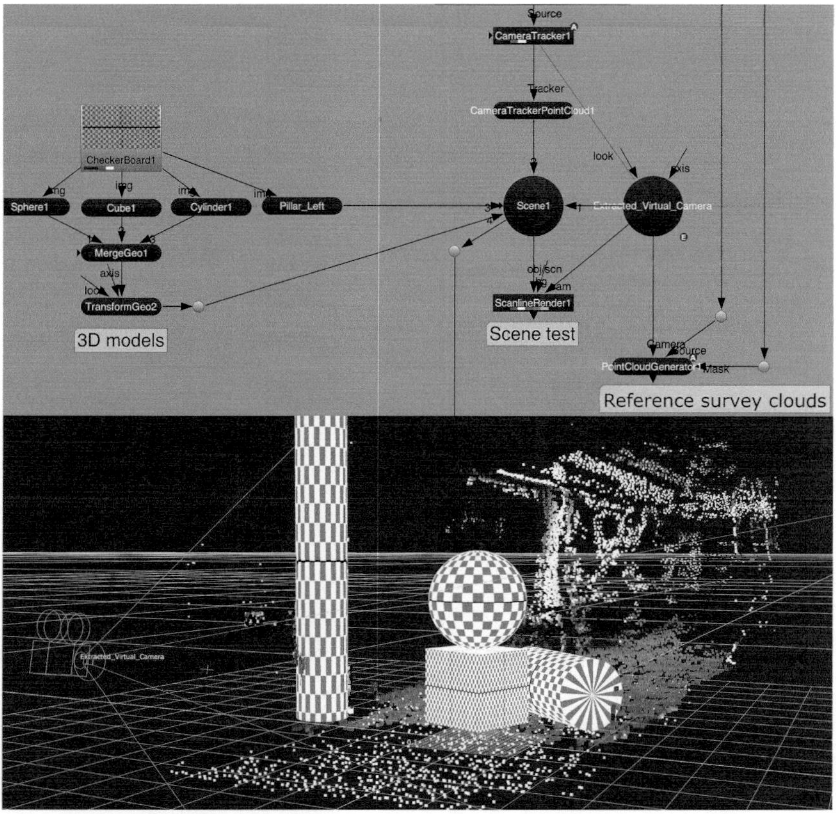

FIGURE 5.49 Node connections and the final result of the 3D camera tracking tests

Note

3D nodes in NukeX have specific characteristics. By default, in the current version of NukeX (16.x), 3D nodes are categorized into two types: 3D Classic and 3D Beta. Unlike 2D nodes, which typically have rectangular shapes, 3D nodes can be either circular or rectangular with rounded corners.

3D models

To conduct additional tests on tracking accuracy, we added four basic 3D nodes to the 3D scene in NukeX: a Sphere, a Cube, and two Cylinders, one of which was named Pillar_Left.

To add 3D geometries such as a cube, click the 3D icon (a grey cube) in the toolbar on the left, then select 3D Classic > Geometry > Cube.

Scene test

The testing scene includes a cluster of 3D tracking clouds, a virtual camera, four reference 3D geometries, and additional reference survey clouds of the scene, as illustrated in the bottom image of Figure 5.49.

Reference survey clouds

A PointCloudGenerator node is added to the scene to generate additional point clouds based on existing 3D camera tracking data, providing further visual detail of the scene's structures.

For full instructions on how to operate these three parts of camera tracking and testing in Case Study 3, please watch the pre-recorded video.

– *Export 3D camera tracking data to Maya*

After completing 3D camera tracking and testing in NukeX, the following data will be exported to Autodesk Maya for further 3D matchmove work:

1. The 3D camera tracking data, including all components in the scene.
2. An overscan background plate.

Connect a WriteGeo node to the Scene1 node, which serves as the hub for all components in the camera tracking scene. Double-click the WriteGeo node to load its parameters into the Properties panel, then tick the following options in the FBX Options section:

☒ geometries

☒ cameras

☒ point clouds

Selecting these three options ensures that the reference 3D models, the virtual camera, and the point cloud data are exported from the scene together.

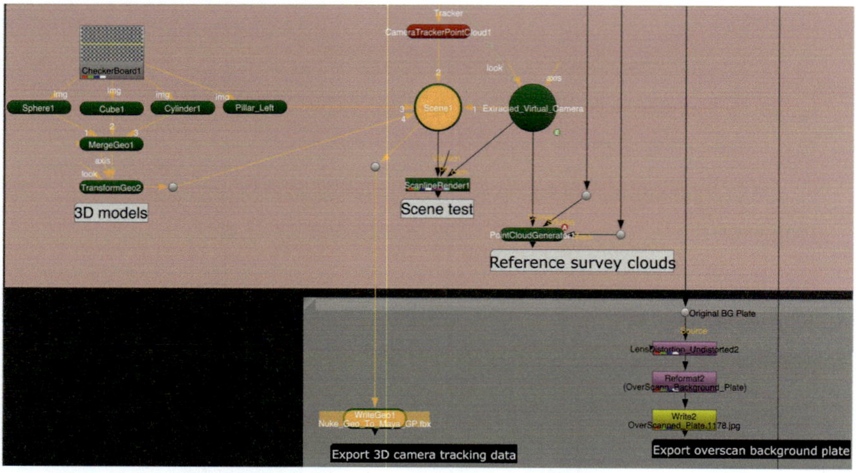

FIGURE 5.50 Exporting 3D camera tracking data

– *Export overscan background plate*

The term "overscan" originates from television imagery. It refers to the portion of an image that extends beyond the edges of the TV screen, helping to prevent black borders from appearing on cathode-ray tube (CRT) displays, where video images might not perfectly align with the screen's edges. Nuke has adopted the concept of overscan to preserve data in areas that extend beyond the image boundaries.

All projects and images have a set aspect ratio, such as Full HD, 2K, or 4K. During image manipulation, compositors inevitably adjust assets and resize images, resulting in overscan sizes that exceed the predetermined project and image dimensions. Figure 5.51 displays a color wheel merged over a gray background. The image shows two aspect ratios on the right side: the upper-right corner shows the current image aspect ratio of 1920 × 1080, while the lower-right corner indicates the project size of HD_1080.

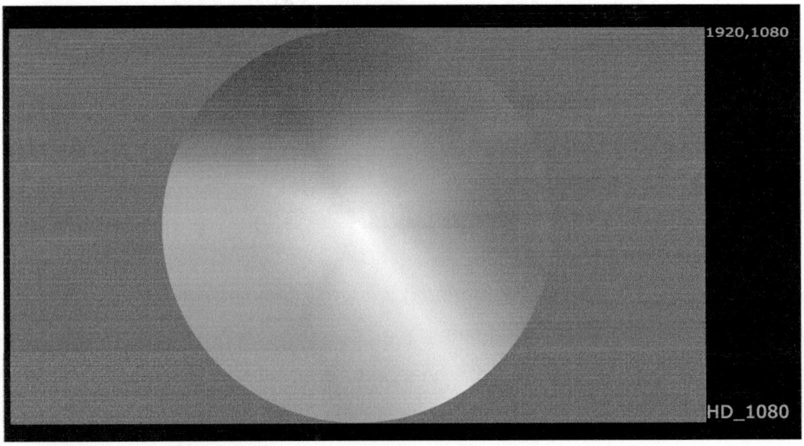

FIGURE 5.51 Original overscan size of the image and the project's aspect ratio

However, an overscan area is produced when the color wheel moves outside the project size of 1920 × 1080. Figure 5.52 shows the color wheel moved to the upper-right corner, creating a new overscan region indicated by diagonal stripes. In this example, the new overscan size is 2420 × 1380, calculated proportionally from the image's lower-left corner coordinates (0,0). The striped area displays an extended overscan field that preserves the information in the upper-right portion of the color wheel. In this case, Figure 5.52 presents two aspect ratios to consider during compositing: the new overscan size of 2420 × 1380 (upper right) and the original project size of 1920 × 1080 (lower right).

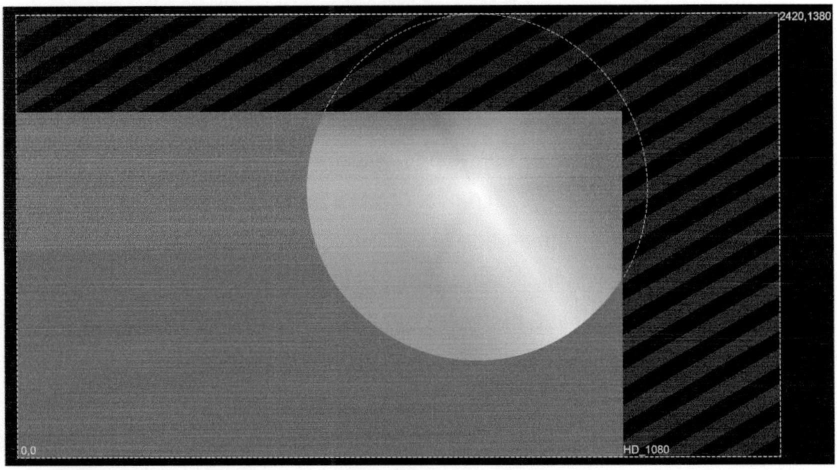

FIGURE 5.52 An overscan region appears when the color wheel extends beyond the project size

Overscan preserves image information that can be reused for later operations. Therefore, a thorough understanding of overscan is essential in compositing. Overscan occurs in numerous instances during image operations, such as when using Transform, Blur, and LensDistortion nodes. Now, let's examine the practical application of overscan.

Figure 5.53 contrasts two identical 3D assets rendered at frame 1190. Image A was rendered with an appropriate overscan size calculated during the rendering process, while Image B was rendered without consideration for overscan. After applying lens distortion to both images, their sizes shrank due to the nature of lens distortion, particularly affecting the boundary areas of the images. This example shows that the cube and cylinder in Image B have lost their bottom areas.

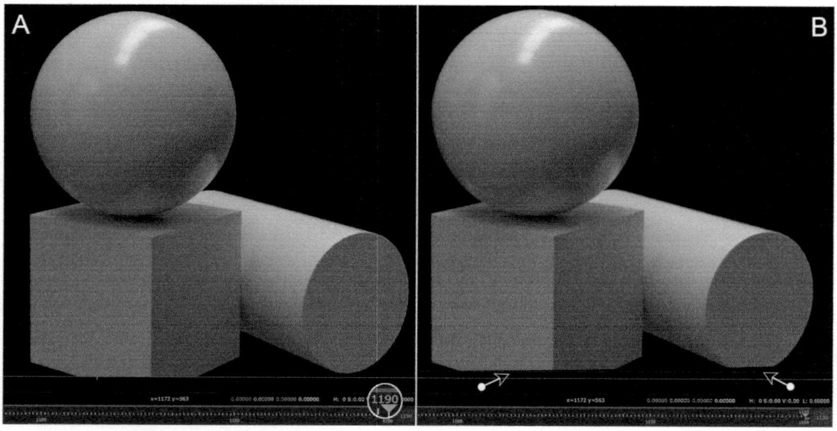

FIGURE 5.53 The geometries in Image B lost their bottom areas after applying lens distortion

With an understanding of overscan, particularly the significant impact of the edge areas of CG images after applying lens distortion, it is essential to calculate an appropriate overscan size when rendering 3D assets. For example, in Case Study 3, after correcting the lens distortion in the live-action footage, the overscan area extends beyond the image boundaries along both the positive and negative X and Y axes. The final overscan size of the background plate is determined by adding the extended values in both directions. This includes X and Y values (1964, 1105) in the upper-right corner and (-44, -25) in the lower-left corner, as shown in Figure 5.54.

Figure 5.54 illustrates the overscan size of the background plate. A black gap is visible between the image boundaries and the dotted line surrounding the image.

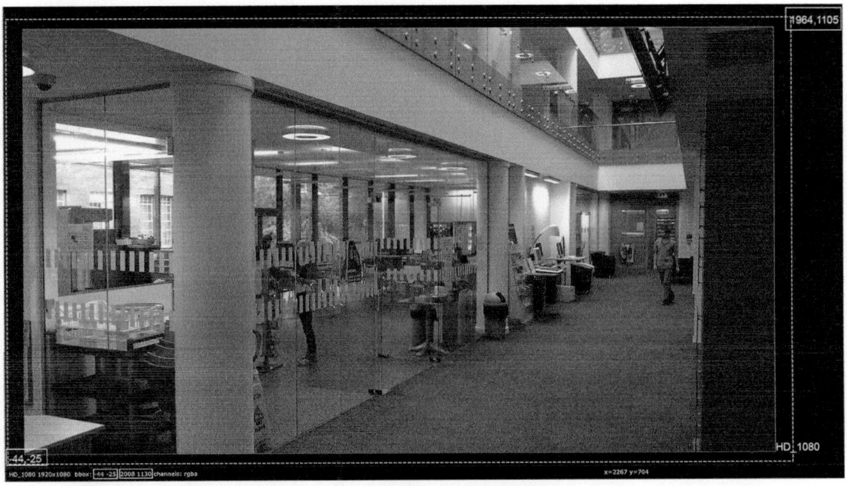

FIGURE 5.54 Final overscan size of the background plate after lens distortion removal

Understanding camera movement within a shot is closely related to overscan size, as 3D assets may be positioned or animated toward the edges of the scene and eventually move out of frame. In such cases, portions of the 3D assets that extend beyond the frame must be reserved within the overscan areas for later use. To accurately render 3D assets, including the embedded overscan, it is necessary to calculate the correct overscan size for use in 3D software during rendering.

By observing the camera movement in this shot, we can see that the camera gradually lifts along the Y-axis and moves diagonally to establish the scene. Therefore, the initial overscan size in Case Study 3 can be calculated by primarily focusing on the Y-axis value, since 3D assets are likely to extend beyond the frame along the Y-axis in this shot. A simple mathematical equation can be used to determine the overscan size, as shown:

1964, **1105** (upper-right corner)

+

44, **25** (lower-left corner)

2008, **1130**

+ 100

Our primary focus in this calculation is the initial height along the Y-axis. Once the height is determined, the overall overscan size for the final rendering settings can be calculated directly in Maya. According to the previous equation, the calculated height is 1130 pixels. However, we add 100 pixels to ensure that the Y-axis overscan size is sufficient, bringing the total to 1230 pixels. After determining the overscan value for the Y-axis, we can calculate the final rendering size for 3D assets using a Maya MEL plug-in, available for download from the project folder. Figure 5.55 shows the final overscan size calculated for rendering 3D assets in Maya.

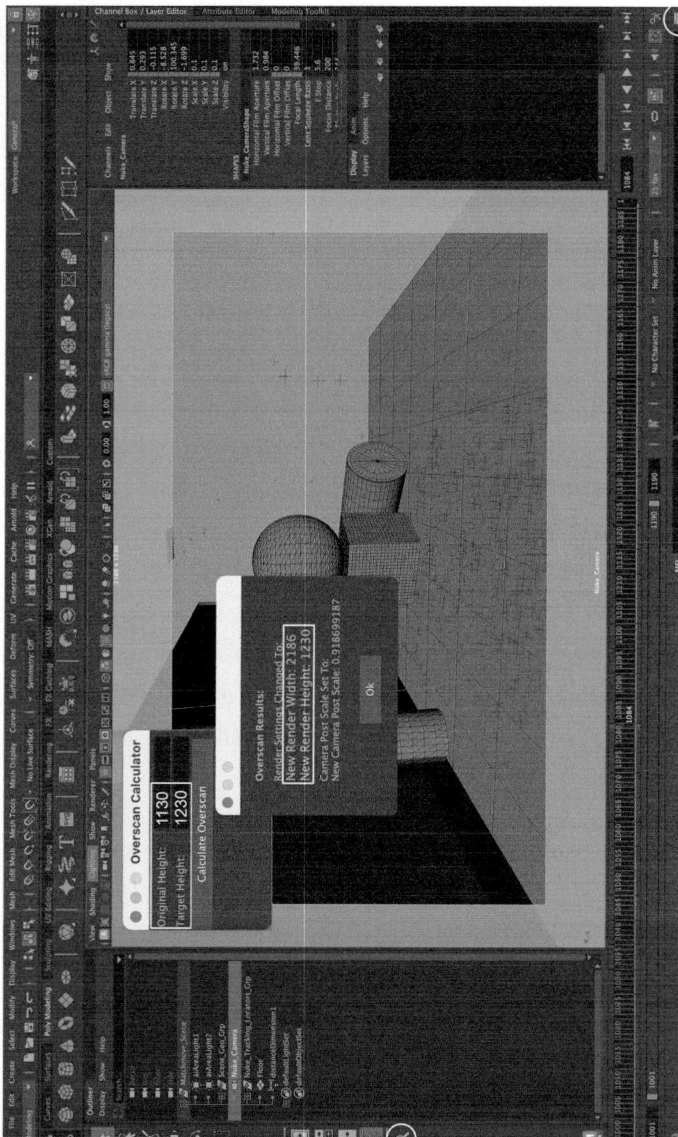

FIGURE 5.55 Final overscan size for rendering 3D elements, calculated using the Maya MEL plug-in

Notes

There are two methods for calculating the overscan size. One method utilizes the Maya MEL plug-in, which is based on the initial overscan size calculated in NukeX. The second method calculates the final overscan size entirely within NukeX, involving a few additional nodes. Both methods are efficient. In Case Study 3, we will demonstrate how to use the Maya MEL plug-in to calculate the final overscan size, while the alternative method will be introduced in Case Study 8 through a more comprehensive workflow.

Before opening any existing Maya files, it is recommended to set up the project. This will allow Maya to access files from the correct folders. To set up an existing Maya project, go to File > Set Project . . .

A pre-recorded introductory video titled "Setting Up Projects in Maya" is available at youtube.com/@InvisibleFilmVFX.

– Use the Maya MEL plug-in to calculate the overscan size.

1. Launch Autodesk Maya.

   Go to File > Open Scene . . . , select Library_Maya3D_MatchMoving_Initial_Overscan.ma, and click Open to load the file into Maya.

   (If you have not set the project yet, go to File > Open Scene . . . , then navigate to: Case_Study_3_Project_File folder > 3_02_Library_Shot_Maya_Data > Library_Shot_3D_Match_moving_in_Maya > Maya_Project > scenes > Library_Maya3D_MatchMoving_Initial_Overscan.ma.)

2. To load the Maya MEL plug-in correctly, first select the imported Nuke tracking camera.

   In the Outliner, click the + icon next to Matchmove_Scene to expand it, then select Nuke_Camera.

3. Click the Script Editor icon located in the lower-right corner of the Maya UI. See the circled icon in Figure 5.55.

4. Once the Script Editor window is open, go to File> Open Script . . . , navigate to the 3_03_Calculate_OverScan_Maya_Mel folder, select the Calculate_Overscan.mel file, and click Open to load it into the Script Editor window. Then, execute the File by selecting Command > Execute.

   This will open the Overscan Calculator window. Refer to Figure 5.55 for reference.

5. The Overscan Calculator window includes two optional fields:

   Original Height

   Target Height

The Original Height field displays 1130, which is the initial overscan height calculated in NukeX.

6. Enter 1230 into the Target Height field and click the Calculate Overscan button. A new dialog window will appear displaying the overscan results:

   New Render Width: 2186

   New Render Height: 1230

   Click the OK button to confirm these results.

   You now have the final overscan size for rendering 3D assets.

   The final overscan size (2186 × 1230) has been calculated. At this point, we need to return to NukeX and proportionally resize the undistorted background plate to match the overscan size (2186 × 1230). To do this, follow these steps in NukeX:

– Render the final overscan plate in NukeX

  Return to the Case_Study_3_LibraryProject_3D_CameraTracking_v1.nk script.)

  To apply the ultimate overscan size (2186 × 1230) to the original background plate, please follow these instructions and refer to Figure 5.56:

  1. Duplicate (Ctrl/Cmd + C) the LensDistortion_Undistorted1 node created in Section 1.3 and paste it (Ctrl/Cmd + V) to create a copied node. The copied node will automatically be named LensDistortion_Undistorted2. Connect it to the original BG plate.
  2. Position the mouse cursor in the Node Graph panel and press the Tab key to search for a Reformat [Transform] node in the search bar.

     Connect the Reformat node after the LensDistortion_Undistorted2 node and adjust its settings in the Properties panel according to Figure 5.56. These settings will generate an overscan background plate of the correct size, matching the overscan size calculated in Maya.
  3. Press the W key to create a Write node and connect it to the Reformat node.

     Render the overscan background plate as a sequence of JPEG images, which are lightweight and can be easily loaded as a reference background plate for match-moving in Maya.

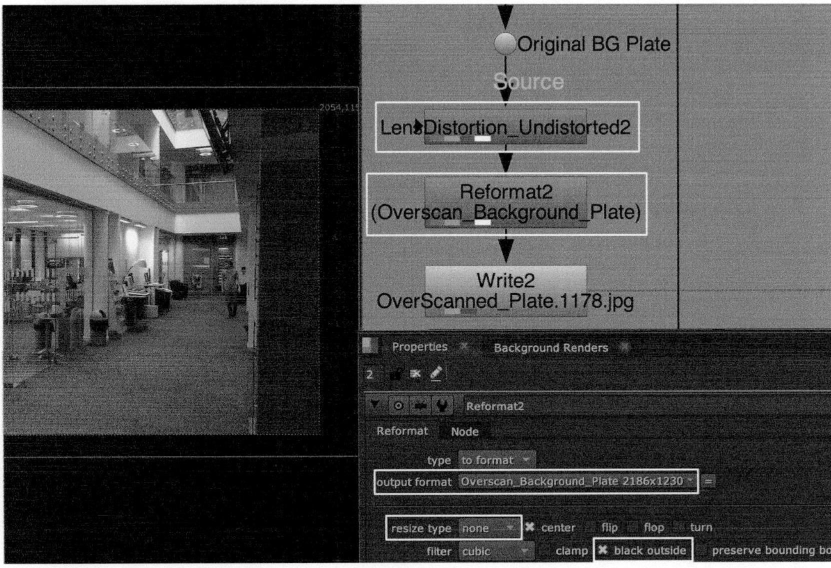

FIGURE 5.56 Node connections and settings for adding the overscan size to the background plate

◦ Part 2: 3D matchmoving, lighting, and rendering in Autodesk Maya

– *3D matchmoving*

When importing elements generated from NukeX in Maya for the first time, you may notice some issues. For example, there may be differences in scene size and locator sizes compared to those in the NukeX scene. These differences occur due to variations in the default working unit measurement settings between Maya and NukeX. To ensure clarity, the complex details in this section are presented in a video format. Please refer to the prerecorded video available at www.youtube.com/@InvisibleFilmVFX. Video title: Case Study 3 | The Library Project.

To successfully conduct matchmoving, we need to double-check for any drifting issues in the scene. If there are no issues, all elements should remain fixed in the same positions on the ground during playback. Additionally, the final plate with overscan, exported from NukeX in JPEG format, should be imported into Maya and used as the reference background for the scene.

To load the overscan background exported from NukeX in JPEG format, follow these steps:

1. Return to the Maya scene used for calculating the final overscan size.
2. Go to Maya's Outliner (located on the left side of the UI), expand Matchmove_Scene, select Nuke_Camera, and open its Attribute Editor (Ctrl + A). Navigate to the imagePlaneShape1 tab. In the Image Plane Attributes section, click the folder icon next to the Image Name field to load the overscan background plate located in the following path:

   3_01_Library_Shot_Nuke_Data > 3_01_004_Overscan_BG_Plate_2186_1230_Reference_For_Maya folder.

Inside this folder, select Overscan_BG_Plate_2186_1230.1001.jpg and click Open to load it into Maya. Once the overscan background plate is loaded, check the Use Image Sequence option box below to enable the loading of image sequences. Figure 5.57 illustrates how the overscan background plate is loaded through the Nuke_Camera Attribute Editor.

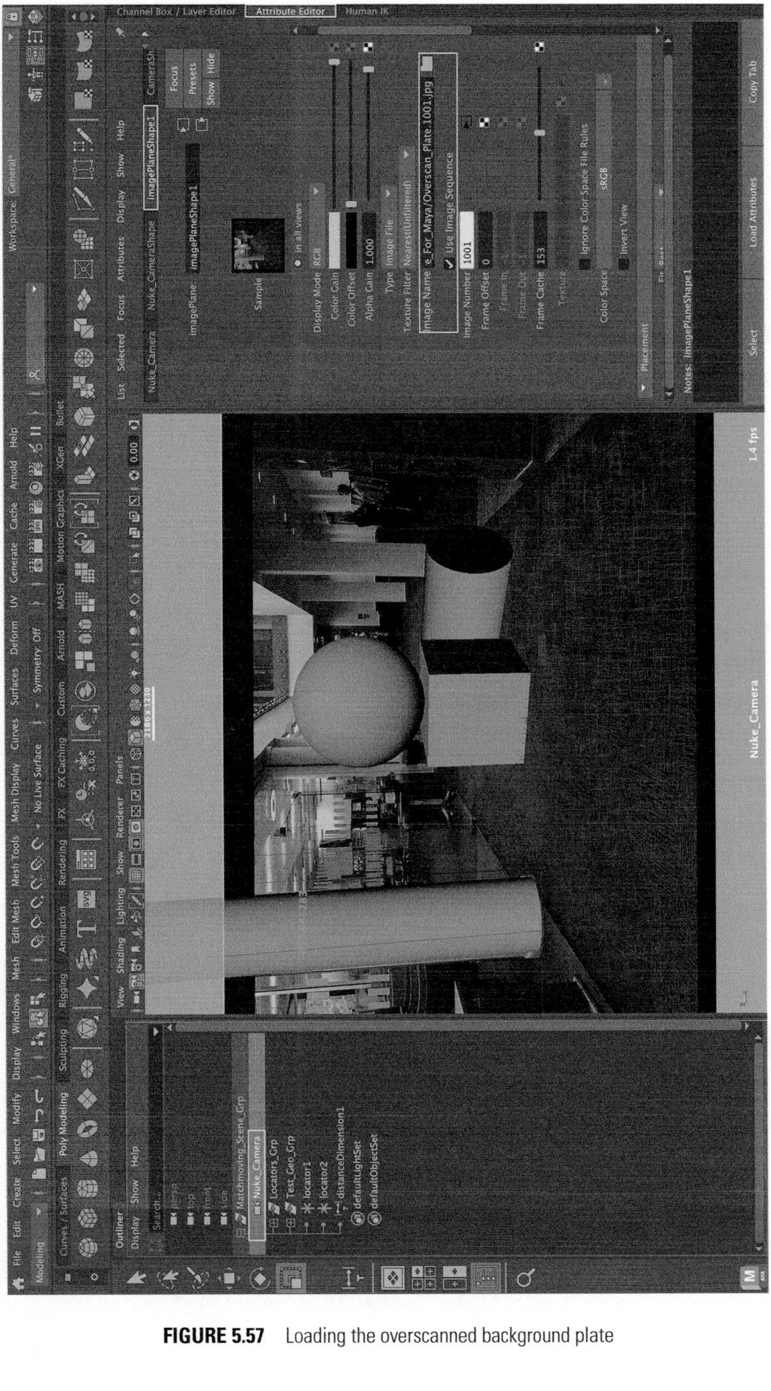

FIGURE 5.57 Loading the overscanned background plate

Now, we can double-check for any drifting issues with the 3D test elements in the scene by quickly scrubbing through the timeline. Additionally, the basic 3D test elements can be replaced with more complex 3D geometries or even dynamic simulations. Furthermore, we need to construct a low-resolution environment that aligns with the building structure in the background plate. This environment will be used to generate global illumination and cast shadows on the 3D characters intended for integration into the scene.

– *Lighting and rendering*

The environmental lighting in this scene primarily comes from the on-set captured HDR image, shown as Image A in Figure 5.58. As introduced in previous chapters, HDR images are 32 bit and can store billions of possible values per channel. By reducing the exposure values of the image, additional details in the highlights become visible, as seen in Images B and C. For instance, in a randomly selected area of the highlights in Image B, the color values for the R, G, and B channels are 7.84432, 8.76225, and 9.02501, respectively. When a 3D object is illuminated using an HDR image, the lighting and reflections emitted by the HDRI surround the 3D objects within the scene, providing realistic illumination and color reflections. This process generates photorealistic lighting for the 3D object, mimicking its presence in the scene during filming.

The default rendering engine in Autodesk Maya is Arnold, a highly advanced Monte Carlo ray tracing renderer renowned for its accuracy and ease of use. A skydome has been created using the Arnold renderer to illuminate 3D elements in the scene, utilizing an on-set captured HDR image as the primary lighting source.

The process of adding the skydome through Arnold involves the following steps:

1. Click Arnold (in the top drop-down menu) > Lights > Skydome Light. This will create a semi-transparent sphere that surrounds the entire 3D scene
2. In the Maya Outliner, select the skydome named "aiSkyDomeLight1" and press Ctrl + A to open its Attribute Editor window.
3. Under the aiSkyDomeLightShape1 tab, in the SkyDomeLight Attributes section, click the square checkerboard icon next to the Color slider to open a separate Create Render Node window. Then, select the File icon from the list on the right-hand side of this dialog. This will open a new panel with a File Attributes section. Click the folder icon at the end of the Image Name slot to load the captured HDR image. Figure 5.59 illustrates the result of applying the HDRI to the skydome.

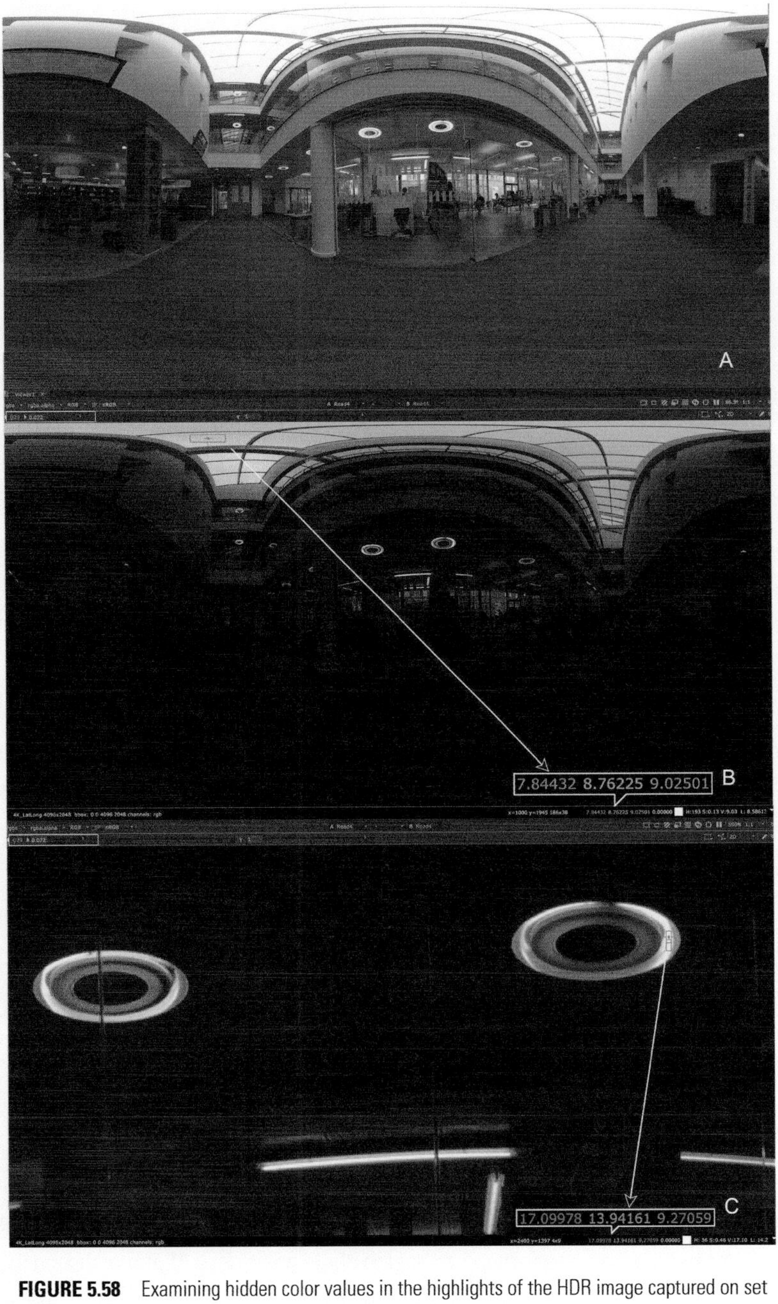

FIGURE 5.58 Examining hidden color values in the highlights of the HDR image captured on set

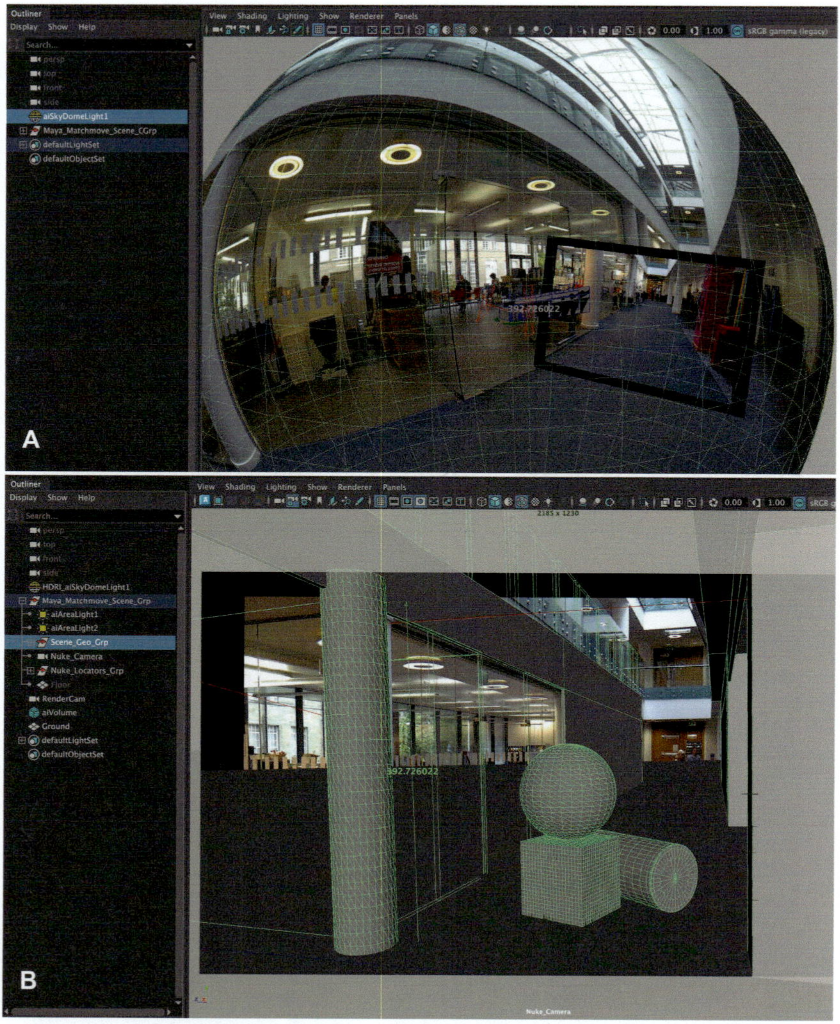

FIGURE 5.59 Image A shows the skydome used to illuminate the 3D elements with the captured HDRI light map

After mapping the HDR image onto the skydome, rotate it until the image aligns with the layout of the overscan background plate. For example, use the skylight on top of the building as a reference to match their positions. Aligning the positions of the skydome and the overscan background plate is important due to the presence of light sources. In this shot, the key light comes from the skylight, while the fill lights come from the ceiling. Therefore, aligning these light sources from the HDR image with the background plate is essential before rendering 3D assets in the scene. Figure 5.59, Image A, shows the skydome that matches the scene of the overscan background plate. At the same time, Image B illustrates the created 3D scene, which includes pillars, a corridor, a glass wall, a floor, a ceiling, and a set of testing geometries placed within the scene.

Rendering 3D assets is crucial for achieving visual realism in compositing. The method of setting up multi-pass rendering may vary depending on the CG lighting and compositing pipelines used in VFX studios. This project will focus specifically on the workflow for integrating CG elements into live-action footage, with more advanced multi-pass rendering examples demonstrated in later chapters.

Figure 5.60 shows a test render used to examine the accuracy of lighting in the 3D scene, including HDRI lighting, a series of fill lights, and color reflections from the HDR image onto the 3D geometries. After confirming the test results, the initial 3D test geometries can be replaced with more intricate elements, such as computer-generated clouds, in the final render for this project.

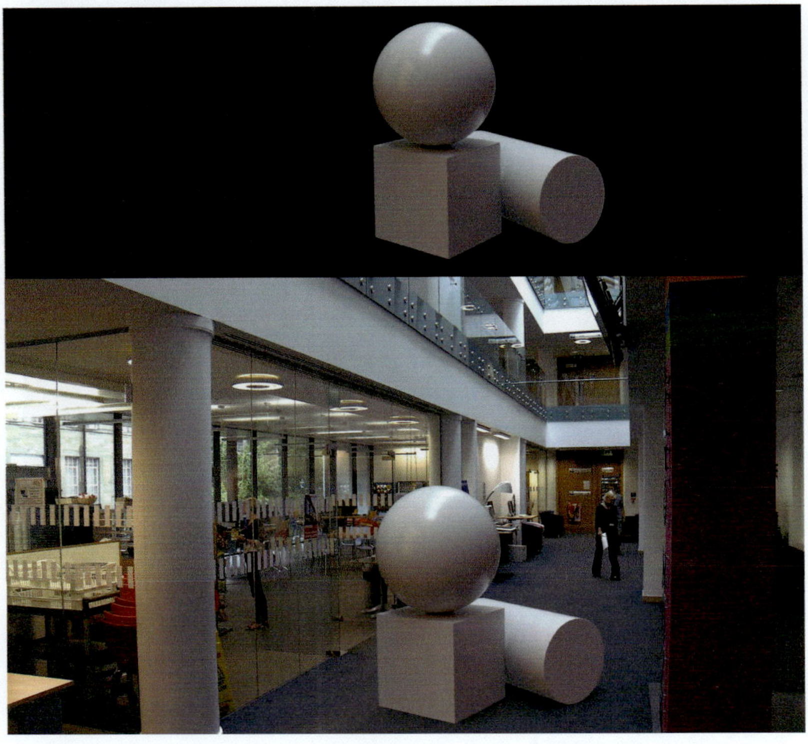

FIGURE 5.60 3D test geometries (top) rendered using the on-set captured HDR image, and a compositing test integrated with the background plate (bottom)

◦ Part 3: Integrating 3D clouds into the original background plate

In the previous sections, we used a set of simple 3D geometries to test the accuracy of camera tracking, lighting, and rendering. To further illustrate the overall workflow based on the results from the previous sections, this section focuses on seamlessly integrating a cluster of 3D clouds into the original shot. The compositing process in this demonstration is divided into six stages, as shown in Figure 5.61.

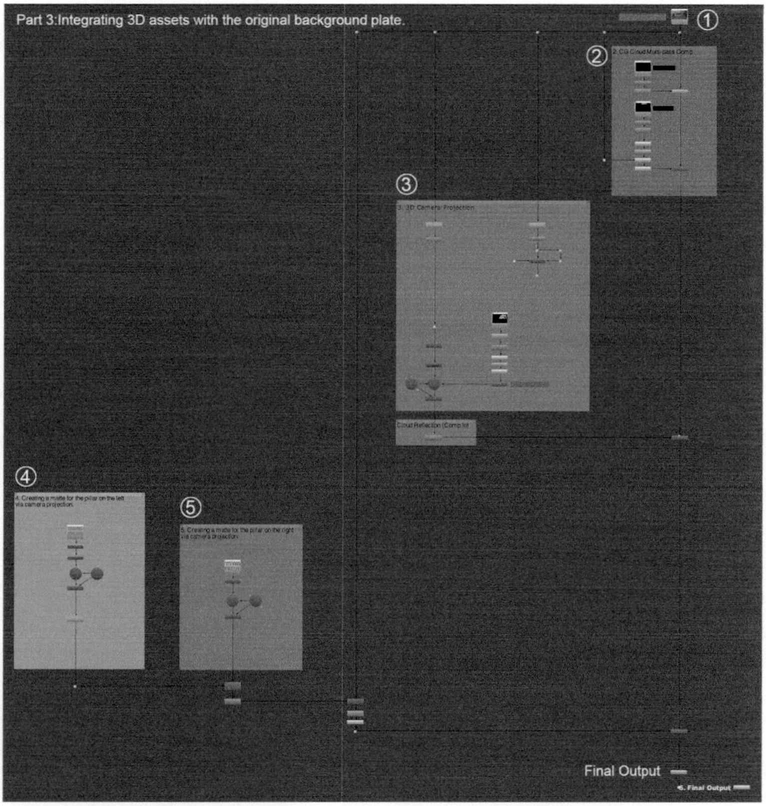

FIGURE 5.61 Compositing script for integrating CG clouds into the background plate in Case Study 3

The outline of the six stages is provided here:

① Background plate

② CG clouds compositing

③ 3D camera projection

④ Creating a matte for the pillar on the left

⑤ Creating a matte for the pillar on the right

⑥ Final output

Notes

1. Before beginning the compositing process, it is important to set up the project. Follow these steps to configure the project settings:

   Go to Edit (menu) > Project Settings . . .

   Use the following parameters to set up the project:

   frame range: 1001–1190

   fps: 25

   full size format: HD_1080 1920 × 1080

2. For educational purposes, the Nuke script used to integrate 3D clouds is provided. It can be found in the 3_01_001_Nuke_Scripts folder:

   Case_Study_3_LibraryProject_3D_Clouds_Final_Comp_v1.nk

① Background plate

The original background plate is imported into Nuke via a Read node.

- Position the mouse cursor in the Node Graph panel and press the R key to bring up the Read File(s) dialog window.
- Navigate to the Case_Study_3_Project_File folder > 3_01_Library_Shot_Nuke_Data > 3_01_002_Background_Plate > Library_BG_Plate.
- Select the sequence and click the Open button to import the background plate.

② CG clouds compositing

To better focus on the workflow of this project, only two render passes are used in the multi-pass compositing process. The details of CG multi-pass compositing will be explored in Case Studies 6, 7, and 8. Figure 5.62 illustrates the integration of the shadow and beauty passes of the CG clouds with the background plate. These two passes can be found in the following folders: Case_Study_3_Project_File > 3_01_Library_Shot_Nuke_Data > 3_01_005_Rendered_3D_Assets > Clouds_Beauty_Pass and Clouds_Shadow_Pass.

– *Shadow pass*

The shadow pass in Figure 5.63 refers to a rendered image containing only the shadows cast by the 3D clouds onto the ground in the scene. The shadow information in this pass is stored in its alpha channel. The image in the upper-left corner shows the shadow pass.

The node connections in the upper-right corner of Figure 5.63 demonstrate the use of a Grade node, with its mask input connected to the shadow pass and its downstream operational nodes (Reformat and LensDistortion). The input to the Grade node is directly connected to the original background plate. This setup allows compositors to use the Grade node to darken areas on the ground covered by the shadow pass, utilizing the alpha channel of the shadow pass. The final compositing result, shown in the lower image of Figure 5.63, reveals a shadow effect cast onto the ground.

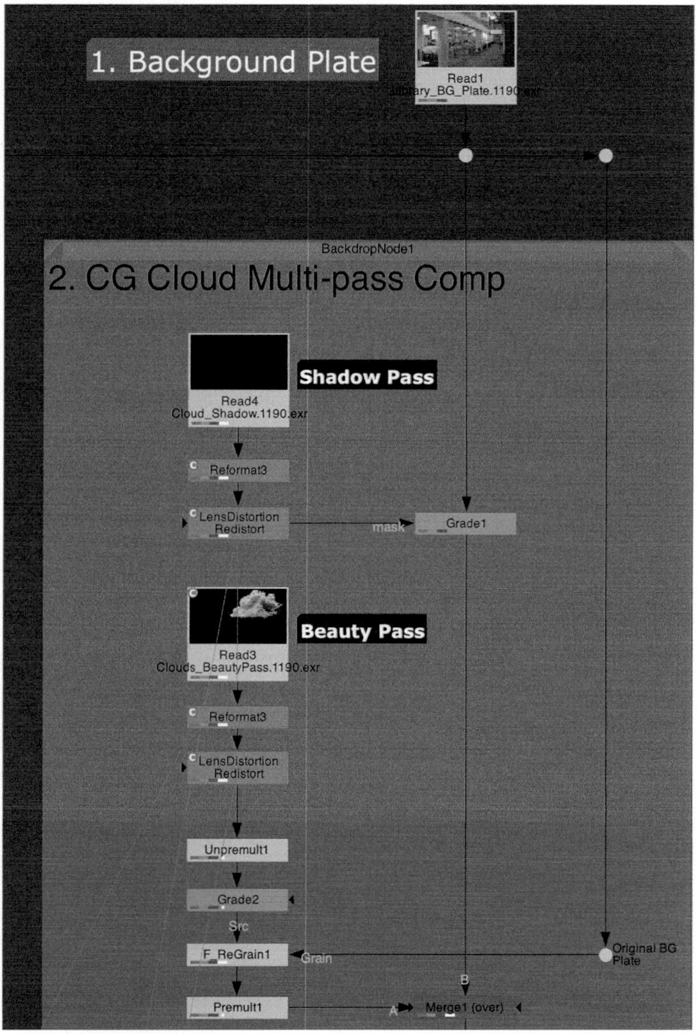

FIGURE 5.62 Node connections for integrating the CG clouds with the background plate

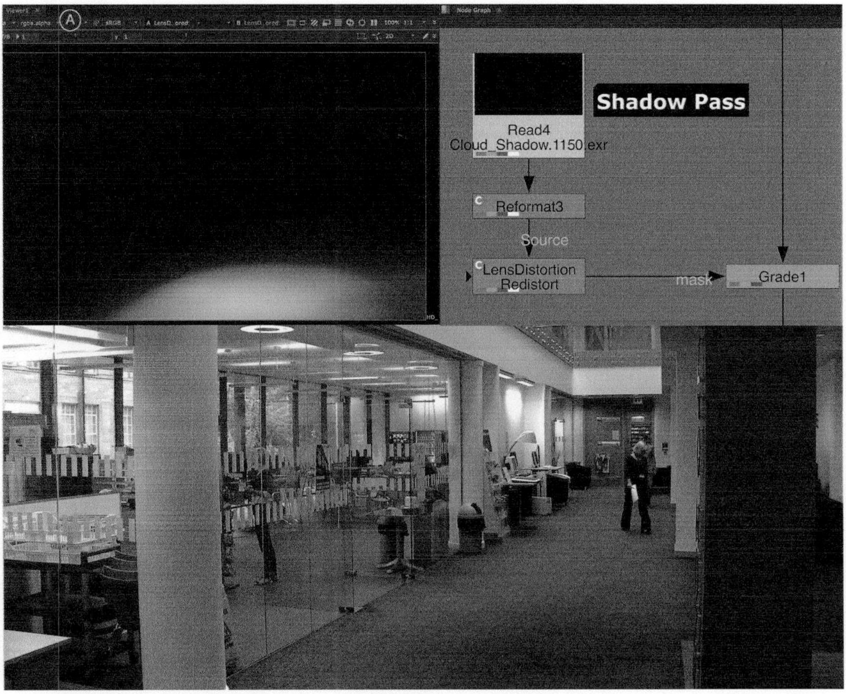

FIGURE 5.63 Shadow pass integrated into the original background plate

Notes

Reformat node

The Reformat node adjusts the aspect ratio of the shadow pass, which was rendered with an overscan size of 2185 × 1230, to match the project's aspect ratio of 1920 × 1080. This ensures that the overscan data beyond the boundaries of the full HD aspect ratio is preserved within the overscan region.

LensDistortion (Redistort) node

The LensDistortion (Redistort) node applies the lens distortion data extracted from the original background plate to the shadow pass.

– *Beauty pass*

A beauty pass represents the final rendered appearance of a 3D asset, typically composed of multiple passes known as arbitrary output variables (AOVs) in customized channels. These include the color pass, specular pass, reflection pass, refraction pass, shadow pass, ID pass, motion vector pass, and other utility render passes. AOVs can be separated from the beauty pass to allow for individual adjustments during compositing. However, to maintain focus on the workflow of this example, we use only a single beauty pass in this script.

As shown in Figure 5.64, the same Reformat and LensDistortion nodes must be applied to the beauty pass to restore the original image's aspect ratio and lens distortion. Additionally, a Grade node is used to fine-tune the color details of the CG clouds. Subsequently, an F_Regrain node is applied to apply the film grain analyzed from the original background plate to the 3D clouds. This process ensures that the CG clouds and the original background plate share a consistent film grain structure.

Additionally, the CG clouds (at the bottom) are integrated with the original background plate. However, two persistent issues remain in the shot: the clouds are not reflected in the glass door, and parts of the clouds should appear behind the front pillars on the right. Addressing these details would enhance the interaction between the CG elements and the scene.

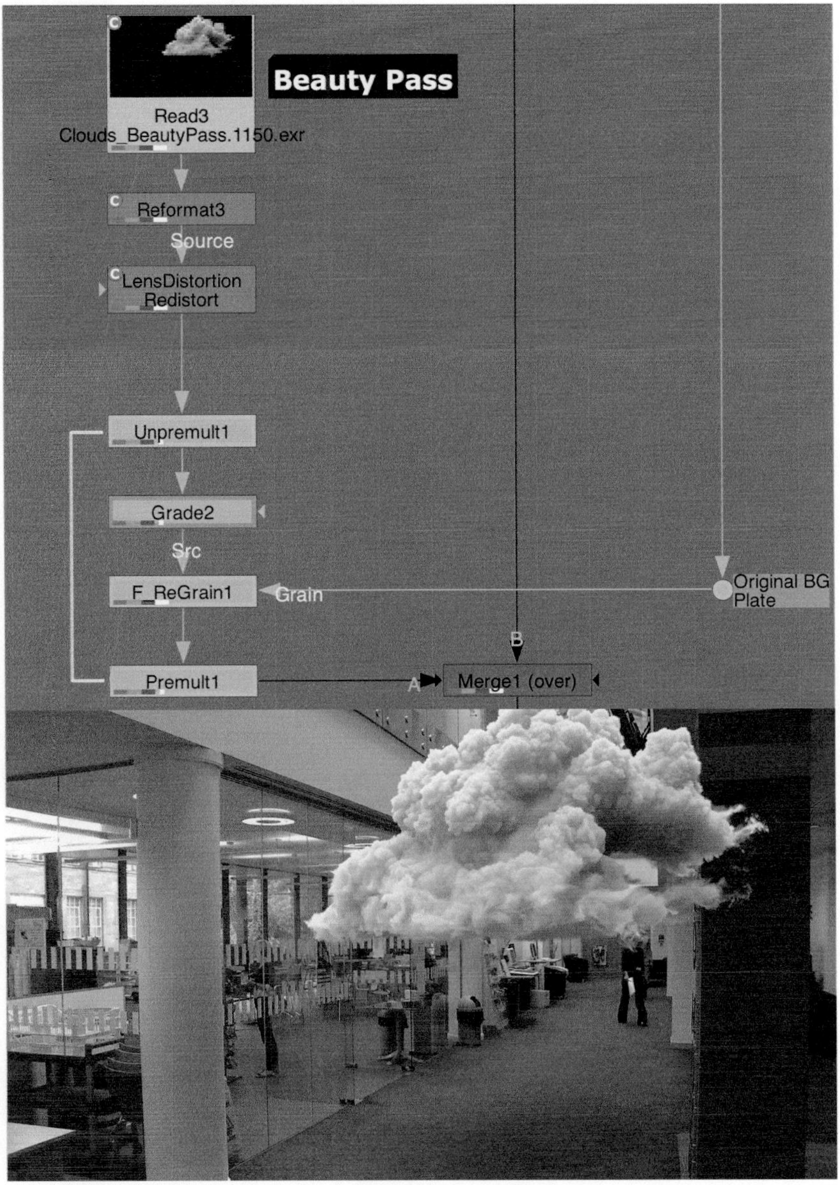

FIGURE 5.64 Node connections for CG cloud integration with the original background plate

Note

The Unpremult and Premult nodes highlighted in Figure 5.64 are critically important for handling unpremultiplied and premultiplied images in compositing. In this portion of the script, the Unpremult node must be placed before the Grade and F_ReGrain nodes, while the Premult node should be added at the end. The concepts of premultiplied and unpremultiplied images will be thoroughly explained during the demonstration of CG multi-pass compositing in Case Study 7.

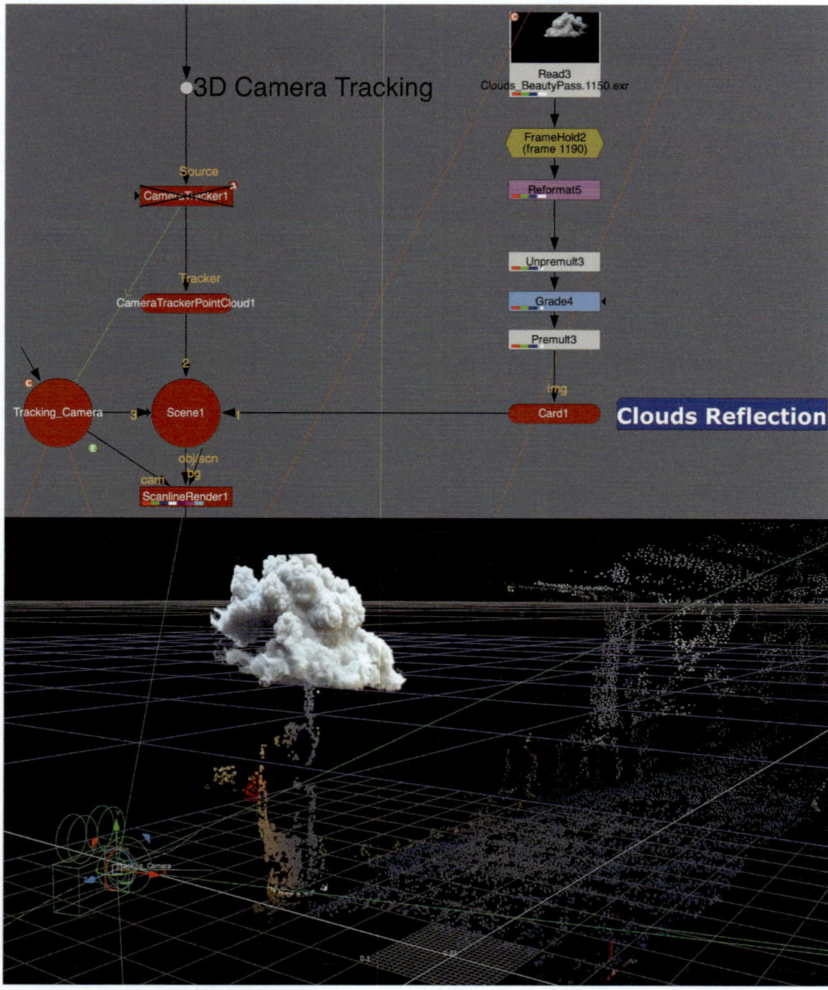

FIGURE 5.65 Projection of CG clouds in Nuke's 3D camera tracking system

③ 3D camera projection

To achieve the camera projection shown in Figure 5.65 using Nuke's 3D system, the following nodes are required:

1. Clone the Clouds_BeautyPass from the upstream of the script using the shortcut Alt (Option) + K. After cloning, an expression link will appear between the original node and the cloned node. This expression link can be temporarily hidden or shown by pressing Alt (Option) + E.
2. Connect a FrameHold node after the cloned Clouds_BeautyPass node. In the Properties panel, set the FrameHold node's frame value to 1190. This node freezes the sequence at the last frame (1190), where the full shape of the clouds is clearly visible in the scene. Since the 3D clouds do not change shape in this instance, only a single frame is needed to process the camera projection.
3. After the FrameHold node, connect a Reformat node to resize the Clouds_BeautyPass from its overscan size (2185 × 1230) to the project output format (1920 × 1080). Configure the following settings in the Properties panel of the Reformat node:

   output format: root.format 1920 × 1080

   resize type: none ☒ flop

   filter: cubic ☒ preserve bounding box

   If additional color corrections are needed for the clouds, connect a Grade node after the Reformat node. Make sure to add an Unpremult node before the Grade node and a Premult node after it, since this 3D clouds asset is a premultiplied image.
4. Position the mouse cursor in the Node Graph panel and press the Tab key to search for the node named "Card [Geometry]" in the search bar. This will create a Card node.

   Connect the Card node after the Premult node. The Card node allows the clouds to be mapped onto it, enabling you to reposition the image within Nuke's 3D space.
5. To access Nuke's 3D system, place the mouse cursor in the Viewer1 panel and press the Tab key. From there, you can adjust the position of the Card in 3D space. For example, in this case, the Card is positioned behind the pillar on the left side of the foreground.

6. Connect the Card node to the Scene1 node of the 3D camera tracking group, which was created and copied from Part 1, to reproject the Card (with the clouds mapped onto it) using the virtual camera (Tracking_Camera) extracted from the original background plate.
7. Before integrating the reprojected 3D clouds with the background plate, it is imported to restore the original lens distortion information. Apply a Lens Distortion (Redistort) node to the projected 3D clouds, as shown in Figure 5.66. The resulting image after the projection can be seen in the bottom image.

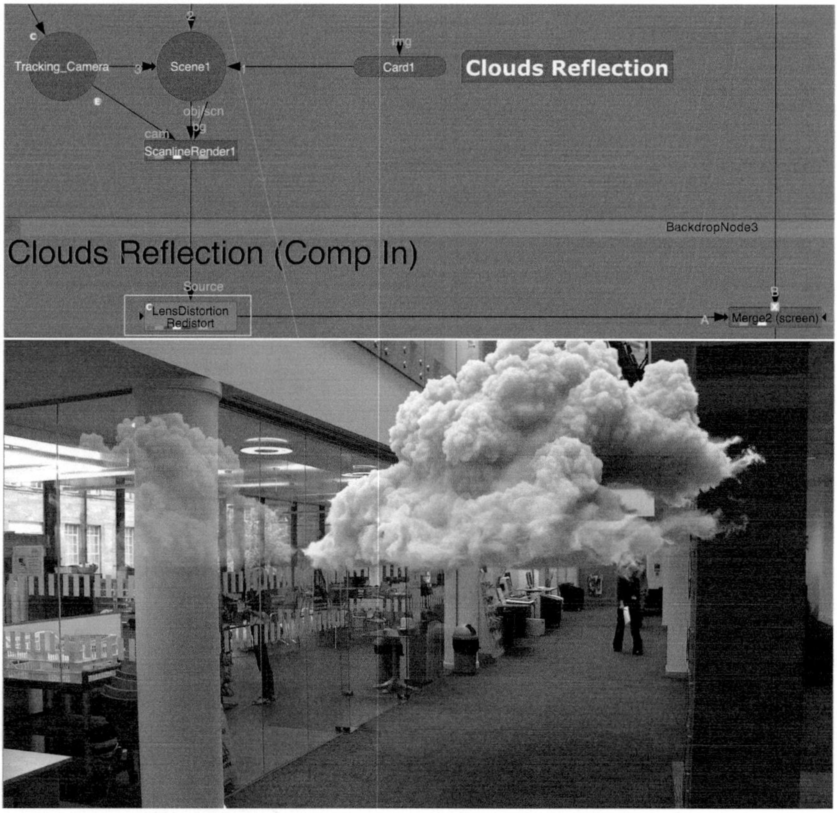

FIGURE 5.66 Initial result of the 3D clouds after camera projection

Note

The 3D virtual camera (Tracking_Camera) does not contain embedded lens distortion information because the original distortion was removed from the background plate before the 3D camera tracking process. As a result, the original lens distortion must be reapplied to the 3D clouds after camera reprojection.

④ Creating a matte for the pillar on the left

After camera projection, it becomes evident that the reprojected 3D clouds overlap with the pillar on the left (see Figure 5.66). However, the reflection of the clouds on the glass door should clearly appear behind the pillar.

To resolve this issue, a carefully created matte for the left pillar is needed. This premultiplied pillar can then be merged back over the original plate to cover the problematic area. Although traditional rotoscoping could be used to create the matte, in this example, Nuke's 3D camera tracking system provides accurate mattes for the foreground pillars.

Figure 5.67 illustrates the node connections used to project the left pillar for matte creation via the camera tracking system. The Left_Pillar node is a 3D cylinder generated in NukeX, serving as a test object for assessing the camera tracking accuracy within the scene. This 3D pillar generates a matte through camera reprojection, which can be used as the required matte for the pillar.

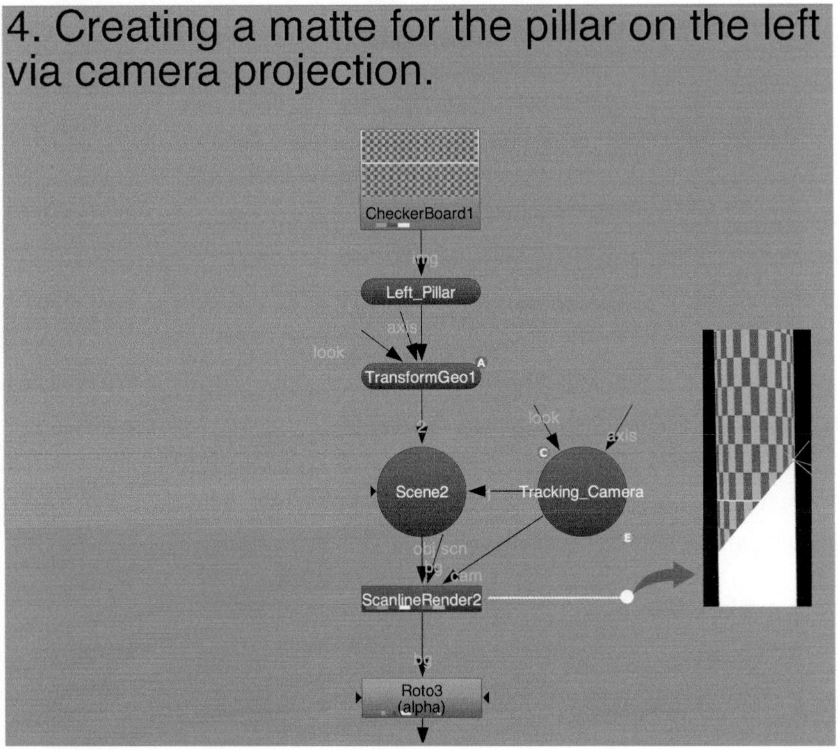

FIGURE 5.67 The required matte for the pillar on the left is created using camera projection

⑤ Creating a matte for the pillar on the right

The same approach is used to create a matte for the foreground pillar on the right using camera projection. Figure 5.68 shows the camera projection setup for the foreground pillars using the NukeX 3D system.

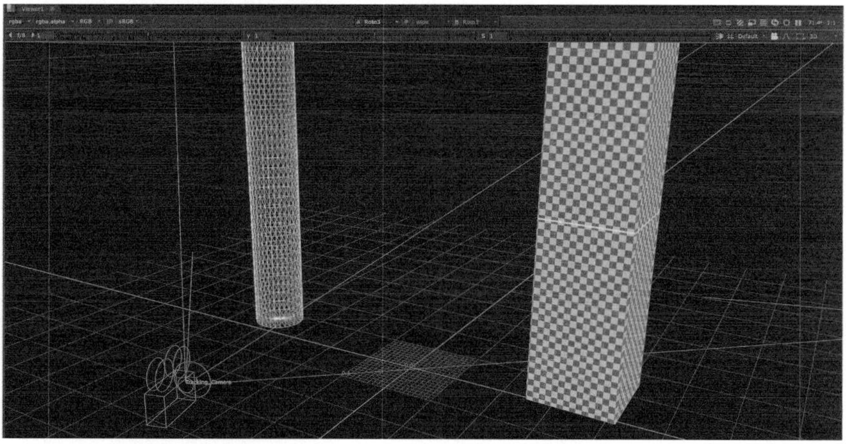

FIGURE 5.68 Camera projection of the foreground pillars

After projecting the 3D models of both foreground pillars using the 3D camera projection system, their outputs are combined into a single 2D matte. Figure 5.69 shows the node connections for combining both camera projections. In this part of the script, a ChannelMerge node is used to combine the mattes of the projected pillars. Following this, a LensDistortion node is connected to apply the original camera lens distortion to the combined matte. The matte is then copied onto the original plate using a Copy node. Finally, a Premult node is used to generate a premultiplied image of the foreground pillars before integrating them with the original background plate. Figure 5.70 shows the final premultiplied foreground pillars before they are merged with the original background plate.

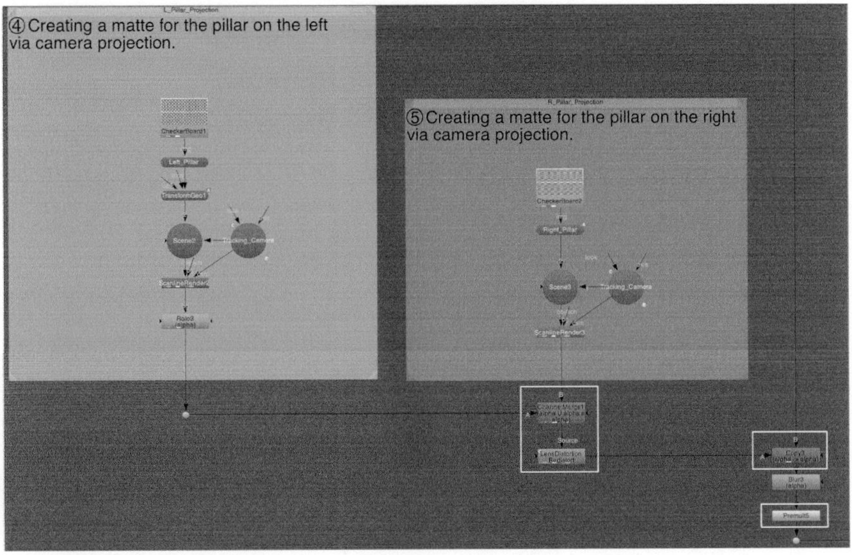

FIGURE 5.69 Node connections for combining both camera projections of the foreground pillars

FIGURE 5.70 Final premultiplied foreground pillars, created using camera projections with lens distortion applied

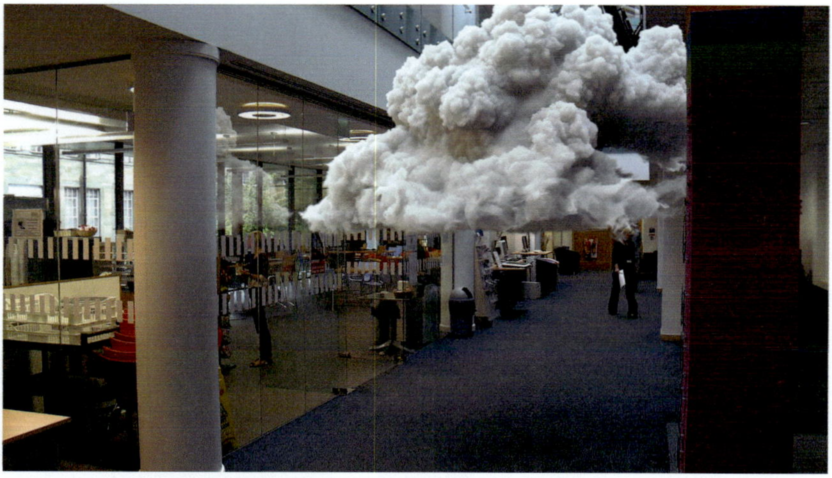

FIGURE 5.71 Final composition of Case Study 3

Despite the small scale of the project, we demonstrated a relatively complete workflow concept between 2D and 3D processes across two major professional applications. This included tasks such as removing lens distortion, creating roto shapes for 3D camera tracking, and testing a variety of 3D assets during camera tracking in NukeX. Additionally, we performed matchmoving and developed a simple 3D environment for HDR image lighting in Autodesk Maya. Finally, we fine-tuned compositing details using the camera projection system in NukeX to seamlessly integrate a group of CG clouds into the original live-action footage.

This project emphasized the importance of on-site filming and data collection, both of which are crucial and can directly impact the final quality of visual effects projects.

Case Study 4

Sky replacement

Key learning points:

> Preparing assets for compositing.

> Understanding the challenges and techniques involved in keying the sky.

> Replacing the sky using camera projection.

> Adding a pothole-damaged road surface to the scene.

Notes

Each case study includes a pre-recorded video tutorial. Watching these videos alongside reading the case studies is strongly recommended to ensure a smooth and comprehensive learning experience for each hands-on project.

Video link: youtube.com/@InvisibleFilmVFX

Video title: Case Study 4 | Sky Replacement

Project file: Case_Study_4_Project_File

The project file is available for download on the book's official webpage.

High-resolution color figures from this project are also available for download on the book's official webpage.

As the projects progress to more advanced stages, we will place greater emphasis on understanding the concepts and workflows of each topic. For more detailed operational demonstrations and instructions, please refer to the accompanying video tutorials.

Thanks to Fxphd (www.fxphd.com) for providing the original background footage shown in Figure 5.72. Please note that the footage used in this project is not available for download. However, the compositing script used in the project is available for download for educational purposes.

• Creative brief and shot analysis

◦ Creative brief

In visual effects production, sky replacement is a common technique used when the original sky is unappealing or does not align with the narrative of the project. In Case Study 4, we aim to demonstrate this process by replacing the sky in the original background plate shown in Figure 5.72.

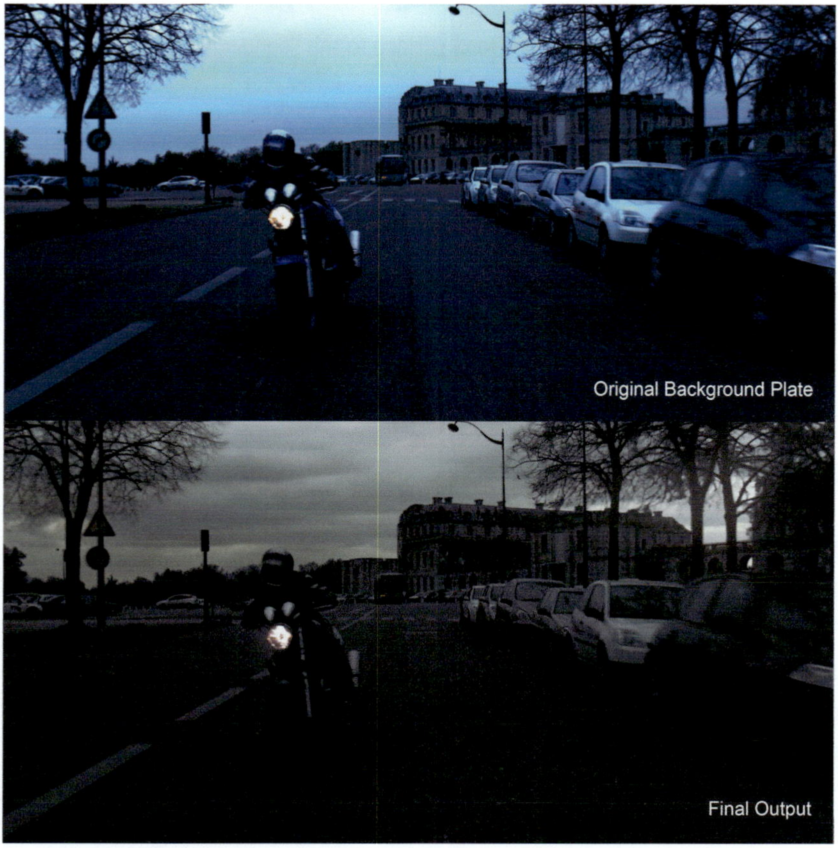

FIGURE 5.72 Comparison between the original background plate and the final visual effects output in Case Study 4. Original background image © Fxphd

o Shot analysis

– *Background plates*

Frame range: 2307–2456 frames.

Image aspect ratio: 1280 × 640

Frame rate: 24 fps

Image bit depth: 10-bit DPX (Digital Picture Exchange)

Required sky replacement image: Not provided

– *Camera information*

Camera model, lens, etc.: Unknown

Lens grid: No lens grids were provided

Camera movement: Tracking shot

o Purpose of this case study

The on-set information provided for this shot is not ideal for a typical production-level project. However, it serves as a practical example of how a VFX shot can be professionally completed with limited on-set data, particularly in low-budget productions or student projects that lack VFX team support during filming.

• Nuke script analysis

The Nuke script in this project consists of five major sections:

- Section ①: Asset preparations
- Section ②: Compositing starts
- Section ③: Creating mattes
- Section ④: Fixing reflections of the original sky on the car roof and motorcycle helmet
- Section ⑤: Adding light wrap and projecting the damaged road surface

Figure 5.73 shows the script layout in Case Study 4. It features two types of connection links between nodes: green lines indicate linked nodes, while brown lines represent cloned nodes.

To temporarily toggle these connection lines on or off, press Alt/Option + E.

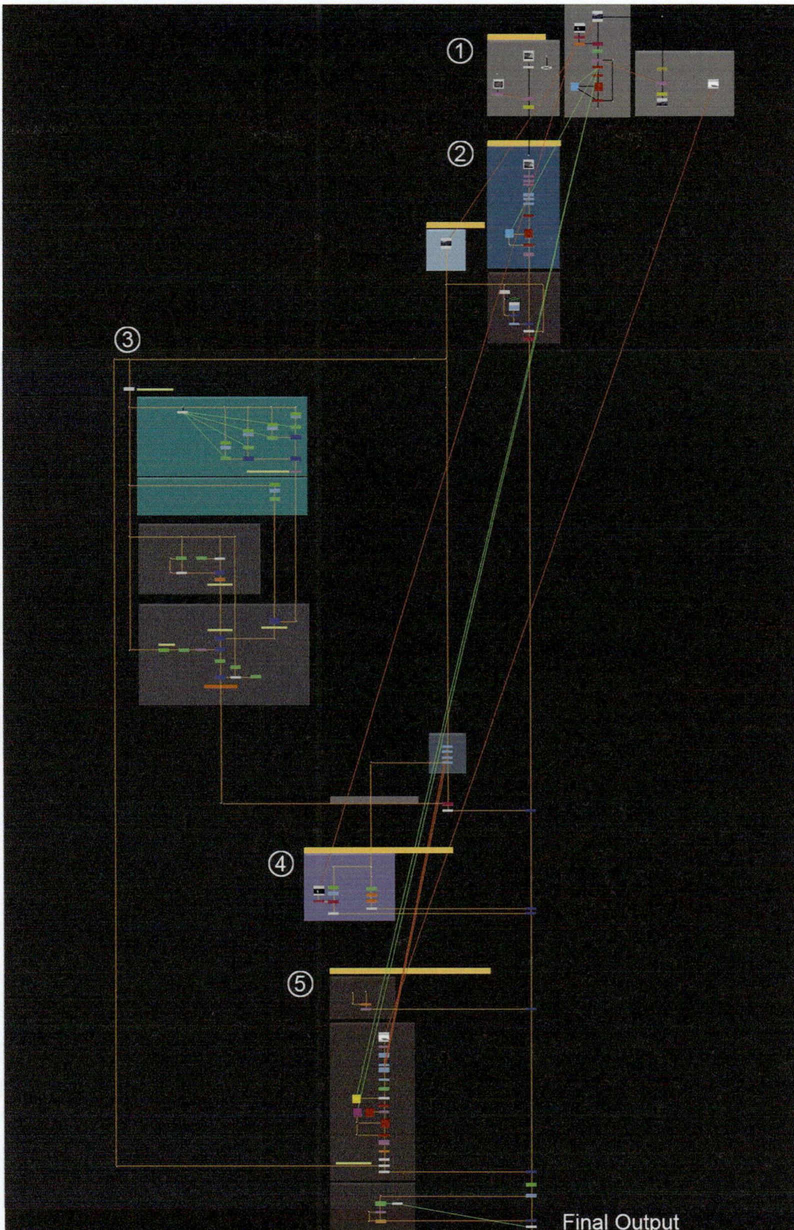

FIGURE 5.73 The overall layout of the Nuke script in Case Study 4

o Section ①: Asset preparations

Before beginning any compositing tasks, a series of essential asset preparations and setups must be completed to ensure production efficiency. These include templates for CG multi-pass renders, screen keying processes, rotoscoping, and other preparatory tasks. While asset preparation in this project is not as complex as in full-scale production environments, understanding the key steps for preparing assets for downstream compositing remains crucial.

Figure 5.74 presents four subsections (1.1 to 1.4) that outline the necessary preparations prior to compositing in Case Study 4.

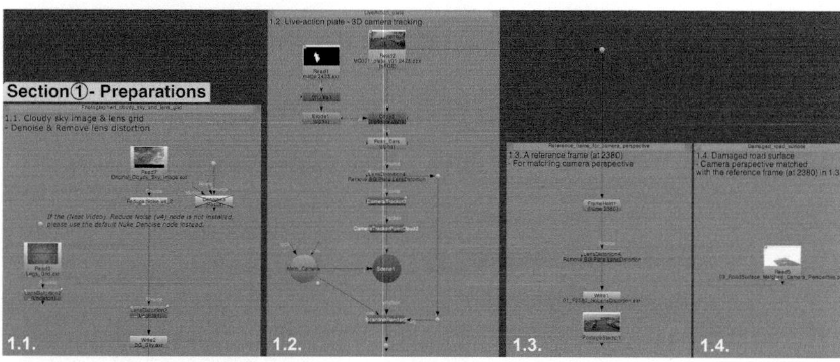

FIGURE 5.74 Asset preparations for compositing in section 1

- *Capture a cloudy sky image and lens grid*

A still image of a cloudy sky with a resolution of 6K (6000 × 4000) was captured, taking into account the camera perspective of the original live-action footage. Additionally, a separate still image of a lens grid was captured. Both the sky image and the lens grid were taken using the same camera body, lens, and focal length settings. Figure 5.75 shows the captured images of the cloudy sky and the lens grid.

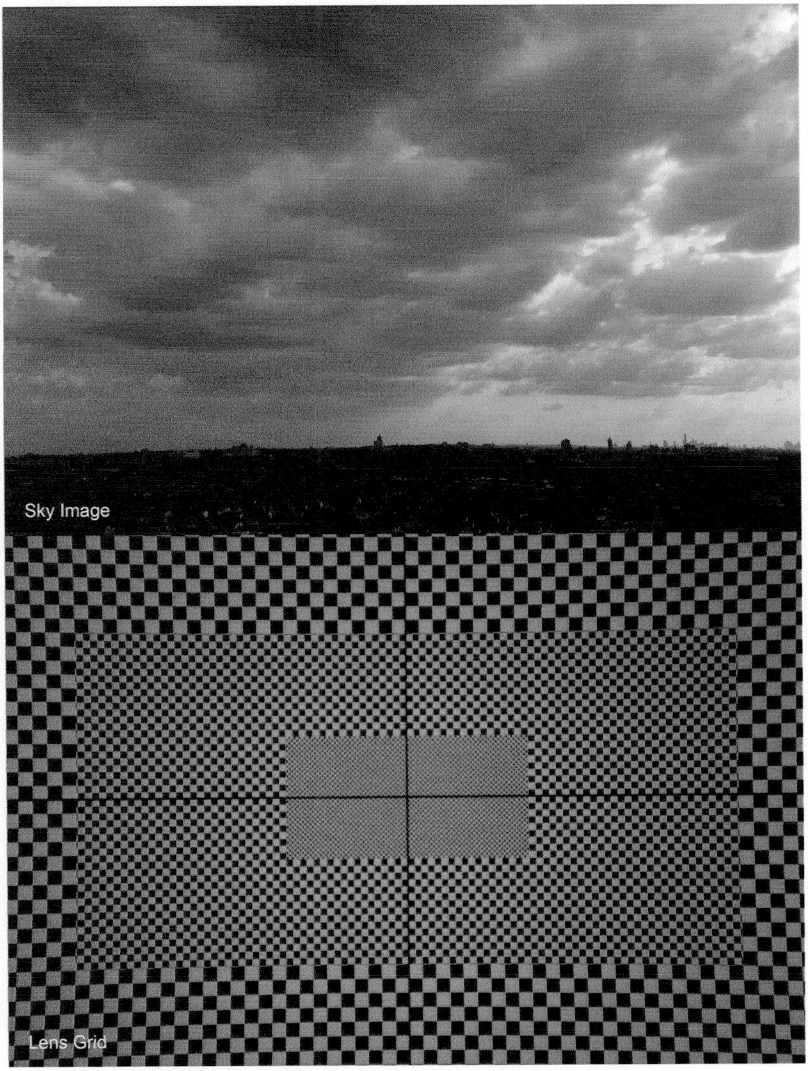

FIGURE 5.75 Both plates were captured using the same camera, lens, and settings

Note

By analyzing the shot, we determined that the clouds in the replaced sky do not require significant movement or shape changes. Therefore, a still image is sufficient for replacing the sky in the original live-action footage. This new sky image will be reprojected using a virtual camera that has been accurately extracted from the original footage. Additionally, the camera model, lens, and focal length settings must remain consistent between the new sky image and the lens grid used during image capture.

Data information of the captured still images:

– *Cloudy sky*

Still image
Image format & color space: OpenEXR in linear sRGB color space
Image bit depth: 16-bit
Image aspect ratio: 6000 × 4000
Focal length: 23 mm (Fujifilm prime lens)
Camera model: Fujifilm X100F

– *Lens grid*

Still image
Color space: sRGB
Image bit depth: 8-bit image
Image aspect ratio: 6000 × 4000
Focal length: 23 mm (Fujifilm prime lens)
Camera model: Fujifilm X100F

Notes

1. Preferably, these images should be captured using full-frame cameras and lenses. However, understanding that many learners may not have access to such equipment, both images were taken using an APS-C camera and a standard prime lens.
2. It is essential to remove any existing film grain and lens distortion data from all assets before compositing. Failure to do so may result in a final composition with mismatched grain and distortion artifacts from different sources. To avoid this, film grain and lens distortion must be removed from the original assets prior to any VFX operations. Later, the same film grain and distortion characteristics extracted from the original live-action footage

should be reapplied to the processed assets before their final integration. This ensures visual consistency between the assets and the live-action footage in the final composition.

Figure 5.76 illustrates the process of removing lens distortion from a captured sky image.

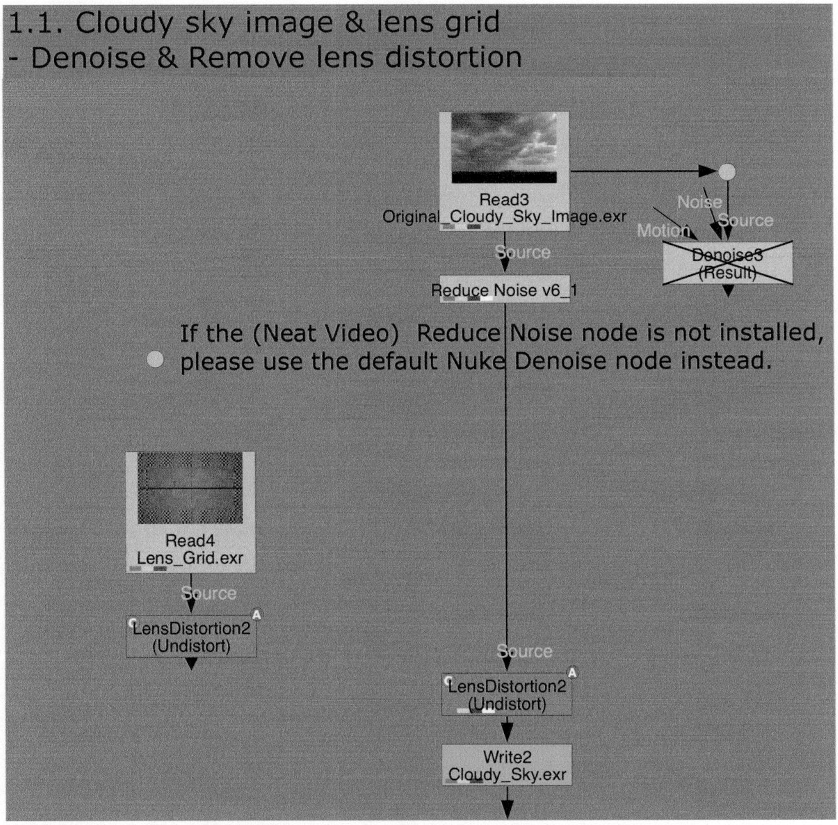

FIGURE 5.76 Node connections for removing film grain and lens distortion

To achieve high-end visual effects shots, studios often use a combination of in-house tools and third-party plug-ins for specific tasks such as denoising. In Figure 5.76, a third-party noise reduction plug-in called Neat Video: Reduce Noise is used to remove film grain from the captured sky image. If this node is not available to you, use the default Denoise node in NukeX instead.

To remove lens distortion from the cloudy sky image shown in Figure 5.76, follow these steps:

Step 1 | Position the mouse cursor in the Node Graph panel, then press the R key to import the following images:

Original_Cloudy_Sky_Image.exr

LensGrid.exr

(Both files are located in the Case_Study_4_Project_File > 4_02_Footage_and_Assets > Photographed_Images folder.)

Step 2 | NukeX provides two nodes for removing lens distortion: a legacy node (LensDistortion [L]) and an updated node (LensDistortion [Transform]). In Case Study 3, we introduced how to activate Nuke's legacy nodes. However, in Case Study 4, we used the LensDistortion [Transform] node to remove lens distortion from the photographed lens grid and cloudy sky images.

To remove lens distortion from the lens grid, follow these steps:

a. In the Node Graph, select the LensGrid.exr node and press the Tab key to open Nuke's search bar. Type LensDistortion [Transform] and press Enter. This adds a LensDistortion node connected to the LensGrid.exr node.
b. Double-click the LensDistortion node to display its parameters in the Properties panel. Navigate to the Analysis tab. In the Grid Detect section, click the Detect button. In the Editing and Drawing section, click the Solve button.
c. In the Overlay section, select None from the dropdown menu.

At this point, lens distortion has been removed from the photographed lens grid.

Step 3 | After removing lens distortion from the LensGrid.exr file, clone the LensDistortion node (using Alt/Option + K) and connect the cloned node after the Reduce Noise v4 (or Denoise) node. This step removes lens distortion from the photographed cloudy sky image. The node connections for these operations are illustrated in Figure 5.76.

Step 4 | Connect a Write node to export the cloudy sky image, ensuring that the original film grain and lens distortion have been removed. Exporting at this stage is beneficial because the Reduce Noise (or Denoise) node performs intensive calculations that can significantly slow down Nuke scripts.

Exporting this segment as a 16-bit OpenEXR sequence and re-importing it into NukeX can improve processing speed for downstream operations.

– *Live-action plate: 3D camera tracking*

The main goal of this section is to accurately extract a virtual camera from the live-action plate. Once this virtual camera is obtained, prepared assets can be reprojected into the scene using Nuke's 3D camera system.

As discussed in previous case studies, any moving elements in the shot must be masked out. Additionally, lens distortion should be removed from the original plate before performing scene tracking. Upon analyzing the shot, we can identify several moving elements, including cars in both the foreground and background, as well as the primary subject – a motorcyclist. In this case, a precise matte of the motorcyclist has been provided separately. This matte can be copied into the alpha channel of the original live-action plate to mask out the motorcyclist, preventing him from being included in the camera tracking. The node connections for this operation are as follows:

Step 1 | Position the mouse cursor in the Node Graph panel, then press the R key to open the Read File(s) dialog window. Import the matte file located in the Case_Study_4_Project_File > 4_02_Footage_and_Assets > Motorcycle_Matte folder.

Step 2 | Once the matte is imported, load the image into the Viewer1 panel by pressing any numeric key on the keyboard. Then, press the letters R, G, B, and A to view each channel individually (make sure your mouse cursor is positioned within the Viewer1 panel).

You will notice that the matte is stored in the R, G, and B channels, but not in the alpha channel.

Step 3 | Select the imported matte file. To transfer the matte to the alpha channel, press the Tab key and type Shuffle [Channel] to create a Shuffle node. In the Properties panel of the Shuffle node, connect rgba.red from the Input Layer section to rgba.alpha in the Output Layer section.

Step 4 | Press the Tab key again and search for Erode (blur) in the search bar. This will bring up an Erode node. Connect the Erode node after the Shuffle node. The Erode node extends the outer edge of the matte, slightly enlarging it beyond its original size. This enlarged matte masks out the moving motorcyclist in the scene, preventing them from being tracked during 3D camera tracking.

Step 5 | Once the enlarged matte for the motorcyclist is created, copy it to the alpha channel of the original live-action plate using a Copy node. Set the Properties panel of the Copy node as follows:

Copy channel: rgba.alpha to rgba.alpha

Step 6 | We also need to create several rough roto shapes and animate them to cover the moving cars in both the foreground and background. To do this, press the O key to bring up a Roto node and connect it after the Copy node. Use the B-Spline tool provided in the Roto node to draw a few roto shapes that cover the moving elements in the shot. Figure 5.77 shows how the Copy node and the Roto node (renamed Roto_Cars) are connected, along with their respective results.

Step 7 | Connect a legacy LensDistortion node after the Roto_Cars node to remove lens distortion from the original live-action plate. Activation and usage of the legacy LensDistortion node were introduced in Case Study 3, where it was used to remove lens distortion from the foreground pillars in the original live-action footage. Please refer to Case Study 3 for details on how to activate and use the node.

Notes

1. When creating roto shapes for 3D camera tracking, it is important to remember that they do not need to match object shapes precisely at the pixel level. However, the shapes should not be too loose either. Overly large or rough roto shapes may result in the loss of valuable tracking features during 3D camera tracking.
2. The lens grid for the live-action plate has not been provided for this project. Given the presence of elements such as traffic lights, buildings, and road surface markings in the scene, these features can be used as references for removing lens distortion due to their straight structures. It is important to note, however, that the results obtained using these features may not be as accurate as those derived from a properly filmed lens grid.

After completing these preparations, it is time to proceed with the 3D camera tracking task. The basic concept of 3D camera tracking was introduced in previous case studies.

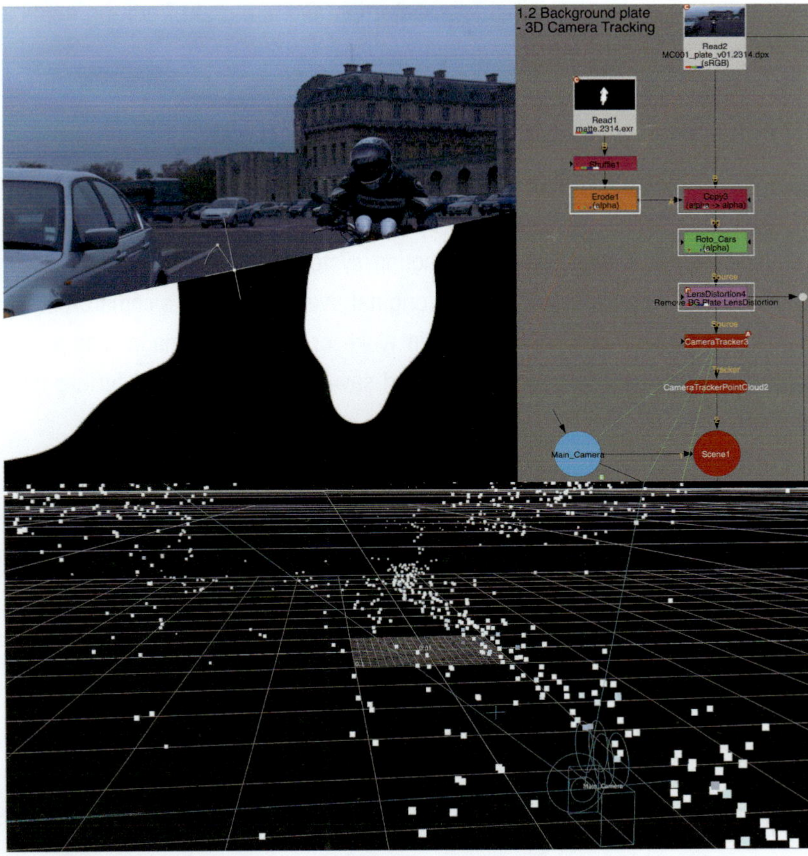

FIGURE 5.77 Node connections and roto shapes (top images) created to generate moving elements, along with the results of 3D camera tracking (bottom image)

– *Extracting a still reference image to match the camera perspective*

According to the narrative of this shot, the motorcyclist appears to swerve to avoid an obstacle on the road around frame 2380. To enhance the visual storytelling and intensify the interaction with the motorcyclist, a potholed road surface is added to the scene. Figure 5.78 (1.3) shows a FrameHold node connected to the original live-action plate, followed by a LensDistortion node. The FrameHold node extracts a still image from frame 2380 of the original background plate, serving as a reference for matching the camera's perspective. The LensDistortion and Denoise nodes are then used to remove original lens distortion and film grain from the extracted still image.

– *The damaged road surface*

The image of the damaged road was captured from a top-down view, manipulated to match the camera perspective of the original live-action plate before being reprojected using Nuke's camera projection system. Figure 5.78 (1.4) shows the damaged road image aligned with the original live-action plate's camera perspective. This alignment can be achieved in Nuke or any other image manipulation application, such as Adobe Photoshop, and saved as a PSD file for further use in compositing.

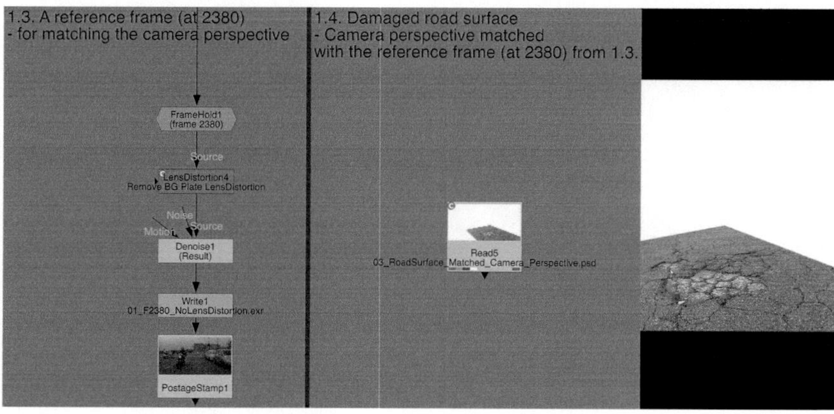

FIGURE 5.78 Result of aligning the damaged road image (1.4) with the camera perspective of the original footage

◦ Section ②: Compositing starts

Integrating assets, including CG and live-action components, into a shot should begin with background elements, then move to the middle ground, and finally to the foreground. In this instance, the key background element is the sky. The buildings and trees are in the middle ground, while the foreground features a motorcyclist and a couple of moving cars.

a. Sky reprojection

In subsection 2.1 (Figure 5.79), the cloudy sky image has its original film grain and lens distortion removed. After this image, three nodes are connected: Reformat1, Transform1, and Transform2. The Reformat1 node is used to scale down the cloudy sky image from its original aspect ratio (6000 × 4000) to match the size of the original background plate (1280 × 640), which also serves as the project format size for Case Study 4. The Transform1 node scales up the sky image to remove the black bars introduced by lens distortion removal around the edges of the cloudy sky. The Transform2 node adds subtle animation to the top area of the image, making the clouds slowly drift from left to right, bringing some movement to this still image. For detailed settings and operational demonstrations of these nodes, please refer to the prerecorded video for Case Study 4.

After the previous nodes, three Grade nodes (Grade1, Grade2, and Grade3) are connected in sequence to color grade the sky image, aligning it with the color-corrected original live-action footage. Grade1 adjusts the white and black points, while Grade2 and Grade3 apply additional color fine-tuning. Finally, the color-graded cloudy sky image is mapped onto a 3D Card node in preparation for camera reprojection.

The camera reprojection rig for the cloudy image consists of four individual nodes: Card1, Copied_Main_Camera_1, Scene, and ScanlineRender. The Copied_Main_Camera_1 node (highlighted in blue) is a duplicate of the 3D camera that was tracked from the live-action footage, as demonstrated in Subsection 1.2.

Note

After mapping the cloudy sky image onto the Card node, place the mouse cursor in the Viewer1 panel and press the Tab key to switch to Nuke's 3D system. You'll notice that the 3D card is initially positioned at the origin of Nuke's grid. Press W to enable the move tool, then drag the card along the Z-axis, pushing it deeper into 3D space to ensure it does not overlap with the projection camera.

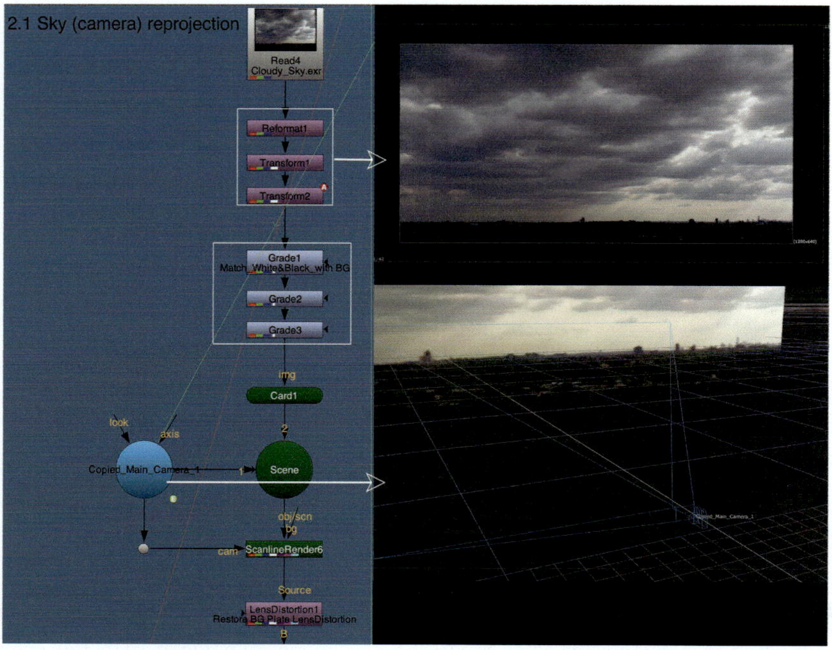

FIGURE 5.79 Node connections for sky reprojection in Nuke's 3D space

The final node in the 2.1 Sky Reprojection section is a legacy LensDistortion node, originally used to remove lens distortion from the live-action footage. In this context, however, its purpose is to reapply the original lens distortion to the reprojected cloudy sky image. To achieve this, simply untick the Undistort checkbox in the LensDistortion tab of the node's Properties panel.

b. Additive keyer

The additive keyer is not typically used to key a plate directly. Instead, its primary function is to blend two images using mathematical operations, helping to preserve fine foreground details within the final composition. For example, in this project, initial keyers in NukeX are used to extract mattes of trees, buildings, and other elements from the background plate. However, this process can miss fine details, such as small tree branches. To recover these lost fine details, the original live-action plate can be directly blended with the projected sky image using an additive keyer. This blended result is then merged beneath the keyed output from the live-action plate, restoring the missing foreground details, especially those semi-transparent fine details in the final composition.

The additive keyer consists of a set of Nuke nodes that perform a series of operations. These nodes can be combined into a gizmo file with multiple inputs, such as FG (foreground), BG (background), and FG clean plate. For detailed information on the node operations associated with the additive keyer, please refer to the green screen keying demonstration in Case Study 5: Additive keyer.

Figure 5.80 displays a set of nodes within the additive keyer gizmo file and shows the final blended result of the live-action footage with the reprojected sky image.

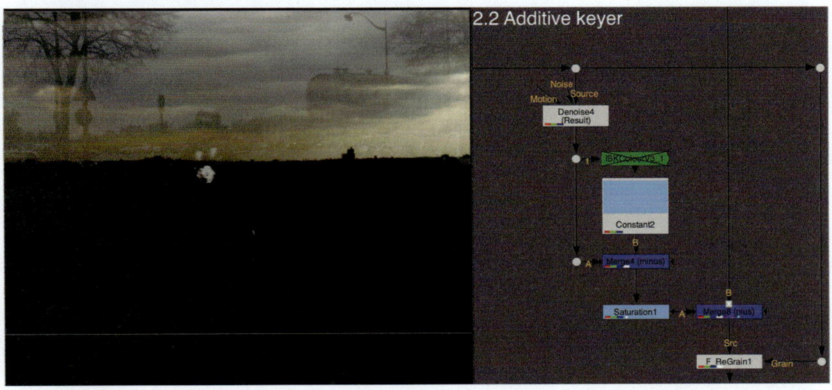

FIGURE 5.80 A set of simplified nodes (right image) within the additive keyer gizmo file and the final blended result (left image)

○ Section ③: Creating mattes

The main objective of this section is to create mattes for trees and buildings, which are essential for effectively generating a sky replacement matte in the shot.

– *The original live-action plate*

The original live-action background plate is provided in 10-bit DPX format. When viewing 10-bit (or higher bit-depth) images on 8-bit monitors without dedicated LUTs, highlights may not display accurately due to the limited color depth of the display.

In this example, to accurately view the background plate using the default sRGB LUT in the Viewer1 panel, follow these steps:

First, import the original live-action plate and double-click the node to display its parameters in the Properties panel. Then, change the Input Transform setting from the default Cineon to sRGB. Figure 5.81 shows a comparison between two 10-bit DPX images processed using different color spaces. The top image uses the default Cineon color space, whereas the bottom one is in the sRGB color space.

Note

It is important to note that converting Input Transform color spaces will alter the original color space of the image. In a production environment, modifying client content requires strict authorization. However, for demonstration purposes in this example, we converted its color space from Cineon to sRGB to ensure it displays correctly in the Viewer1 panel, which uses the default sRGB color space, without requiring a custom LUT.

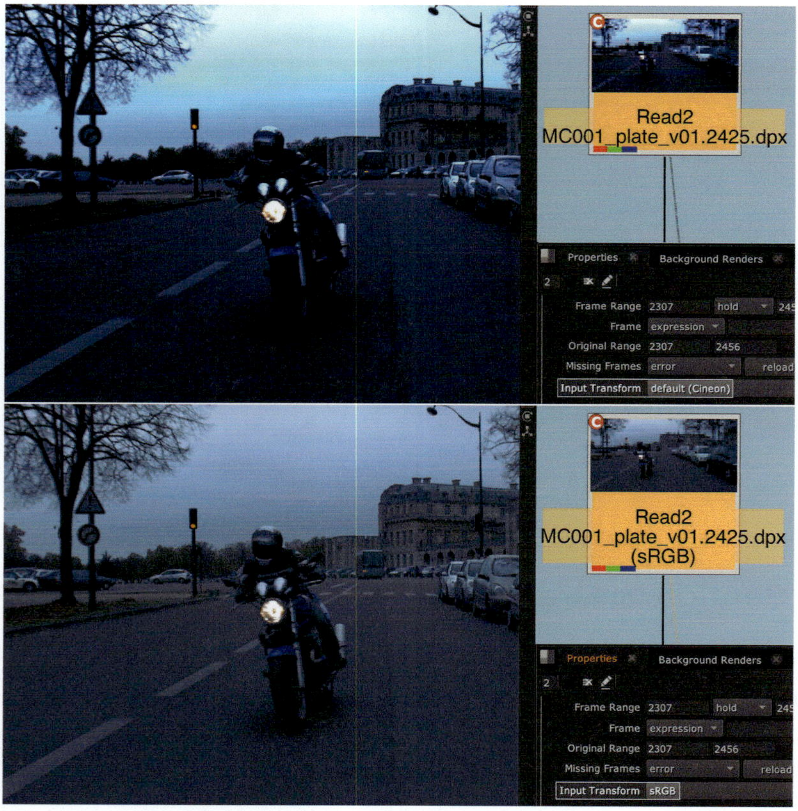

FIGURE 5.81 The same DPX-format images displayed with different color spaces in the Viewer1 panel

– *Creating mattes for the trees on the left side of the road*

A simple keying technique will be demonstrated to generate mattes for the treetops on the left side of the road. However, before proceeding with these keying tasks, it is important to address the following issues:

Issue 1:

The uneven luminance of the sky from top to bottom.

Potential solution:

Uniform lighting lit on screens is crucial for effective keying. However, in practice, the sky's natural luminance is unevenly distributed. For instance, the upper regions of the sky typically vary in brightness compared to areas near the horizon. As a result, keying should be adjusted regionally to account for differences across various parts of the trees. To produce a high-quality matte under such conditions, it is important to generate separate mattes for different parts of the sky and trees. These individual mattes can then be composited into a single, unified matte.

Additionally, if the footage is grainy, film grain should be removed prior to keying and tracking, as it can negatively impact the accuracy and overall quality of both processes.

Issue 2:

Since this is a tracking shot with continuous camera movement, the individual mattes separated by Roto nodes for different parts of the trees must match the camera motion.

Potential solution:

Use a 2D Tracker node to track the trees and apply the tracking data to drive the individual roto shapes that separate the mattes.

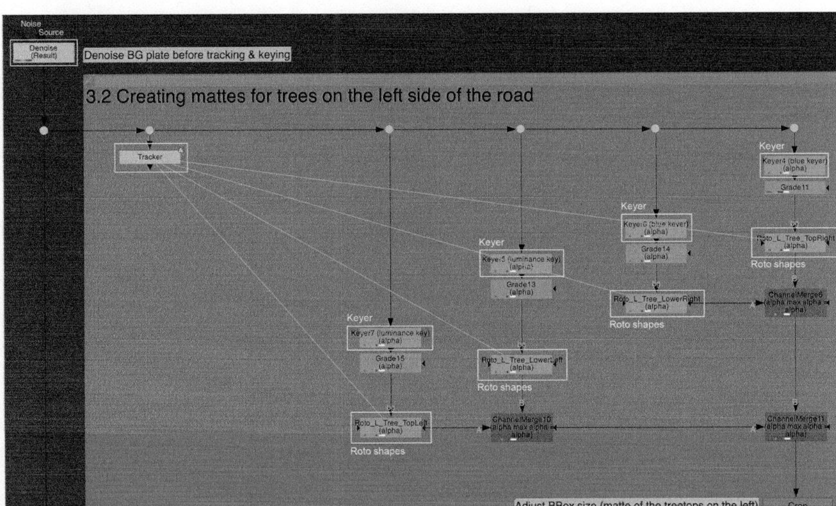

FIGURE 5.82 Node connections used to create separate mattes for different sections of the treetops on the left side of the road

In Figure 5.82, a Denoise node (located in the upper-left corner) was used to remove film grain from the original live-action background plate. A Tracker node was then employed to follow the camera's movement, which drove four Roto nodes created for the treetops. Additionally, four Keyer nodes were used separately to key the shapes isolated by these Roto nodes for the treetops. The final matte for the treetops was created by combining the individual mattes using two ChannelMerge nodes.

– *Creating mattes for the trees on the right side of the road*

Figure 5.83 shows the final mattes created for the treetops in the scene. The matte on the left consists of four individual mattes, each corresponding to different portions of the treetops. Another matte, located on the right side of the road, is generated using a Keyer node and then refined with a Grade node to enhance the contrast in its alpha channel.

To better understand the keying process demonstrated in this example, please refer to the relevant demonstrations in the pre-recorded video for Case Study 4. The video provides additional operational details on the node connections illustrated in Figures 5.82 and 5.83.

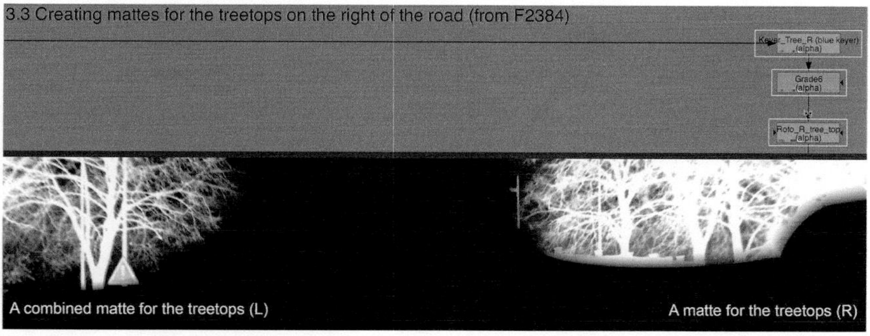

FIGURE 5.83 Mattes created for the treetops

The same keying method can be applied to create mattes for the background buildings in the scene. However, the edges of the buildings in the matte should be treated slightly differently from those of the foreground treetops, as the treetops require a soft matte to preserve the fine details of the branches.

- *Creating mattes for the buildings in the background*

Mattes for the buildings are created using two Keylight nodes. One node isolates the silhouette of the buildings and trees along the horizon. The other Keylight node generates a matte for the bridge's guardrails. These two mattes are then combined into a single composite matte, as shown in Figure 5.84.

Note

At this stage, the keying process should prioritize enhancing the details of the buildings and tree silhouettes on the horizon. Any black holes that appear in the white area of the matte can be addressed later using a garbage matte.

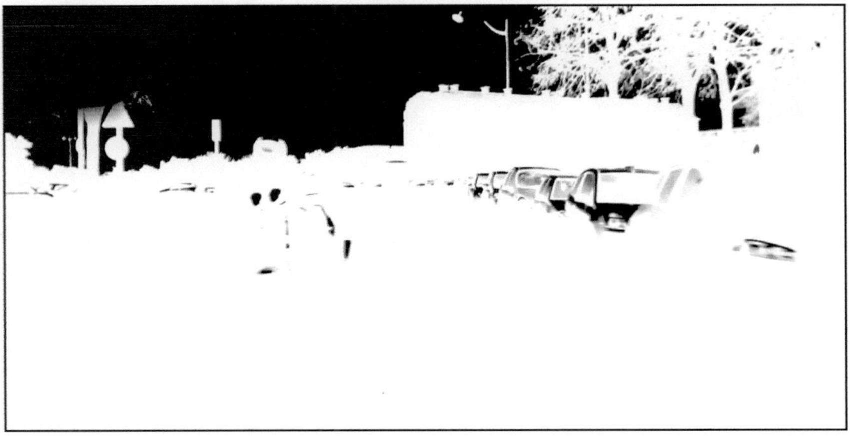

FIGURE 5.84 An initial matte was generated for the edges of the buildings and trees along the horizon

- *Combining mattes*

Once the individual mattes for the treetops and the buildings on the horizon have been created, we begin integrating them and addressing any remaining issues in the inner area of the matte. For instance, a garbage matte is used to cover black holes in regions that should be fully opaque (white). Finally, a couple of ChannelMerge nodes are used to combine all the separate mattes into a single matte.

Figure 5.85 shows the node connections used to combine the mattes for the buildings and other elements. The final combined matte for the shot is shown in the lower image.

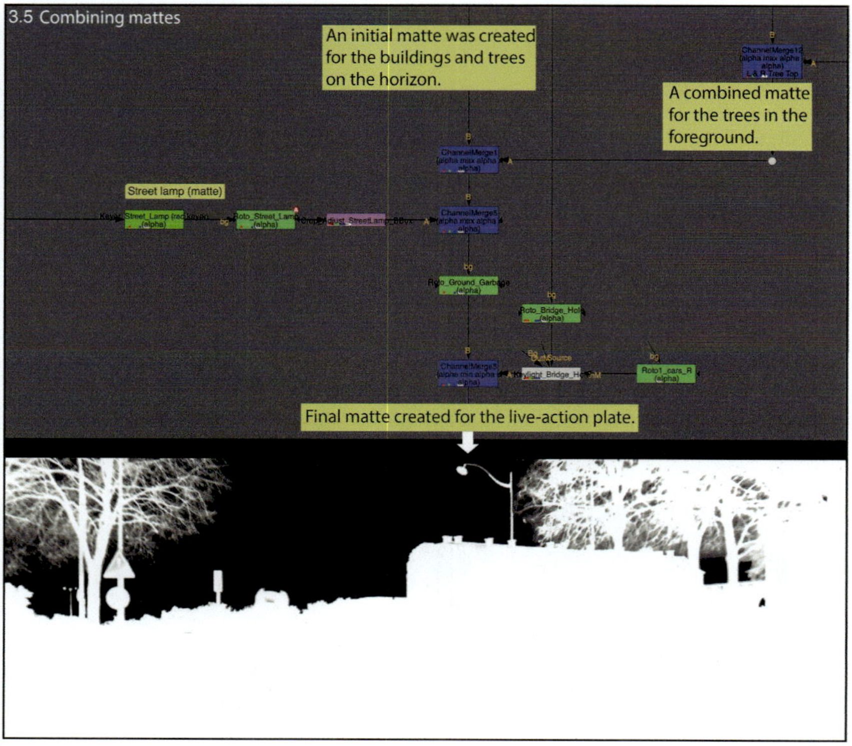

FIGURE 5.85 Node connections used to combine mattes and generate the final matte for the live-action plate

– *Applying color corrections to the live-action plate*

This subsection contains four nodes: HueCorrect1, HueCorrect2, ColorLookup1, and Grade8, which are used to color correct the original background plate. Figure 5.86 shows the node connections involved in this process and includes a before and after comparison.

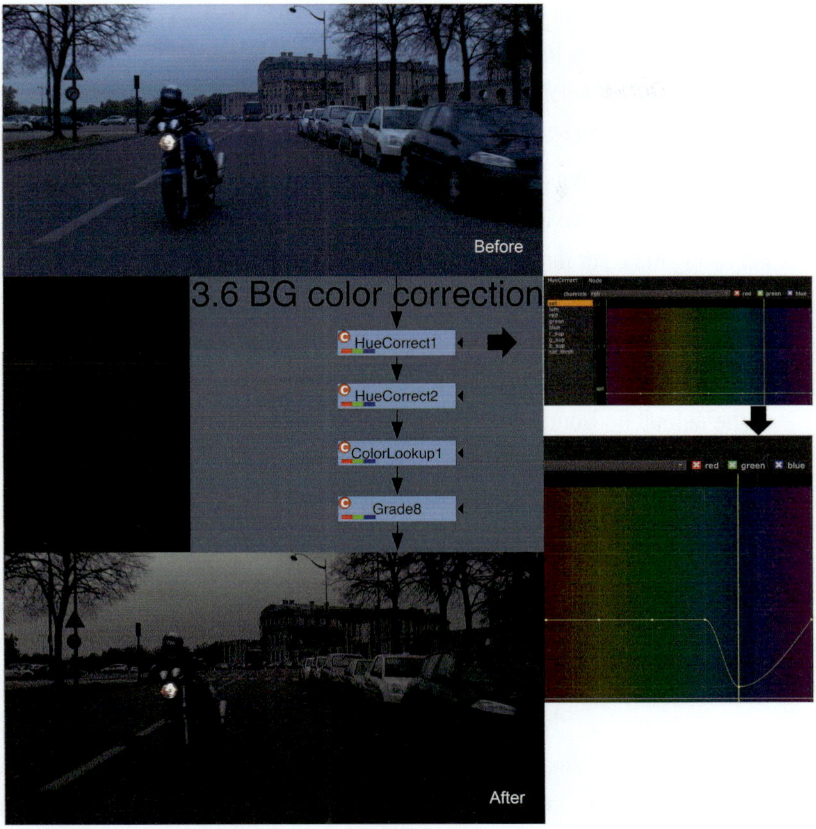

FIGURE 5.86 A comparison between the original background plate and the result after color correction

Note

Instead of using a single node, multiple nodes are employed to perform color corrections on the original live-action plate. This approach allows each node to handle a specific aspect of the color correction process. For example, if the client requests additional adjustments, it is easier to modify the results by tweaking individual nodes rather than redoing all the color operations within a single node. In this section of the script, for instance, the initial HueCorrect1 node is used to reduce the saturation of the predominant blue tones in the image.

The following steps provide a practical example of how the HueCorrect1 node operates in this section of the script.

1. Press the Tab key, type HueCorrect [Color] in the search bar, and connect this node directly to the original live-action plate.

2. With the node still selected, press any numeric key to load the plate into the Viewer1 panel. Then, in the Properties panel of the HueCorrect1 node, select "sat" from the left column. By default, this will display a horizontal line with several control points, as shown in the top image on the right side of Figure 5.86.
3. Move your mouse cursor over the image in the Viewer1 panel. A vertical yellow line will move in the color spectrum field of the Properties panel, indicating the color range corresponding to the cursor's current position in the image. In this example, the vertical yellow line likely appears in the blue range, as the image has an overall blue tone. To add a control point, press and hold Ctrl + Alt (or Option + Cmd on Mac), then click at the intersection of the default horizontal and vertical lines in the color spectrum field of the Properties panel. Once the control point is added, drag it downward to reduce the image's overall saturation. The result of this adjustment is shown in the bottom images of Figure 5.86.

After applying color corrections to the live-action plate, a Copy node is used to insert the final combined matte into the alpha channel of the color-corrected plate (as shown in the lower image of Figure 5.86). A Premult node is then placed below the Copy node to convert the plate into a premultiplied image, effectively removing the original sky area. Finally, this premultiplied background plate can be merged with the reprojected sky image, where the additive keyer is applied, using an AddMix node. Figure 5.87 illustrates the node connections used in this part of the process.

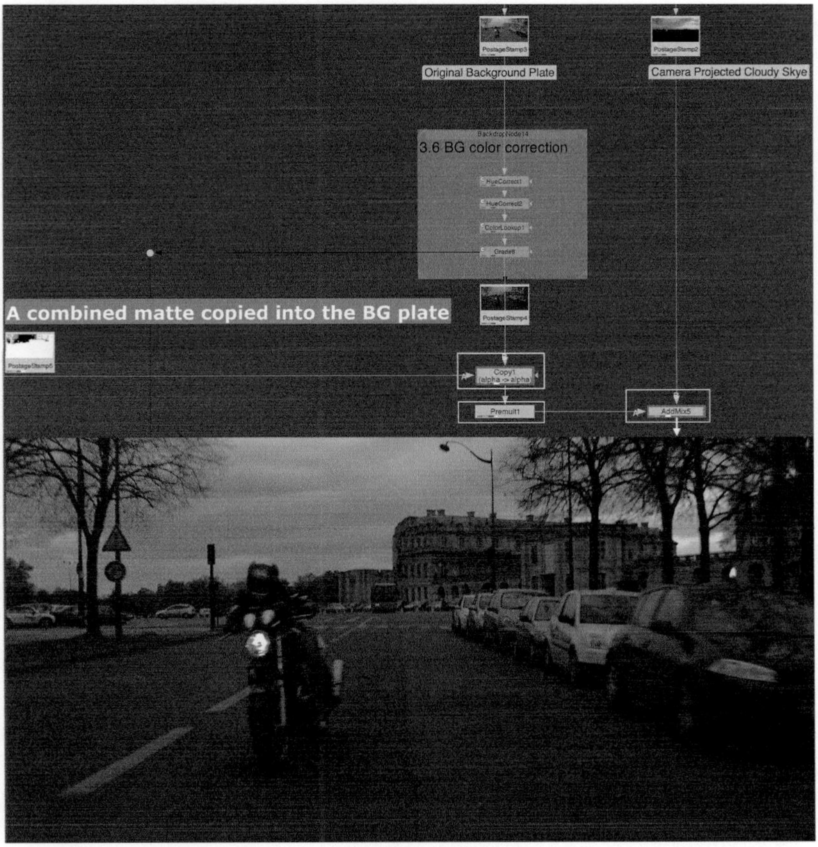

FIGURE 5.87 An initial result of integrating the reprojected sky image into the live-action plate

o Section ④: Fixing reflections of the original sky on the car roof and motorcycle helmet

– *Fixing car roof and helmet reflections*

This subsection aims to address the semi-transparent reflection issues on the car roof and the top of the motorcycle helmet. These issues result from semi-transparent mattes created during the keying of the live-action background plate. One potential solution is to reconstruct the car roof and helmet, then integrate them back into the shot to cover the affected areas. Figure 5.88 shows the node connections used to correct the reflection issues on both the car roof and the motorcycle helmet.

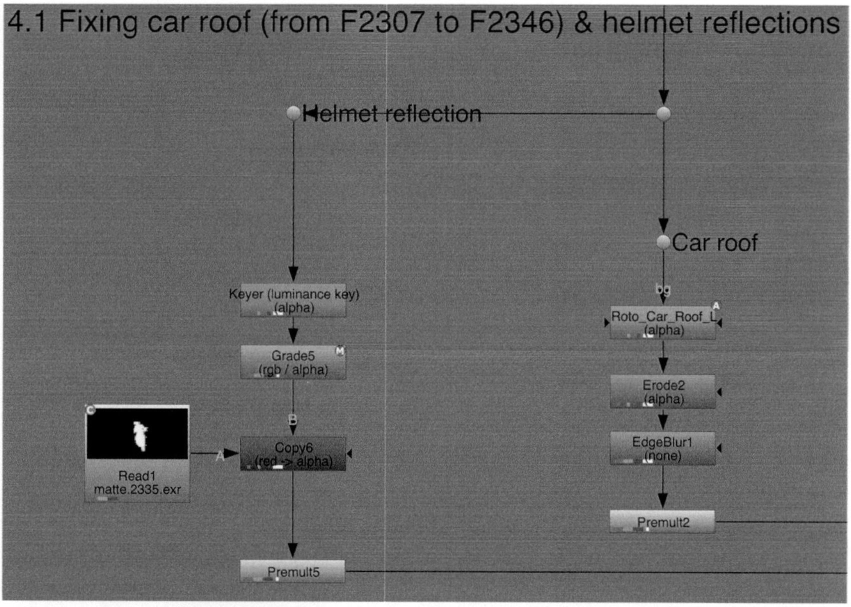

FIGURE 5.88 Node connections for fixing the car roof and helmet reflection issues

The script in this section is divided into two parts: one for recovering the car roof and the other for rebuilding the helmet reflection.

Recovering car roof

On the left side of the foreground, the semi-transparent car roof is visible from the beginning of the shot until frame 2347. To address this, we need to create an animated roto shape that covers this frame range. The process of creating this roto shape involves the following steps:

1. Press the O key to create a Roto node and connect it to the color-corrected live-action plate. The rotoscoping of the car roof must be done with pixel-level precision, closely following its contours.
2. After the rotoscoping process is precisely completed within the required frame range, connect a Premult node to generate a premultiplied image for the area defined by the rotoshape, then merge it back over the color-corrected live-action plate.

Rebuilding the helmet reflection

We can use a combination of keying and roto shapes to reconstruct the helmet reflection by following these steps:

1. Press the Tab key, search for Keyer [Keyer], and connect the Keyer node to the color-corrected live-action plate.
2. Press the A key to switch to the Keyer's alpha channel. Double-click the Keyer node to open its Properties panel. Increase the luminance contrast in the alpha channel by narrowing the gap between the A and B vertical yellow lines. This will generate a matte in the alpha channel.
3. Add a Grade node after the Keyer node.

   In this example, we fine-tuned the Gain and Multiply values in the Grade node's Properties panel. Also, ensure that the mask channel option is set to rgba.alpha so that the color grading only affects the areas defined by the Keyer node.
4. Add a Copy node after the Grade node to transfer the original matte provided to the motorcyclist from its red channel (rgb.red) to the alpha channel of the newly corrected background plate. Then, connect a Premult node after the Copy node to generate a premultiplied image of the motorcyclist. Lastly, merge this result over the projected sky background composition using an AddMix node to fix the semi-transparent helmet issue.

○ Section ⑤: Applying a light wrap effect and projecting the damaged road image

– *Implementing a light wrap effect*

The light wrap is a natural effect that occurs when light falls onto an object from behind, creating a soft silhouette around it. This phenomenon becomes more prominent when the object is illuminated in a dim environment, often allowing the light to seep into the object's silhouette. A light wrap can seamlessly blend elements into an environment and enhance visual realism when applied appropriately in compositing. Figure 5.89 compares the results before and after applying the light wrap effect using a LightWrap node. The image on the right shows the natural light wrap effect produced by the bright light source in the background sky.

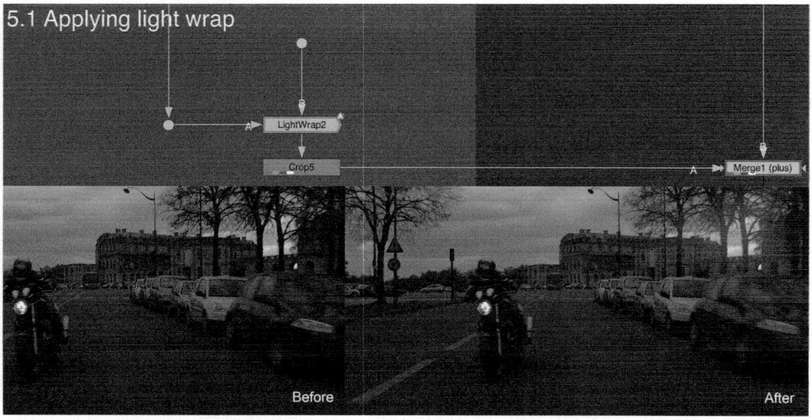

FIGURE 5.89 A before-and-after comparison of the light wrap effect in the final composite

– *Reprojecting the damaged road image*

This subsection explains the use of camera reprojection, a process that involves creating a still camera by duplicating the virtual moving camera extracted from the live-action footage. This still camera is then used to project the image of the damaged road surface prepared in Section 1. Once the reprojection is complete, the original virtual camera is used to re-film the projected still image, thereby reintroducing camera movement.

Camera reprojection in this example involves several stages, as shown in Figure 5.90. It begins with color grading the image of the damaged road.

1. We used two color grading nodes, as highlighted in the "Color Grading" section. After the damaged road image, the first Grade node (named Grade_match_black_white_points) is used to fine-tune the image's black and white values and adjust the overall color tint to match the sky replacement composition. The second Grade node (Grade_gamma) is used to balance the image's gamma values in specific frames.
2. Following the initial color grading, four additional color correction nodes (HueCorrect1, HueCorrect2, and ColorLookup), originally used for grading the live-action background plate, are cloned and applied here to further grade the image of the damaged road. This ensures that the road surface closely matches the color-graded composition.

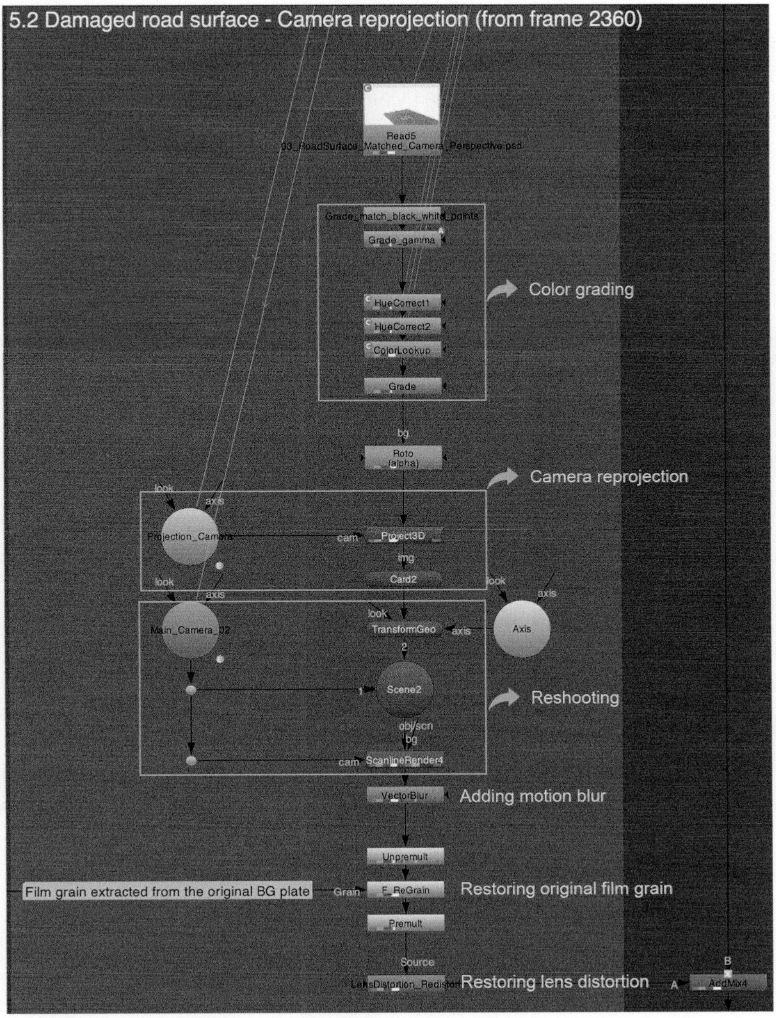

FIGURE 5.90 Node connections for the camera reprojection of the damaged road surface

3. Press the O key to add a Roto node. Use the Roto node to define a projected area of the image. In the Properties panel, change the premultiply drop-down menu from None to rgb. This will produce a premultiplied image based on the result of the Roto node.
4. Two cameras are used in the camera reprojection process.

   The yellow color-coded camera (Projection_Camera) is a duplicate of the virtual camera extracted from the original live-action footage, with its translation and rotation animation data removed at frame 2375. As a result, it functions as a static projection camera for the damaged road image.

The blue color-coded camera (Main_Camera_2) is another copy of the extracted virtual camera, but it retains its full animation data. This camera reintroduces the original camera movement to the projected image of the damaged road before it is integrated into the sky replacement composition. The relationship between these two cameras is illustrated in Figure 5.91.

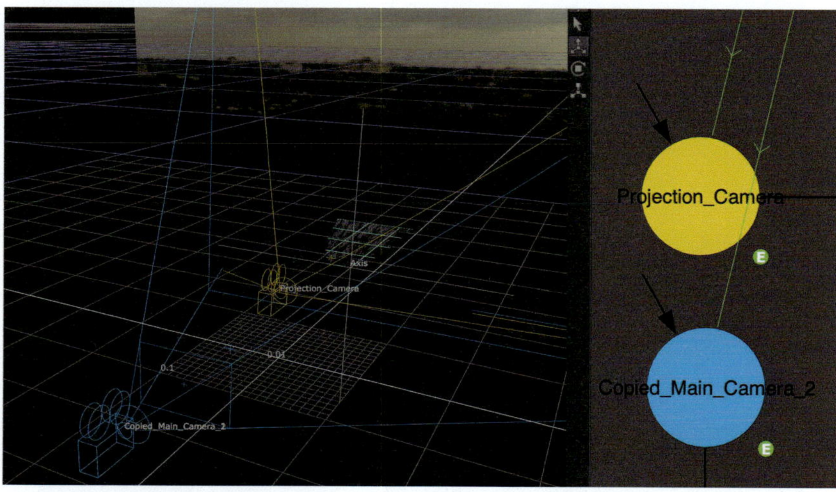

FIGURE 5.91 Camera reprojection for the damaged road surface in the 3D system of NukeX

5. After camera reprojection, the ScanlineRender node generates motion data for the damaged road image. Connect a VectorBlur node after the ScanlineRender node to apply motion blur to the projected image, matching the motion blur of the original live-action plate. Additionally, apply the original film grain and lens effects to the reprojected image. Finally, merge the reprojected image into the sky replacement composition using an Addmix node. At this stage, global color grading is applied to the composition as a creative decision. For detailed instructions on camera projection in Case Study 4, please refer to the pre-recorded video.

– *Adding a light beam & lens flare*

In the final stage, adding a light beam and lens flare to the motorcycle's headlight can further enhance the naturalism after the sky replacement shot. Because the motorcycle moves through the scene, a 2D Tracker node can be used to accurately track the headlight and apply that data to the light beam and lens flare. This ensures both effects remain precisely synchronized with the headlight's movement. The node connections for this process are illustrated in Figure 5.92.

As shown, a Roto node (Roto_F2307) is used to draw a circular shape that matches the motorcycle's headlight, allowing the VolumeRays node to generate a light beam based on this defined shape.

The Tracker1 node tracked the movement of the headlight and is used to drive both the movement of the roto shape and the lens flare created by the Flare node to follow the motorcycle.

Once the light beam is generated by the VolumeRays node, a Merge (plus) node is used to integrate it into the final composition.

Finally, a Remove node is applied to remove the unnecessary alpha channel from the composition before the final output.

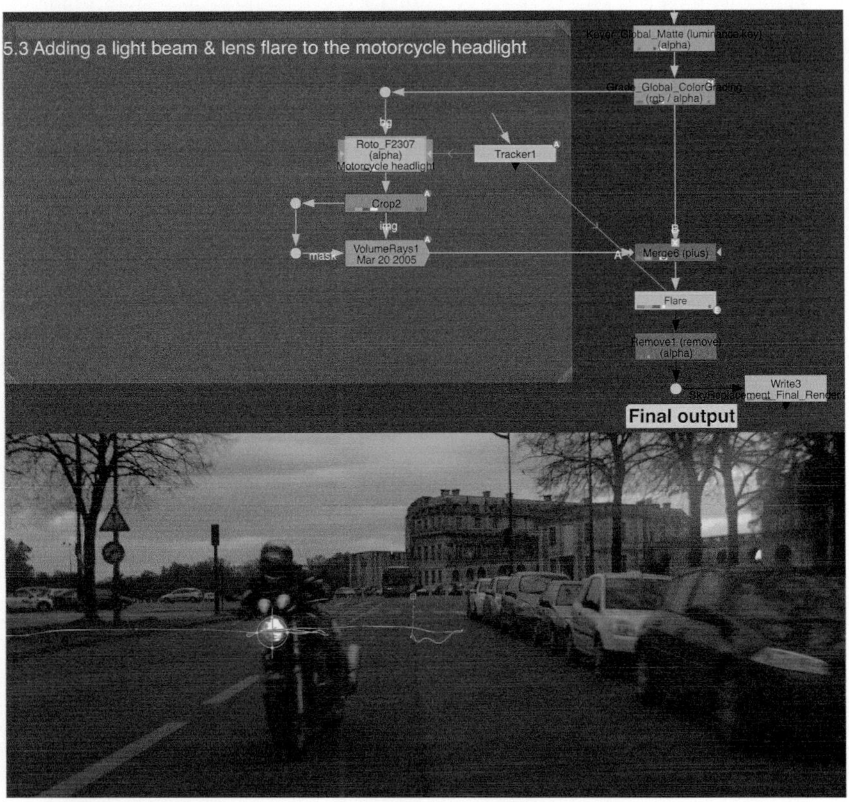

FIGURE 5.92 Adding a light beam and lens flare to the motorcycle's headlight and finishing the VFX shot

Case Study 5

Essential concepts of keying in compositing

Key learning points:

> The importance of chroma subsampling for keying.

> Common types of mattes used in keying.

> An example of green screen keying.

> Additive keyer.

Notes

Each case study includes a pre-recorded video tutorial. Watching these videos alongside reading the case studies is strongly recommended to ensure a smooth and comprehensive learning experience for each hands-on project.

Video link: youtube.com/@InvisibleFilmVFX

Video title: Case Study 5 | Essential Concepts of Keying in Compositing

Project file: Case_Study_5_Project_File

The project file is available for download on the book's official webpage.

High-resolution color figures from this project are also available for download on the book's official webpage.

• A fundamental understanding of green/blue screen keying

Green or blue screen keying is a visual effects technique used to separate an object from its background by leveraging the chroma range of the footage to generate a grayscale image known as a matte. Most modern digital cameras use sensors equipped with a Bayer filter, which makes them twice as sensitive to green chrominance compared to blue or red when capturing brightness. As a result, contemporary digital cameras are more responsive to green chroma, allowing them to capture more subtle and intricate details when using green screens.

• The importance of chroma subsampling for keying

Chroma subsampling is a compression technique that can potentially affect the quality of results in green and blue screen keying. It is used in digital video signals to reduce file size by lowering color resolution while preserving luminance. Chroma subsampling is expressed using the Y′CbCr color space, which consists of one luma component (Y′) and two chroma components: Cb (blue-difference) and Cr (red-difference). Since the human visual system is more sensitive to luminance than color, the luma component is prioritized in chroma subsampling.

To better understand this in practice, consider our common experience with output media files, such as QuickTime clips, where we often encounter compression options when selecting quality settings. For instance, sampling ratios like 4:4:4, 4:2:2, and 4:1:1 describe the relationship between luma and chroma sampling in a video signal. A 4:4:4 ratio indicates no chroma subsampling, meaning each component is sampled at the same rate. In contrast, a 4:2:2 ratio means the chroma channels (Cb and Cr) are sampled at half the rate of the luma (Y′), resulting in reduced color detail. Consequently, keying footage with 4:2:2 subsampling typically produces lower-quality results than footage with 4:4:4 sampling. Figure 5.93 compares the image quality between 4:4:4 and 4:2:2 sampling ratios.

As introduced in previous chapters, visual effects productions typically use OpenEXR format image sequences exported by the editorial department based on raw live-action footage. This workflow preserves the highest possible quality of the original live-action footage, which is especially important for keying and compositing.

FIGURE 5.93 A comparison of 4:4:4 and 4:2:2 chroma subsampling rates

• Common types of mattes used in keying

Keying methods can vary between compositors in visual effects studios, but general guidelines exist for creating mattes using different approaches within production pipelines. VFX projects are handled on a shot-by-shot basis, and each shot involving green, blue, or other color screens may require various types of mattes, such as soft mattes, hard mattes, core mattes, and garbage mattes. In many cases, a single key is not sufficient to produce a high-quality matte for all elements, including detailed hair or fur, clothing edges, or sharp props. As a result, these different elements often need to be treated separately during the keying process.

◦ Soft matte

A soft matte includes semi-transparency and intricate edge details, such as those found in hair and fur. VFX artists should focus on the edges of the matte to preserve as much detail as possible during the keying process.

◦ Hard matte

A hard matte refers to a matte with relatively sharp, well-defined edges, such as those found around solid objects. The goals of keying to create a hard matte should differ from those used to create a soft matte.

◦ Core matte

As previously introduced, a matte consists of three regions: white, black, and gray. The white area is fully opaque, the black area is completely transparent, and the gray areas are semi-transparent. These three attributes of a matte enable the seamless integration of images. A core matte is an inner matte used to correct defects caused by imperfect keying, such as black holes that may appear in the inner areas of the matte after the keying process.

◦ Garbage matte

A garbage matte is a rough mask used to exclude unwanted elements, such as light stands, studio equipment, or other reference objects, from a green screen shot during the keying process.

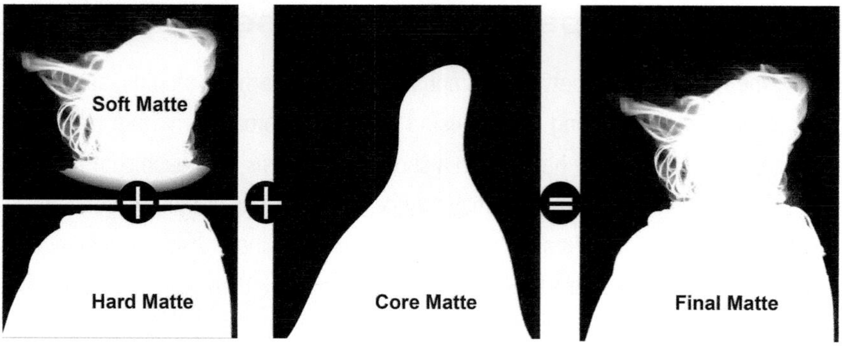

FIGURE 5.94 Combining different types of mattes into a single matte (from left to right)

- **Footage analysis**

◦ Green screen plate

Frame range: 1001–1241 frames

Image aspect ratio: 4096 × 2160

Frame rate: 24 fps

Image bit depth: 16-bit OpenEXR

Color space: Linear

◦ Camera information

Camera: Sony F65

Camera lens | Focal length: Unknow

Camera movement: Handheld

◦ Background image

Image aspect ratio: 7952 × 5304

Camera model: Sony a7R II

Focal length: 16 mm

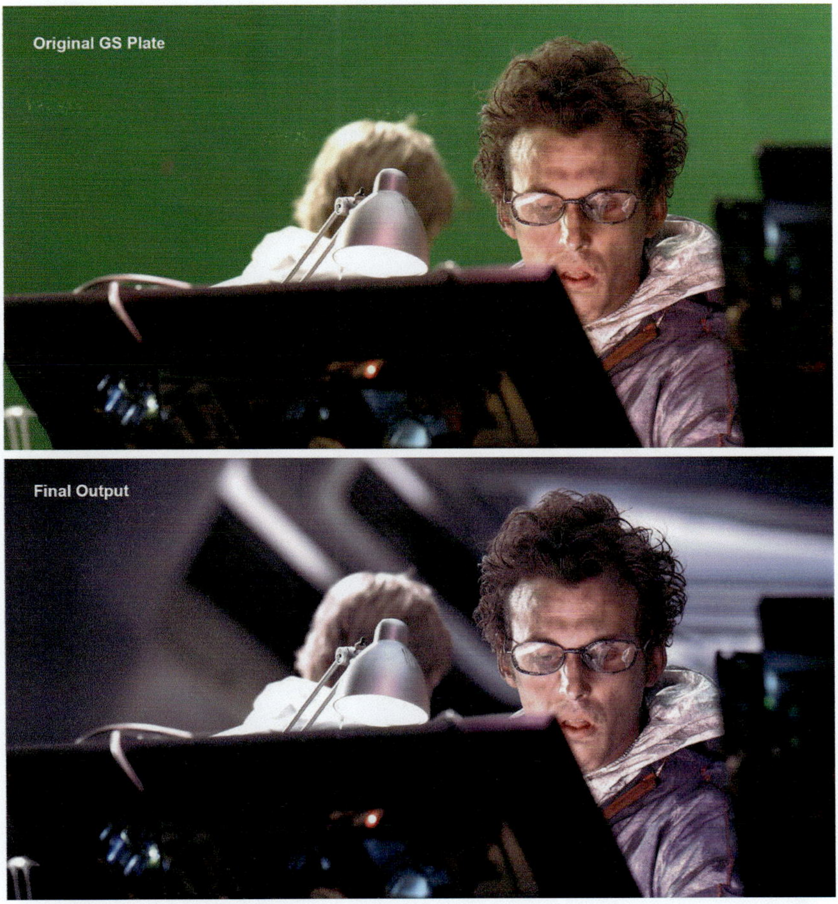

FIGURE 5.95 A comparison between the original plate and the final output of Case Study 5. Original green screen footage © mango.blender.org

• Nuke script analysis

The Nuke script for Case Study 5, shown in Figure 5.96, includes a LUT preparation section for the shot, along with eight keying and compositing sections.

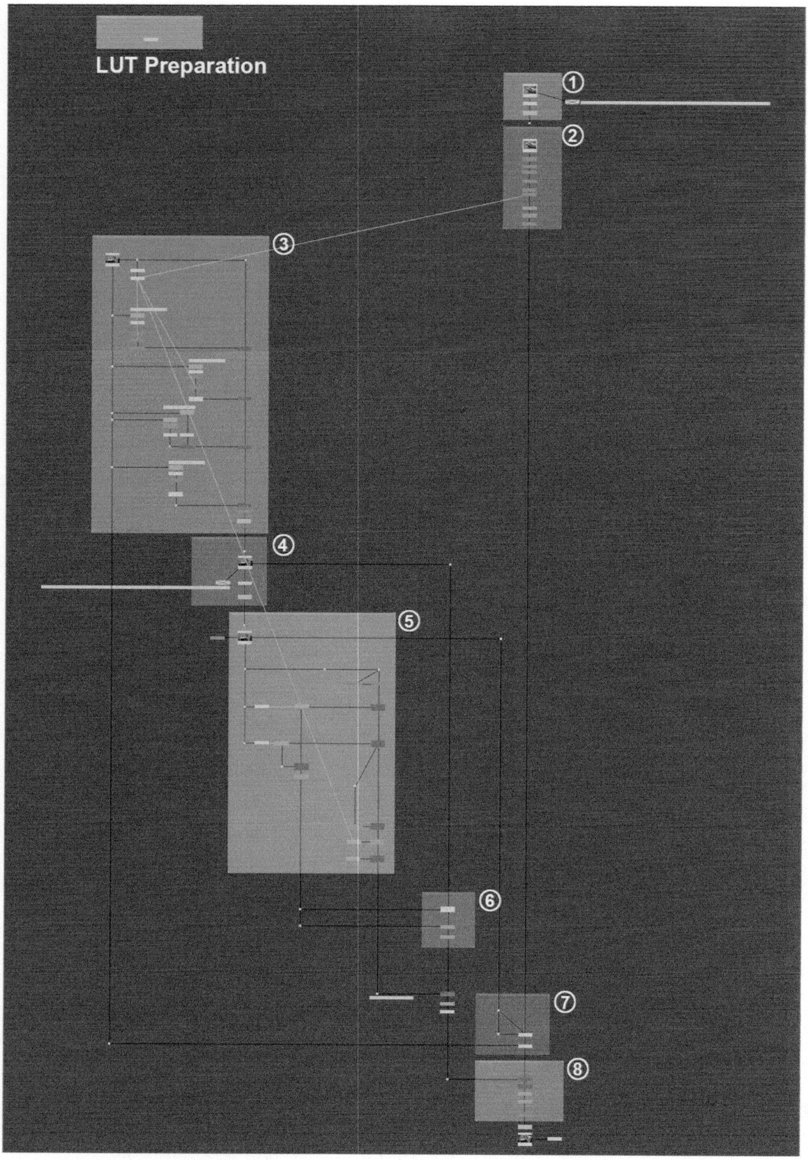

FIGURE 5.96 The overall layout of the Nuke script used for green screen keying in Case Study 5

○ Creating a custom LUT (lookup table) for the shot

Setting up LUTs was introduced in Chapter 4 through the hands-on example (I). In Case Study 5, we apply the same principles to create a custom LUT node named

VIEWER_INPUT, which is used in the Viewer1 panel to display image details in highlights on 8-bit monitors. Figure 5.97 shows the VIEWER_INPUT group node, which includes the Colorspace1 and Exposure1 nodes. The bottom-left result displays the original green screen plate with the default sRGB LUT applied in the Viewer1 panel, while the bottom-right result shows the same plate with the custom LUT applied.

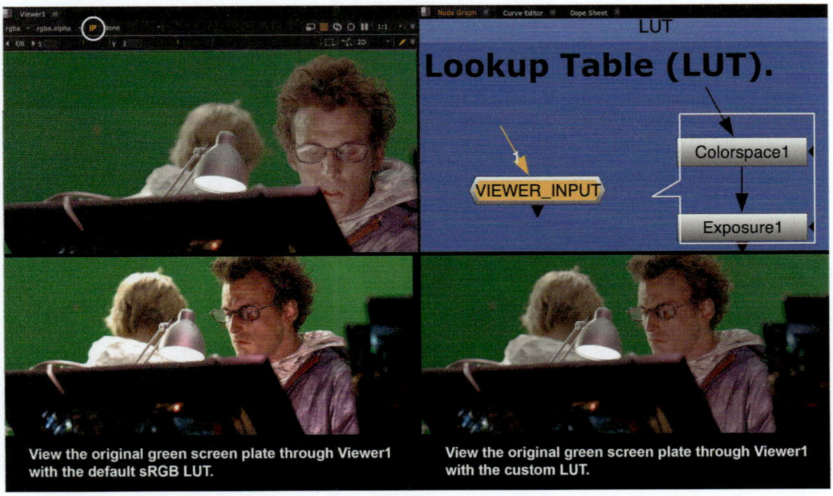

FIGURE 5.97 Comparison of results before and after applying the custom LUT node

In previous chapters, we introduced the concept of 8-bit and higher bit depths in relation to digital images and display panels. We also learned that 8-bit images cannot represent color depths greater than 1. The same principles apply to displays, meaning that highlight details stored in higher bit depths cannot be accurately shown on 8-bit monitors. With this brief review in mind, let us now build this VIEWER_INPUT node.

Within the VIEWER_INPUT node, as shown in Figure 5.97, the Colorspace1 node converts the green screen plate from its default linear space to a logarithmic one. This conversion enhances the visibility of highlight details, particularly in regions that appear blown out on 8-bit monitors.

The Exposure1 node then reduces the image's luminance values. In logarithmic space, these values are typically elevated, often resulting in a milky, flat appearance. Adjusting the exposure at this stage helps achieve a more visually appealing image.

To create the VIEWER_INPUT node, follow these steps:

1. Position the mouse cursor in the Node Graph panel, press the R key to open the Read File(s) dialog window, and navigate to the following folder to import the OpenEXR green screen plate:

   Case_Study_5_Project_File > 5_01_Green_Screen_Plate > A003C007_120507_Green_Screen_Plate

   After importing the green screen plate, press any numeric key on your keyboard (for example, 1) to load the plate into the Viewer1 panel. At this point, the green screen plate should resemble the lower left image in Figure 5.97. The highlights, particularly on the back of the head and the white hoodie worn by the character on the left, appear blown out.
2. Ensure the mouse cursor is in the Node Graph panel, press the Tab key to search for Colorspace [Color] in the search field, and then connect this node to the Green_Screen_Plate node. Double-click the Colorspace node to load its parameters into the Properties panel. Set the following options:

   input: Linear

   output: Cineon
3. After converting the image to the Cineon color space, it appears milky at this stage. To correct this, click on viewerProcess, located to the right of the IP icon above the Viewer1 panel, and change it from its default setting of sRGB to None. The image should now look better, although it may still appear slightly flat.

   To enhance the contrast, connect an Exposure node after the Colorspace node and set the following parameters in its Properties panel:

   blackpoint: -3

   red: 0.03

   green: 0.03

   blue: 0.03
4. The image should now appear normal, with improved contrast and full detail in the highlights. Select both nodes, then press Ctrl/Cmd + G to group them.

5. With the new group selected, press the N key to rename the node to:

   VIEWER_INPUT

   VIEWER_INPUT is the default name for the input_process node in NukeX. When a custom LUT node is named VIEWER_INPUT, the input_process (IP) icon above the Viewer1 panel automatically activates, applying the custom LUT.
6. After activating the IP icon, disconnect the node connection between the green screen plate and the VIEWER_INPUT node. This step ensures that the LUT is applied only in the Viewer panel, without affecting the native color space of the green screen plate.

◦ Section ①: Removing film grain from the background image

This part of the script uses a third-party plugin, Neat Video Reduce Noise Node, to remove film grain from the original green screen plate. If the plugin is unavailable, please use Nuke's default Denoise node as an alternative.

To use the Denoise node, follow these steps:

1. Ensure that the mouse cursor is positioned in the Node Graph panel. Press the Tab key and search for the Denoise [Filter] node. Connect the Source input of the Denoise node to the original green screen plate.

   By default, an analysis square region for the Denoise node appears in the bottom-left corner of the Viewer1 panel. Reposition the analysis box over a flat area that is free of patterns. The Denoise node will automatically analyze the noise structure in this region and remove noise from the plate.
2. After removing the film grain, use a Write node to export the denoised background plate in the OpenEXR file format. Then, re-import the image into NukeX for further compositing operations. This approach avoids redundant calculations within the script and improves Nuke's processing performance. The node connections used for removing film grain are shown in Figure 5.98. The background image used in this project was provided courtesy of Photobash (https://photobash.gumroad.com/l/futuristic-interiors).

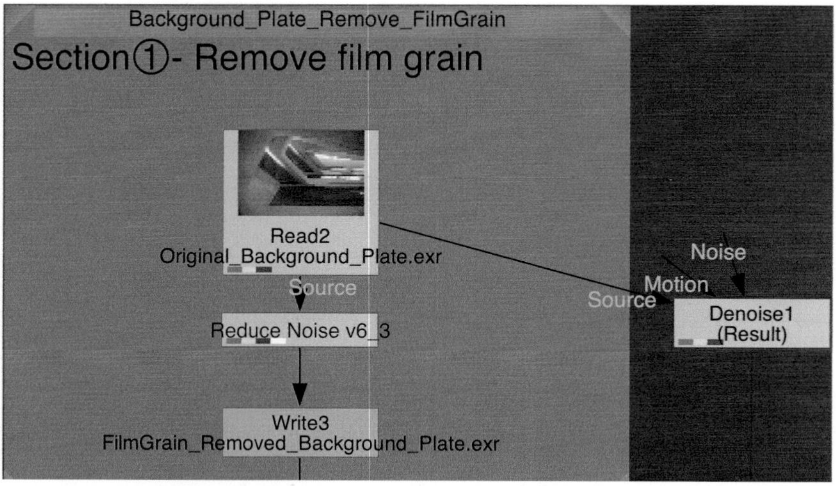

FIGURE 5.98 Removing film grain from the original background image

Notes

At this stage, removing the film grain from the background image is necessary for two reasons:

1. The background image was captured using a Sony a7R II camera, whereas the green screen footage was shot with a Sony F65 camera, resulting in different film grain characteristics.
2. The background image is a still frame with static film grain, while the green screen plate is a sequence of images containing randomized film grain patterns. Combining two different types of film grain in a single composition would be visually inconsistent. Therefore, to maintain film grain consistency in the final composition, the static grain in the background image must be removed and replaced with grain extracted from the green screen plate.

- **Section ②: Removing lens distortion from the background image**
  - It is crucial to maintain consistent lens distortion across all assets and live-action footage in the final composition. In this example, the camera attributes of the background image must match those of the green screen plate. Therefore, a LensDistortion node (named Remove_Original_Lens_Distortion)

is used to remove the original lens distortion from the background image (see Figure 5.99), as it was captured using a different camera, lens, and focal length. These differences result in lens distortion that does not match the green screen plate.

- Next, a new Lens Distortion node (Apply_GreenScreen_Lens_Distortion) is applied to the undistorted background image. This distortion is calculated based on the original green screen plate to ensure that the background image matches the lens distortion of the plate. After applying the lens distortion, connect a Crop node to reduce the enlarged bounding box size caused by the distortion.
- The aspect ratio of the background image is 7952/5304, which is significantly wider than the green screen plate's aspect ratio of 4096/2160. Therefore, after the Crop node, a Reformat node is used to scale down the background image to match the green screen plate's aspect ratio.

To align the camera perspective with the green screen plate and match the camera movement, two Transform nodes are added after the Reformat node. The Transform_Position_Scale node adjusts the scale, while Transform_MatchMove2, driven by a Tracker node, applies the green screen plate's camera movement to the background image.

The background image is then color graded using a Grade node (Grade_Match_FG_Colors) to match the overall color tint of the green screen plate, as required for the storytelling in this shot. Finally, a Defocus node is applied to create an out-of-focus effect on the background image. See Figure 5.99.

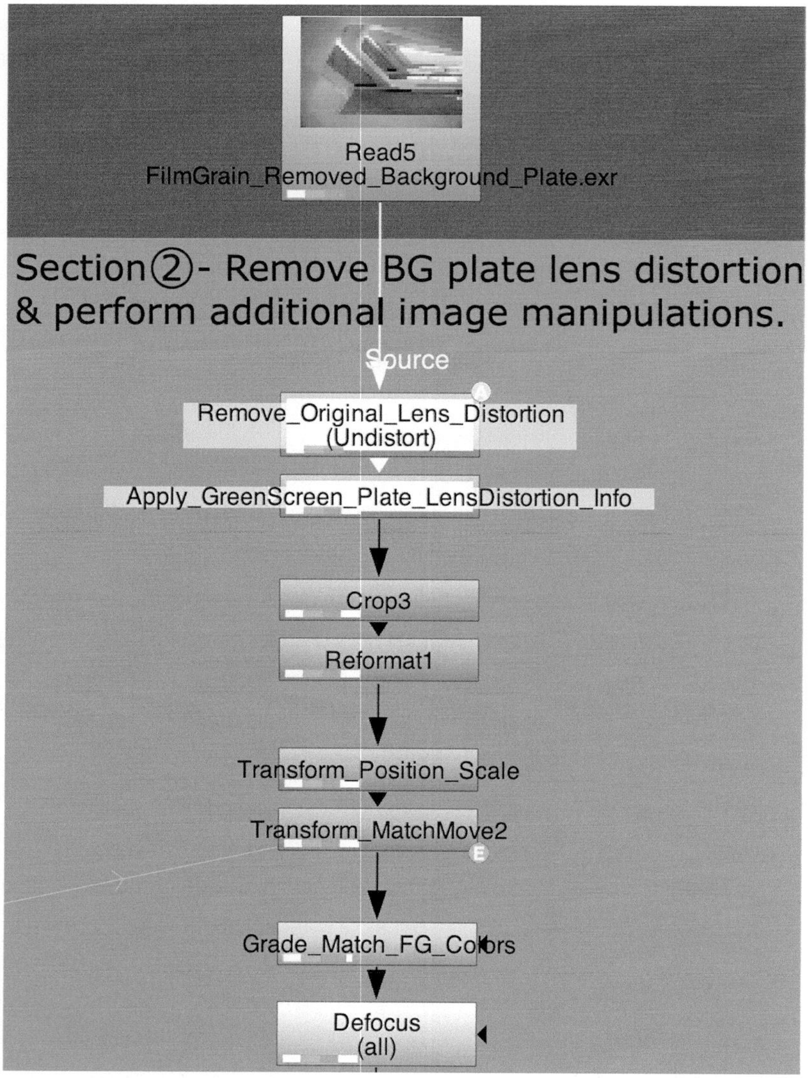

FIGURE 5.99 Node connections used to prepare the background image

◦ Section ③: Removing tracking markers from the green screen plate

Placing tracking markers on green or blue screens, as well as in the surrounding environment, is common practice when shooting visual effects plates. These markers come in various shapes and are positioned flat against the screen or on nearby elements. This setup allows tracking software to accurately analyze the markers for both 2D and 3D camera movement. Markers on the screen should have slightly different hues and luminance levels compared to the green or blue background to ensure visibility without interfering with the keying process. In contrast, markers placed outside the screen can use high-contrast, monochromatic patterns such as sharp black-and-white designs, which help the camera detect parallax and improve the accuracy of 3D tracking.

Tracking markers placed on green or blue screens can complicate the keying process, particularly when they overlap with fine details such as semi-transparent areas like hair or motion blur. In Figure 5.100, several tracking markers are visible on a green screen plate, and some intersect with the actors in various frames. These markers should be carefully removed before performing any keying operations.

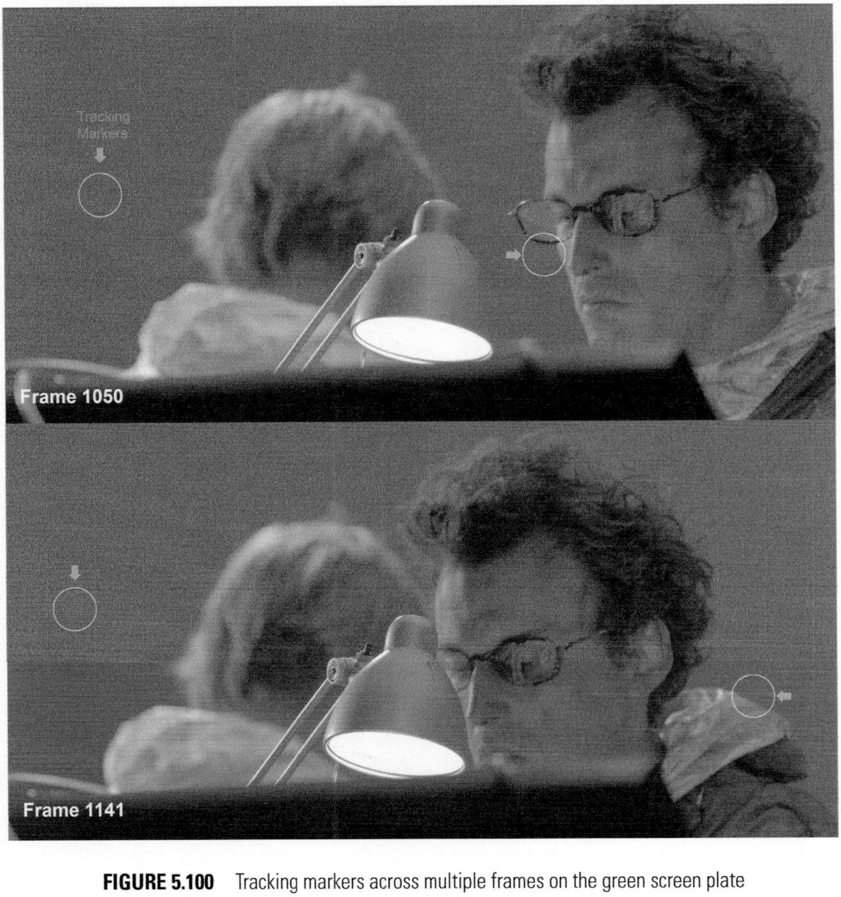

FIGURE 5.100 Tracking markers across multiple frames on the green screen plate

Notes

In general, there are two types of tracking tasks: 2D tracking and 3D tracking.

2D feature tracking occurs along the X and Y axes of the shot. In contrast, 3D tracking captures details in the foreground, middle ground, and background of the scene. As a result, a well-structured scene with an appropriate camera perspective can lead to efficient and accurate camera tracking.

To ensure camera tracking accuracy, it is important to place tracking markers on green or blue screens. Adding reference tracking details between the camera and the green or blue screens, such as extra tracking markers on light stands, also helps the tracking software understand the positions of objects in 3D space.

Using the green screen plate from Case Study 5 as an example, we can observe a series of details: the backside of the computer display in the foreground, features on the table lamp in the middle ground, and tracking markers on the green screen in the background. These features are distributed throughout the foreground, middle ground, and background, enabling the tracking software to determine how elements are positioned in 3D space within the scene and how they relate to the camera.

Figure 5.101 illustrates the node construction process used to remove tracking markers from the green screen plate. The removal begins in the upper left corner and progresses toward the lower right. According to the script, this process involves four groups of node sets, highlighted in yellow, each corresponding to the removal of tracking markers in different areas and at various frames of the green screen.

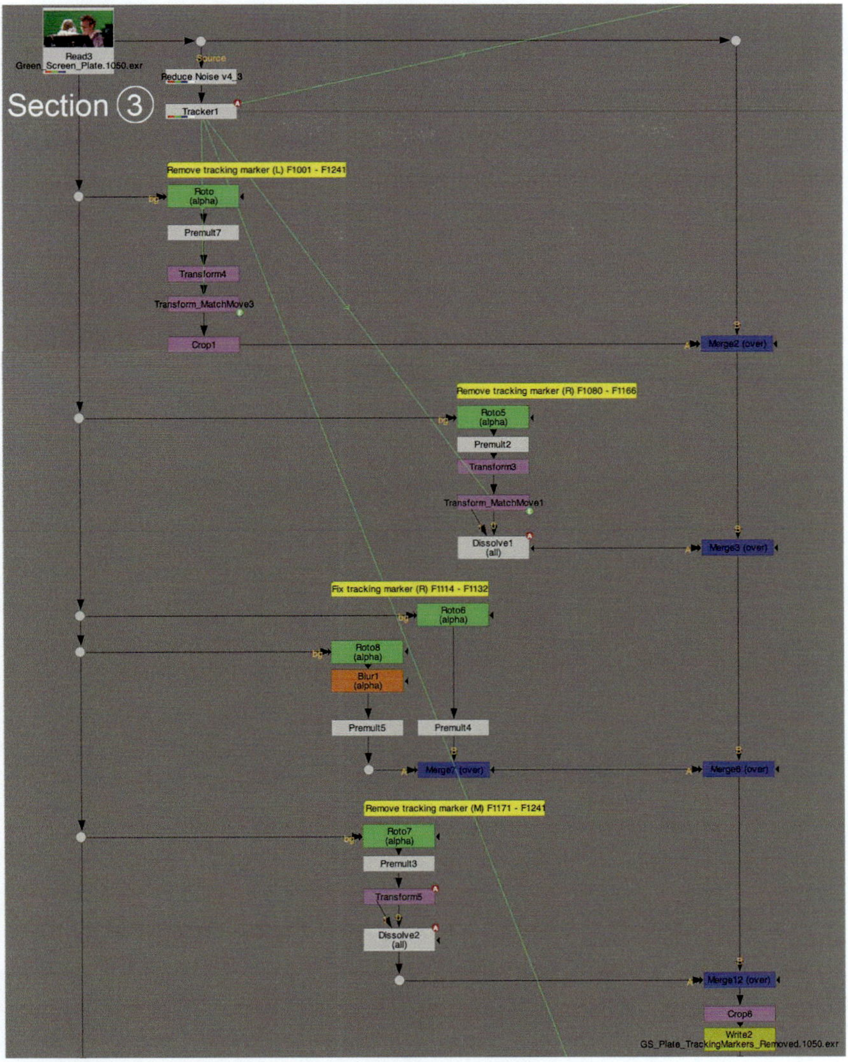

FIGURE 5.101 Operations for removing tracking markers from the green screen plate

– *Conducting 2D tracking*

The basic concept for removing a tracking marker from green/blue screen plates involves selecting an area using a Roto node from a nearby region of the tracker, extracting it to create a clean patch, and then using this patch to cover the tracking marker on the original green screen.

In this particular shot, the green screen plate includes camera movement. By using 2D tracking, we can obtain tracking data to drive the generated clean patch so that it matches the camera's movement. Therefore, after removing the film grain from the original green screen plate, we used a Tracker node (named Tracker1) to analyze the 2D movement of the camera throughout the shot.

After completing the 2D tracking analysis, we can generate several Transform_MatchMove nodes from the tracking results. These nodes are then used to drive the movement of all clean patches in downstream operations. This is why several green expression links can be seen emanating from the Tracker1 node and connecting to downstream Transform_MatchMove nodes in Figure 5.101.

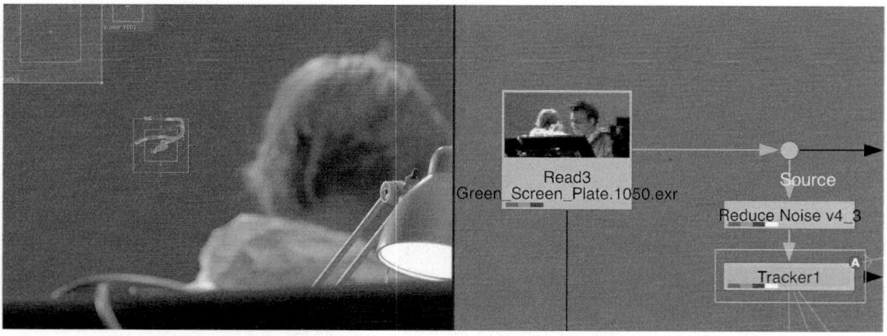

FIGURE 5.102 Using a Tracker node to analyze the camera's 2D movement

– Removing the tracking marker from frames 1001 to 1241

In this example, we will use a tracking marker located on the left side of the original green screen plate to demonstrate how tracking markers are removed from green screen footage.

Step 1 | Connect a Roto node directly to the original green screen plate. Draw a circle in a clean area next to the tracking marker that needs to be removed, as indicated by the red circle in Image A of Figure 5.103. Ensure that the circle is large enough to cover the tracking marker.

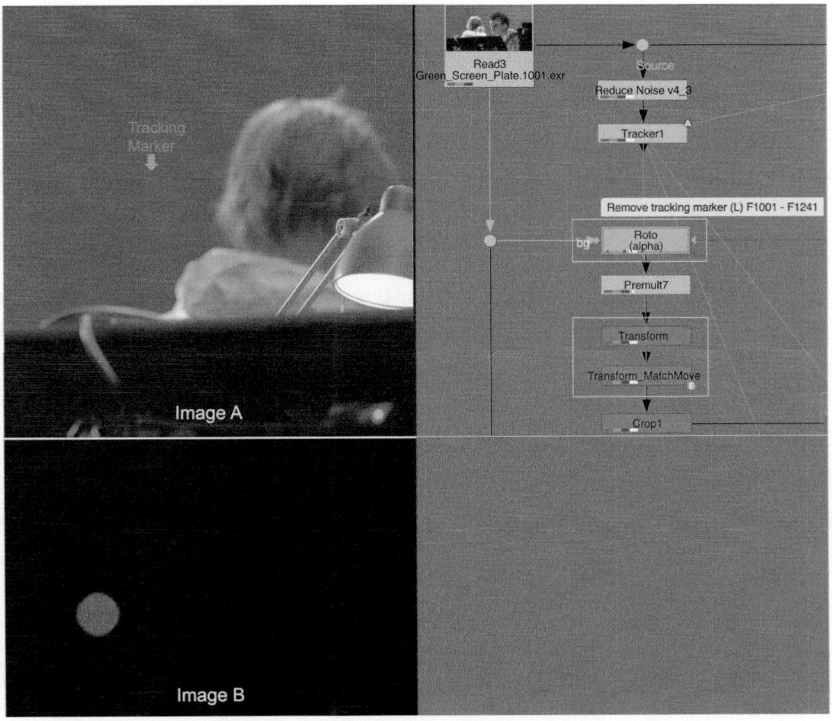

FIGURE 5.103 Drawing a circular area around the tracking marker on the original green screen using a Roto node

Step 2 | After the Roto node, add a Premult node. This node multiplies the RGB channels by the alpha channel, converting the defined circle into a premultiplied image, as shown in Figure 5.103, Image B.

Step 3 | After the Premult node, add a Transform node to reposition the premultiplied green screen patch over the tracking marker on the original green screen plate. This ensures that the patch effectively covers the tracking marker when it is later merged.

Step 4 | Use the Tracker1 node created upstream to generate a Transform_MatchMove node (see Figure 5.103) and connect it after the Transform node above. The Transform_MatchMove node applies the original camera movement, tracked from the green screen plate to the clean green screen patch, allowing it to follow the same movement consistently throughout the entire shot.

Be aware that Transform nodes can generate large bounding boxes, which may slow down Nuke's performance. For instance, a large black area with no image information might be included within the green screen patch, leading to unnecessary processing. To avoid this, use a Crop node to limit the bounding box size of the clean patch.

Step 5 | Add a Merge node. Connect the A input of the Merge node to the Crop node, and the B input to the original green screen plate.

Erasing tracking markers that are partially obscured by an object can be challenging, as demonstrated by the marker behind the actor's hoodie in frame 1140, shown in Image A of Figure 5.104. To remove the tracking marker, repeat the process outlined in Steps 1 through 5. Next, use a Roto node to create a premultiplied patch for the missing portion of the hoodie (see Image C). Merge this patch with Image B to generate Image D, as illustrated in Figure 5.104.

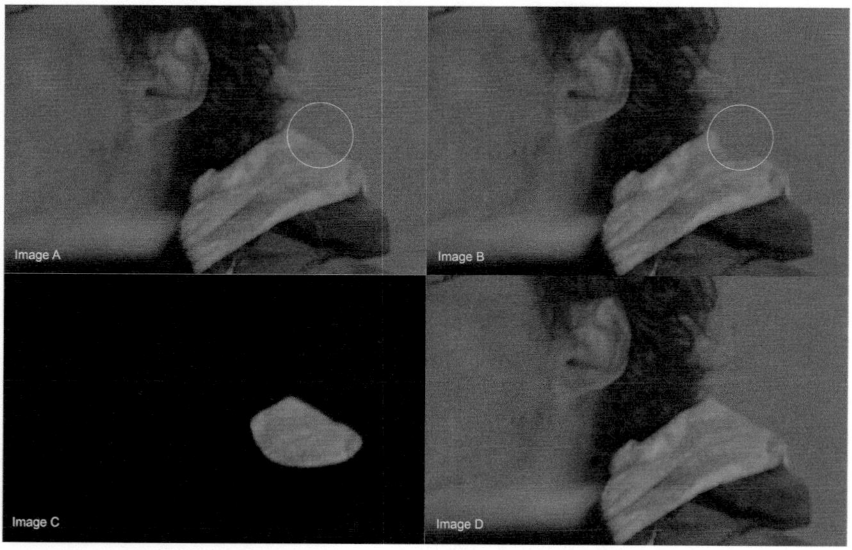

FIGURE 5.104 An example of removing a partially covered tracking marker

Note
At this stage, the green screen plate retains its original film grain, with only the tracking markers removed.

○ Section ④: Removing film grain from the green screen plate

– Once all tracking markers have been removed from the original green screen plate, use a Write node to export the plate as a sequence of OpenEXR images. This step helps avoid reprocessing the marker removal nodes and may improve Nuke's performance.

- Reimport the newly created green screen plate (with the tracking markers removed) into NukeX. Before keying, remove the film grain to enhance keying accuracy.
- Connect a Denoise node to the reimported green screen plate to remove its film grain. After denoising, connect a Write node to render the result as a sequence of OpenEXR images. The plate is now ready for green screen keying.

○ Section ⑤: Keying and generating mattes

The process of creating mattes described in this section involves the use of soft matte, hard matte, and core matte techniques to generate individual mattes. These individual mattes can then be combined to form a single, complete matte.

The creation process begins with the green screen plate, from which tracking markers and film grain have been removed in previous steps.

The keying process is divided into three stages, as follows:

- A set of IBKColour and IBKGizmo nodes is used to key a basic matte, focusing on the soft edges around elements in the green screen plate.
- After creating the initial matte, two Roto nodes (Monitor_Roto_R and Monitor_Roto_L) are used to generate separate garbage mattes. These mattes cover black holes that appear in the inner areas of the monitors' matte. Additionally, two Tracker nodes (Tracker_R and Tracker_L) are employed to track the monitors and apply shakiness to the garbage mattes, ensuring they match the movement of the monitors.
- Once these individual mattes are ready, two ChannelMerge nodes (ChannelMerge1 and ChannelMerge2) are used to combine them into a single, complete matte. These steps are highlighted by the white rectangular shapes in Figure 5.105.

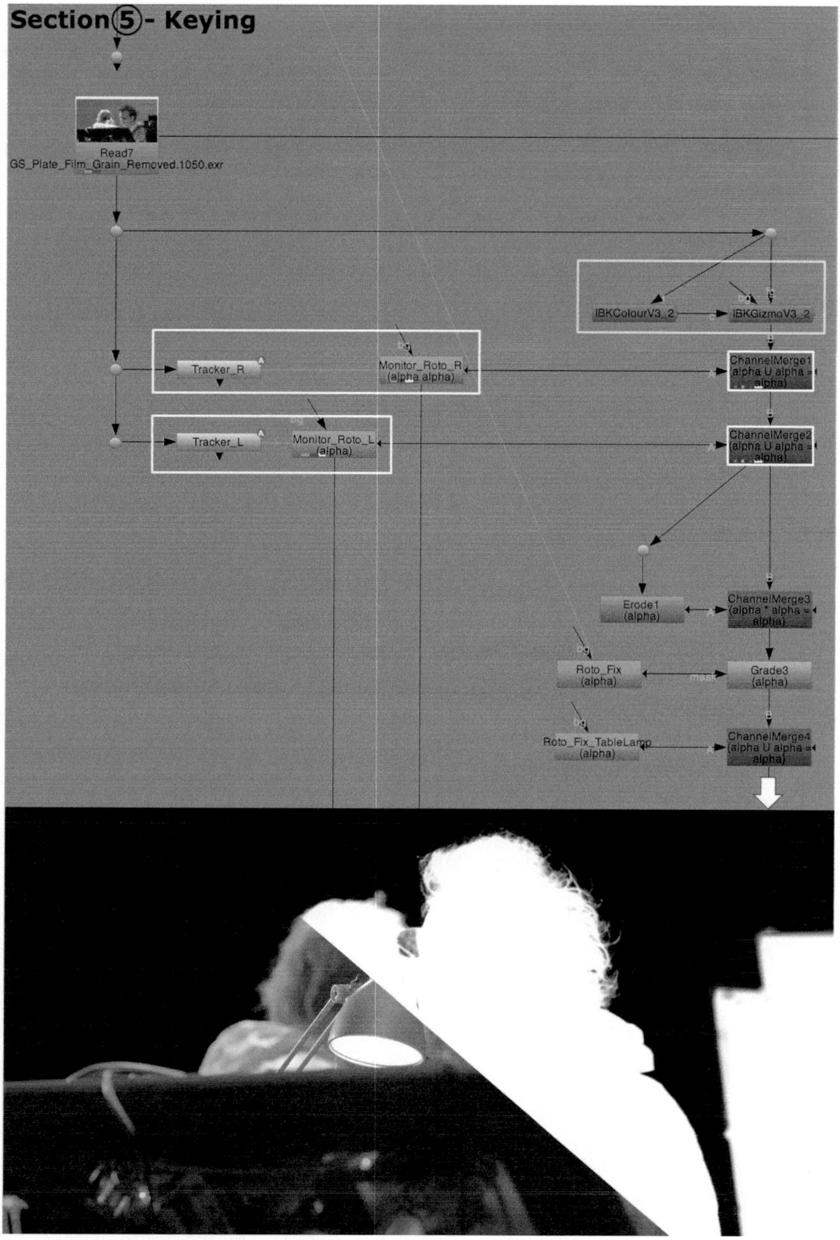

FIGURE 5.105 Keying and creating mattes for the green screen plate

Up to this point, an initial complete matte has been created. However, there is an issue hidden within the black area of the matte. To reveal it in the Viewer1 panel, please follow these steps:

1. Select the ChannelMerge2 node and press any number key on the keyboard to load it into the Viewer1 panel. Then, place your mouse cursor inside Viewer1 and press the A key to switch to the alpha channel. The generated matte of the green screen plate should now be visible.
2. Increase the gamma slider above the Viewer1 panel from its default value of 1 to 4. This will expose uneven values in the black area, which should ideally be completely black.

Note

After keying a matte, use the gamma slider to double-check that the black area in the alpha channel is filled with a solid black value of 0. Typically, increasing the gamma slider by 3 or 4 stops is sufficient to verify this. This step is important due to its role in the digital intermediate (DI) process. The matte should contain solid values: white areas must be fully opaque, while black areas should have a value of 0 to indicate complete transparency during compositing. Poorly keyed mattes, especially in the white and black areas of the alpha channel, may become visible during the DI process.

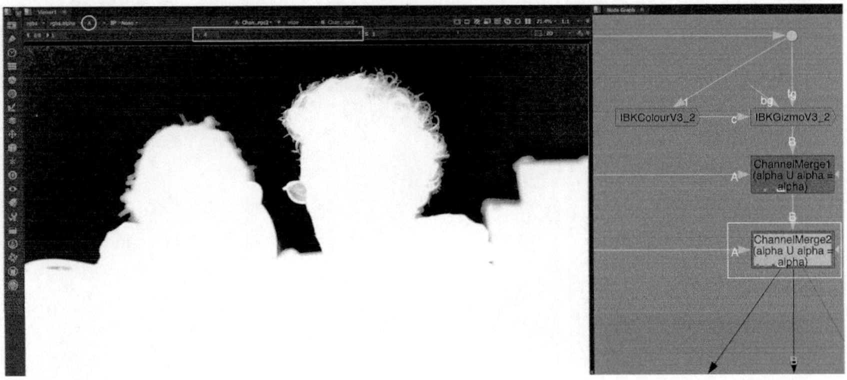

FIGURE 5.106 Examining black values in the alpha channel of the generated matte

Figure 5.106 illustrates uneven black values in the alpha channel, which may cause issues during the DI process. To improve the quality of the black areas in the current matte, we can generate a new matte with evenly distributed black values and use it to multiply the existing matte. The underlying math is straightforward: 0 × any value = 0. This operation helps to minimize the impact of uneven black values in the alpha channel.

Once a qualified matte for the green screen plate has been created, we will proceed to the next step: green screen despill.

◦ Section ⑥: A commonly used professional method for despill

This section features three important nodes, as shown in Figure 5.107. The result of the green screen despill appears at the bottom of the image, with its matte stored in the alpha channel.

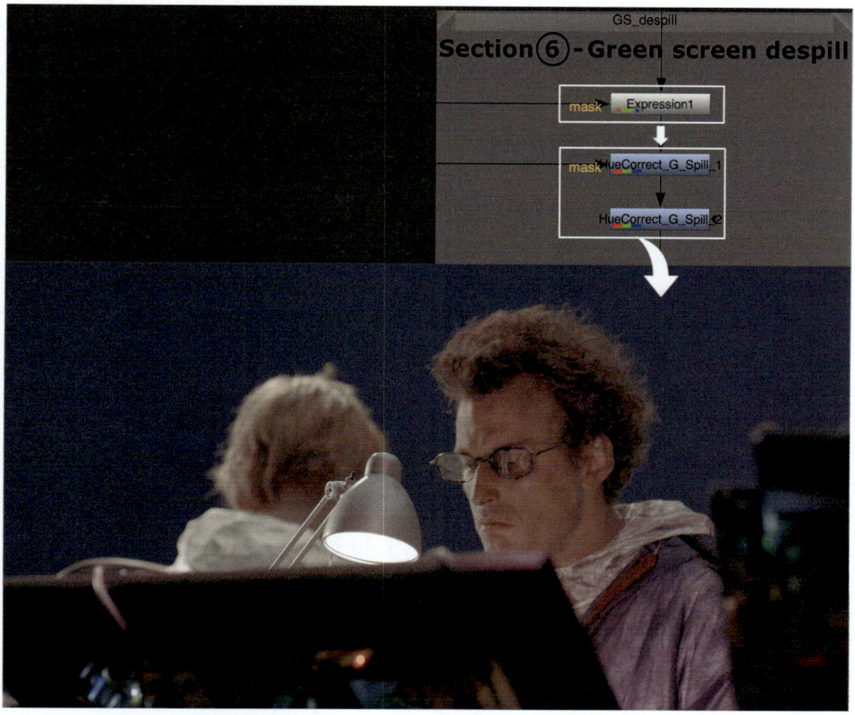

FIGURE 5.107 Node setup for green screen despill and the resulting image

In this part of the script, an Expression node is used to remove the green color from the green screen plate, and the result is further refined using two HueCorrect nodes. Once the green is eliminated from the plate, the green screen becomes a neutral gray. Finally, the combined matte created in the upstream section is copied into the alpha channel of this neutral gray plate using a Copy node.

– *Screen despill using expression nodes*

1. Connect an Expression node directly to the green screen plate from which the tracking markers have been removed, ensuring that the original film grain on the plate remains untouched.
2. Double-click the Expression node to load its parameters in the Properties panel. In this example, we aim to remove the green spill from the green screen plate. The equation used for the green channel in the Expression node is as follows:

   g > (r + b)/2? (r + b)/2: g

   This expression means that if the green channel value is greater than half the sum of the red and blue channel values, it will be replaced with that average; otherwise, it will remain unchanged.

   Similarly, a comparable equation can be used for blue screen despill. The following expression can be applied to the blue channel in the Expression node when using a blue screen plate.

   b > (r + g)/2? (r + g)/2: b
3. The mask input of the Expression node, as shown in Figure 5.107, connects to the mattes generated for the monitors to exclude them from the scene. This ensures that the green spill correction affects only the green screen and the two characters, while preventing the green lights behind the monitors from being altered by the Expression node.
4. The HueCorrection nodes are used to fine-tune subtle details in specific areas that the Expression nodes might not address, such as color reflections on foreground elements.
5. Add a Copy node to transfer the combined matte created in the upstream section into the alpha channel of this neutral gray plate.

6. After the Copy node, a Grade node is used to fine-tune the color of the neutral gray plate.
7. Next, a Premult node is applied to multiply the image's RGB values by its alpha channel. The node connections and the resulting image are shown in Figure 5.108.

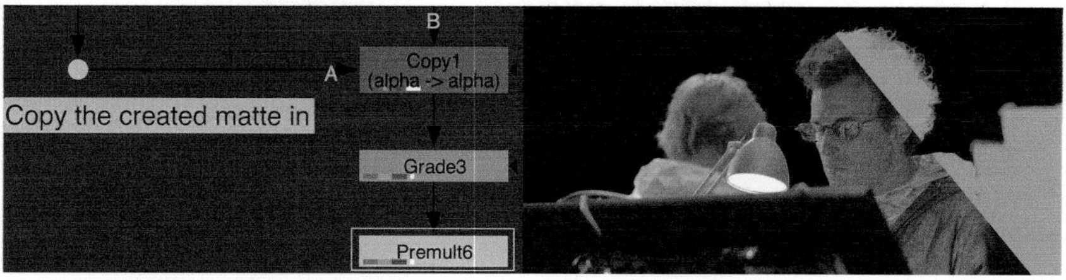

FIGURE 5.108 Node connections after the Copy node, along with the resulting premultiplied image

○ Section ⑦: Additive keyer

The Additive_Keyer is a custom Nuke gizmo that typically includes three input connections: FG_Input (foreground input), BG_Input (background input), and Clean_Plate_Input. This node operates through a series of mathematical operations. In this section, we will focus on the core concept behind its functionality.

The FG_Input connects to the green screen plate, from which tracking markers and film grain have been removed. The BG_Input connects the background image. The Clean_Plate_Input generates a clean plate using an IBKColour node that is embedded within the Additive_Keyer gizmo. Figure 5.109 illustrates the input connections of the Additive_Keyer node, as well as the resulting composite of the green screen plate and the background image.

To examine the nodes included in the gizmo, follow these steps:

- If you are using NukeX 16 or later, click the plus sign in the lower-right corner of the gizmo to expand it.
- If you are using an older version of NukeX, select the gizmo node, then go to Edit > Node > Group > Open Group Node Graph. Figure 5.110 shows the overall structure of the nodes and operations contained within the gizmo.

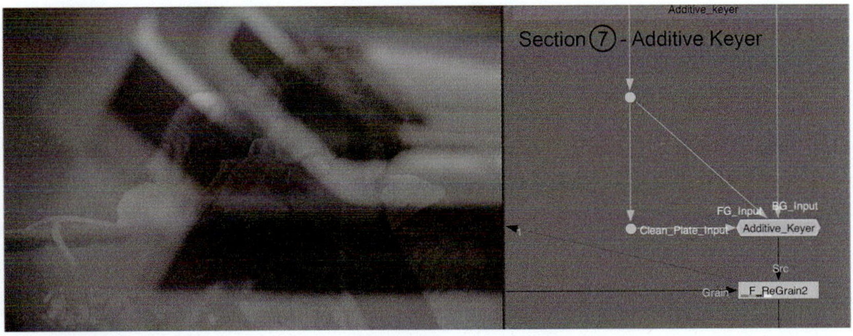

FIGURE 5.109 Input connections of the Additive_Keyer node and its resulting output

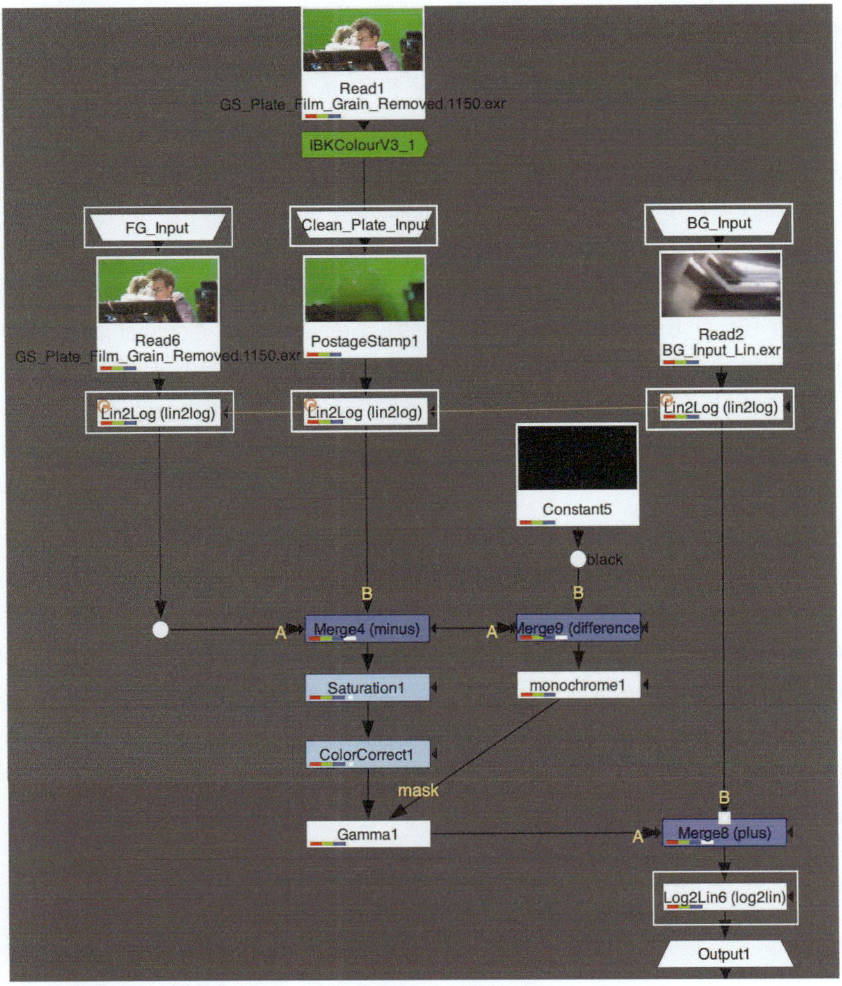

FIGURE 5.110 Operating nodes and connections inside the Additive_Keyer gizmo node

Note

As discussed earlier, visual effects pipelines primarily operate in a linear color space, and Foundry NukeX is designed to work within this space, whether using its default color management system or the ACES OCIO color management system. However, the Additive_Keyer gizmo operates in logarithmic space due to the nature of its required mathematical operations. As shown in Figure 5.110, three Lin2Log nodes are used to convert OpenEXR images from linear to logarithmic space before applying mathematical nodes. Once processing is complete, the result must be converted back to linear space. To do this, a Log2Lin node is applied before the final output.

◦ Section ⑧: Final output

Following the Additive_Keyer node, an F_ReGrain node is applied to extract and reintroduce the original film grain to the blended image, maintaining consistency with the grain of the original green screen plate.

After the F_ReGrain node, connect an AddMix node, as shown in Figure 5.111, to integrate the premultiplied green screen plate with the background image generated by the Additive_Keyer. Following the AddMix node, apply two Grade nodes (Grade_Global_Grading_1 and Grade_Global_Grading_2) for global color grading, enhancing the visual storytelling. Additionally, use a Reformat node to ensure the final output meets the required aspect ratio before exporting the composition.

Note

In a visual effects studio environment, rendered outputs are typically produced in two formats: QuickTime files for internal VFX dailies and OpenEXR files for production delivery. Consequently, during the rendering process, a QuickTime file with the client-approved LUT embedded is also generated for each shot to facilitate shot tracking and feedback, enabling supervisors and clients to review and provide comments. Once approved, shots are delivered in their original full-resolution formats, often as OpenEXR files or in another format specified by the post-production pipeline or client.

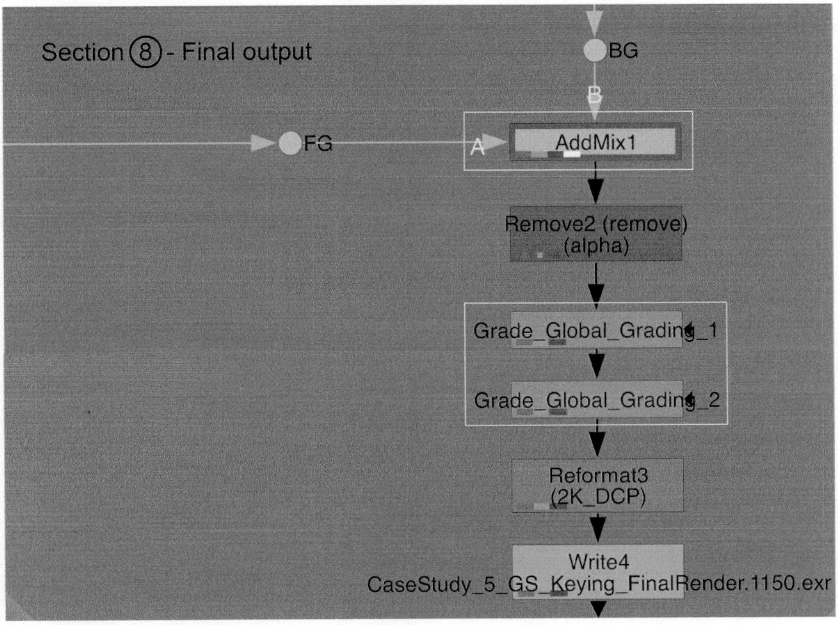

FIGURE 5.111 Node connections for the final output of Case Study 5

Case Study 6

Creating a VFX shot for the classic film *The Lavender Hill Mob*

Key learning points:

- > Footage and production analysis.
- > 3D camera tracking.
- > Matte generation and clean plate creation.
- > Creating 3D elements.
- > 3D match-moving.
- > CG multi-pass compositing.

Notes

Each case study includes a pre-recorded video tutorial. Watching these videos alongside reading the case studies is strongly recommended to ensure a smooth and comprehensive learning experience for each hands-on project.

Video link: youtube.com/@InvisibleFilmVFX

Video title: Case Study 6 | Creating a VFX Shot for the Classic Film The Lavender Hill Mob

Project file: Case_Study_6_Project_File

The project file is available for download on the book's official webpage.

High-resolution color figures from this project are also available for download on the book's official webpage.

This project demonstrates the key concepts and operational steps involved in seamlessly replacing one of the Eiffel Tower toys with a 3D Coca-Cola glass bottle in a shot from *The Lavender Hill Mob* (1951). The creative process includes rotoscoping, creating clean plates, removing lens distortion, tracking in NukeX, generating a CG bottle and elements for 3D matchmoving in Autodesk Maya, and final compositing in NukeX.

Images from *The Lavender Hill Mob* used in this project are licensed by StudioCanal.

Figure 5.112 displays the original footage, in which an actor repeatedly takes toy Eiffel Towers from a suitcase and hands them to eagerly awaiting pupils. The frequent hand movements in this shot pose a challenge for achieving the intended visual effects.

Figure 5.113 shows the final visual effects scene, which is based on the original footage.

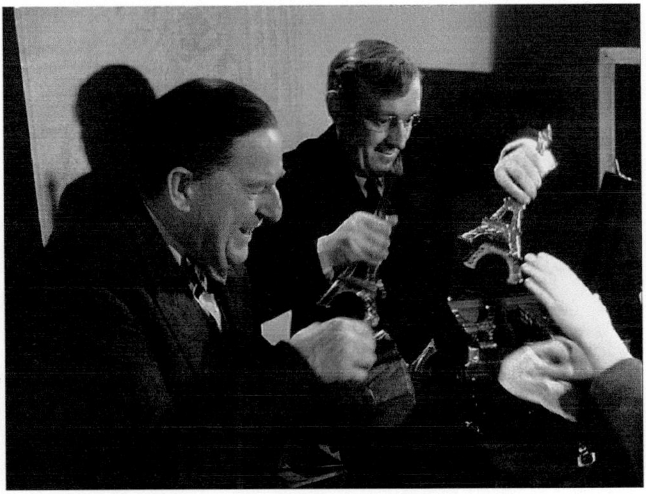

FIGURE 5.112 Original shot from *The Lavender Hill Mob* (1951). © StudioCanal

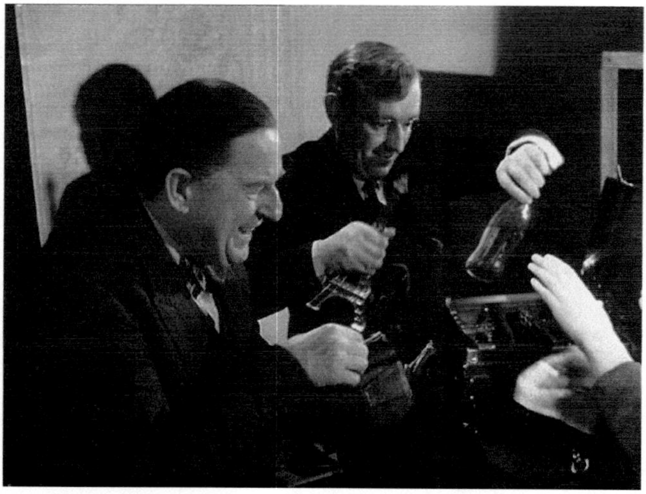

FIGURE 5.113 Final output of the VFX shot from Case Study 6

• Footage and production analysis

o Footage information

Footage length: 400 frames

Image aspect ratio: 768 × 576 (used in this project)

Negative format: 35 mm

Camera model: Unknown

Camera lens: Unknow Spherical

o Production analysis

To seamlessly integrate the CG glass bottle into the scene and make it appear as though the character is naturally holding it, the following approach should be carefully considered:

First, use rotoscoping techniques to isolate the hands that deliver and receive the toy between the actor and the student in the original footage.

Second, remove the toy tower and any related elements to create clean background patches. Then, generate a 3D Coke bottle that matches the original animation and lighting, ensuring it blends naturally into the scene.

Finally, composite the isolated hands over the CG bottle to seamlessly complete the VFX shot.

This sandwich method of integrating CG elements enables the seamless replacement of the toy tower with the glass bottle. The VFX shot is reconstructed using three key layers: a clean plate with the toy tower removed (bottom layer), the CG Coke bottle (middle layer), and the restored original footage of both hands (top layer).

Based on the concept described previously, we will develop the following assets:

– *Rotoscoping hands in the footage*

1. Create a matte for the student's hand in the foreground, including movements such as receiving, grabbing, and holding the toy tower.
2. Create a matte for the left hand of the actor on the right as he removes the toy tower from the suitcase and hands it to the student.

- *Clean plate*

Remove the toy tower and its shadows cast on the actor's chest, the back wall, and the wallet from the original footage. Figure 5.114 presents three reference frames (165, 179, and 183) that highlight the elements to be removed (outlined in white) across frames 135 to 185.

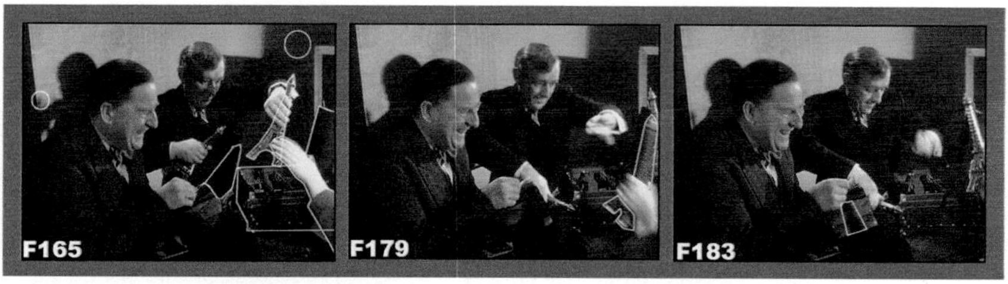

FIGURE 5.114 Elements requiring removal from frames 135 to 185

- *A 3D Coke glass bottle*

A 3D Coke glass bottle will be created and animated to precisely match the movement of the toy tower and the lighting conditions in the original scene.

◦ Examples of the required 2D assets

Figure 5.115 shows the generated mattes (A) for the hands, along with the clean plate where the toy tower and its shadows have been removed from the scene.

Image C compares the accuracy of the mattes with the original footage.

For testing purposes, Image D shows the original image of both hands composited onto the clean plate. Note that the toy tower has been successfully removed. At this stage, a 3D glass bottle will be integrated into the scene.

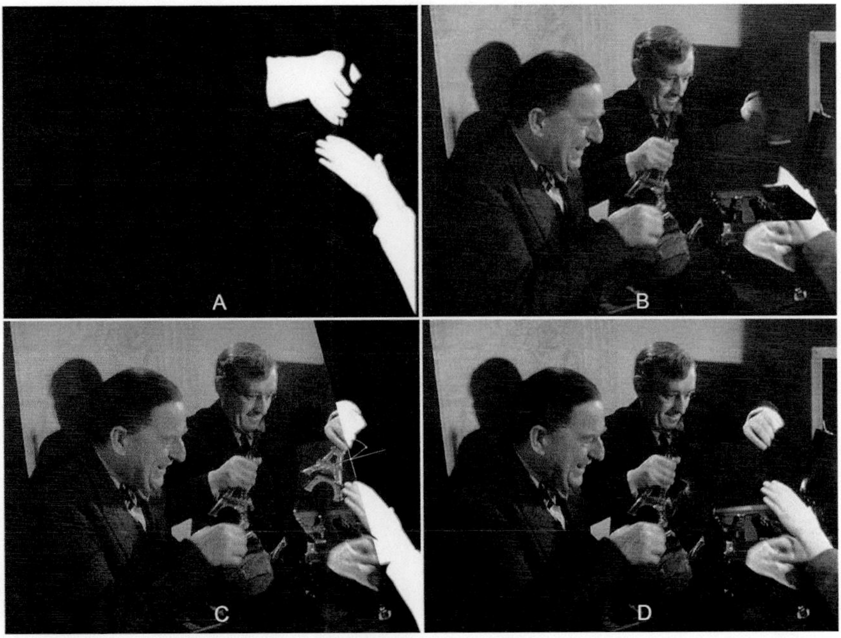

FIGURE 5.115 Testing the required mattes and clean plate for compositing

This project involves two separate Nuke scripts.

Nuke script 1: 3D camera tracking

A virtual camera is extracted from the shot and used to matchmove the animation of the 3D Coke glass bottle in Autodesk Maya. The script, shown on the left in Figure 5.116, demonstrates 3D camera tracking used to extract the virtual camera from the footage.

Nuke script 2: Compositing

This stage of the Nuke workflow includes rotoscoping, generating clean patches and a clean plate, and multi-pass compositing of 3D renders to integrate all assets into the final composition.

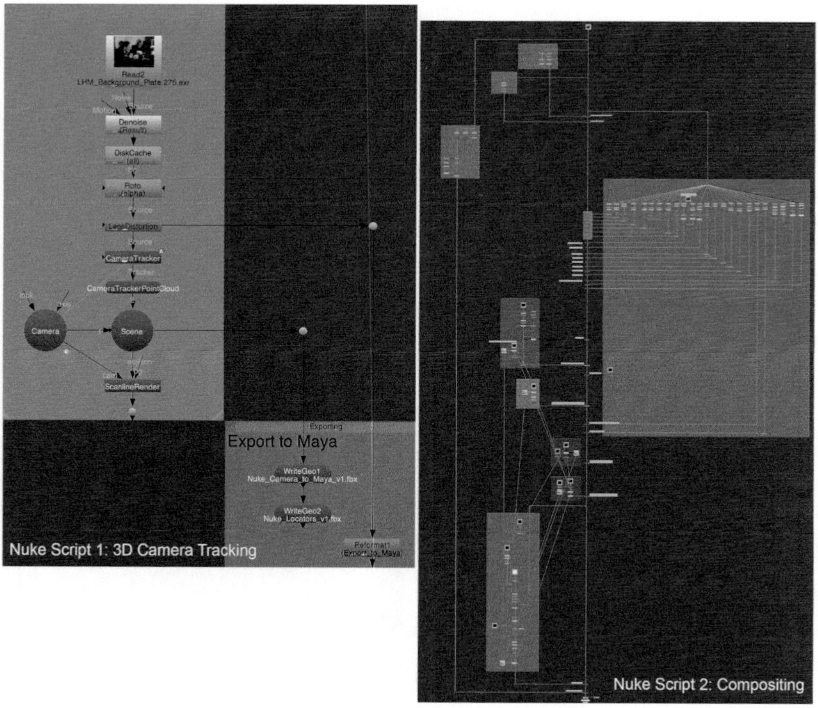

FIGURE 5.116 Nuke scripts used in Case Study 6. Script 1–3D Camera Tracking (left); Script 2 – Final Compositing (right)

• Nuke script 1: 3D camera tracking

In this project, the 3D camera tracking differs from that in previous projects because the camera is stationary rather than moving.

o Preparations before 3D camera tracking

A Denoise node was used to remove film grain from the original shot. Before starting 3D camera tracking, it is important to mask out any moving objects in the scene. This ensures accurate tracking, since the goal is to track the scene itself rather than individual objects. To achieve this, a Roto node was connected to create two rough masks in the alpha channel of the undistorted plate. These masks exclude all moving elements during tracking, allowing NukeX to focus on the static parts of the scene.

Next, a legacy LensDistortion node was used to remove lens distortion from the original shot. In this node, the Line Analysis operation was applied by drawing several horizontal and vertical lines along the window frame in the upper-right corner and the edges of the suitcase at frame 345. These reference lines helped NukeX accurately calculate and remove the lens distortion.

Note

Legacy nodes in NukeX were introduced in earlier projects. For a detailed demonstration of how to activate the legacy LensDistortion node, refer to Case Study 3 (Figure 5.46).

o 3D camera tracking

The process of 3D camera tracking was thoroughly covered in previous chapters. However, a few settings should be clarified when configuring the CameraTracker node. Since this is a static shot, set the Camera Motion option to Rotation Only. To do this, double-click the CameraTracker node and navigate to the Properties panel > CameraTracker tab > Camera Motion, and set it to Rotation Only. Figure 5.117 illustrates the node connections used to set up the camera tracking node. The Denoise, Roto, and Lens Distortion nodes are applied before the 3D camera tracking setup.

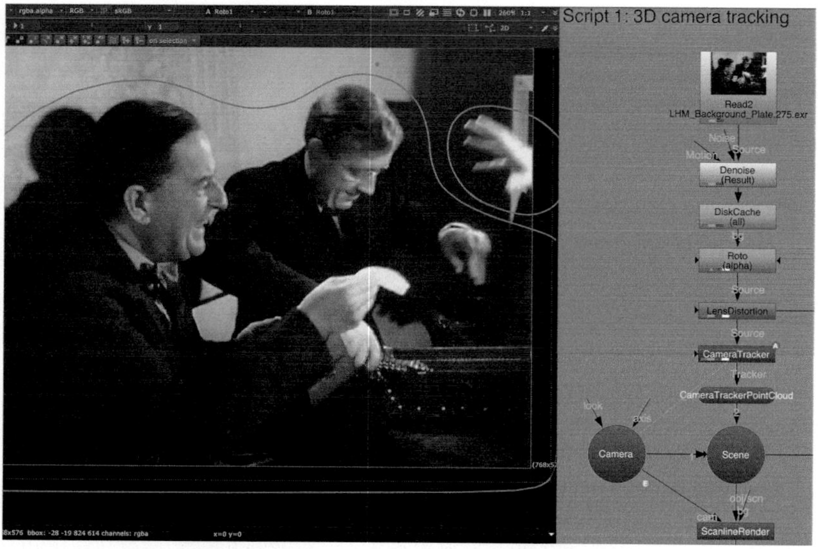

FIGURE 5.117 Node connections for 3D camera tracking

After completing the 3D camera tracking, the following assets are exported for further match-moving in 3D applications:

1. A virtual camera
2. Point clouds
3. An overscan plate (with film grain and lens distortion removed)

Two separate WriteGeo nodes are used to export the virtual camera and tracking point clouds. Additionally, a Reformat node is applied to resize the background plate to match the overscan dimensions. The overscan plate is then exported as a sequence of JPEG images using a Write node.

These exported files serve as reference data for 3D match-moving, modeling, animation, and lighting setup in Autodesk Maya. Figure 5.118 illustrates the node connections used to export these assets in NukeX.

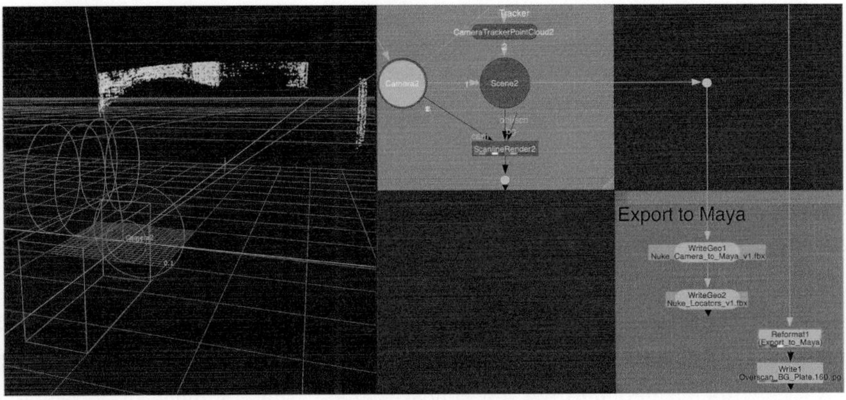

FIGURE 5.118 3D camera tracking result (left) and corresponding nodes used to export reference data (right)

Note

The virtual camera and tracking clouds were exported as FBX files, especially to preserve the animation data in the virtual camera. The overscan background plate was rendered as an uncompressed JPEG image sequence, which is lightweight and easy to load into 3D applications for reference during matchmoving.

• Nuke script 2: Compositing

Because the camera remains stationary in this shot, the most effective method for generating a clean plate involves exploiting the positional changes of moving objects across frames. The concept is straightforward: as an object moves from one frame to another, areas of the background that were previously obscured become visible. For instance, when an object shifts from frame 10 to frame 20, frame 10 reveals the background where the object initially appeared. Similarly, as the object moves from frame 20 to frame 30, frame 20 exposes newly visible background regions. By systematically analyzing these changes, a clean plate can be reconstructed directly from the source footage. This approach is particularly well-suited to static shots. Figure 5.119 illustrates this process, highlighting the object's movement and the corresponding background reveals across sequential frames.

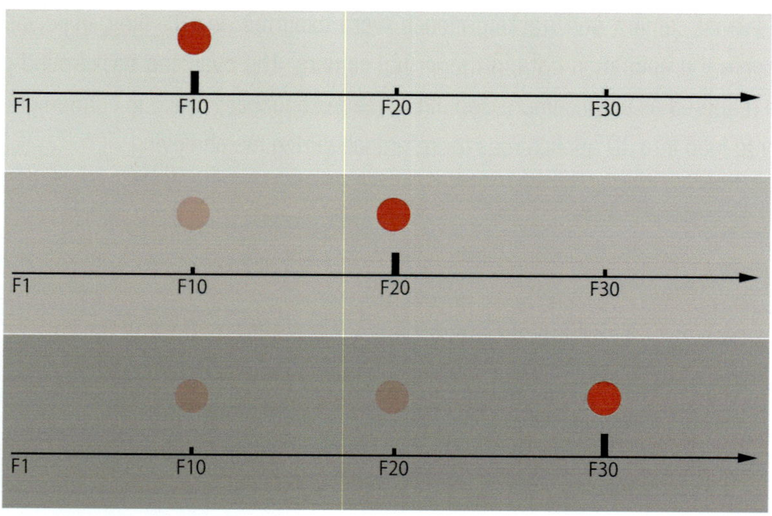

FIGURE 5.119 The concept of object movement and background reveal across sequential frames

◦ Section ①: Removing shadows on the wall (F160–F180)

The toy tower casts shadows in two distinct areas on the wall, highlighted by the white circles in frame 164 of Image 1 in Figure 5.120. Between frames 160 and 180, the toy tower moves while the camera remains static. This static camera is crucial for the shadow removal process, which proceeds as follows:

- To remove the shadows in frame 164, two TimeOffset nodes (L and R, as shown in Image 2) are used to shift frame 164 to nearby frames where the wall is not shadowed. Two Roto and Premult nodes are then applied to create two separate clean patches for the shadowed areas in the offset frames. This approach is effective because the camera remains static while the object's position changes, as illustrated in Figure 5.119.
- Next, the two clean patches are combined using a Merge (over) node, as shown in the final node of Image 2 in Figure 5.120. The resulting merged patches are displayed in Image 3.
- Finally, another Merge (over) node is used to composite the combined clean patches (Image 3) over the original background plate (Image 1), replacing the wall shadows with clean patches, as shown in Image 4.

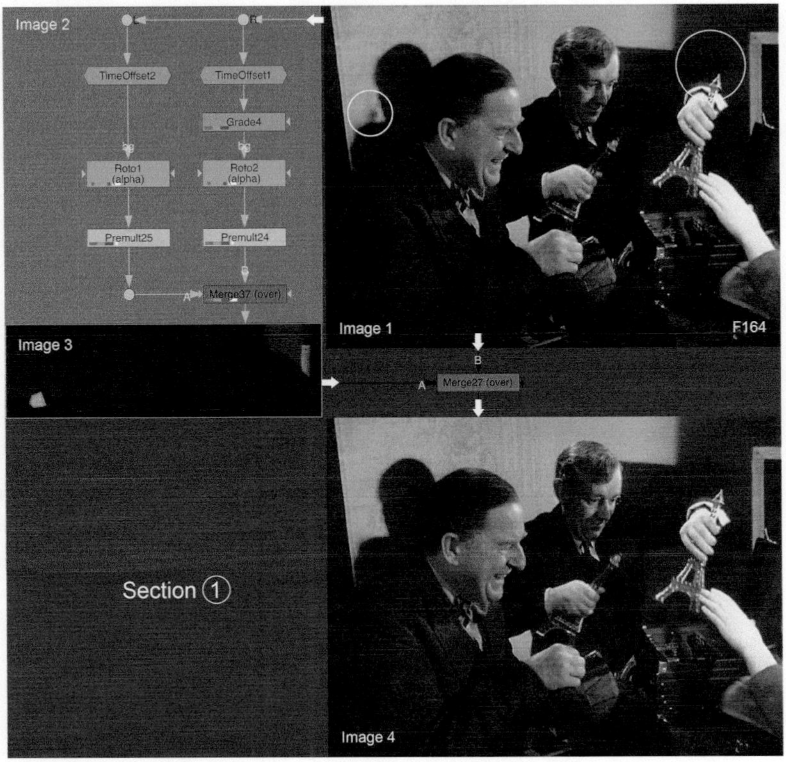

FIGURE 5.120 Removing shadows from the wall in the background plate between frames 160 and 180

◦ Section ②: Erasing the toy tower held by the student (F177–F183)

Figure 5.121 shows four nodes used to erase the toy tower from frames 177 to 183. The toy tower was initially held by the man in the middle and was later picked up by the student. In frame 177, the man's cuff and part of his fingers, which were originally hidden behind the toy tower, were also reconstructed. A key technique demonstrated here is the use of the TimeOffset node, which offsets the footage by two frames backward (-2) to create a clean patch without the glass bottle. For detailed instructions, refer to the pre-recorded demo video.

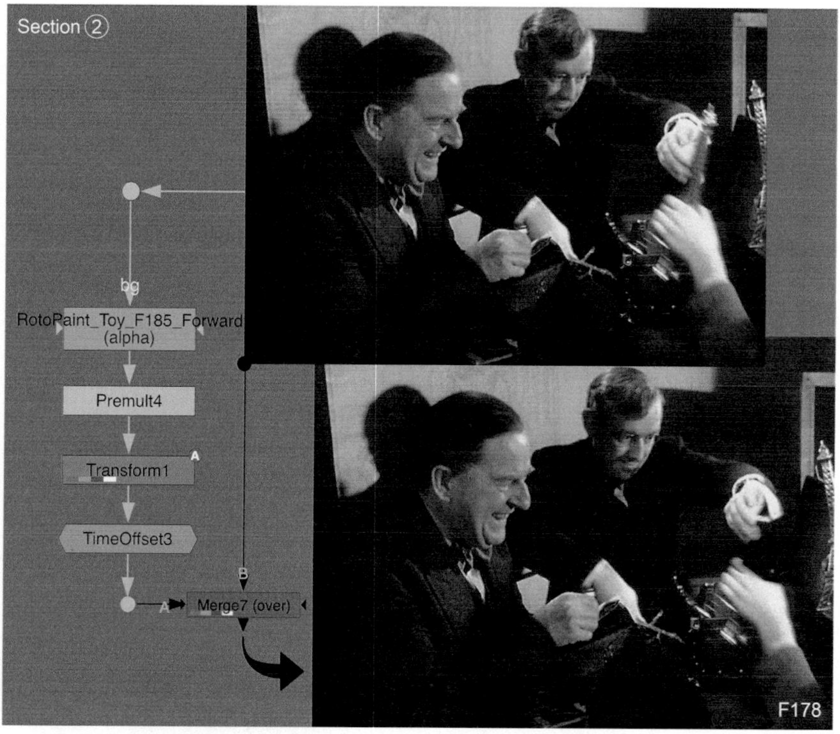

FIGURE 5.121 Removing the toy tower held by the man and the student from the original footage (frames 177–183)

○ Section ③: Creating mattes for the hands (F101–F191)

Section 3 involves roto shapes, painted patches, and fixes for other elements in the shot. In Figure 5.122, the top six nodes are used to generate mattes. The two Roto nodes highlighted within the white rectangle contain separate roto shapes created for the man's and the student's hands, covering frames 137 to 181. After these operations, a Premult node is applied at the end to extract both hands from the original plate. In the final composition, these extracted elements will be composited back on top to obscure the Coke glass bottle after it has been integrated with the original plate.

Watching the provided instructional video and downloading the Nuke project file to explore how these nodes work is the best way to learn.

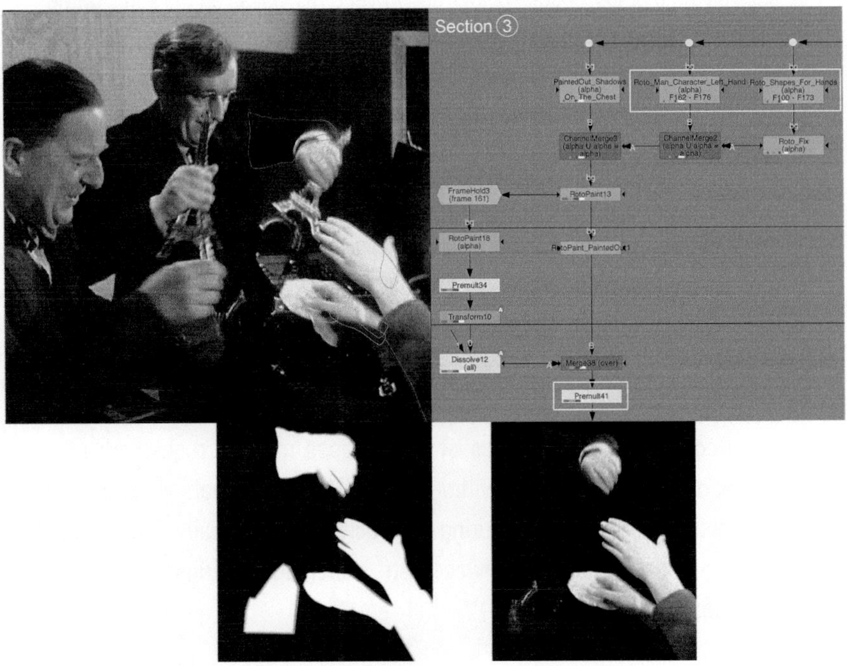

FIGURE 5.122 Node connections and mattes created for the hands

The concept of rotoscoping techniques was introduced in the section on the fundamental understanding of mattes in compositing at the beginning of this chapter. Although specific elements may vary from shot to shot, certain principles can still be applied consistently across all shots. For example, before beginning any rotoscoping tasks, we can analyze the shot by considering the following factors:

- Analyze how to break down the natural structure of the hands into different units based on their movement. In this particular example, neither hand underwent significant changes in overall shape during movement. Therefore, we only separated the thumb from the rest of the hand for each character during the rotoscoping process.

  However, in many cases, hand shapes and motion patterns can be more complex. In such situations, roto shapes should be subdivided into components such as the thumbs, fingers, palms, and lower arms, based on the joints of the hand. This approach allows for greater flexibility in adapting roto shapes to changes in hand structure. Otherwise, creating roto shapes as a single unit can make it difficult to capture each major pose and movement of the hands accurately, potentially resulting in unstable or jittery edges in the final matte across all frames.
- Identify the motion patterns of the hands in the scene, including key poses and transitions. Understanding these key poses and major transitions before rotoscoping allows artists to focus on the keyframes of movement, while leaving the in-between frames to be calculated by rotoscoping software and computers.

Note

In visual effects studios, two types of roto shapes may be requested: one that includes motion blur and another without it. This flexibility enables compositors to adjust the motion blur as needed during compositing. Additionally, roto shapes created for this purpose must be highly accurate, matching the original object shapes down to the pixel level.

○ Section ④: Create clean patches for the wall and the suitcase

In this section, a series of TimeOffset and Roto nodes were used to generate clean patches for various areas of the wall and suitcase. As expected, after replacing the toy tower with a glass bottle, the shadows cast on elements in the scene needed to appear semi-transparent. Therefore, the shadows originally cast by the toy tower had to be removed. By applying TimeOffset and Roto nodes across different frames, clean patches were created along the path of the toy tower's movement. These patches were then integrated into the original plate using Merge (over) nodes, resulting in a clean plate. Figure 5.123 illustrates node connections of this process.

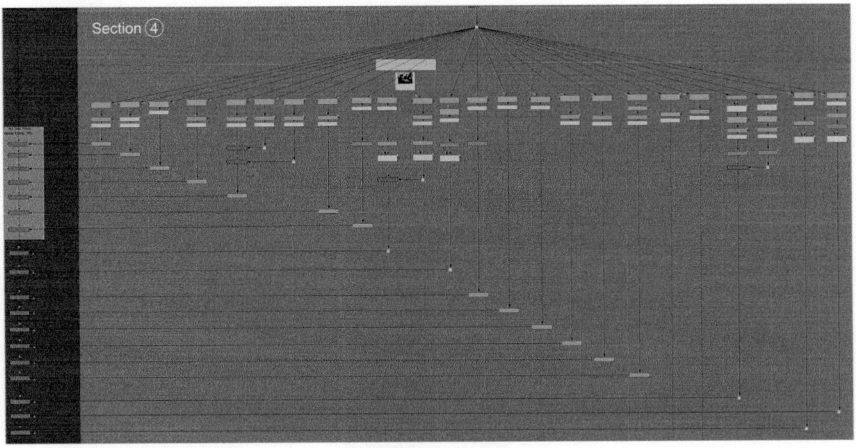

FIGURE 5.123 Nodes used for creating clean patches on the wall and the suitcase

• Creating the 3D Coca-Cola bottle

The Lavender Hill Mob was released in 1951. To replace the toy tower with a CG Coke bottle in the scene and achieve invisible visual effects, it is also important to ensure that the shape of the CG glass bottle matches the style of Coke bottles produced during that era. Such attention to detail is essential for creating convincing results. In many VFX shots, subtle elements can bring an entire scene to life.

After conducting research, we found that the Coke bottle used between 1951 and 1958 was known as the "Hobbleskirt" Coke bottle (6 FL OZ). It featured an embossed Coca-Cola logo and was sealed with a red bottle cap. With this historical reference established, a 3D model of the bottle was created using the polygon modeling method. This model, along with camera tracking data from NukeX, was used for 3D match-moving and animation tasks in Maya.

Figure 5.124 shows the final 3D model, created based on a reference image of a Coke bottle produced around 1951.

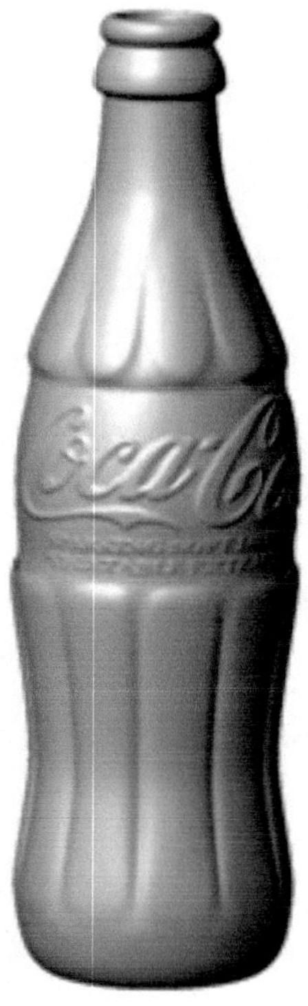

FIGURE 5.124 The 3D Coke bottle created based on the Hobbleskirt Coke bottle (6 fl oz)

○ 3D matchmoving and animation in Maya

Import the virtual camera, tracking point clouds, and the reference background plate as part of the 3D camera tracking data into Maya. Use the Distance Tool (Create > Measure Tools > Distance Tool) to measure and rescale elements in the scene, ensuring they align with the real-world scale shown by the imported reference background plate. In this example, we use the known size of the Coke bottle as a basic reference to estimate the scale of the suitcase and the overall scene.

This step is essential for achieving a physically based rendering (PBR) result. Figure 5.125 illustrates the process, including imported camera tracking files, scale measurements, matchmoving of the 3D Coke bottle, and the final animation.

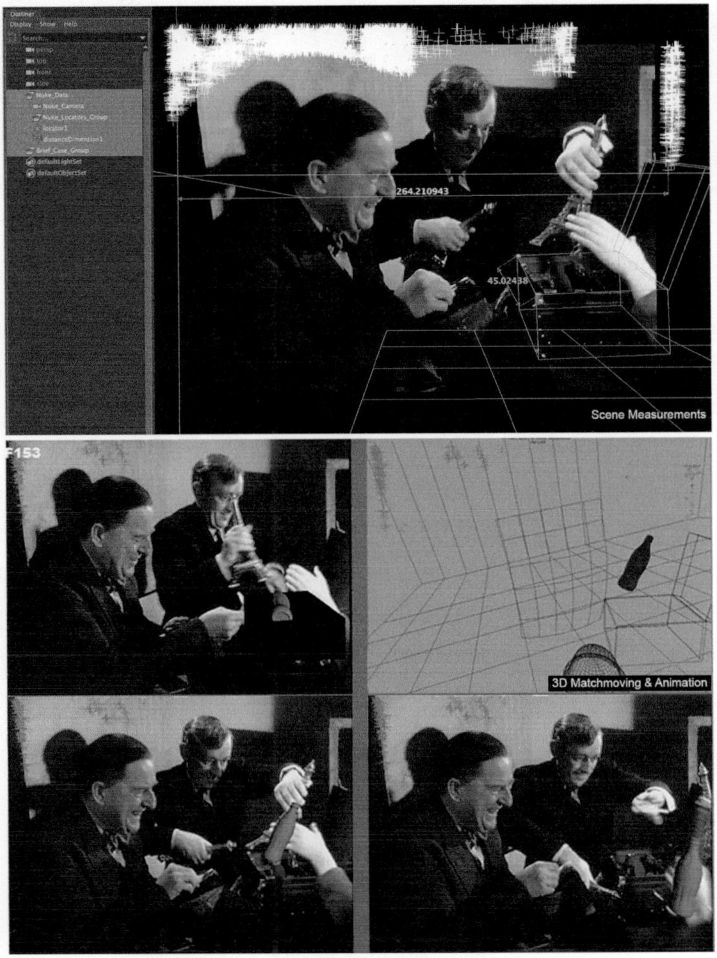

FIGURE 5.125 3D matchmoving and animation of the Coke bottle

∘ Final rendering and compositing

As we know, light rays passing through transparent objects such as glass bottles can form caustics. These caustics are influenced by the curvature of the object's surface and are projected onto another surface according to the principles of physical optics. To simulate and render realistic caustics, a series of tests were conducted. Figure 5.126 shows the results of a study on caustics using a glass Coke bottle.

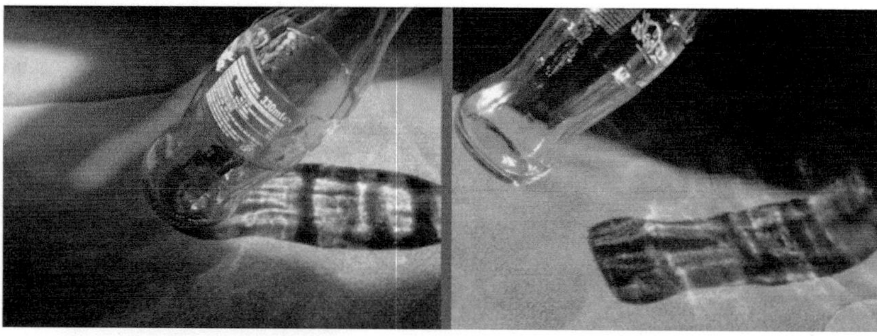

FIGURE 5.126 Reference images for analyzing caustics on a glass Coke bottle

After matchmoving and animating in Maya, the 3D Coke bottle was rendered as multi-pass arbitrary output variables (AOVs) for final compositing. These passes include specular, reflection, refraction, occlusion, Fresnel, shadow, caustics, normal, and motion vector. The purpose of using these passes is to reconstruct and enhance the details of the 3D bottle, enabling seamless integration with the original footage during compositing. In Figure 5.127, Image A illustrates the integration of the 3D Coke bottle with the clean plate, while Image B displays the final composition.

For a more in-depth understanding of AOV multi-pass compositing, refer to Case Study 7.

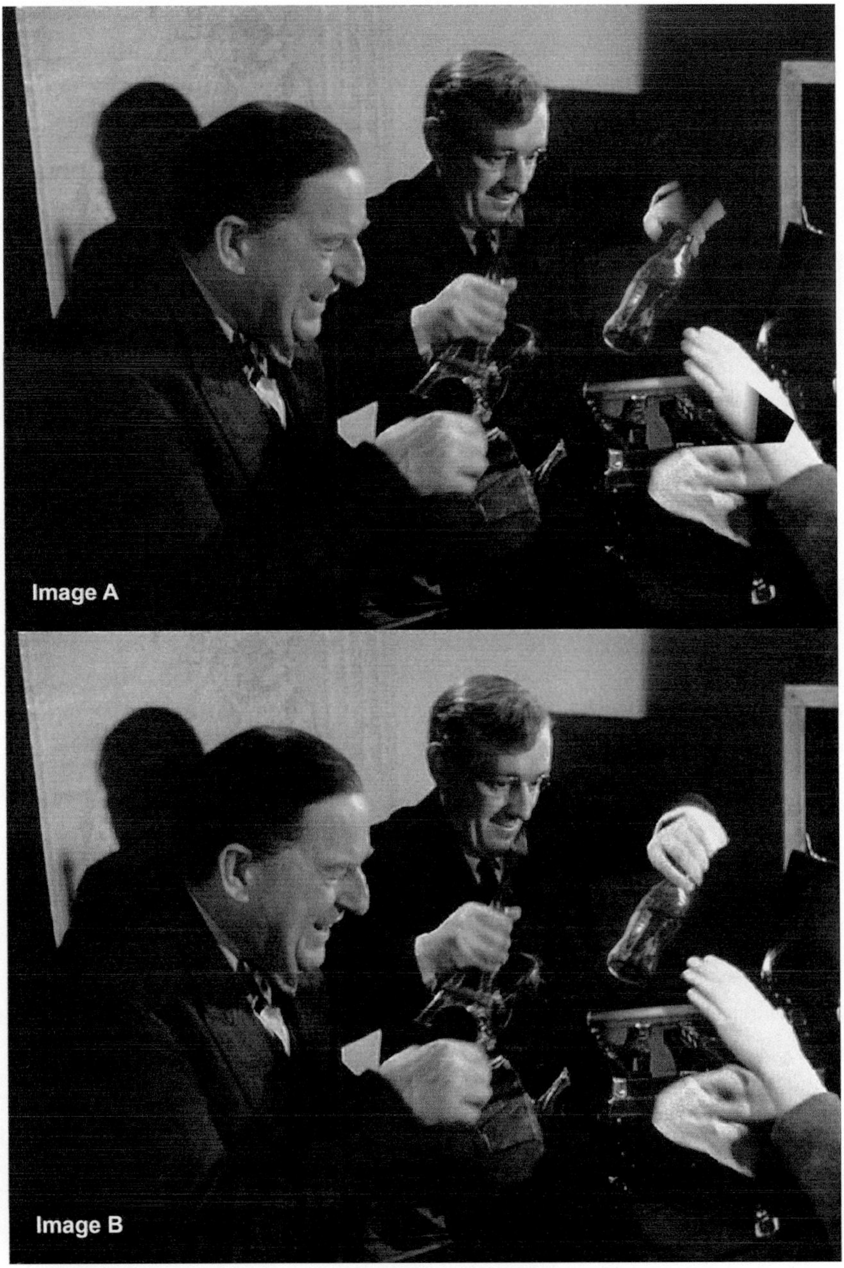

FIGURE 5.127 Image A illustrates the integration of the 3D Coke bottle with the clean plate, while Image B presents the final VFX shot

Case Study 7

The CG shoe project: seamless integration of CG elements with low-end footage

Key learning points:

> Workflow between applications in Case Study 7.

> Understanding factors when working with low-end footage.

> CG multi-pass compositing.

Notes

Each case study includes a pre-recorded video tutorial. Watching these videos alongside reading the case studies is strongly recommended to ensure a smooth and comprehensive learning experience for each hands-on project.

Video link: youtube.com/@InvisibleFilmVFX

Video title: Case Study 7 | The CG Shoe Project: Seamlessly Integrating CG Elements with Lower-End Footage

Project file: Case_Study_7_Project_File

The project file is available for download on the book's official webpage. High-resolution color figures from this project are also available for download on the book's official webpage.

As the projects progress to more advanced stages, we will place greater emphasis on understanding the concepts and workflows of each topic. For more detailed operational demonstrations and instructions, please refer to the accompanying video tutorials.

• Production analysis

For many learners, working with high-end footage in exercises is always desirable. However, for professional VFX artists, particularly those working on feature films, the primary goal is to achieve realism and match the quality of the live-action footage. Ultimately, all elements in the scene should be integrated so seamlessly that they appear to have been filmed at the same time, with the same camera, and in the same environment, and with all the native characteristics of the original live-action footage.

The objective of Case Study 7 is to integrate a CG casual shoe into low-quality live-action footage while achieving photorealism in all aspects, including replicating flaws and common issues such as compression artifacts and chromatic aberration. The project also demonstrates 3D camera tracking and key concepts such as casual shoe modeling, texturing, HDRI lighting, and multi-pass compositing.

By simulating the constraints often encountered in low-budget VFX production workflows, this case study is designed to help learners understand and apply:

1. A cross-application workflow
2. Practical techniques for integrating 3D elements into low-quality live-action footage and multi-pass compositing.

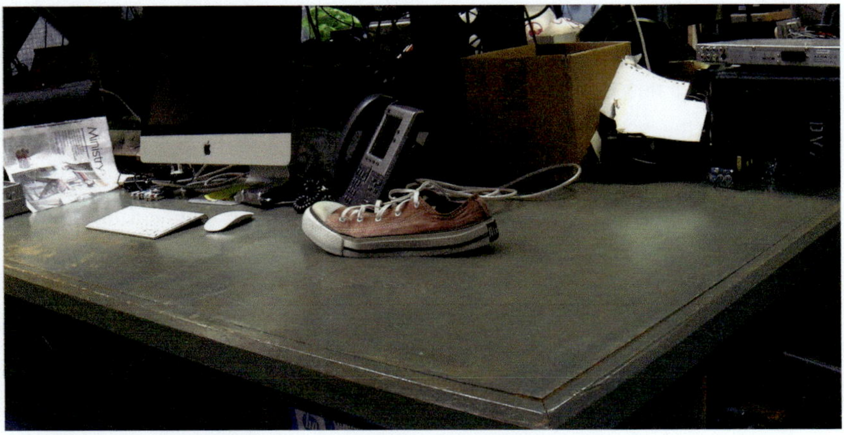

FIGURE 5.128 Final compositing result in Case Study 7

∘ Footage analysis

– *Background plate information*

Frame range: 1–100

Image aspect ratio: 1920 × 1080

Frame rate: 24 fps

Image bit depth: 8-bit JPEG

– *Camera information*

Camera model, lens, etc.: Unknown

Lens grid: Not provided

Camera movement: Handheld

∘ Shot analysis

The background plate for this project was captured using a Sony camera and converted into an 8-bit JPEG sequence. As discussed in previous chapters, 8-bit images contain limited color information and struggle to retain detail, especially in highlights. Additionally, compression introduces noticeable artifacts in the background plate. For example, black edges are visible around objects such as the keyboard and mouse. Chromatic aberration is also apparent in certain areas, particularly along the edges of the newspaper. While these imperfections may seem minor, it is necessary to replicate them in the CG assets to match the characteristics of the original background plate. Therefore, during compositing, the CG assets must be intentionally degraded to reproduce the artifacts present in the background plate. Figure 5.129 illustrates certain issues present in the original background plate.

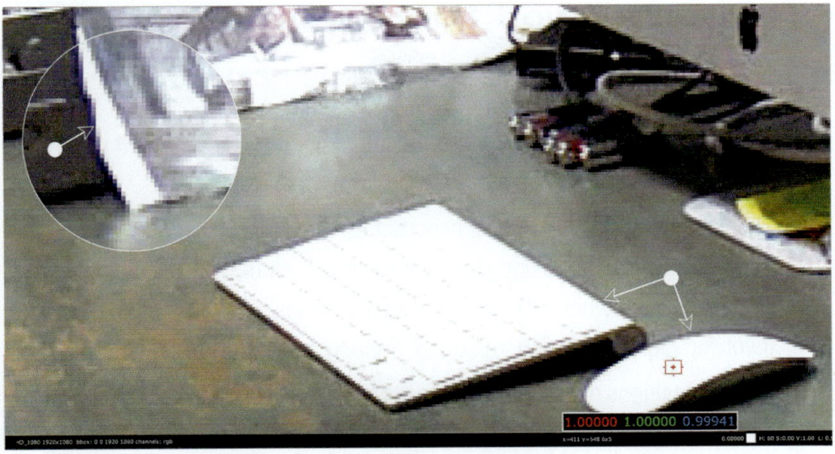

FIGURE 5.129 Image artifacts in the original background plate due to compression

• The overall workflow across applications

The project began with the preparation of the original background plate:

1. Lens distortion was removed from the plate, and a virtual camera was extracted using the 3D camera tracking system in NukeX.
2. The camera tracking data was exported to Maya for further 3D match-moving, along with the undistorted background plate, which included overscan. Meanwhile, 3D models of casual shoes were created in Maya, involving digital sculpting, texturing, lighting, and multi-pass rendering.
3. The original lens distortion data was then reapplied to the rendered 3D assets before integrating them with the original background plate.

The main workflow for this process is illustrated in Figure 5.130.

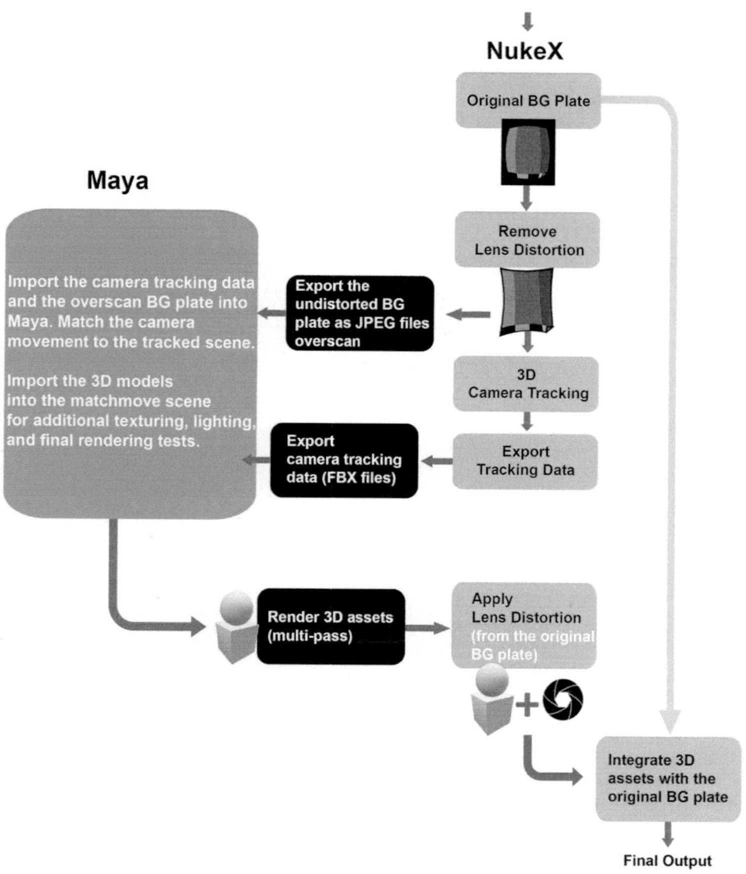

FIGURE 5.130 Flowchart of the major stages in Case Study 7

o 3D camera tracking and matchmoving

In Case Study 7, 3D camera tracking followed the same concept and operational process introduced in the previous case studies. Before performing the 3D camera tracking, a Denoise node was applied to remove film grain from the original background plate. This step helped reduce inaccuracies in the tracking results caused by heavy film grain. Next, a legacy LensDistortion node was used to remove lens distortion, using the table edges as reference lines. Additionally, a Roto node was employed to mask the reflection of the computer screen in the scene, preventing it from affecting the 3D camera tracking. After the initial tracking, a PoissonMesh node was used to create a reference 3D mesh. This mesh, along with the extracted camera, tracking point clouds, and the overscan background plate, was exported to Autodesk Maya for further 3D matchmoving.

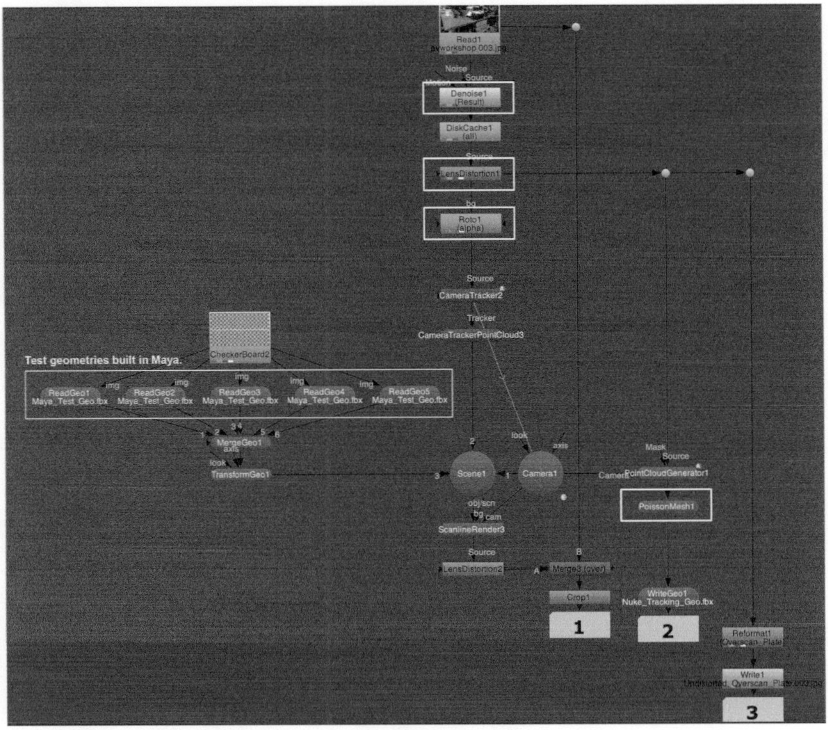

FIGURE 5.131 The 3D camera tracking script and its node connections

During the 3D match-moving process, several 3D cones were created in Maya to test camera alignment. These shapes were then exported to Nuke's 3D system for final evaluation, where the accuracy of the match-moving results against the background plate was assessed. Simultaneously, a pair of 3D casual shoes was modeled in Autodesk Maya using reference photos as a guide. The following section provides a brief outline of the workflow used to build the 3D models.

• Creating 3D shoes in Maya

The creation of 3D assets, including models, textures, lighting, animation, and final rendering, is a vital component of visual effects production.

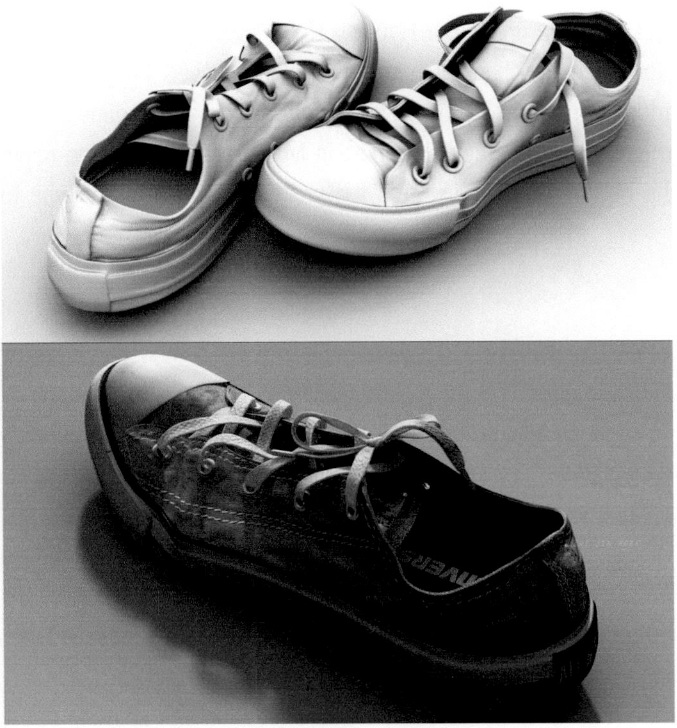

FIGURE 5.132 Final 3D models of the casual shoes, including texturing and lighting tests

Figure 5.132 shows a pair of 3D shoes created for this project. The upper image displays the 3D models with sculpted shoe details, while the lower image presents a test render that demonstrates the texturing and lighting of the shoes.

As discussed in previous chapters, the process of gathering reference images and initial models can be effectively supported by 3D scanning tools and applications, which are widely used in VFX production. However, in this demonstration, we used a more traditional approach to explore some of the key principles involved in the process.

◦ Shooting reference images and create 3D models

The traditional method of capturing reference images is used in this example. Unlike the LiDAR scanning process, this approach takes more time to capture reference objects. However, it allows for thorough documentation by capturing additional images of the reference objects on set, which are used for 3D texturing in later stages. The top images in Figure 5.133 show the front, back, top, and side views of the reference shoes with lens distortion removed. Since no scan data was available for the reference shoes, we measured their actual dimensions and used this information to scale the 3D models in Maya, as shown in the middle image. Finally, the bottom image illustrates the process of creating textures for the 3D shoes.

Note

To understand the essential principles, this project demonstrates the traditional process of capturing reference images. However, for your own projects, it is recommended to combine texture painting with procedural creation techniques. Texture resolutions can vary from 2K to 4K, 8K, or higher, depending on where the key 3D elements appear and how they will be used in the scene.

Next, use a digital camera or smartphone to scan the model and generate a true-scale 3D version, which can then be imported into your preferred 3D application for retopology. This approach can provide more data and improve workflow efficiency.

If you are familiar with procedural texture creation and painting software such as Adobe Substance Designer, Substance Painter, or Foundry's Mari, using procedural methods to create textures is a common industry practice for producing high-quality texture maps.

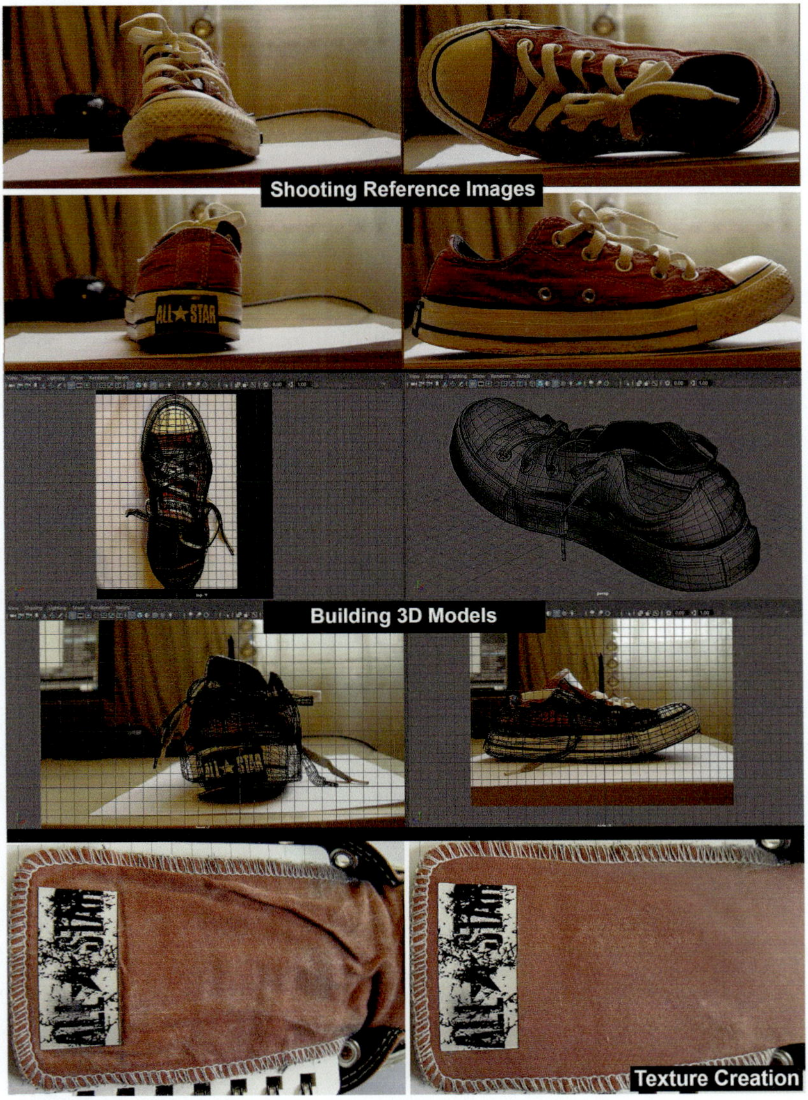

FIGURE 5.133 Capturing reference images and developing 3D models and textures for the shoes

○ Creating texture maps

A series of 4K photos was captured from various angles to serve as reference images for building the 3D shoes. These photos can also be used to generate textures for the 3D models. However, any highlights, reflections, or shadows must be removed if the photos are not cross-polarized. For a detailed explanation of cross-polarized imagery, refer to the "Texture Shoot for Characters and Props" section in

Chapter 4. If you have access to advanced equipment such as a polarized lens filter and polarized studio lighting, consider capturing cross-polarized reference photos to enhance texture quality.

Why were 4K texture images chosen for this project over other resolutions, such as 2K or 8K?

For 3D texture artists, creating textures at the highest possible resolution is often ideal. However, in production pipelines, efficiency is crucial, and the level of detail in both textures and 3D models must be carefully considered. In this case, the choice of the most appropriate texture resolution for the 3D model was based on two key factors:

- The final output resolution of the project.
- The distance of the 3D object from the camera.

The final output resolution for this shot is based on the original plate's aspect ratio, which is Full HD (1920 × 1080). Additionally, the distance between the 3D object and the camera intentionally varies between the middle ground and foreground throughout the animation. In other words, the 3D shoe will appear in both medium shots and close-ups. Therefore, appropriate texture resolutions should range between 2K and 4K. Using lower-resolution textures may result in pixelation during close-ups, while excessively high resolutions, such as 6K or 8K, can unnecessarily slow down the production process.

The bottom image in Figure 5.133 shows an example (left) captured for texture creation. It was taken under overcast conditions to minimize directional lighting and shadows. However, visible self-shadows caused by wrinkles on the shoe's surface are still present. As a result, such images cannot be used directly as texture maps. The image on the right shows a work-in-progress result in which the wrinkles and self-shadows have been removed.

Additionally, experimenting with current AI tools may further enhance the 3D texturing process in some cases. In this example, Google Gemini AI Nano Banana Pro was used to initially remove major wrinkles from the shoe tongue in the original image (lower left in Figure 5.133), followed by manual final touches using painting tools such as Adobe Photoshop (lower right).

o Illuminating the scene using an HDR image

To take advantage of Arnold's physically based rendering system in Autodesk Maya, we captured a high dynamic range image while filming the background plate. The HDRI was then aligned with the positions of six ceiling lights in the scene and mapped onto a skydome to illuminate the CG shoe.

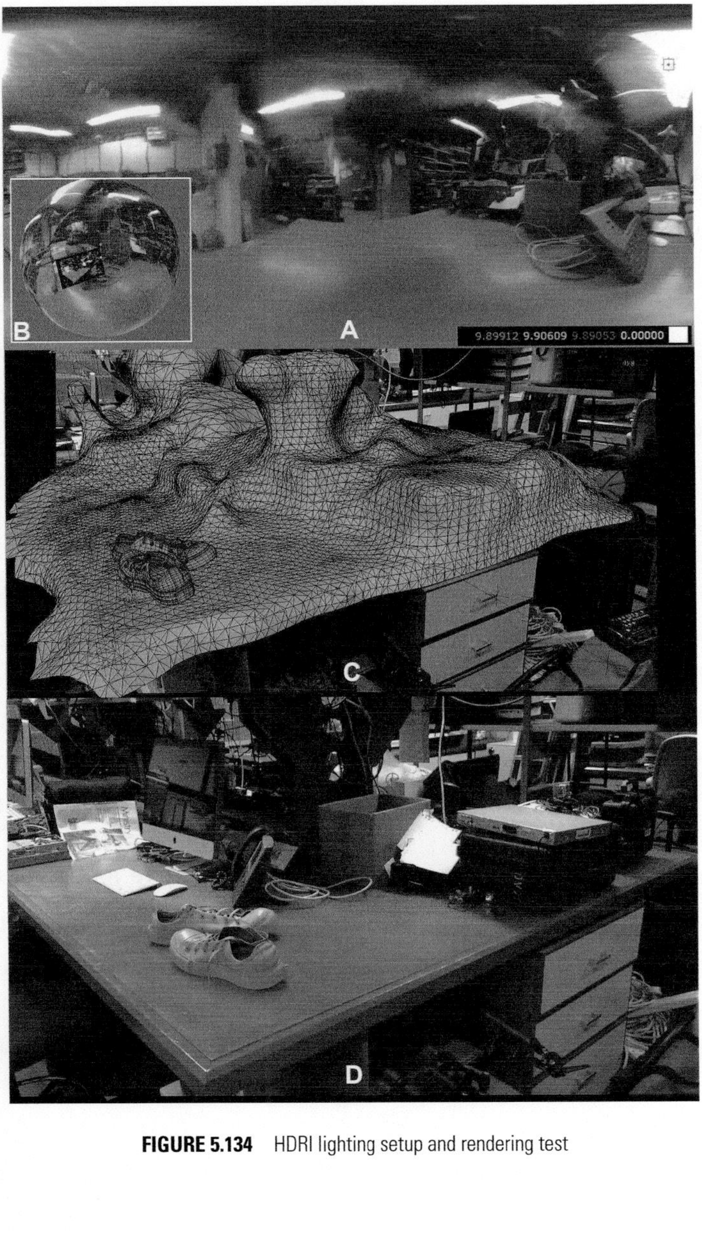

FIGURE 5.134 HDRI lighting setup and rendering test

Figure 5.134 illustrates the HDR image (A), the skydome (B), the 3D matchmoving alignment (C), and the final lighting test for a pair of CG shoes (D).

As shown in Image A, the RGB color values of one of the ceiling lights are 9.89912, 9.90609, and 9.89053. These high dynamic values, preserved in the image, are crucial for accurately lighting the CG elements in the scene. Additionally, the 3D mesh in Image C was generated using the PoissonMesh node based on tracking point clouds from the scene. Aligning this 3D mesh with the live-action footage creates a real-scale 3D environment, allowing for the easy placement of test geometries. Image D displays the result of a lighting test on the 3D shoes.

◦ Multi-pass renders

Multi-pass rendering and compositing allow 3D artists and compositors to work flexibly on individual passes, efficiently refining the final composition of CG elements integrated with live-action footage. For instance, when changes are required in a CG element, compositors can easily make adjustments using the available passes or request additional ones from the 3D department. This workflow significantly improves production efficiency. In contrast, when CG elements are rendered as a single image with all passes combined, any further updates require re-rendering the entire element. This process can be extremely time-consuming, especially under tight production deadlines.

Multi-pass compositing utilizes arbitrary output variables, with the specific types of passes varying depending on the rendering engine used in production pipelines. For instance, RenderMan is widely used in visual effects studios to render CG elements in feature films. AOVs are typically grouped into categories such as lighting, color, utility, and others, with each category containing specific passes. For example, a typical set of passes rendered with Pixar's RenderMan includes primary passes, multiLight passes (which group lights in Katana-rendered scenes for various functions), multiDiffuse passes, multiSpecular passes, diffuse direct and indirect passes, specular direct and indirect passes, transmission, scatter, color, occlusion, depth, world position, reference position, normals, ID passes, UV maps, vector motion passes, and more.

In this project, we rendered the following passes using Maya's default rendering engine, Arnold.

– *Beauty pass (primary pass)*

The Beauty pass serves as the primary container for various multi-passes within its channels, including lighting, color, and utility passes. Although the Beauty pass is not used directly in compositing, it plays a crucial role as a reference throughout both the rendering and compositing stages. Therefore, when combining all the multi-passes to reconstruct the Beauty pass, the result should match the original as expected.

– *Matte*

A matte pass refers to a mask embedded in the alpha channel of a 3D asset after rendering. It plays a vital role in compositing, as it is used to isolate specific elements or areas of an image for further manipulation, such as color grading or pre-multiplication.

– *Diffuse (no shadow) & Specular (no shadow)*

By adding the Diffuse and Specular passes (without shadows), we can create a composition that incorporates both the diffuse and specular elements of the CG shoe.

– *Indirect*

Lighting passes can be categorized into direct and indirect types. A direct lighting pass represents light that travels directly from a source and hits the surfaces of 3D geometry in the scene. An indirect lighting pass, on the other hand, refers to ambient or bounced light, where light reflects off surfaces in the environment and contributes to the overall illumination.

– *Shadow*

In this example, a shadow pass refers to self-cast shadows. For instance, shoelaces may cast shadows onto the uppers of CG shoes.

– *Reflection*

In the real world, almost everything exhibits some degree of reflection due to lighting and material properties. In this example, the reflection pass includes reflections from various shoe materials, such as the metal eyelets, shoelaces, rubber soles, and the canvas fabric itself.

- *Occlusion*

Occlusion becomes noticeable, particularly when an object comes into contact with other objects. In these cases, the contact areas exhibit soft shadows resulting from the scattering of ambient light.

- *Fresnel*

The Fresnel effect describes how the intensity of light reflection varies depending on the viewing angle. For instance, when a sphere's surface faces directly toward the camera (i.e., at a near-zero viewing angle), it typically exhibits minimal specular reflections. In contrast, surfaces viewed at glancing angles tend to show stronger specular reflections of the environment. This effect can be achieved in a Fresnel pass to help blend the edges of CG objects with their surrounding environment.

- *ID pass A & ID pass B*

Two groups of ID passes were generated for this project: ID pass A and ID pass B, each using primary colors to designate different parts of the CG shoe. Each part can then be treated as an individual matte for further image adjustments, such as color correction.

- *Shadow on the table*

The shadow of the CG shoe is cast onto the table surface within the HDRI lighting environment.

- *Motion vector*

A motion vector pass can generate realistic motion blur based on the movement of objects or the camera. In this project, although the CG shoe is rendered without animation, the camera's movement can still produce motion blur on all static CG elements in the scene. Therefore, the CG shoe should exhibit motion blur consistent with that seen in the footage.

Figure 5.135 presents a contact sheet of the rendered AOV passes from Case Study 7.

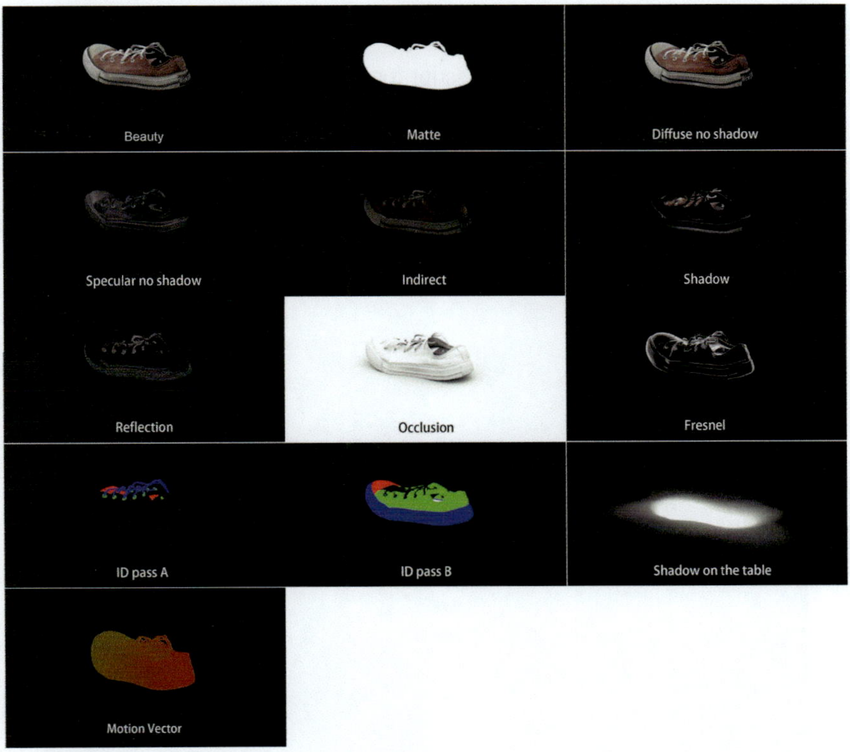

FIGURE 5.135 Arbitrary output variable passes rendered for the 3D shoe

• Compositing scripts

Figure 5.136 shows the compositing script for Case Study 7, which features multi-pass compositing. The script is organized into four main sections:

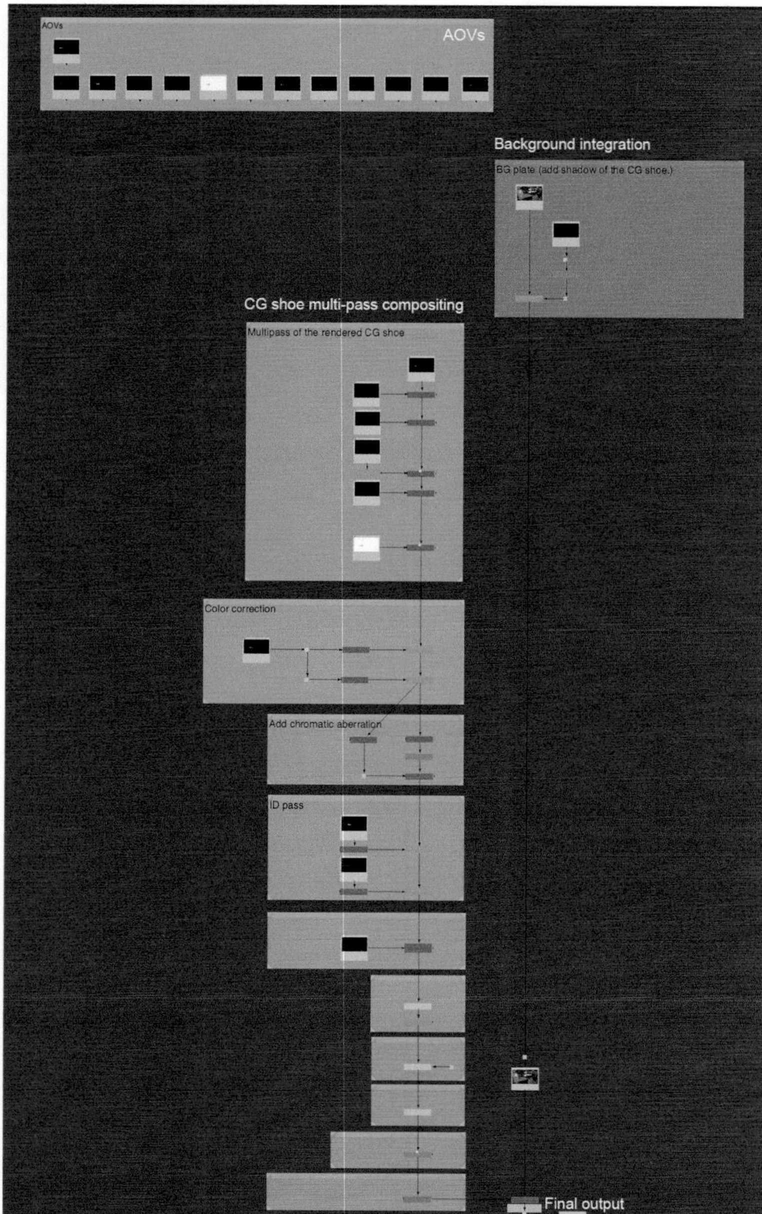

FIGURE 5.136 Compositing script for Case Study 7

o Integrating 3D assets into the background plate

To integrate 3D assets with the original background plate, we first need to apply the same lens distortion present in the background plate to the rendered AOV passes before compositing them.

Figure 5.137 illustrates the integrated shadow of the shoe within the original background plate. A LensDistortion node is added after the shadow pass (Shadow_on_the_table pass). This node contains lens distortion data extracted from the original background plate and is used to apply the same lens distortion to the shadow cast by the 3D shoe onto the table.

Additionally, a Grade node is connected directly after the original background plate to darken the shadow cast by the CG shoe onto the table. The grading is controlled through the Mask input of the Grade node, using the shadow information embedded in the alpha channel of the rendered shadow pass.

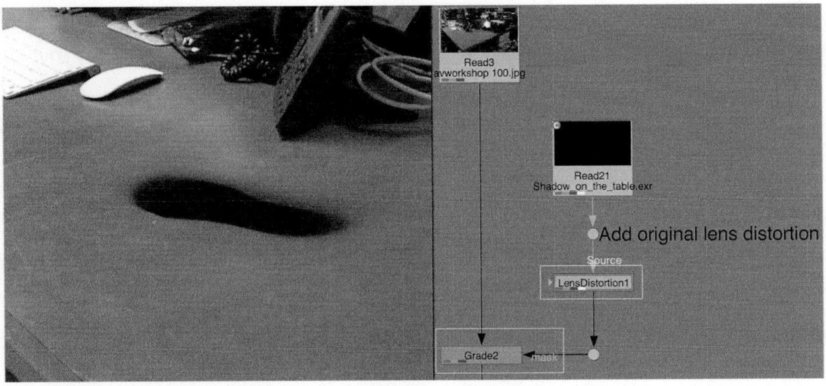

FIGURE 5.137 Integration of the 3D shoe's shadow with the original background plate

o CG shoe multi-pass compositing

There are two common approaches used for handling CG multi-passes in compositing:

- Rendering AOV passes separately.
- Rendering a Master Beauty pass with all other AOV passes embedded within its channels.

The choice between these two approaches may depend on the pipelines used by each studio. However, regardless of the chosen method in multi-pass compositing, all AOV passes must be recombined, and the final composition should match the Master Beauty pass, which serves as the reference.

In this example, the DiffuseNoShadow_pass, SpecularNoShadow_pass, and Indirect_pass were first combined using Merge (plus) nodes to build the base lighting of the CG shoe.

Next, a Merge (difference) node was used to add the shoe's self-shadows.

The Reflection_pass was then added using another Merge (plus) node, enhancing surface detail.

Finally, the Occlusion_pass was integrated with a Merge (multiply) node to introduce soft contact shadows, helping the shoe sit more naturally in the scene.

These multi-pass compositing steps are shown in the top image of Figure 5.138.

○ Creating the blown-out image highlights

The goal of color correction in this example is to intentionally degrade certain image qualities to match the look of the original background plate. This process includes replicating visual flaws present in the footage, such as blown highlights and artifacts resulting from heavy compression in an 8-bit image. It also involves recreating chromatic aberration found in the original footage.

The middle section of Figure 5.138 shows two separate Shuffle nodes used to transfer the red and blue channels of the MasterBeauty pass into the alpha channels of their respective Shuffle nodes. These are then connected to the mask inputs of two Grade nodes. By adjusting the gain and multiply values of each Grade node, we can simulate blown-out highlights on the CG shoe. The result is shown in the bottom image.

Note

As mentioned earlier, the MasterBeauty pass is used solely as a reference during compositing. However, we can extract individual channels, such as the red and blue channels, to assist with other operations. For example, in Figure 5.139, the red and blue channels of the Beauty pass are used as separate mattes for additional color correction via two Grade nodes. This approach allows us to create blown-out highlights in two distinct areas. In this scenario, the brightest areas are located around the shoe's toes and laces. Adjusting the gain and multiply values of each Grade node primarily influences the higher-luminance regions of both color channels, producing blown-out highlights on the CG shoe.

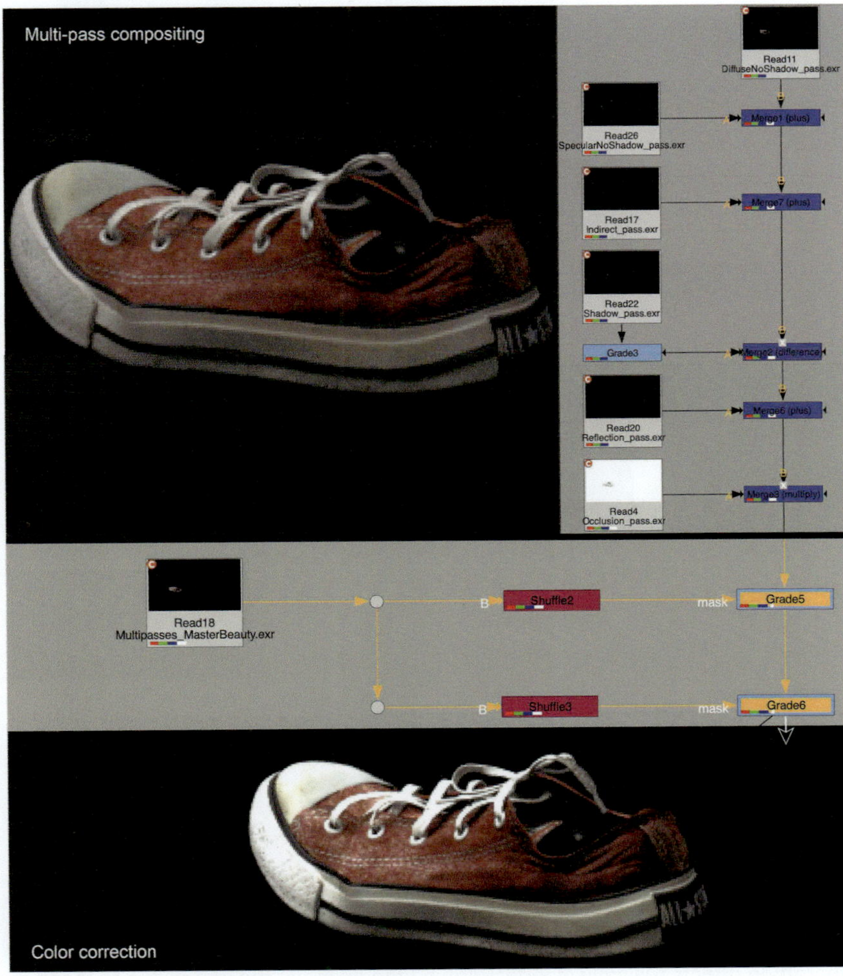

FIGURE 5.138 Nodes used for multi-pass compositing (top) and simulated blown-out highlights on the CG shoe (bottom)

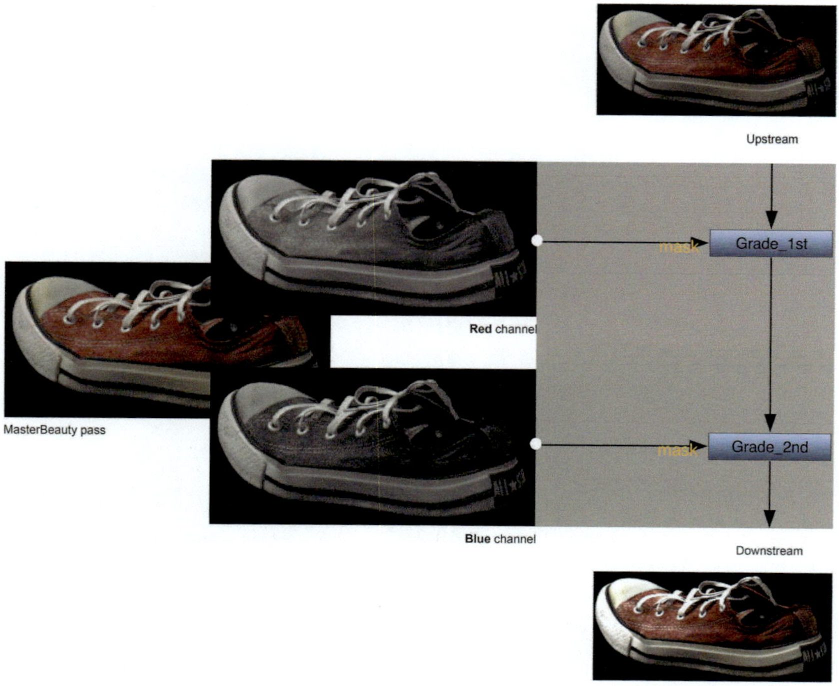

FIGURE 5.139 Using two different color channels as mattes to simulate blown-out highlights on the CG shoe via the mask inputs of two Grade nodes

o Creating chromatic aberration

Chromatic aberration is an optical phenomenon that frequently appears in live-action footage, especially when filmed with wide-angle lenses. Apparent chromatic aberration effects typically manifest around the edges of the image due to the varying refractive indices of different wavelengths of light. There are two types of chromatic aberration: transverse and axial.

Figure 5.140 illustrates the principles of chromatic aberration in Image A. It shows that light rays farther from the camera sensor's central axis (indicated by the dotted line) lead to greater separation between red, green, and blue colors. As a practical example, Image B demonstrates visible chromatic aberration in the footage, with noticeable blue and yellow fringing that indicates transverse chromatic aberration.

To create a realistic composition, we need to match the chromatic aberration of the footage with that of the CG shoe, making it appear as though the CG shoe was originally part of the scene during filming.

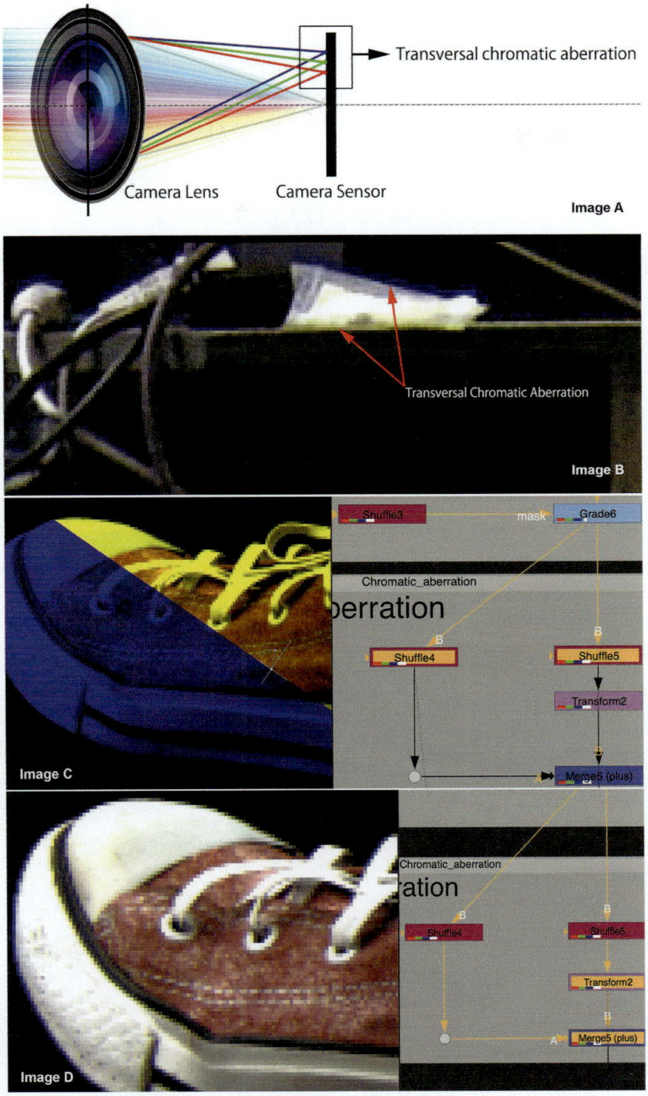

FIGURE 5.140 Principles and practical techniques for creating chromatic aberration effects

To replicate the chromatic aberration effect on the CG shoe, split the R, G, and B channels of the upstream-composited CG shoe using two Shuffle nodes, as shown in Figure 5.140 (Image C). In the Properties panel of the first Shuffle node (Shuffle4), connect the red and green channels from the Input Layer to the Output Layer. In the second Shuffle node (Shuffle5), connect only the blue channel. Then, use a Merge (plus) node to recombine the outputs of both Shuffle nodes. Next, add a Transform node below Shuffle5. In the Properties panel of the Transform node, slightly increase the scale to offset the blue channel's position, separating it visually from the red and green channels. Image D shows the final chromatic aberration effect created on the CG shoe.

∘ Color correction with ID passes

We created two ID passes for the 3D shoe:

ID pass A covers the shoelaces, eyelets, and tongue, each assigned a different primary color.

ID pass B includes the toe cap, upper, and sole, also using three distinct primary colors.

Each ID pass can be separated using a Shuffle node and connected to the mask input of a Grade node, allowing targeted color corrections to specific areas. See Figure 5.141.

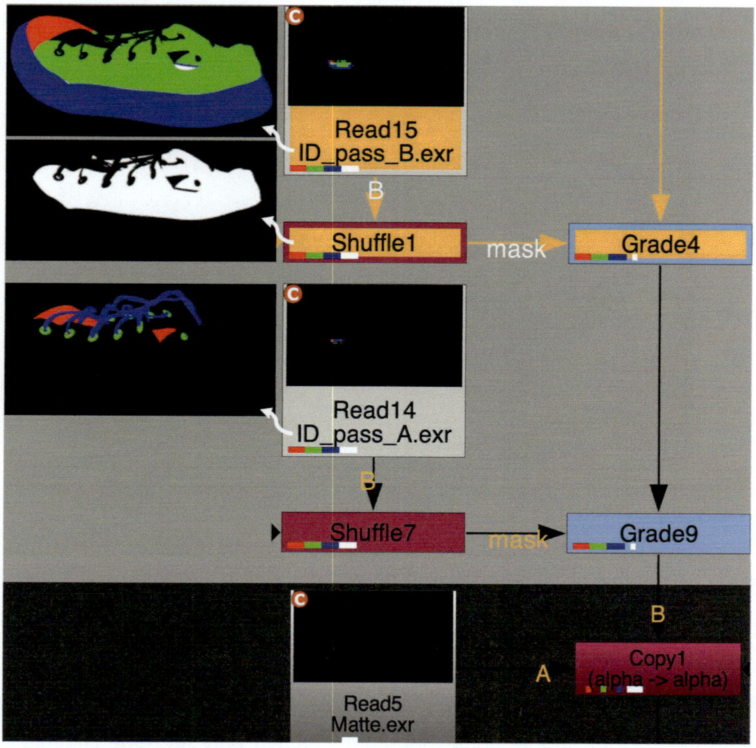

FIGURE 5.141 ID passes are separated using Shuffle nodes, allowing targeted color correction through the mask input of Grade nodes

After the Grade (Grade9) node, as shown in Figure 5.141, connect a Copy node to transfer the matte of the 3D shoe to the alpha channel of the shoe composition. From this point forward, the composition is considered a premultiplied image.

o Understanding premultiplied vs. unpremultiplied images

3D applications typically render premultiplied images by default. This means that a rendered CG asset includes an RGB color image and a grayscale matte stored in the alpha channel of the image. The RGB image and its matte are precisely aligned in terms of size, shape, transparency, and other relevant attributes. Image A in the upper left corner of Figure 5.142 shows a premultiplied image alongside its matte in the alpha channel. The shape and transparency of the RGB image align perfectly with those of the alpha channel. Conversely, an unpremultiplied image can be identified by comparing the shapes, sizes, and edge transparency of objects in the RGB image with those embedded in the alpha channel. Image B in the same image shows an unpremultiplied image, where the edge transparency between the RGB image and its alpha channel is different.

In compositing, working with premultiplied assets is inevitable. Here is the rule for handling premultiplied images:

If an image is premultiplied, it must be converted to an unpremultiplied state before performing any color grading or applying film grain. After these adjustments, the image should be converted back to a premultiplied state before any further downstream processing. Failure to follow these premultiplication and unpremultiplication guidelines during compositing can result in unexpected artifacts. Images C-1 and C-2 in Figure 5.142 illustrate two common mistakes made by novice compositors: black or white edges appearing around objects in the composition.

– *Black edge artifacts*

The black edge visible in Image C-1 is caused by an incorrect premultiplication operation.

If a premultiplied image is mistakenly treated as unpremultiplied, applying an additional premultiplication will result in black edges. In other words, the image ends up being premultiplied twice during compositing. For example, if the edge of a premultiplied image has values of 0.5, and the image is mistakenly treated as unpremultiplied, applying premultiplication again results in the following calculation:

$$0.5 \times 0.5 = 0.25$$

As a result, its value becomes 0.25, which is half of the original value, making it appear darker than intended. This reduction in brightness around the edges of the image causes visible black edges in the final composite. Similar principles apply to the issue of producing a white edge.

– *White edge artifacts*

If an unpremultiplied image is mistakenly divided by its alpha channel again, the pixel values will increase. For example, in an unpremultiplied image, a pixel might have RGB values of 1 and an alpha value of 0.5. If the image is incorrectly treated as premultiplied and processed with an Unpremult node, which performs a division operation, the calculation will be:

$$1 \div 0.5 = 2$$

Since the value of 2 is higher than the surrounding pixel values, the result appears brighter, creating white edges around the asset. Refer to Image C-2 in Figure 5.142 for a visual illustration.

In the upper-right image of Figure 5.142, the first node (Copy1) is used to copy the matte of the CG shoe into the alpha channel of the multi-pass compositing pipe. After that, the CG shoe composition becomes a premultiplied image. To avoid black edge artifacts during color grading, it must be unpremultiplied. Therefore, an Unpremult node is placed immediately after the Copy1 node. Next, Saturation and F_ReGrain nodes are added to perform color grading and apply film grain, ensuring the CG shoe matches the grain structure of the background plate.

Note

When applying film grain to CG assets, the focus is typically on the visible image areas, while the black (transparent) regions are often overlooked. However, increasing the gamma slider (located above the Viewer1 panel) can reveal hidden film grain in these black areas, as shown in Image B at the bottom of Figure 5.142. Compositing this result over the original live-action footage, which already contains film grain, can cause the grain to appear doubled and produce an incorrect final output.

In this example, the Saturation and F_ReGrain operations should be applied between the Unpremult and Premult nodes.

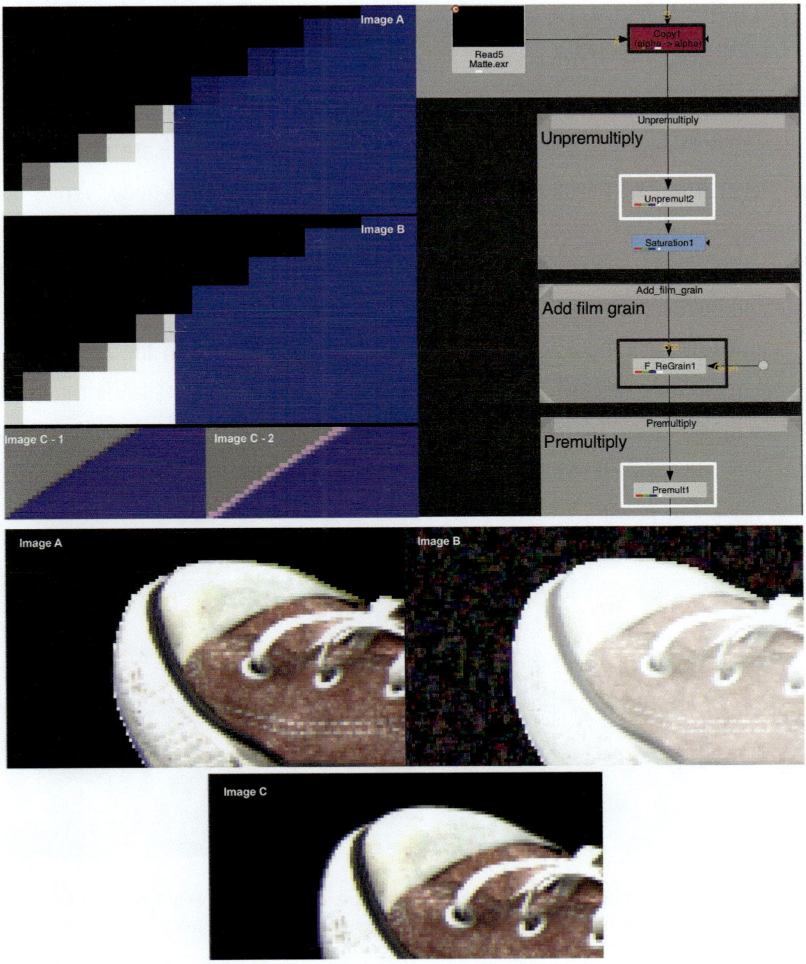

FIGURE 5.142 Understanding premultiplied and unpremultiplied images and their applications

The bottom image in Figure 5.142 compares three results obtained by applying the same film grain to the same CG shoe rendering. Images A and B show unpremultiplied results. In Image A, the black area appears normal; however, when the gamma value is increased, the film grain hidden in the black becomes clearly visible, as shown in Image B. This can result in the grain being doubled when the image is composited over live-action footage in the final composition. To remove the grain from the black areas, a Premult node must be applied after the F_ReGrain node, as highlighted in Figure 5.142. Image C shows the correct result after applying the Premult node.

◦ Adding image artifacts to the CG shoe composition

During shot analysis, we observed compression artifacts in the background plate, particularly around the edges of elements in the scene. To replicate this effect on the CG shoe, a Sharpen node can be applied after the Premult node. While color grading premultiplied images typically causes unwanted black edges and can compromise the final composition, in this specific case, we intentionally introduce black edges on the CG shoe to match the background artifacts.

Figure 5.143 compares two compositing outcomes based on the placement of the Sharpen node relative to the Premult node. Result 1 demonstrates the correct approach, with the Sharpen node applied before Premult, preserving proper edge treatment. Result 2 shows visible black edges around the toe box profile of the CG shoe, caused by placing the Sharpen node after the Premult node.

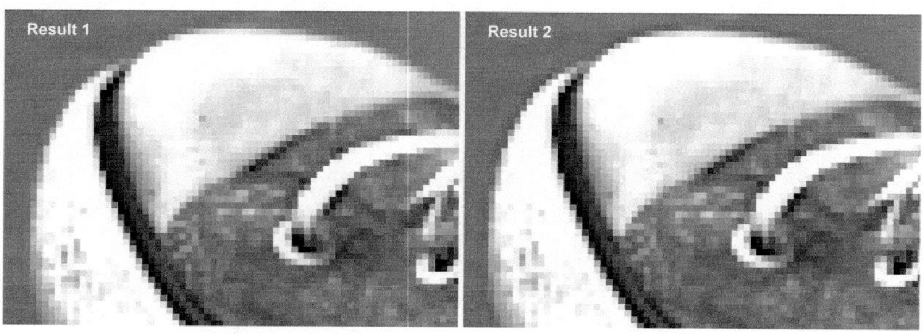

FIGURE 5.143 Comparison of two compositing results. Result 1 shows clean edges around the CG shoe, while Result 2 displays intentional black edging around the toe box

◦ Adding lens distortion to the CG shoe and finalizing the composition

After completing multi-pass compositing for the CG shoe, add a LensDistortion node to reapply the original lens distortion extracted from the background plate. Do this before integrating the CG shoe with the plate. Finally, use a Merge (over) node to composite the CG shoe into the background plate, which already includes its shadows.

Project Summary:

The successful completion of Case Study 7 involved the following steps:

- The project began with 3D camera tracking of the background plate. Once tracking was completed, several critical components were exported, including the virtual camera, tracking point clouds, 3D test geometries, and an undistorted overscan background plate. These files were then imported into Autodesk Maya for 3D matchmoving.

- Meanwhile, a pair of 3D casual shoes was created. This process involved capturing reference images, measuring the shoe dimensions, and shooting high-resolution texture images. Once the 3D models were completed, they were imported into the matchmove scene for further setup, including lighting, texturing, and animation tests. Finally, multi-pass AOVs of the 3D shoes were rendered for later compositing in NukeX.
- The final compositing phase involved integrating the rendered passes with the live-action footage. This stage was crucial for achieving the level of photorealism that was the primary objective of this visual effects shot.

Case Study 8

The space capsule project

Key learning points:

> Determining appropriate shooting methods based on the shot script.
> Shooting live-action footage and capturing on-set reference data.
> Editorial workflow for live-action footage.
> Preparing for 3D camera tracking.
> Performing 3D camera tracking in SynthEyes.
> Matchmoving the background plate in Maya.
> Creating the 3D space capsule.
> Applying textures and conducting lighting tests.
> Rendering in multiple passes for compositing.
> Compositing in NukeX and final output.

Notes

Each case study includes a pre-recorded video tutorial. Watching these videos alongside reading the case studies is strongly recommended to ensure a smooth and comprehensive learning experience for each hands-on project.

Video link: youtube.com/@InvisibleFilmVFX

Video title: Case Study 8 | The Space Capsule Project

Project file: Case_Study_8_Project_File

The project file is available for download on the book's official webpage. High-resolution color figures from this project are also available for download on the book's official webpage.

Case Study 8 aims to showcase key stages and potential workflows involved in visual effects production. While the project is small in scale, it draws on knowledge from previous chapters of this book, providing a clear example of how core concepts are applied in practice and helping to develop an overall understanding of workflows that may support your future projects.

Learning content involved in this project:

- Determining appropriate shooting methods based on the shot script
- Shooting live-action footage and capturing on-set reference data
- Editorial workflow for live-action footage
- Preparing for 3D camera tracking
- Performing 3D camera tracking in SynthEyes
- Matchmoving the background plate in Maya
- Creating the 3D space capsule
- Applying textures and conducting lighting tests
- Rendering in multiple passes for compositing
- Compositing in NukeX and final output preparation

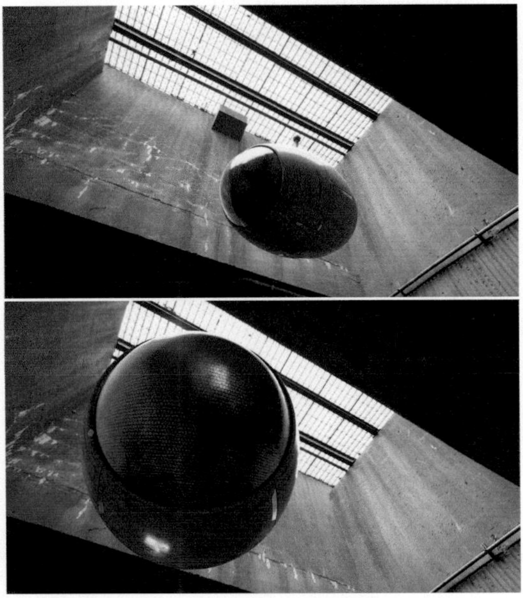

FIGURE 5.144 Final rendering of the space capsule project

• Determining appropriate shooting methods based on the shot script

Shot Script

He stumbled into a pedestrian tunnel, where dim lighting cast shadows, and a pair of soft orange lights at the top bathed the area in a warm glow, offering a subtle sense of security. Positioned in the heart of the tunnel, a ray of light projected from the sky through the skylight above. The unexpected peacefulness drew him, and he swayed as he walked towards it. As he slowly approached the vicinity of the skylight, an oval-shaped aircraft suddenly appeared above him, meticulously scrutinizing him. It was as if it were encountering a being like him for the very first time. He and the aircraft were so close that he could distinctly see the mesh-like structure inside its pupils and the accumulated dust on its body. Clearly, it had been in this place for quite some time.

The following production requirements have been identified based on the script:
Shooting method
Handheld camera work in this scene creates a sense of instability, effectively reflecting the protagonist's inner turmoil and insecurity.
Shooting location and time
Inside a pedestrian tunnel at midday in winter.

• Shooting live-action footage and capturing on-set reference data

Once the most suitable shooting method had been identified, on-set filming took place, and the following data were collected during the process.

o Camera-related settings

The camera used for this shot was a Sony A7CR, which features a full-frame sensor capable of capturing 4:2:2 10-bit live-action footage using the full sensor width at specific frame rates.

– *Project frame rate and aspect ratio*

23.976 fps

3840 × 2160

Knowing the specific camera model is important for matchmove artists, as it can determine the camera sensor size, which is essential for accurate 3D camera tracking.

Using the same camera, lens, and settings throughout filming ensures consistency between the live-action footage and the lens grid, which is necessary for removing lens distortion during visual effects production.

– *Lens model and focal length*

This shot was filmed with a full-frame Sony 20-mm G prime lens.

Focal length: 20 mm

Note

Footage captured by cameras, especially high-end professional models, can preserve shooting information in the metadata. However, when using consumer-level cameras that do not retain all settings in the metadata, it is advisable to manually record the camera settings during shooting.

o Shooting a lens grid

A lens grid may be filmed separately. However, it must be captured using the same camera settings, lens, and focal length as those used for the live-action footage in this project. This is essential to ensure the accurate removal of lens distortion from the live-action material using the lens grid. Figure 5.145 illustrates the key steps involved in filming the lens grid for this project.

As introduced in previous chapters, when filming a lens grid, the camera should be positioned vertically facing the monitor to avoid potential perspective issues. Image A in Figure 5.145 demonstrates the correct camera alignment. Image B shows the maximum area of the checkerboard that should be captured. Image C displays the final recorded lens grid, which was filmed for approximately 10 seconds using the same camera, lens, focal length, and frames-per-second (fps) settings as those used for shooting the live-action footage.

Notes

1. The lens grid should be captured as a 10-second video clip rather than a still image, since camera sensors may have different aspect ratios for video and photography in consumer cameras. During framing, ensure the maximum visible area of the lens grid board is captured to best reveal lens distortion, but avoid including any objects or patterns outside its edges.
2. In this example, the original footage was exported from DaVinci Resolve; however, if your media codecs are compatible with Nuke, it is recommended to export the footage as image sequences directly in NukeX for optimal workflow efficiency.

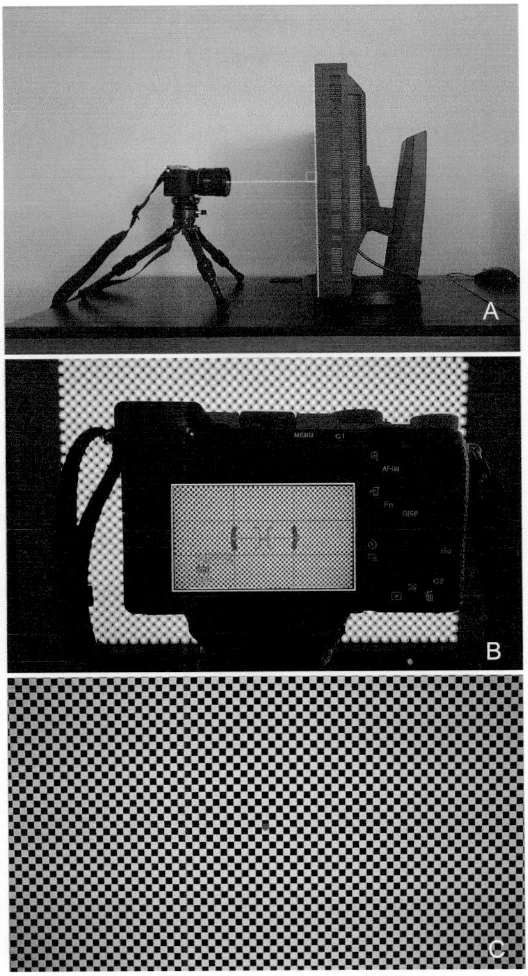

FIGURE 5.145 Recommended approaches for filming a lens grid displayed on a computer screen

◦ Footage color space

To take advantage of the camera's color space capabilities, we recorded the background footage in the S-Log3/S-Gamut3 color space with 10-bit image depth. This choice was made because the shoot took place inside a pedestrian tunnel, which featured high contrast between highlights and shadows. The S-Log3/S-Gamut3 color space, combined with 10-bit depth, allowed for easier recovery of highlight details during post-production.

Figure 5.146 shows the original footage captured for this project. Although it may appear somewhat flat when viewed on sRGB computer monitors, this is expected. The footage will be converted to the ACEScg color space during the editing process, ensuring accurate color representation in the final compositing stage.

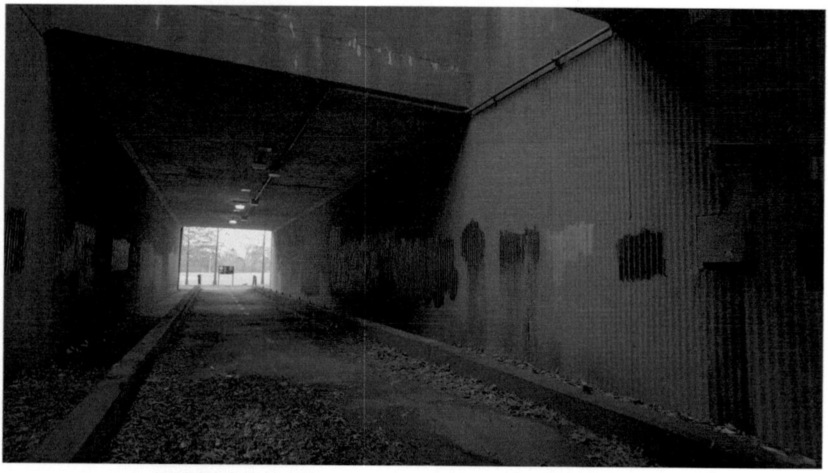

FIGURE 5.146 Original footage filmed in S-Log3/S-Gamut3 color space with 10-bit depth

∘ Capturing reference photos on-site

- Capture reference images at the start and end points of the camera movement when filming live-action footage. These images or videos help clarify the camera's motion, including details like its height from the ground, and serve as valuable references for camera tracking.
- Take multiple angles of both wide and tight shots for on-set reference.

  Capturing on-set reference images from various angles will help other team members better understand the filming environment. Although this is a personal project, gathering these reference images is strongly recommended for potential downstream use.

∘ Capturing high dynamic range images

A series of high dynamic range images was captured to create a 360-degree HDRI environmental light map. During the capture process, multiple exposures were taken from the same position and later combined into a single HDR image. This image was saved in 32-bit OpenEXR format in the sRGB color space, then converted to the ACEScg color space for lighting the CG space capsule in Maya.

Image A in Figure 5.147 displays a series of DNG-format images with varying exposures, captured by an Insta360 X5 camera from the same spot within the tunnel. Image B presents two reference examples of HDR image capture. When shooting HDR, the (Insta360) camera should be positioned as close as possible to the location where the 3D space capsule will appear in the final VFX shot. In this case, the capsule floats beneath the skylight. Positioning the camera in this way ensures that the HDRI captures accurate lighting and color reflections in the relevant area. The resulting light map is then used to illuminate the 3D space capsule scene.

Notes

1. Capture reference images and take on-set notes when shooting HDR images, including the exposure values between each bracketed shot.
2. Minimize the time gap between filming live-action footage and capturing HDR images. Significant delays can lead to lighting inconsistencies, especially in environments with uncontrollable lighting conditions, such as outdoor locations.

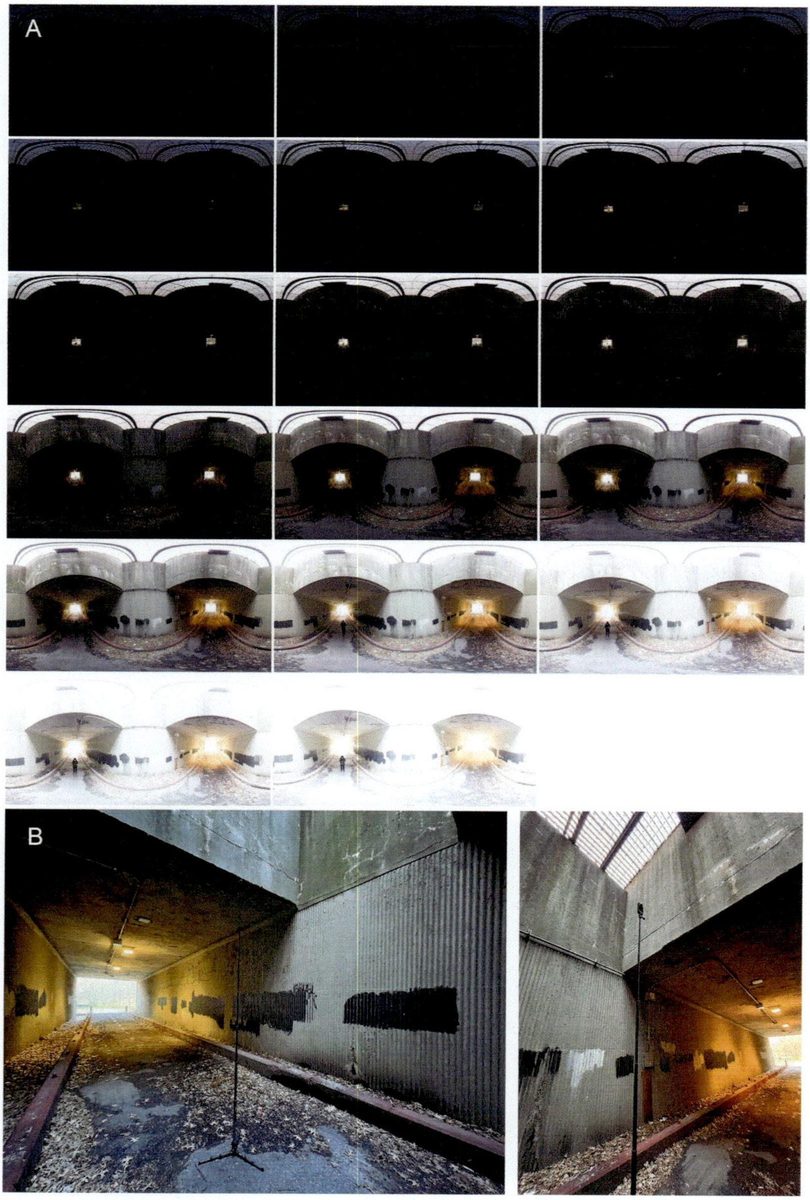

FIGURE 5.147 The process of capturing a 360-degree HDR image for Case Study 8

Figure 5.148 presents a comparison of the 360-degree HDR light map created for Case Study 8. The top image is shown in the linear sRGB color space, while the bottom image is in the ACEScg color space. When comparing the two, the HDR light map in the linear sRGB color space appears slightly warmer and more saturated. In contrast, the ACEScg version looks more neutral and less saturated.

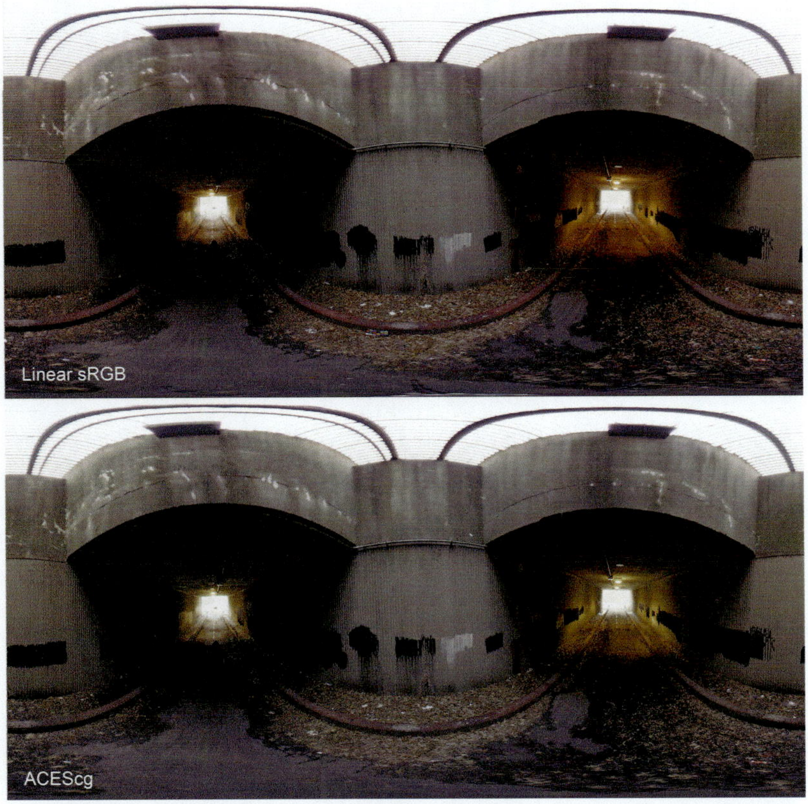

FIGURE 5.148 Final HDR image converted from linear sRGB to ACEScg color space

◦ Scanning the tunnel for a full-scale 3D model

A 1:1 scale 3D-scanned model of the tunnel was created for this shot using the Insta360 X5 camera and Matterport software. The model was then reconstructed in Autodesk Maya and used as the 3D environment for the project. To ensure the accuracy of the final rendering, the actual dimensions of the tunnel were carefully measured with a digital measuring device and used as a reference. These measurements helped align the scale of the 3D model with the tunnel's real-world dimensions. The need for a real-life scale scan stems from the fact that modern professional 3D software relies on physically based rendering engines to achieve realistic results.

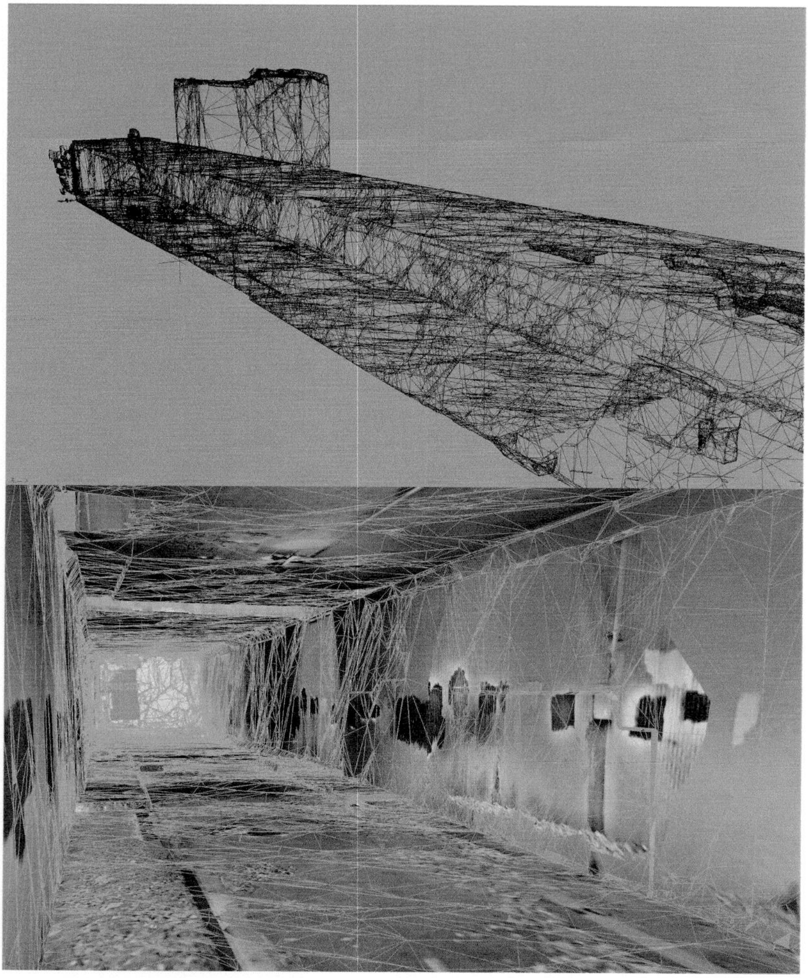

FIGURE 5.149 The scanned 3D model of the tunnel at real-life scale

• Editorial workflow for live-action footage

The editorial process for the live-action footage in this project was carried out in DaVinci Resolve, which allowed for the use of the latest ACES color management during both editing and file export. Additionally, based on our prior experience with visual effects shot editing, the original media files needed to be converted into image sequences during the editorial phase. For this project, the VFX shot was exported as an OpenEXR image sequence with the ACES2065–1 color space embedded and later converted to the ACEScg color space in NukeX for compositing. Naturally, if your footage codecs are compatible with NukeX, you can convert the original media directly into OpenEXR image sequences in the ACEScg color space within NukeX.

Figure 5.150 shows the exported OpenEXR background plate in the ACES2065–1 color space, along with its converted version in the ACEScg color space for compositing. The shot consists of 539 frames, ranging from frame 1001 to frame 1540. From a professional standpoint, this is considered a relatively long VFX shot.

VFX editorial typically keeps shots at reasonable lengths for both technical and artistic reasons. Excessively long shots can cause issues such as inconsistent camera movement and patterns, which complicate 3D camera tracking and may result in tracking difficulties.

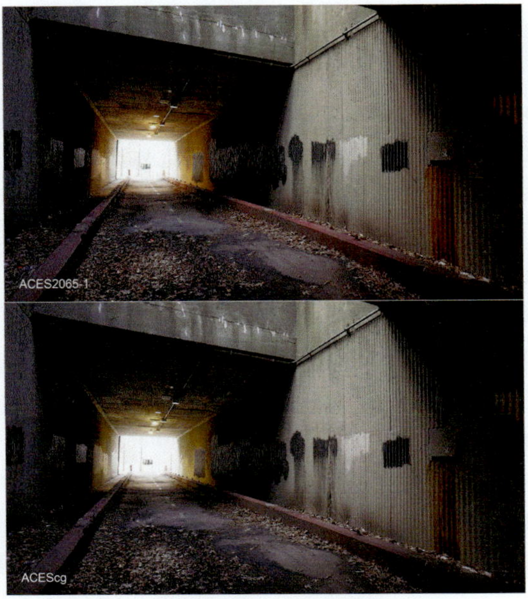

FIGURE 5.150 Comparison of the background plate in ACES2065–1 and ACEScg color spaces as displayed on standard computer monitors

• Preparing for 3D camera tracking

After preparing the background plate, another critical step before performing 3D camera tracking is to remove lens distortion from the footage. Since a lens grid was filmed using the same settings, we can analyze it to extract distortion data and apply that data to the background plate, effectively removing its inherent distortion. For an example of how this process is applied in Case Study 8, refer to the node connections shown in Figure 5.151.

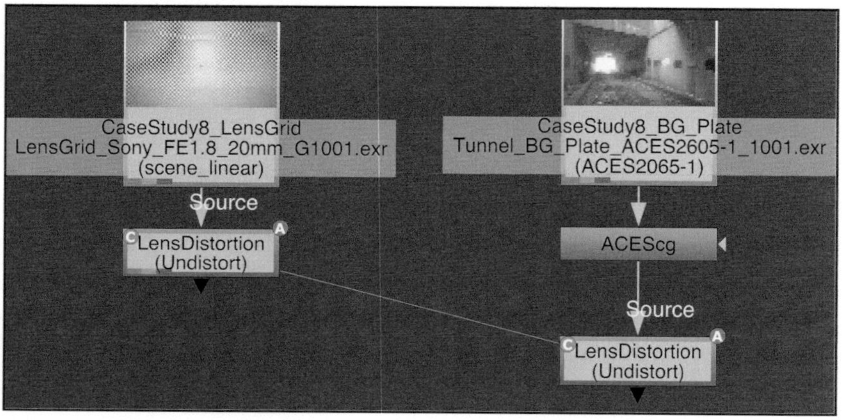

FIGURE 5.151 Removing lens distortion from the background plate

As illustrated in Figure 5.151, the thumbnail in the top-left corner shows the lens grid file connected to a LensDistortion node, which is used to remove lens distortion. Since the lens grid was filmed using the same camera settings as the background plate, the same LensDistortion (Undistort) data can also be applied to remove distortion from the background plate. As shown, a thin line connects both LensDistortion (Undistort) nodes, each marked with the letter "C" in the top-left corner, indicating that these nodes are clones of each other and perform the same operation on different images.

After removing lens distortion from the background plate, the image becomes undistorted, and its overall scale slightly expands beyond the original aspect ratio. This expanded portion is retained within the overscan areas. For 3D camera tracking, it is necessary to calculate the full size of the undistorted image, including the overscan areas.

In this example, the undistorted background plate shows expanded coordinates: X = 3874 and Y = 2175 at the top right, and X = -34 and Y = -15 at the bottom left. To determine the dimensions of the fully undistorted image, including the overscan area, we can use the following method:

X (3874) + X (-34) = 3908
Y (2175) + Y (-15) = 2190

The final aspect ratio of the undistorted image is 3908 by 2190. This aspect ratio will be used for 3D camera tracking and rendering settings in the 3D animation scene for Case Study 8. Once the aspect ratio of the undistorted background image has been determined, export the image sequence for use in 3D camera tracking. In this example, the third-party matchmoving application SynthEyes is used. Therefore, export the background image as a sequence of 8-bit JPEG files, which are lightweight and can be quickly loaded into matchmoving and 3D animation applications.

• Performing 3D camera tracking in SynthEyes

To demonstrate the workflow, the 3D camera tracking task in Case Study 8 is performed using SynthEyes. However, if you are familiar with 3DEqualizer or other professional matchmoving software, or if you wish to experiment with this process in NukeX, you are encouraged to explore those options. Figure 5.152 shows the results of the camera tracking for Case Study 8.

As mentioned in the editorial section, each VFX shot should maintain a reasonable duration. In this instance, the handheld camera moves forward in a point-of-view (POV) motion through the tunnel, then quickly tilts upward to reveal the skylight. As a result, the shot features two distinct camera movement patterns. From a professional standpoint, it would be more effective to divide this into two separate shots, each with a consistent camera movement, to enable more accurate camera tracking. However, we retained the entire shot to illustrate the challenges it presents for 3D camera tracking. As expected, the lowest achievable tracking error for this shot is approximately 0.6, which is acceptable, as the value remains below 1.

Additionally, as shown in the tracking diagnostic bar in Figure 5.152, a red error peak occurs around frame 1140, corresponding to the change of the camera movement. If the shot were split into two segments around frame 1140 and tracked separately, the final tracking accuracy could likely be improved, potentially resulting in an even lower tracking error.

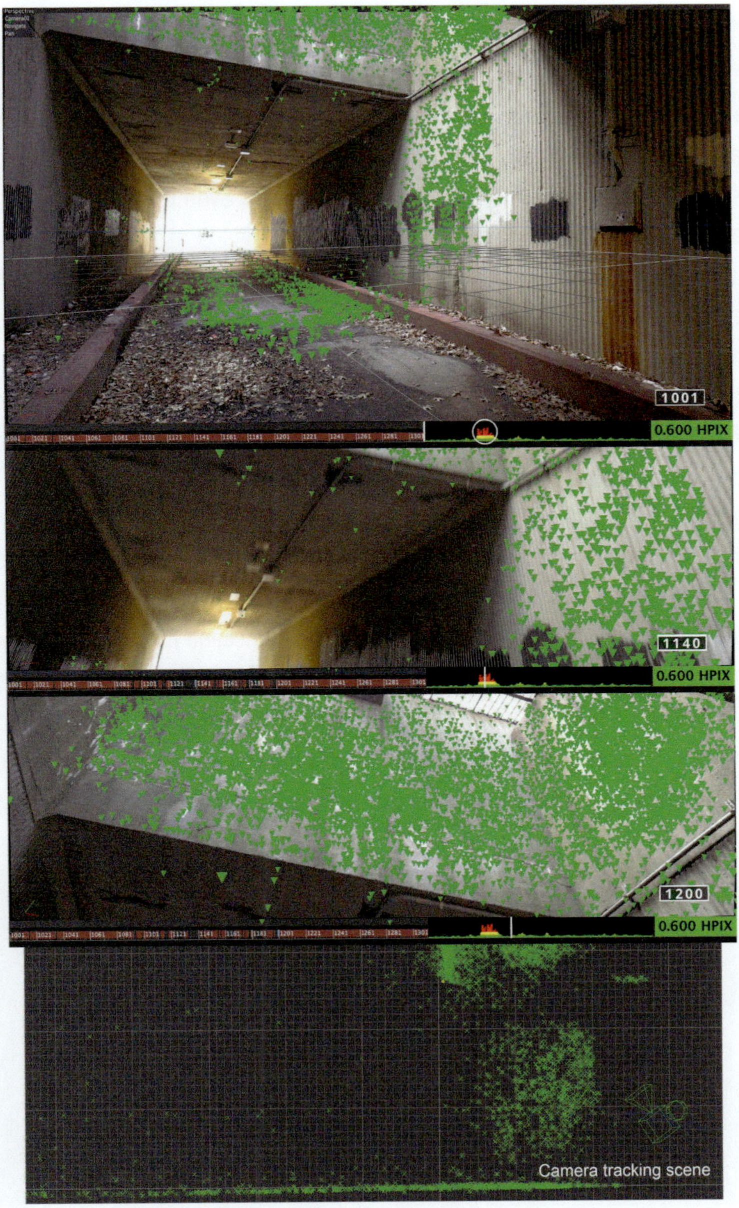

FIGURE 5.152 3D camera tracking examples in SynthEyes

Note

After successfully tracking the camera, scale the entire scene to real-world dimensions using on-set measurement references. For further explanation of 3D camera tracking operations in SynthEyes, please refer to the demonstration video.

• Camera matchmoving in Maya

After completing the camera tracking process, several key components need to be exported, including the extracted virtual camera, tracking features (locators), and any available test geometry. In this example, SynthEyes packages these components into a native Maya (.ma) file. After loading the SynthEyes tracking data into Maya, verify the following:

The on-set scale was measured in meters. Please double-check that the default scene units in Maya are also set to meters. To verify the scene measurement units in Maya, follow these steps:

Go to Windows > Settings/Preferences > Preferences. In the Preferences dialog window, select Settings from the left-hand column. Under Working Units, set the Linear dropdown menu to meter, then click Save.

The real-world scale of the camera tracking scene should match the on-set measurements. To measure the scale of the camera tracking scene in Maya, go to Create > Measure Tool > Distance Tool.

As shown in Figure 5.153, the 3D camera tracking scene has been imported into Maya. The width (approximately 6 meters) and height (approximately 4 meters) of the tunnel were measured using the Distance Tool to ensure they match the on-set dimensions. Once the scene scale is aligned, simple geometries can be added for various tests, such as 3D scene layout and animation blocking.

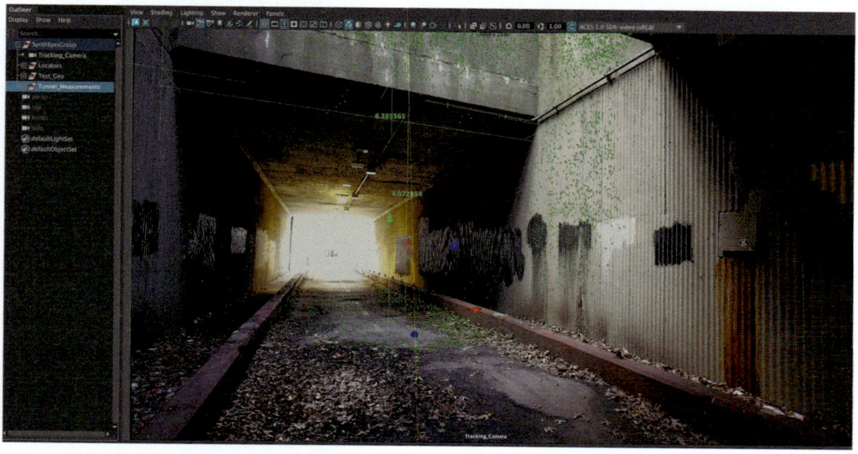

FIGURE 5.153 The camera tracking scene has been measured and scaled to match real-world dimensions

• Creating the 3D space capsule

In general, before finalizing a CG character, its conceptual design is thoroughly developed in alignment with the project's storytelling. This process typically includes brainstorming, sketching, color studies, visual development, and more. However, our focus here is on demonstrating the transformation of the main CG character from a 2D blueprint into a 3D model. Figure 5.154 shows the side, front, and top views of the 2D blueprint of the space capsule (upper image). The UV-unwrapped 3D model, with checker patterns applied, is shown in the lower right.

Note

Ensure that the views are properly aligned in terms of size and detail. Misalignment can lead to unnecessary confusion during the modeling process.

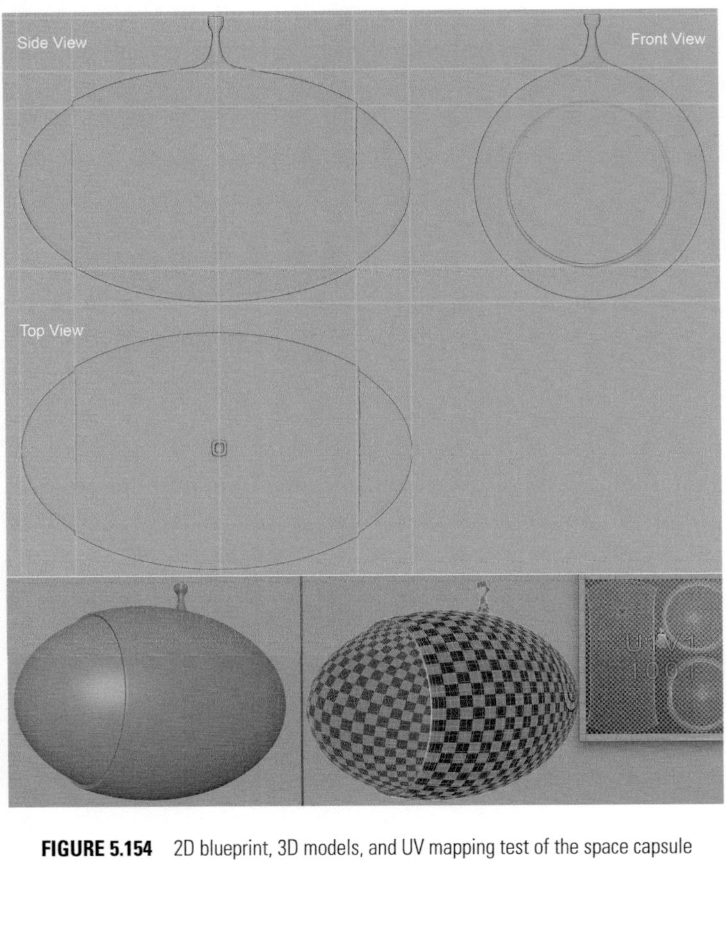

FIGURE 5.154 2D blueprint, 3D models, and UV mapping test of the space capsule

The 3D animation in this project is relatively simple, as this shot features only one CG character. Keyframes are used to animate the space capsule as it moves through the tunnel. However, a crucial aspect of this shot is the interaction of environmental lighting between the tunnel and the CG space capsule, which features reflective surface materials. To achieve visual realism in the final shot, photorealistic textures and physically accurate lighting and reflections are essential.

• Texturing and lighting

With the advent of more advanced technologies and hardware in the industry, whether for creating photorealistic scenes in film or other types of interactive visual productions, it has become crucial to achieve realistic textures for 3D elements and implement physically accurate lighting that integrates seamlessly with the environment. These enhancements can significantly boost visual immersion for both audiences and participants.

o Creating textures for the 3D space capsule

Texture creation for the space capsule was carried out using Adobe Substance 3D Painter. However, VFX productions often involve complex scenes with multiple CG characters, requiring additional tools to suit specific production pipelines. These tools include widely used software such as Foundry Mari, Adobe Substance 3D Painter, and others.

To create textures in Substance Painter, the 3D model needed to be exported in a format compatible with the software. For this project, the UV layout was divided into three parts in Maya: the main body and the two side caps. The model was then exported as either an OBJ (.obj) or FBX (.fbx) file.

It is worth noting that collaborating on projects across departments and studios may require more efficient methods to maximize production potential at every stage, particularly when creating assets for high-end feature films. For instance, the UDIM texturing workflow is commonly used to enhance UV mapping. Additionally, adopting the USDZ/USD (Universal Scene Description) format facilitates the exchange of 3D computer graphics data throughout the production pipeline.

Figure 5.155 shows a snapshot of the textures created for the 3D space capsule in Adobe Substance 3D Painter, with key passes of the final texture displayed to the right of the image.

Notes

1. The workflow for creating textures for the 3D space capsule used ACES color management. All textures were exported in the 16-bit ACES Linear sRGB color space. The texture resolution for the capsule body was rendered at 8K, while the side caps were rendered at 4K.

2. Before applying color-related textures in Maya, such as the Base Color texture for the space capsule, the textures were converted from ACES Linear sRGB to ACEScg using NukeX.
3. Utility passes such as Height, Metallic, Roughness, and Normal were retained in their raw form during the texturing process in Autodesk Maya.

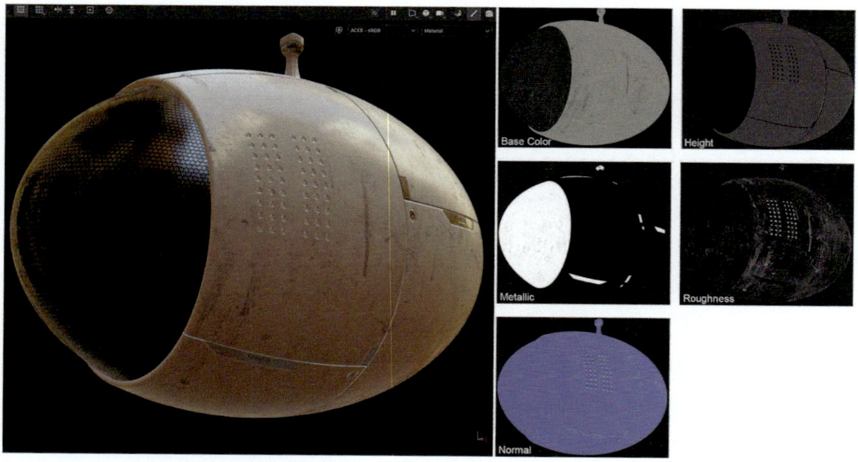

FIGURE 5.155 Final textures created for the 3D space capsule model

○ Simulating environmental lighting using the captured HDRI

In 3D scenes, a spherical skydome mapped with a 360-degree HDR image is commonly used for environment lighting. For this project, we adopted the same approach, using the created HDRI lighting map to illuminate the 3D scene through a spherical skydome. However, during testing, we observed that the environmental structures, lighting, and shadows on the surface of the 3D space capsule were not accurately represented, particularly the shadows cast on the capsule did not align with the tunnel's structure as it passed beneath it.

Upon reviewing the live-action footage, distinct hard-edged structures are visible within the tube-shaped tunnel. These details should be accurately reflected on the surface of the 3D space capsule. However, the sphere-shaped sky dome cannot reproduce this precise lighting result, as it lacks the specific structural details of the tunnel. This discrepancy becomes evident when certain parts of the tunnel cast shadows on the 3D space capsule.

Recognizing that the traditional HDRI lighting setup is unsuitable in this case, we are now exploring whether the HDR map designed for the tunnel can be projected onto the accurately scanned and reconstructed 3D tunnel model in Maya. If feasible, this method would ensure perfect alignment between the HDRI and the 3D tunnel model, providing both the correct light source and the necessary 3D structures for the space capsule scene.

To achieve this, we used an additional camera in Maya to project the 360-degree HDRI onto the reconstructed tunnel model, which was built at a 1:1 scale based on scans of the actual tunnel on set. As a result, the HDRI maps accurately projected onto the tunnel, aligning precisely with its structures. With this setup, we can place the 3D capsule inside the tunnel and achieve highly accurate environmental lighting.

Figure 5.156 shows two images. The top image displays the 360-degree HDRI projected onto the reconstructed 3D model of the tunnel, which was used to illuminate the 3D space capsule. The bottom image presents the view through the tracked camera, with the live-action footage serving as a reference background in Maya. The textured and animated 3D space capsule was placed within the projected HDRI environment for lighting and multi-pass rendering.

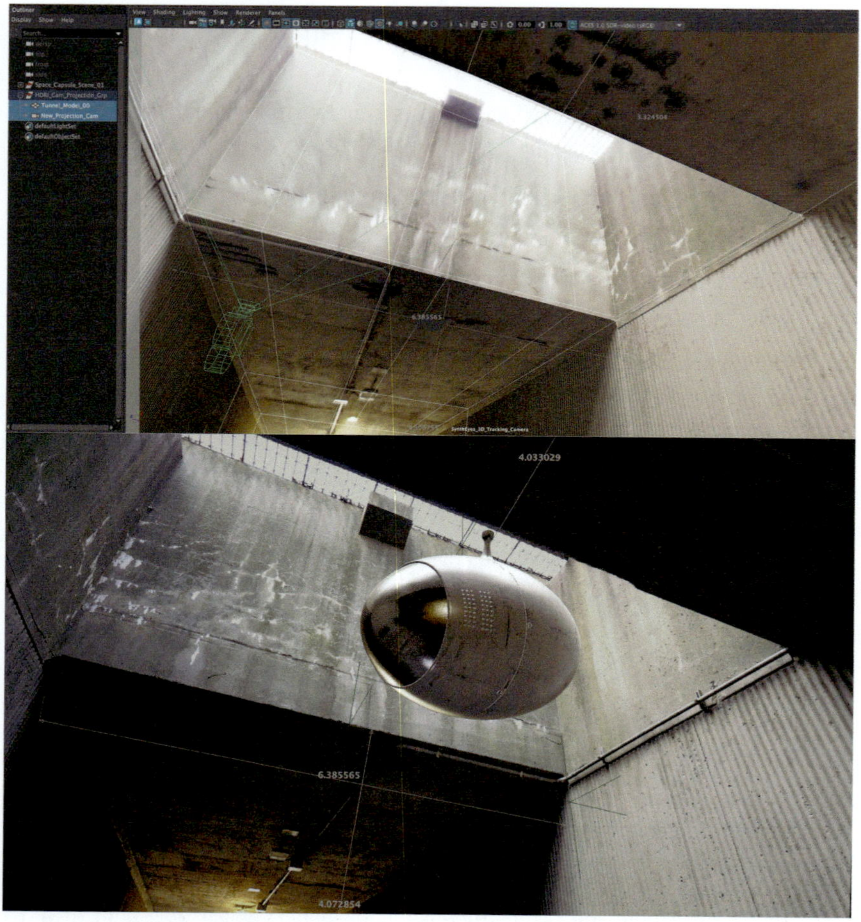

FIGURE 5.156 HDRI projected onto the 3D model (top); space capsule placed in the HDRI environment for animation, lighting, and rendering (bottom)

• Multi-pass rendering and final compositing

○ Multi-pass renders

Once the animation is finalized, the next phase involves multi-pass rendering of the CG space capsule for integration with the live-action background footage during compositing. The specific configuration of multi-pass rendering may vary depending on the rendering engine and production pipeline. For this project, several AOV passes were rendered using Maya's default Arnold renderer. The example images in Figure 5.157 illustrate a series of render passes produced for the space capsule.

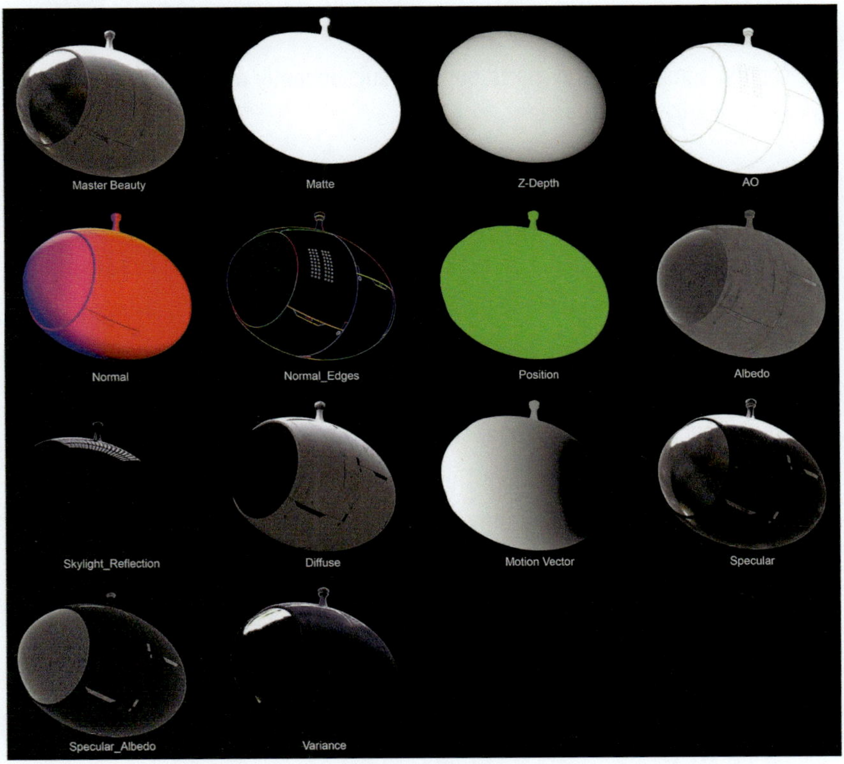

FIGURE 5.157 Multi-pass renders of the 3D space capsule in Case Study 8

After rendering, we finally reached the stage of integrating CG assets (foreground) with the live-action footage (background plate). Now, let's explore the key aspects of the final compositing process in Case Study 8.

Depending on the scale of each project, more complex scenes typically involve a greater number of render passes. This results in extensive CG compositing sections within the compositing scripts, especially in films and high-end television productions with heavy VFX requirements. However, given the scale of visual effects required in Case Study 8, a more streamlined set of render passes was used during compositing. Figure 5.158 illustrates the overall compositing script for Case Study 8.

◦ Final compositing script

The Nuke compositing script in Case Study 8 was built in NukeX 17.0v1 (using fn-nuke_studio-config-v3.0.0_aces-v2.0_ocio-v2.4) and is organized into two main parts:

– *Preparations*

This section consists of four parts outlined subsequently and detailed in the project's preliminary overview.

1. Color neutralization: Convert the color spaces of live-action footage and 3D assets related to the color pass to the ACEScg color space.
2. Remove lens distortion: Use the captured lens grid to remove lens distortion from the live-action footage before performing 3D camera tracking.
3. Prepare the undistorted background plate: Prepare the undistorted background plate (live-action footage) for 3D camera tracking, ensuring its overscan size meets the requirements for rendering 3D assets.
4. Confirm multi-pass rendering: This step may vary depending on how the passes were generated. If the multi-passes were rendered into a single file, separate each pass using Shuffle nodes. Then, reconstruct them for additional image adjustments during the compositing stage as needed.

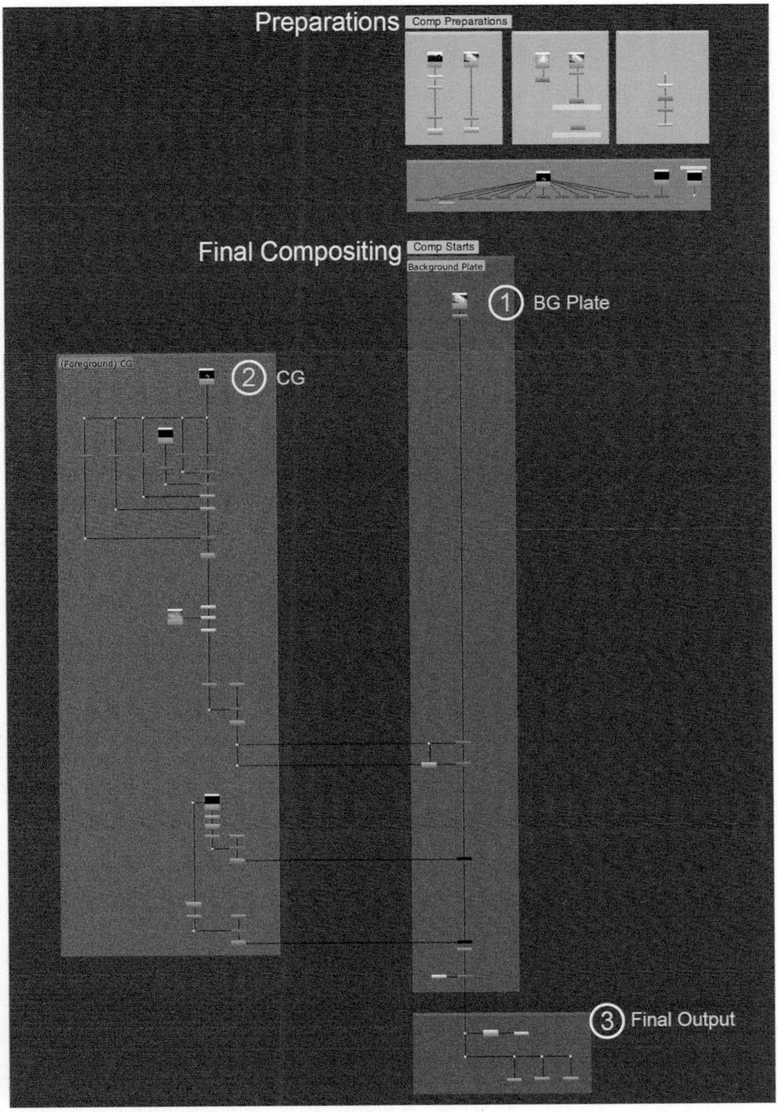

FIGURE 5.158 Final compositing script for Case Study 8

– *Final compositing*

This section consists of three sections: the background plate, multi-pass renders of the space capsule, and the final output.

Section ①: Background (BG) Plate

Color management in modern visual effects production is governed by the ACEScg workflow, which applies to both compositing and the CG assets involved. The background plate was delivered in OpenEXR format using the ACES2065–1 color space and needed to be converted to ACEScg for compositing. Therefore, at this stage, the background plate is transformed from its original color space to ACEScg using an OCIOColorSpace node.

Section ②: (Foreground) CG

A single AOV file was rendered in Arnold, containing all the necessary passes (see Figure 5.157) for compositing. In this section, a series of Shuffle nodes is used to extract individual passes from the AOV file. This multi-pass compositing workflow is especially useful, as it enables artists to apply targeted color corrections and image adjustments to specific elements. Such flexibility offers significant creative control over the final appearance of the CG character. The following notes are important to consider during this stage:

Notes

1. To recombine the individual passes into the original result shown in the AOV file, use Merge nodes with the plus and multiply operations. For example, apply a Merge (plus) node to add the Specular pass to the Diffuse pass. Similarly, use the Merge (multiply) operation to integrate ambient occlusion shadows into the CG space capsule.
2. There are two methods for calculating the overscan size when rendering multi-pass sequences.

   The first method involves calculating the initial overscan size after lens removal and using a MEL plugin to determine the final aspect ratio in Maya, as described in the relevant section of Case Study 3.

   The second method uses Nuke nodes to calculate the final overscan size for rendering in Maya after lens removal, followed by a reverse calculation during compositing to align the CG elements with the original background footage.
3. To realistically integrate CG elements into live-action footage, the CG must match all visual characteristics of the original footage, including film grain. However, CG renders do not inherently contain the film grain found in live-action shots. Therefore, the film grain extracted from the original footage should be applied to the CG renders. In this project, the same camera, lens, and settings used to film the live-action scenes were also used to capture a ColorChecker Passport positioned on set. This ColorChecker Passport was later used to analyze and replicate the film grain structure.

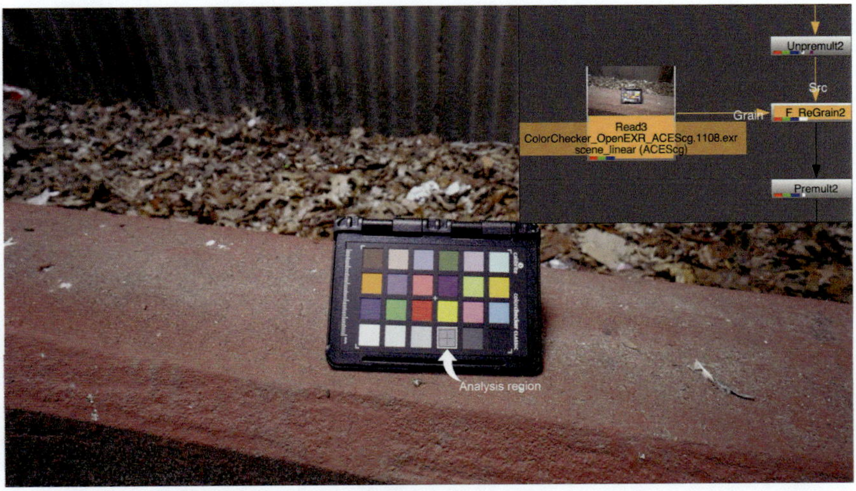

FIGURE 5.159 A ColorChecker Passport was filmed to assist in the analysis of film grain

Section ③: Final output

The final output of the project must conform to the required color spaces. VFX productions typically use the ACEScg color space. However, various media platforms have their own specific color spaces for display purposes. Therefore, the final project should be converted to color spaces that match the specifications of the respective media platforms. For demonstration purposes, the final output of this project includes the following color space conversions:

ACES2065–1

Since the live-action footage (background plate) was originally delivered in the ACES2065–1 color space, the final output must be converted back to ACES2065–1 after compositing in the ACEScg color space. This conversion ensures that the final output remains compatible with the original format and aligns seamlessly with the non-VFX shots during editorial and other post-production processes.

sRGB – Display

Output to this color space for shots intended for viewing on computer displays or online distribution.

S-Log3/S-Gamut3

Use this color space to revert the final VFX shot to its original S-Log3/S-Gamut3 format, as set in the camera during filming.

Note

When compositing shots in production, it is crucial to preserve the original quality of the client's live-action plates in the final output. To ensure this, a pixel-level comparison between the original and composited versions can be performed. From a professional standpoint, only the areas where visual effects have been applied should show differences, while the rest should remain unchanged.

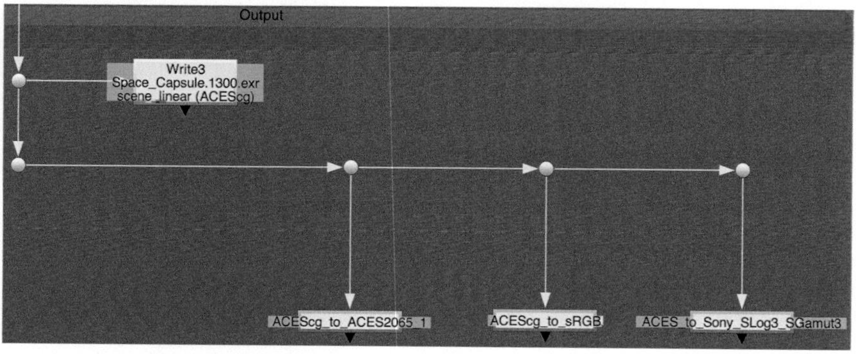

FIGURE 5.160 Examples of the final output color spaces in Case Study 8

Nuke script examples for high-profile feature film shots

• Nuke compositing script – example 1

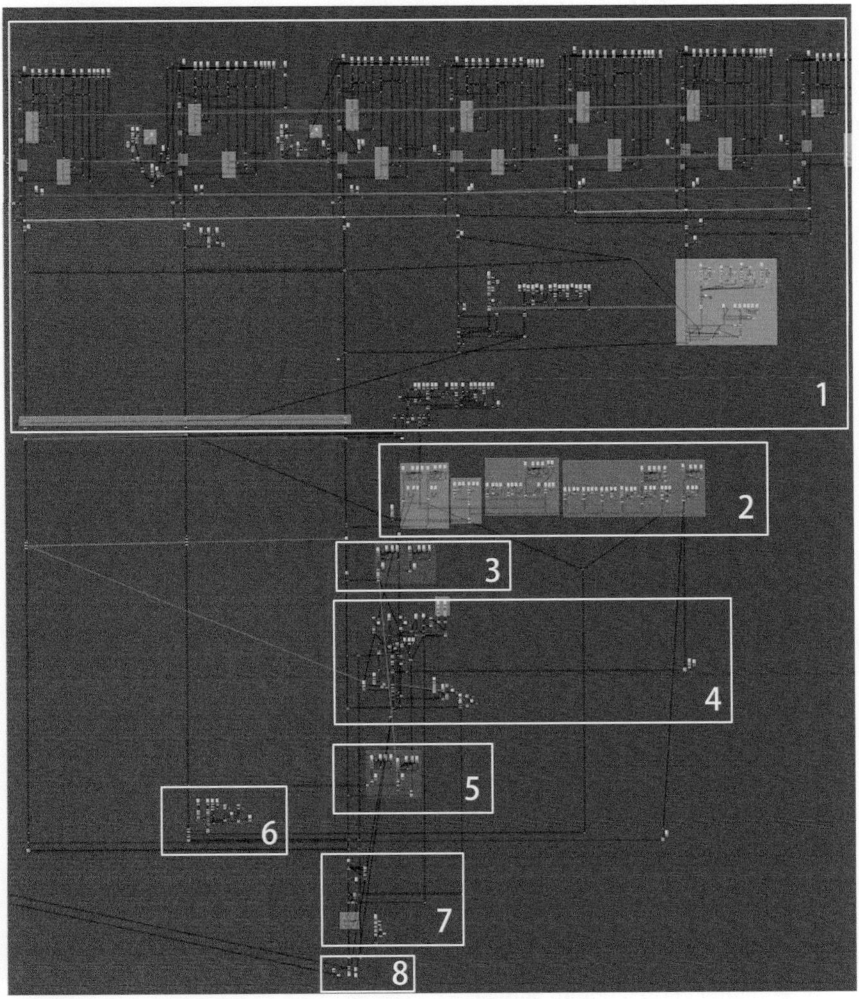

FIGURE 5.161 Nuke script examples for high-profile feature film shots – example 1

Digital compositing is a crucial stage in visual effects production. Compositors often manage hundreds of nodes and assets from various departments within a single shot, making effective script management essential. In large-scale visual effects facilities, projects are frequently shared across multiple studios, even within a single shot. This section explores two production-level examples of Nuke scripts.

Figure 5.161 showcases a script created for a fight scene in a feature film. In this shot, a human character battles a group of alien creatures on a battlefield. The live-action plate was filmed without the use of green or blue screens, requiring the roto/prep department to generate accurate roto shapes of the actor throughout the shot. In this case, rotoscoping was essential to ensure the seamless integration of CG aliens appearing both in front of and behind the human character during the fight.

The overall complexity of this production-level compositing script is significant. For this shot, the script is divided into eight sections:

1. Multi-pass render setups

   This section includes setups for multi-pass renders of the CG creatures, covering aspects such as lighting, color, and utility AOV passes. It can serve as a template aligned with the studio's AOV rendering pipeline. In some cases, this section may be provided by other studios working on the same CG creatures within the shot.
2. Ground elements

   This section includes elements such as dust and stones splashing on the ground during the fight. These elements can be a combination of CG elements and live-action assets.
3. Background blood splashes

   This section includes blood splashes from CG creatures engaged in background battle sequences, adding dynamic visual impact to the scene.
4. Integration of CG creatures

   This section involves integrating CG creatures into the live-action plate.
5. Foreground blood splashes

   This section features blood splashing from CG creatures positioned in the foreground.
6. Foreground CG creature details

   This section provides additional details for the CG creatures in the foreground.
7. Chromatic aberration

   This section applies chromatic aberration to the CG elements.
8. Final output and grading

   This section presents the final output along with the corresponding neutral grade.

• Nuke compositing script – example 2

Figure 5.162 presents a comprehensive Nuke script that integrates CG multi-passes and green screen keying elements. According to the shot's narrative, a human character runs from a forest in the background toward a wild prairie in the foreground. A blue screen plate of the character was filmed separately by an external vendor. Additionally, a CG creature chases the character through the wild prairie, which features dense bushes in the middle ground.

The Nuke script is organized into four main sections, arranged from top to bottom: a digital matte painting of the sky, CG elements in the background, CG creatures in the middle ground, and the green screen live-action plate in the foreground. These sections are outlined as follows:

1. Digital matte painting of the sky

   This section involves projecting a sky image created by the Digital Matte Painting (DMP) department.

2. Integration of background CG elements

   This section includes eight sub-sections, covering multi-light passes, color passes, and utility passes, all organized according to their distance from the camera. Background elements such as mountains and trees on the horizon are placed at the top of the script, while middle ground and foreground elements appear closer to the bottom.

3. Blue screen plate with the main character

   This section focuses on generating a matte for the blue screen plate featuring the main human character and integrating CG elements into the shot.

4. Incorporation of foreground dust and smoke effects

   This section involves adding additional foreground elements such as dust and smoke to the final composition. Finally, a camera shake effect is applied to simulate the look of handheld footage.

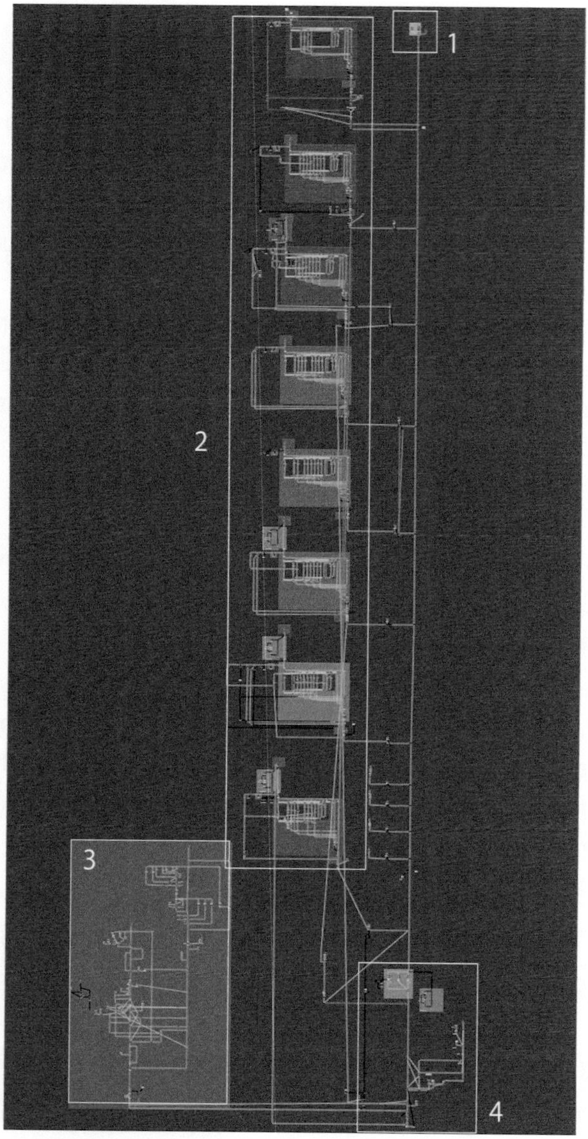

FIGURE 5.162 Nuke script examples for high-profile feature film shots – example 2

Chapter Six

Entry-level roles and job applications at leading VFX studios

Key learning points

> Gain a clear understanding of how to create effective demo reels and navigate the job application process within the visual effects industry.

DOI: 10.4324/9781003224617-6

• Entry-level roles and job applications at leading VFX studios

The standard for visual effects production in film remains consistently high. For entry-level job seekers, it is crucial to demonstrate a strong understanding of the VFX production workflow and the necessary skills when applying for any position at a VFX studio. This chapter focuses on key considerations for creating an entry-level demo reel. While film compositing is used as a specific example, the core principles discussed are applicable to roles across various departments within visual effects studios.

1. Avoid attempting to showcase Hollywood-level blockbuster projects in your demo reels.

   As entry-level candidates, studios typically do not expect reels with overly complex scenes that would require a team of skilled artists to produce. It is preferable to showcase high-quality yet straightforward projects aligned with potential tasks assigned to junior artists. A strong visual effects demo reel can reflect your solid production skills and professional understanding of creating assets required for visual effects shots, even if the projects are relatively simple.

2. Control the overall duration of your demo reel.

   Keep your demo reel within a reasonable length, as hiring managers and department heads often have limited time to review each reel. For junior-level compositing reels, the recommended duration is 1 to 2 minutes.

3. Place your strongest work at the beginning of your demo reel.

   Start your demo reel with your most impressive piece. The opening shots should clearly demonstrate your professional skills and understanding in the specific areas relevant to the position you're applying for. For example, a compositing demo reel should highlight capabilities in rotoscoping, removing unwanted elements, keying, 2D and 3D camera tracking, and multi-pass compositing.

   While some of these tasks may not typically be assigned to junior-level artists early in production, demonstrating a strong understanding of the pipeline and solid problem-solving skills can set you apart from other candidates. Industry professionals will notice even a brief, well-executed detail that showcases professional-level ability and distinctiveness.

For example, Case Study 6 in Chapter 5 highlights the visual effects work on *The Lavender Hill Mob*, including tasks such as rotoscoping, generating clean plates, camera tracking, 3D matchmoving, modeling, animation, and multi-pass compositing. Watch Case Study 6 | VFX Shot Breakdown at youtube.com/@InvisibleFilmVFX.

These VFX tasks not only showcase your technical skills but also demonstrate a solid understanding of the VFX pipeline. Additionally, be sure to use accurate professional terminology when explaining key operations in your reels, if applicable.

4. Things to keep in mind when editing your demo reels.

   When editing your demo reel, keep in mind that visual effects companies may have different expectations than motion graphic design studios. Avoid overusing motion graphic titles and background music, as these elements can distract from the professional content of your reel. Instead, aim for a polished, professional presentation that highlights your skills. Showcase different aspects of your learning process to demonstrate your potential in the specific field you are targeting.

   Pay close attention to the pacing and rhythm of your technical demonstrations. If you choose to include background music to enhance the overall tone, keep in mind that some professionals prefer muted audio to avoid distractions. Make sure your reel plays at a reasonable speed, neither too fast nor too slow. Ultimately, the main objective should be to highlight the quality and substance of your work rather than embellishing the reel with unnecessary effects or design elements.

Note:

During the early stages of your job search, take time to research the companies you are interested in. Start by visiting their official websites to review the specific requirements for demo reels, job applications, and training opportunities. As you explore different companies, pay attention to recurring requirements or expectations. As discussed in earlier chapters, VFX studios often collaborate on projects, which leads to shared production pipelines. Consequently, many studios look for similar skills and knowledge in potential candidates.

In professional practice, studio department heads and recruiters often view AI-generated content in demo reels as a red flag, particularly when it misrepresents an artist's foundational skills or raises legal or copyright concerns. Any use of AI must therefore be clearly disclosed. The majority of the reel should demonstrate original, artist-driven work, emphasizing problem-solving ability and "unique human expression" that cannot be replicated by automated AI tools.

5. Keep knocking, and the door will open to you.

   Visual effects studios typically do not advertise entry-level openings on their websites year-round. However, this does not reflect a lack of demand for these positions. Many major studios offer apprenticeships and internships, so it is important to check their official websites regularly for application windows, which usually align with specific training periods each year. Given the high level of competition among students, demo reels are often required when applying. Therefore, it is crucial to develop a job-hunting strategy and timeline for your final year of study.

After submitting your demo reels for a junior-level role, especially at large VFX studios, immediate responses are uncommon. The waiting period can sometimes last several months. During this time, keep your reels updated, and if the wait becomes prolonged, consider staying in touch with the studio by sending updated versions. Since visual effects work is project-based, new job opportunities frequently arise. Showing professional passion and persistence can significantly improve your chances. Additionally, consulting professional organizations, such as the official websites of leading VFX studios, is highly recommended for entry-level VFX artists to better understand the essential skills required and to showcase them effectively in their demo reels for job applications.

Lastly, thank you once again for your support of this book. As both a higher education practitioner and a working visual effects artist, I sincerely hope this book inspires the next generation and offers meaningful guidance for professional development in the field of visual effects.

By applying the knowledge and insights shared in these pages, I am confident that you can take meaningful steps toward a successful career in the visual effects industry, just as many of the students I have mentored over the years have.
I wish you every success on your learning journey.

Index

Note: Page numbers in *italics* indicate a figure.

For Product Safety Concerns and Information please contact our EU representative GPSR@taylorandfrancis.com Taylor & Francis Verlag GmbH, Kaufingerstraße 24, 80331 München, Germany